Judith Rauscher
Ecopoetic Place-Making

Literary Ecologies | Volume 1

Editorial

In the age of the Anthropocene and in the face of climate crisis, societal perceptions of the environment, the way it is talked about, and how it is represented aesthetically are changing. In Literary Studies, scholars increasingly focus on the relationship between humans and nature, on how the latter manifests itself as an important element in literature, and on how literature influences the ecological discourse of its time.

Building on ongoing discussions in Ecocriticism, the **Literary Ecologies** series examines the interplay between literature and the environment. It aims to illuminate perceptions and conceptions of the environment from ancient times to the present day as well as the tense relationship between humans and nature in different forms of literary expression. Special interest is also given to the complex relationship between human and non-human actors, which is increasingly gaining importance in debates about climate change, species extinction, and other forms of environmental degradation.

The series is not limited to analyses of fictional literature, but also integrates investigations of ecological narratives in non-fiction as well as theoretical discussions relevant to Ecocriticism itself. Possible topics and research fields in the series include Plant and Animal Studies, Petro- and Ecocriticism, Climate Fiction, Nature Writing, Ecopoetry and Literatures of the Anthropocene.

Judith Rauscher is assistant professor (Juniorprofessorin) of American Literature and Culture at the Universität zu Köln. She holds an M.A. in Comparative Literature from Dartmouth College, an M.A. in English and American Studies and a Ph.D. in American Studies from the Otto-Friedrich-Universität Bamberg. Her research focuses on contemporary American poetry, ecocriticism, Mobility Studies, American speculative fiction, and Gender Studies.

Judith Rauscher

Ecopoetic Place-Making

Nature and Mobility in Contemporary American Poetry

[transcript]

Funding: Most of the research for this book was carried out as part of the project "The Environmental Imagination of Mobility: Nature and Migration in Contemporary American Poetry," funded by the German Research Foundation (DFG). It was further supported by short-term grants from the Women's Office of the University of Bamberg, the German Academic Exchange Service (DAAD), and the Bavarian American Academy (BAA).

Thesis: The dissertation on which this book is based was accepted as Ph.D. thesis by the Faculty of Humanities of the Otto-Friedrich Universität Bamberg. It was revised in part while I was a postdoc at the University of Bamberg and in part while I was assistant professor at the University of Cologne.

Bibliographic information published by the Deutsche Nationalbibliothek
The Deutsche Nationalbibliothek lists this publication in the Deutsche Nationalbibliografie; detailed bibliographic data are available in the Internet at http://dnb.d-nb.de

First published in 2023 by transcript Verlag, Bielefeld
© Judith Rauscher

Cover layout: Maria Arndt, Bielefeld
Cover illustration: Image by ArthurHidden on Freepik

Print-ISBN 978-3-8376-6934-3
PDF-ISBN 978-3-8394-6934-7
https://doi.org/10.14361/9783839469347
ISSN of series: 2941-4210
eISSN of series: 2941-4229

Contents

Acknowledgements

I am writing these acknowledgements knowing that this book owes its existence to many fortunate circumstances and encounters. I am also writing this in the hope that some of the conversations that have inspired this book will continue and that I will get a chance to express my gratitude to many of the people mentioned below more directly in the not-so-distant future. In some way, then, these acknowledgements are a to do list for me: I want to thank all of you in person when we meet again and I hope it will be sooner rather than later!

It took me a long time to write this book, much longer than is common in German Academia, which requires people to publish their dissertations and usually encourages them to do so within two years after their Ph.D. defense. This is not what I did. The reasons for why I took longer to turn my dissertation into a book are diverse. The COVID pandemic, a major work-related move, and a demanding new position are three of them, but there are others. Another way of looking at it is that I was lucky, because I was able to take the time to rework parts of my manuscript in ways that would not have been possible had I published this book back in 2020 or 2021. Many emerging scholars in German Academia do not have this opportunity. I was lucky, because my employment situation has been extraordinarily stable in a system notorious for precarious, short-term contracts that force untenured scholars to publish quickly in order to keep their positions. I am grateful to the people who have provided this stability for me when they could easily have chosen not to do so and to those people in my life who have supported me in all the small and big ways that have allowed me to succeed in those situations in which my career depended on others' evaluation of my work. I do not take this support for granted and if I have sometimes not been forthcoming enough with expressing my gratitude, I hope that these acknowledgements can make good on some of these failings.

This book would not have been possible without the people who read the entire manuscript or drafts of individual chapters. I want to thank my advisor, Christine Gerhardt for countless conversations and her meticulous comments on large parts of my dissertation as well as my second reader, Sylvia Mayer, for helpful suggestions on possible revisions in addition to her detailed reader report. Thank you, Mareike Spychala, Claire Scott, Melissa Zeiger, Leontien Potthoff, Jian Chyng Tu, Kathrin

Lachenmaier, Julia Hahn-Klose, Izel Ercanoglu, Rumeysa Ceylan, and Verena Wurth for reading parts of what is now this book, and Mahshid Mayar for reading it all. Mahshid, your expertise and help with revising the final version of *Ecopoetic Place-Making* was invaluable. I also want to thank the reviewers and editors of the journals that published my earlier reflections on the poets treated in this book as well as the anonymous reviewers at Bloomsbury Press who found valuable material in my book proposal and also suggested things that should be reconsidered or explored further. Thank you, Greg Garrard and Richard Kerridge for considering my proposal and my apologies that external circumstances made it so that I could not publish my book in your series. At the same time, I am extremely grateful to the editors at transcript Verlag who decided to pick up my book for their new environmental humanities series.

This book would also not have been possible without institutional support. The dissertation on which this book is based was in large parts written as part of the DFG-funded project "The Environmental Imagination of Mobility: Nature and Migration in Contemporary American Poetry," led by Christine Gerhardt (University of Bamberg). Research that entered this book was further supported by grants from the Women's Office of the University of Bamberg, the German Academic Exchange Service (DAAD), and the Bavarian American Academy (BAA). I am immensely grateful that I was able to spend time at Dartmouth College and Duke University thanks to these grants which allowed me to have conversations about my project with Melissa Zeiger, Colleen Boggs, Nisha Kommattam, and Claire Scott, building relationships that will, I hope, continue into the future. I also want to thank the members of my Ph.D. committee, Andrea Bartl, Christine Gerhardt, Iris Herrmann (all three University of Bamberg), and Sylvia Mayer (University of Bayreuth) as well as the administrative staff at the University of Bamberg who patiently answered all my questions about the submission and publication process of my dissertation.

The dissertation that formed the basis of this book was written under the supervision and guidance of Christine Gerhardt at the University of Bamberg. We still sometimes joke about the traditional German word for Ph.D. advisor, *Doktormutter/ Doktorvater* ("Ph.D. Mother/ Ph.D. Father"), and it is true that some of the implications of this designation are misleading, if not outright problematic. For me, having Christine Gerhardt as my *Doktormutter* meant having an advisor and a mentor who took interest in my development as an academic and supported me when I needed support, but also taught me a lot about navigating academia on my own, either by example or by sharing some of her own experiences. Christine, there are so many things I would like to thank you for, too many to mention them here. Let's talk about some of them during a walk.

Having a *Doktormutter* and working at the University of Bamberg for eight years meant having "Ph.D. siblings," including ones at other universities, and many lovely colleagues. Thank you, Laura Oehme (University of Bayreuth) for being my Ph.D.

sister by another *Doktormutter* and taking me with you to my first DGfA conference, Theresa Roth for having been my Ph.D. sisters from what feels like the first hour; Mareike Spychala for being not only my Ph.D. sister but one of my best friends, and to Lorena Bickert, Susen Halank, and Yıldız Aşar for making me regret having to leave Bamberg too soon to be around as your big Ph.D. sister for long. Thank you to Nicole Konopka for letting me share your office and telling the most distracting stories. I am also immensely grateful to my former British Literature and French Literature professors at the University of Bamberg, Christoph Houswitschka and Dina De Rentiis, for giving me my first student assistant positions and to my former instructors, Beatrix Hesse and Bettina Full, for recommending me for these positions. Thank you also to my former British Literature colleagues at the University of Bamberg, Susan Brähler, Kerstin-Anja Münderlein, and Johannes Weber, for the productive collaboration between our teams and all the fun department events. Thank you to everyone at the Women's Office of the University of Bamberg for taking me in for a year and especially to Johanna Bamberg-Reinwand, my brain-twin, for welcoming me into the office you were running so expertly. Last but not least: thank you to my friends in the "Mensagruppe" for keeping me entertained and sane during all those years in Bamberg and for still doing it now, even after I moved away.

In 2011, I went to my first PGF conference. For ten years afterwards, the Postgraduate Forum (PGF) of the German Association for American Studies (DGfA) was my principal academic home away from Bamberg. In many ways, it continues to be that home, even though I'm no longer technically a 'Postgraduate,' because of the lasting friendships that I made with my peers in American Studies at numerous PGF conferences and at the annual meetings of the DGfA. Thank you to everyone who I worked and was in contact with during my time as PGF representative in the past years, but especially to Linda Heß and Nele Sawallisch for accompanying me on this academic journey (as well as the occasional literal journey), to Kathrin Horn and Wiebke Kartheus for being two of the smartest and coolest people I know, and to Lexi Hauke, Maxi Albrecht, and Jiann-Chyng Tu for all the times you listened and had my back. See you at the next DGfA dance party (or on another fun occasion of your choice)!

I finished the first full draft of this book when I was still a postdoc at the University of Bamberg. Now I am assistant professor (Juniorprofessorin) at the University of Cologne. While I initially thought that changing universities could only mean having less wonderful colleagues, this has not been the case. Thank you to all my colleagues at the English Department I and adjacent departments who made me feel welcome when I joined the University of Cologne in the middle of a global pandemic. Thank you, Esther Fritsch, Beate Abel, Philipp Hofmann, and Bärbel Eltschig for explaining the department to me when I arrived and for still occasionally doing it today. Thank you to the American studies team around Hanjo Berressem as well as to all my other colleagues at the English Departments I and II, in GeStiK and in MESH who helped me transition into my position as assistant professor of American Literature and Culture at the University of Cologne. Thank you to my Cologne North American History colleagues Anke Ortlepp and Silke Hackenesch and to our Bonn colleagues for the constructive collaboration on the North American Studies M.A. My most deep-felt thanks to Andrea Gutenberg for your support and friendship from the minute I arrived in Cologne and to Johanna Pitetti-Heil, Susanne Gruß, and Mahshid Mayar, for your support and friendship from the moment you joined the department. Thank you, Johanna and Susanne, for working with me on *gender forum: An Internet Journal for Gender Studies*. Last but not least, thank you to the past and current members of my team for the amazing work you have been doing in the past three years, specifically Julia Hahn-Klose, Izel Ercanoglu, Tensae Desta, Maheen Muzaffar, Leontien Potthoff, Kilian Schmitt, Rumeysa Ceylan, Burak Sezer, Sara Tewelde-Negassi, Verena Wurth and Mahshid Mayar.

Finally, I would like to thank my family for encouraging me when I needed encouragement and for reminding me that there is life outside academia when I needed reminding. Thank you to my mother Christa Rauscher, my father Klaus Rauscher, and my twin sister Christine Rauscher. Last but not least, thank you to my wife Stefanie Künzel-Rauscher. The four of you were there for me, when I wrote the very first word of this book and you are still there, for which I am deeply grateful.

Introduction: Ecopoetic Place-Making in Contemporary American Poetry

Anthropogenic environmental change and the uneven global effects of mass mobility, each with their own unique histories and long-term effects on life on the planet, are two of the most urgent challenges of the twenty-first century. Contemporary American poetry can help us understand some of the complex ways in which these two challenges are interrelated. When connecting environmental change and mass mobility, both public and scholarly debates frequently focus on the phenomenon of climate refugees and environmental migrants, that is, on individuals who have been displaced by climate change or environmental degradation. A similar trend can be observed when environmental crisis and human mobility are discussed in works of literature and popular culture, especially in the United States. Whether in Hollywood blockbusters such as Roland Emmerich's *The Day After Tomorrow* (2004), documentary films such as Al Gore's *An Inconvenient Truth* (2006), or contemporary works of science fiction such as Paolo Bacigalupi's *The Water Knife* (2015), climate refugees have become a powerful shorthand for the ways in which environmental change and matters of mobility are imagined together. Yet, as is necessarily the case with this kind of shorthand, the figure of the climate refugee cannot capture the complex interplay between environmental issues and human mobility. Understanding these complexities is crucial, however, because the sedentary lifestyle idealized by traditional environmentalist discourses, most strands of ecocriticism, and the dominant traditions of ecopoetry has often been unattainable for large parts of the world's population and will only become more so as oceans continue to rise and deserts continue to spread. In particular, idealized notions of emplacement as attachment to one's chosen place of residence resulting from long-term inhabitation have little in common with the lived experiences of displaced peoples who are forced to move due to floods, droughts, famine, and armed conflicts over dwindling resources, or prevented from doing so by borders, walls, or patrol boats, whether in the United States or elsewhere. Attending to the intersections of environmental issues and human mobility matters too, because econativist arguments that link (pseudo-)ecological, racist, and anti-immigrant discourses continue to resurface in times of national and global crisis and are all too easily used to attack marginalized communities of color in particular, whether they are actually on the move or merely unwanted in their current place of residence. Reading contemporary American poetry about nature and mobility by poets with different migratory backgrounds, I argue in this study, can help us to counter such arguments and enrich existing models for how to live place-conscious and sustainable lives. As I will show in the following, the poetry of Craig Santos Perez, Juliana Spahr, Derek Walcott, Agha Shahid Ali, and Etel Adnan proposes mobile environmental imaginaries that rely on critical notions of belonging and offer alternative perspectives on how meaningful place-attachments can be formed in the context of displacement. In doing so, the ecopoetries of migration I discuss in *Ecopoetic Place-Making* envision ways of being in the world that are both more eco-ethical and more just.

Moving Beyond the Figure of the Climate Refugee in Contemporary Poetry

Like contemporary filmmakers and novelists, many contemporary poets too approach the interdependences between global environmental change and human mobility by evoking the figure of the climate refugee. A well-known example is the Marshallese poet and climate activist Kathy Jetñil-Kijiner who performed one of her poems about climate refugees, "Dear Matafele Peinem," at the opening ceremony of the United Nations Climate Summit in 2014. Later included in Jetñil-Kijiner's debut collection *Iep Jaltōk: Poems from a Marshallese Daughter* (2017), "Dear Matafele Peinem" draws attention to the threat that rising sea-levels pose to small island nations and their Indigenous populations, who "will wander / rootless/ with only / a passport / to call home" (70). The poem is addressed to the poet's daughter and promises the child that "no one's gonna become/ a climate change refugee" (71), only to retract that promise, at least partly, immediately afterwards: "or should i say/ no one else" (71). If there is hope in the poem that the drowning of the Marshall Islands and similar places may still be prevented so her daughter will not be displaced and lose access to the land her ancestors inhabited, it arises at least in part from the speaker's anger and desperation over world leaders' reluctance to take the necessary measures to protect Indigenous lives and cultures, an anger and desperation partially concealed in the poem for the child's sake but nonetheless articulated through the careful use of imagery and insistent placement of line-breaks.

Desperation and anger also play a role in Niyi Osundare's short poem "Katrina's Diaspora" (2011), which addresses the fate of those inhabitants of New Orleans displaced by the infamous 2005 category 5 hurricane in a detached yet strained voice. Focusing on the past rather than on the future, the Nigerian-born poet links the "desperate dislocation" (43) of African American families after Katrina to a longer history of Black dispersal and racism in the American "Babylon" (43), implying that the population *"known to the Press as 'Katrina Refugees'"* (43; emphasis original) had been made "[h]omeless again" by being forced into "placeless destinations" (43). Awareness of a longer racialized history of anthropogenic environmental change and the structures of discrimination and oppression manifesting in histories of human displacement also permeates Craig Santos Perez's poem "Praise Song for Oceania" (2016). An Indigenous poet like Jetñil-Kijiner, Perez, whose work I discuss in my first chapter, first published "Praise Song" on the occasion of World Oceans Day 2016. Rather than concentrating primarily on climate refugees, his poem evokes many different kinds of environmental change and environmental degradation as well as many different kinds of displacement, migration, and mobility. It thus exemplifies the kind of poetry I analyze in *Ecopoetic Place-Making*.

Drawing from the poem "The Sea is History" by Derek Walcott, whose epic poem *Omeros* (1990) I discuss in my third chapter, Perez's "Praise Song" depicts the ocean as a complex ecosystem and as a repository of histories shaped by *"migrant routes"* and *"submarine roots"* (*Habitat Threshold* 68, emphasis original). In a tone that is simultaneously sincere and bitterly ironic, the poem praises the ocean for its *"capacity to survive/ our trawling boats"* and its ability *"to dilute/ our heavy metals and greenhouse gases/ sewage and radioactive waste/ pollutants and plastics"* (67, emphasis original). More than that, in a variation on the central theme of Walcott's poem, Perez figures the ocean not merely as "history" but as a *"library of drowned stories"* and *"vast archive of desire"* (67, emphasis original) that holds *"lost treasures"* but also constitutes a *"watery grave"* for more than one *"human reef of bones"* (67, emphasis original). Alluding to many different (hi)stories of violence and displacement, but also emphasizing that these (hi)stories must be (re)discovered and (re)told in order to unfold their transformative power, Perez evokes the environmental devastation and human suffering caused by centuries of Euro-American colonial exploitation in the Pacific and beyond. In his poem, the figure of the climate refugee appears as one among many other human subjects whose relationship to the more-than-human world has been marked by experiences of mobility and histories of displacement. It is this kind of multidirectional and multifaceted poetry—a "polytemporal" and "polyspatial" poetry (Ramazani, *Poetry in a Global Age* 8) that considers a broad range of mobilities and an equally broad range of natural phenomena—that I focus on in this book.

When Perez's poem mentions *"those who map you [Oceania] aqua nullius"* and *"scar"* the ocean's *"middle passages"* (*Habitat Threshold* 66, emphasis original), the harm caused by *"lustful tourism"* (68, emphasis original), or the increasing vulnerability of the inhabitants of *"coastal villages"* and *"low-lying islands"* (69, emphasis original) to rising sea levels, it distinguishes different kinds of environmental harm and different kinds of mobility. It also introduces an important distinction between the perpetrators and the victims of exploitation and injustice. Implying that this distinction is crucial but not necessarily clear-cut or stable, "Praise Song" moves from a universal "we" at the beginning of the poem ("our *heavy metals and green-*

house gases") to a very specific collective "we" at the end of the poem: Indigenous peoples of the world's ocean(s). Their cultures, identities, and everyday lives, the poem suggests, are bound to the ocean not only as an endangered ecosystem and a place of many different (hi)stories and cultural practices but also as a powerful idea that gestures toward more sustainable futures. Asking the world's oceans for forgiveness for the destruction caused by (parts of) humanity, the speaker expresses the *"hope"* (71, emphasis original) that the Indigenous peoples of Oceania will unite around a *"common heritage"* (72, emphasis original) and a shared commitment to protect this endangered *"blue planet / one world ocean"* (72, emphasis original). While the poem thus strongly suggests that the *"trans-oceanic / past present future flowing / through our blood"* (72, emphasis original) it conjures through song must be centered on Indigenous experiences and ways of knowing, it also implies that the alternative understanding and enactment of human-nature relations that this transoceanic community is based on may have important lessons to offer to non-Indigenous peoples who are looking for, or perhaps even depending for survival on developing more sustainable ways of living with the ocean.

Those invested in the project of environmental and cultural restoration that stands at the heart of Perez's text and the alternative way of living with the ocean it imagines, "Praise Song" insists, must take seriously the ocean both as a physical place and as a *"powerful metaphor"* (*Habitat Threshold* 72, emphasis original), that is, as a material and as a socio-cultural formation with many different, at times conflicting meanings. By integrating all of these dimensions into his poem Perez evokes a *"vision of belonging"* (72, emphasis original) that is in equal measures constituted and disrupted by environmental degradation and (forced) mobilities. This mobile vision of belonging relies on the archival as well as the utopian possibilities of poetry and it points to what Perez, in a 2017 version "Praise Song" published in *The Missing Slate*, refers to as a "horizon/ of care" (n. p.). This horizon of care is ecological insofar as it insists that human and non-human destinies are inextricably entwined and that any hope for more sustainable and more just futures must be based on radically new ethical principles and political arrangements that poetry can help us to imagine. As Perez's poem illustrates, environmental perspectives that acknowledge the experiences and histories of displacement as well as the diverse cultures of mobility of Indigenous and otherwise marginalized peoples are central to such an endeavor.

Ecopoetic Place-Making examines the complex visions of belonging and the ecological horizons of care evoked in contemporary American poetry about nature and mobility. It explores how poetic texts written by poets with different migratory backgrounds reimagine human-nature relations from various perspectives of mobility. The migrant poets I read are CHamoru poet Craig Santos Perez, Anglo-American poet Juliana Spahr, Caribbean poet Derek Walcott, Kashmiri-American poet Agha Shahid Ali, and Lebanese American poet Etel Adnan. The relationships of migratory subjects to the natural world, the works of these poets insist, are complex and fraught with histories of gendered, class-based, racial, colonial, and indeed environmental violence, raising questions about conventional notions of place-based belonging, identity, and community as well as about what it means for people on the move to encounter and engage with the more-than-human world. Instead of focusing primarily on experiences of deterritorialization or a sense of placelessness of the kind often evoked in relation to (post)modern American literature in general and migrant literatures in particular (see Halttunen, Harding, Zelinsky, or Verghese), the poets I have selected evoke human-nature relations that are meaningful in environmental terms not merely *in spite of*, but precisely *because of* the experiences of mobility that shape these relations. Their works counter the idea that literatures of migration are produced predominantly in an abstract, decidedly urban space of cultural hybridity and transnational networks in which "physical geography is of no longer much importance" (Verghese xiv), even if, as Indian-American migrant poet Abraham Verghese puts it in his foreword to *Contours of the Heart: South Asians Map North America* (1996) by referencing William Carlos Williams, there are moments when "everything in [the migrant poet's] world seems to depend on the jasmine blooming" (xv).

The idea that migratory lives and literatures are doubly removed from the natural world is problematic from an environmental standpoint, because, as ecocritics have long argued in other contexts, such a view feeds into the very "crisis of the imagination" (Buell, *The Environmental Imagination* 2) that is at least partly responsible for our present global environmental crisis. Describing (post)modern cultures in general and migrant cultures in particular as always already deterritorialized and detached from place constitutes a reductive overgeneralization that prevents close examination of how these texts represent the natural world and non-urban environments. As Ursula K. Heise famously noted in *Sense of Place and Sense of Planet* (2008), processes of globalization have not done away with forms of culture invested in a "sense of place" (8). Rather, they have led to the production of "new forms of culture that are premised [....] on ties to territories and systems that are understood to encompass the planet as a whole" (*Sense of Place* 10). While I consider notions of "ecocosmopolitanism" (Heise, *Sense of Place* 10) when they are expressed in the poetry I analyze, I am overall more interested in how "local places," including those whose names we do not frequently hear and whose coordinates we are not sure about, continue to matter in contemporary American poetries of migration. This choice results from the fact that, even though the works of poetry I discuss here contradict the idea that experiences of migration must necessarily lead to a sense of placelessness, they also do not necessarily evoke a "sense of planet" (Heise, *Sense of Place* 21). Instead, they imagine meaningful "glocal" human-place relations in the context of mobility, that is, human-place relations that acknowledge the powerful pull that the local continues to exert on the global and vice versa (Heise, *Sense of Place* 51; Buell, *The Future*

92) together with the continued importance that local natural environments hold for migratory subjects.

The poets whose work I analyze in *Ecopoetic Place-Making* are migrants of various national, cultural, ethnic, and racial backgrounds. Highly educated and affiliated with institutions of higher education both in the U.S. and elsewhere, they write from migratory positions of relative privilege, taking a long and often critical view of American ideas and practices surrounding issues of nature and mobility. Rather than serving as a refuge from the human world or as sites for detached contemplation, the landscapes they evoke in their poems reveal a complex layering of place and equally complex histories of displacement, calling into question traditional definitions of place as a closed and stable site of human attachment and engagement. Their poems feature migrant speakers who struggle to develop, regain, or maintain meaningful relationships to the more-than-human world as they explore the many ways in which human-nature relations are shaped by physical and geographical movement, whether voluntary or forced. By creatively reimagining such relationships from varying perspectives of im/mobility, a poetic project I conceptualize in this book as *ecopoetic place-making*, their works testify to the potential as well as the limits of poetry as a means to produce environmental imaginaries fit for our contemporary age of converging global environmental and mobility crises. By engaging with issues of nature and mobility in the United States in the context of longer histories of violence as well as the pervasive structures of oppression these histories have produced, their poems evoke ecopoetic place-making as a restorative or constitutive practice for more-than-human communities and human-nature relations in a particular place. At the same time, they evoke contexts in which practices of place-making turn destructive, that is to say, contexts in which place-making becomes place-*taking*, harming rather than supporting the flourishing of local environments and communities. When read with a double focus on issues of nature and mobility, the works of contemporary American poetry that I analyze in *Ecopoetic Place-Making* reveal both the potential and the limits of ecopoetic place-making in light of different experiences of mobility and histories of displacement. In doing so, they not only point to less parochial and more inclusive forms of belonging and community formation; they also serve as valuable sources of environmental insight for our contemporary world on the move.

Theorizing Nature and Mobility in Contemporary American Poetry

Employing the terms *nature* and *mobility* side by side in an analysis of contemporary American poetry may seem paradoxical in that the term and idea of *nature* has largely fallen out of favor with scholars in American studies, while *mobility* is one of the field's current buzzwords. Ecocritics, too, have been urged to let go of the idea of "nature" after environmental thinkers proclaimed its untimely end.[1] In his influ-ential study *Ecology without Nature* (2007), Timothy Morton argues, for example, that "the very idea of 'nature' which so many hold dear will have to wither away in an 'eco-logical' state of human society. Strange as it may sound, the idea of nature is getting in the way of properly ecological forms of culture, philosophy, politics, and art" (1). Like other ecocritics before and after him, Morton rejects the idea of "nature" in favor of that of "ecology" because, as he sees it, the former "impedes a proper relationship with the earth and its lifeforms [... that would] include ethics and science" due to its "confusing, ideological intensity" (*Ecology* 2). While I do not mean to deny that a more nuanced understanding of the principles of ecology and a more in-depth knowledge of the findings of contemporary environmental science can produce more sustain-able and ethical ways of living, history as well as current public debates about cli-mate change teach that they do not necessarily do so. As many scholars writing on the subject have noted, the knowledge produced by the natural and environmen-tal sciences, like any form of knowledge, can all too easily be decoupled from ethics or yoked to political agendas that clash with principles of sustainability and, even more frequently perhaps, with principles of environmental justice. What is more, scientific knowledge can easily be ignored or, even when understood, fail to move people to action. A more complex understanding of ecology is thus by no means a guarantee for more "ecological" forms of ethics or politics. Reversely, I would ar-gue that even if the idea of "nature" possesses a "confusing, ideological intensity," as Morton notes, it can nonetheless produce what environmentalists or ecocritics would view as a "proper" ethics and politics: one that secures a better future for life on this planet, or simply *a future* as one might have to phrase it at this point in his-tory. For such an environmental ethics and politics to emerge and to remain viable in a world in which science sometimes matters less for social and political processes than other forms of culture and in which both the most environmentally beneficial and the most harmful politics are not necessarily based on any easily recognizable or coherent ethics, ideas of nature and conceptualizations of human-nature relations must be discussed in a manner that does justice to their complexity and encourages a critical interrogation of the histories and ideologies that shape them. Poetry, I posit, is a medium that is well suited for precisely this purpose.

---

1   For a detailed discussion of arguments concerning the "end of nature" by such theorists as Bill McKibben (*The End of Nature*, 1989), Carolyn Merchant (*The Death of Nature: Women, Ecol-ogy, and the Scientific Revolution* 1980) and Bruno Latour (*The Politics of Nature*, 2004) and its relation to the "end of history" famously proclaimed ("The End of History" 1989) and then again retracted (*Identity: The Demand for Dignity and the Politics of Resentment*, 2018) by Francis Fukuyama, see, for example, Margaret Ronda's chapter on "Mourning and Melancholia at the End of Nature" from her study *Remainders: American Poetry at Nature's End* (2018).

In *The Ecological Thought* (2012), Morton goes into more detail about why he charges the idea of "nature" with a "confusing, ideological intensity": again like others before and after him, he associates it with "hierarchy, authority, harmony, purity, neutrality, and mystery" (3), which is why, he comments, he sometimes uses "a capital N to highlight [nature's] 'unnatural' qualities" (3). This distinction between "nature" and "Nature" is a crucial one to make, and one that must be made consistently for the concept to be useful. In what follows, I use the word *Nature* with a capitalized *N* to refer to what philosopher Kate Soper has described as the "metaphysical concept" (*What is Nature* 155). This metaphysical Nature is also what ecocritic Lawrence Buell—in drawing on cultural critic Raymond Williams—identifies as "the capitalized Nature of classical mythology or eighteenth-century Deism" (Buell, *The Future* 143), which has lived on in American (proto-)environmental discourse from the Enlightenment onward. In order to distinguish this metaphysical idea of Nature from the material world of physical experience, I refer to the latter by using the term *nature* with a small *n*. This material nature includes what Soper calls the "realist concept" (*What is Nature* 155) of nature, that is, the "structures, processes and causal powers that are constantly operative within the world" (155) or, put differently, the ecological systems and phenomena studied by science. It also encompasses the "'lay' or 'surface' concept" (Soper 156) of nature, that is, the "ordinarily observable features of the world" (156), or the nonhuman environment we encounter every day, during a walk in the neighborhood, our daily car drive or bicycle ride to work, or a weekend hike. Contemporary American poetry invested in nature and mobility features all of these dimensions of N/nature. Indeed, the works of poetry I discuss in *Ecopoetic Place-Making* provide deeply generative material for analysis exactly because they engage not only with the natural world as observed by more or less mobile subjects, or with the material ecologies that are examined in ever more detail by science, but because they also engage with mythical Nature as it has been contemplated, whether skeptically or reverently, by philosophers and poets through the ages. In this sense, then, I am interested less in the death or impossibility of *nature* in the Anthropocene than in the afterlife of *Nature* and in the presence (and indeed in some cases the strange possibilities and utter aliveness) of material and observable *natures* in contemporary American poetry of migration.

Ever since the emergence of ecocriticism as a scholarly discipline, ecocritics have engaged critically with the many different dimensions and meanings of N/nature. They have asked how notions of an essential dichotomy between human beings and the natural world must be rethought, when technoscientific advances are allowing biogenetic manipulations of unprecedented degree and when microp-ollutants whose long-term effects on the human body are yet to be determined have been proven to travel as freely between ecosystems as they travel between ecosystems and our bodies. Already before the so-called materialist turn in the humanities, ecocritics had challenged ideas of nature as that which is separate from us or that which is *not* us. Drawing from earlier ecofeminist and Marxist-feminist theorizations of materiality as well as from New Materialist paradigms, Stacy Alaimo's influential study *Bodily Natures* (2010), for instance, demonstrates the porosity of the boundaries between human and nonhuman "natures" in an effort to gauge "the possibilities for more robust and complex conceptions of the materiality of human bodies and the more-than-human world" (2). Such a reconceptualization of materiality is necessary, she argues, because in an age of global environmental crisis, ethics are "not merely social but material" (Alaimo, *Bodily Natures* 2), which is to say that they depend on "the emergent, ultimately unmappable landscapes of interacting biological, climatic, economic, and political forces" (2). Acknowledging the porosity of bodily selves vis-à-vis the world that environs them, Alaimo emphasizes, is "an ethical matter" that must ultimately lead to an "epistemological shift" in the form of a dismantling of anthropocentric and environmentally destructive fantasies about human mastery over the physical world (*Bodily Natures* 17). Discussing Muriel Rukeyser's groundbreaking poem sequence "Book of the Dead" (1938) amongst other environmental(ist) texts, Alaimo insists that literature and other forms of cultural expression can help to produce such an epistemological shift by fostering critical awareness about the precarious position of human bodies in an increasingly toxic world. My readings of Juliana Spahr's and Etel Adnan's poetry demonstrate how such an argument can be made for poetry that is invested in issues of nature and mobility. In related but also very different ways, the works of these two poets of migration demonstrate that the N/nature represented in contemporary American poetry can come to encompass the precarious materiality of human bodies, including the cognitive-somatic processes that take place in these bodies. Put differently, contemporary American poetry about nature and mobility not only features metaphysical Nature, nonhuman ecologies, and everyday physical environments, it sometimes also foregrounds entanglements of more-than-human and human natures.

While contemporary American poetries of migration evoke all kinds of human and nonhuman natures, they remain particularly invested in everyday experiences of nonhuman environments. In order to analyze these everyday experiences of nonhuman environments, I draw on theories of place as discussed in spatial and environmental literary studies. My use of the term *place*—like that of many ecocritics—follows human geographer Yi-Fu Tuan, who defines place as "an organized world of meaning" (*Space and Place* 179) characterized by a certain "boundedness" (54) and as space made "concrete" by experience (18) and memory (154). Although I rely on Tuan's basic distinction between space and place, I take issue, as others have before me, with his descriptions of place as a "pause" (6) and as "a calm center of established values" (54) that stands in contrast to "space" which he defines as "that which allows movement" (6). While I thus use the term *place* because it denotes concreteness, boundedness, and a fullness of meaning, I also draw from theorizations of place that do not define places as the obverse of mobility, such as Doreen Massey's influential description of a "global sense of place" ("A Global Sense of Place" 28; *For Space* 131). As Karen Halttunen noted in her 2005 presidential address to the American Studies Association (ASA) on the continued importance of questions of place for the field, Massey's conceptualization of place is productive for cultural and literary analysis because it is "not closed but open, not essentialist but hybrid, not reactionary but progressive, not static but dynamic" (Halttunen, "Groundwork" 2). In Massey, as well as in the works of scholars inspired by her writing, a global sense of place is frequently conceived of as an urban phenomenon, that is, as the product of human engagement with the city as a cosmopolitan space (Halttunen "Groundwork" 2). It would be wrong to claim that this idea does not register in contemporary American poetries of migration. Indeed, I could have analyzed collections that depict human and nonhuman mobilities in urban environments, such as Ed Roberson's *City Eclogue* (2006), Aracelis Girmay's *Kingdom Animalia* (2011), or Harriett Mullen's *Urban Tumbleweed* (2013). Yet, one of the main objectives of this study is to show how non-urban environments and their representations in poetries of migration, too, can become sites of an open, hybrid, progressive, and dynamic sense of place, when reconsidered from perspectives of mobility.

One of the reasons why analyses of space and place in literature frequently focus on urban environments is because they tend to rely heavily on thinkers such as Michel de Certeau, Henry Lefebvre, and Edward Soja, who developed their theories of spatiality by analyzing the (post)modern city. More useful for my purposes, then, are approaches to place offered by critical regionalism, a field of study that investigates representations of complex place-formations and non-urban environments by foregrounding issues of race and histories of dispossession. Taking seriously the interventions of critical regionalism for a study of contemporary American poetry about nature and mobility means reading representations of U.S.-American places in these works through what Stephen Tatum has described as a "newer field imaginary" ("Postfrontier Horizons" 461)—an imaginary that "involves subaltern voices and alternative histories" (461). One of the matters at stake in such a newer field imaginary, Tatum indicates, then, is a thoroughgoing exploration of how identity affects people's relationship to place and vice versa.

As Krista Comer contends in "Exceptionalism, Other Wests, Critical Regionalism" (2011), "one unstated issue under discussion [in critical regionalism and New Western criticism] concerns identity and its politics and their relationship to an *ethics of place*" (160, emphasis added). In Comer's understanding, such an ethics of place should be less oriented toward the non-human "environment" and more "toward the interface among people, communities or places and their constitution with and through discourse, materialist geography, and in-place structures of feeling" (173). One larger point I want to make in *Ecopoetic Place-Making* is that in an age of global environmental crisis shaped by human (and nonhuman) mass migration within and across borders, an ethics of place invested in the multidimensional associations between people, communities, and places also has to be an environmental ethics of place invested in the more-than-human world. In particular, it has to be an ethics of place that interrogates how histories of displacement and experiences of mobility, together with "in-place structures of feeling" (Comer 173), affect humans' relationships to and engagements with the nonhuman world of the places they encounter.

In the preface to his poetry collection *No Nature* (1992), poet Gary Snyder notes that nature is not easily defined because it "will not fulfill our conceptions or assumptions" but instead "dodge our expectations and theoretical models" (v). The same can be said about mobility. Yet, mobilities must be studied, not least since increased mobility, or perhaps rather increasingly conflicted regimes of im/mobility, are often taken to be one of the defining characteristics of our current age, such as when James Clifford describes postmodernity as an era defined by a "new world order of mobility" (*Routes* 1).[2] The nascent field of cultural mobility studies provides the necessary tools to discuss the different forms of mobility that characterize this new world order of mobility and their representations in literature. In *On the Move: Mobility in the Modern Western World* (2006), human geographer and poet Tim Cresswell productively suggests that "*movement* can be thought of as abstracted mobility (mobility abstracted from contexts of power)" (2; emphasis original). Mobility, in this conception, is movement in social, political, and cultural contexts of power and thus "movement plus meaning" (Cresswell 3). Mobility, Cresswell outlines, is "practiced," "experienced," and "embodied" (3), which makes it "the dynamic equivalent of *place*" (3; emphasis original). If one views mobility not merely as "a thing in the world, an empirical reality" (3), but in fact as "socially produced motion" (3), any analysis of mobility has to pay attention to how the meanings of different kinds of mobility are "conveyed through a diverse array of representational strategies" (3). Contemporary mobility scholarship, in other words, is situated at "the interface between mobile physical bodies on the one hand, and the represented mobilities on the other" (Cresswell 4).

Mimi Sheller and John Urry, two key figures of the "new mobilities paradigm" in the social sciences, too, emphasize that the analysis of mobilities requires both interrogation of "the relation between local and global 'power geometries'" and an

---

2   While scholars such as James Clifford, Rosi Braidotti (*Nomadic Subjects* 2), or Kevin Robins ("Encountering Globalization" 195) link mobility to globalization and thus to postmodernity, other scholars delineate a longer history for our current "world order of mobility." Marshall Berman (*All That Is Solid Melts into Air: The Experience of Modernity*, 1988), Zygmunt Baumann (*Liquid Modernity*, 2000), Tim Cresswell (*On the Move*, 2006, esp. 10–20) and Richard Sennett (*Flesh and Stone: The Body and the City in Western Civilization*, 1994, esp. 255–56) regard mobility as a phenomenon that emerged with the Renaissance and Enlightenment and was transformed during the nineteenth and twentieth century.

examination of the relation "between the physical and symbolic dimensions of cultures of mobility" (211). By investigating such relations, Sheller and Urry suggest, the new mobility studies they propose can help us understand how people imagine "the 'atmosphere of place'" together with how they experience the "'feeling' of particular kinds of movement" (218), questions, they note, that are also "often a concern in the *poetry and literature of exile and displacement*" (218; emphasis added). By analyzing the works of contemporary American poets of migration who foreground both the atmosphere and feeling of place, or what ecocritics will often call "sense of place" (see Buell, *The Future* 77; Heise *Sense of Place*), then, my study not only draws from insights of new mobilities scholarship in cultural studies and the social sciences; it also seeks to generate insights of value for the critical debates surrounding mobile cultures and cultural mobility in these fields as well as in the humanities at large.

American studies, and especially American studies in Europe, is one of the scholarly disciplines in which cultural and literary mobility studies have generated ongoing and fruitful debates.[3] In his introduction to *Cultural Mobility: A Manifesto* (2009), a collaborative publication by literary and cultural studies scholars from North America and Europe, Stephen Greenblatt emphasizes the need to "rethink fundamental conceptions about the fate of culture in an age of global mobility" ("Cultural Mobility" 1–2). He calls for an examination of "cultural mobility" across disciplinary limits and especially in literary studies, where, as he asserts, the phenomenon of mobility has so far only been addressed in passing ("Cultural Mobility" 3–4). In his closing statement to the same publication, Greenblatt establishes several axioms for the study of cultural mobility in and beyond literature, axioms indebted to the work of scholars such as John Urry and Mimi Sheller. In drawing from sociology, geography, and adjacent fields, Greenblatt argues, literary and cultural mobility studies must examine the "literal" or physical "*movements* of people, objects, images, texts, and ideas" as well as the "metaphorical" movements connected to these mobilities "A Mobility Studies Manifesto" 250; emphasis original). Scholars invested in literary and cultural mobility studies, he suggests, must examine how structural and institutional constraints, as well as the pull of the local, shape experiences and representations of mobilities ("A Mobility Studies Manifesto" 252) and theorize how cultures of mobility remain "strikingly enmeshed in particular times and places" (252), both symbolically and materially.

---

3   See, for instance, Alexandra Ganser's study *Roads of Her Own: Gendered Space and Mobility in American Women's Road Narratives, 1970–2000* (2009); the essay collection *Pirates, Drifters, Fugitives: Figures of Mobility in the US and Beyond* (2012), edited by Heike Paul, Alexandra Ganser, and Katharina Gerund; Ann Brigham's monograph *American Road Narratives: Reimagining Mobility in Literature and Film* (2015); and Julia Leyda's recent study *American Mobilities: Geographies of Class, Race, and Gender in US Culture* (2016).

Examining mobilities along with their constraints and "enmeshments"—a term popularized in the environmental and mobility humanities not least due to Timothy Morton's use of the metaphor of the "mesh" in *The Ecological Thought* (2012)—requires paying close attention to the specific material, historical, social, and cultural contexts that shape represented mobilities as well as to the human-nature relations these representations (re-)produce. To give examples from the texts discussed in this study: it makes a difference whether the mobile subject depicted in a given text is a Black Caribbean poet who takes a road-trip through the U.S.-South to visit the place where the Trail of Tears started, as in one section of Derek Walcott's book-length poem *Omeros* (1990), or whether the mobile subject is a transnational migrant and air-traveler who contemplates the desert landscapes and colonial history of the American Southwest during take-off, as in Agha Shahid Ali's poem "Leaving Sonora" (1991). It matters whether the mobile subject is a Lebanese exile walking by the Pacific Ocean and remembering the Mediterranean Sea of her childhood, as in Etel Adnan's poetry, or an Anglo-American woman from the continental United States who becomes acutely aware of her complicity in existing structures of colonial domination and capitalist exploitation after she moves to Hawai'i, as in Juliana Spahr's works. Just as the differences in the represented mobilities and enmeshments matter, so does exploring the differences between the environmental imaginaries of mobility that emerge in the texts of migrant poets who are positioned differently in relation to the social, cultural, and physical environments they move to, through, and away from.

While scholars working in third wave postcolonial and transnational ecocriticism have been discussing places as porous formations open to all kinds of transnational movements at least since the early 2000s (Slovic 7), issues surrounding human mobility have only more recently become a matter of more systematic investigation in these fields. In such writings, the concept of "migration" has sometimes been favored, because, as Ursula K. Heise points out, it is "more ecologically grounded" than other concepts linked to geographical mobility such as "nomadism" or "vagabondage" (*Sense of Place* 31). In one of the landmark studies of second-wave ecocriticism, *The Future of Environmental Criticism* (2005), Lawrence Buell called on ecocritics to account for the ways in which displacement, diaspora, and migration challenge traditional notions of "sense of place" and sustainable living (64). Two scholars in particular, one might argue, have responded to this call to action, addressing the revision of place-sense through displacement in ways that are especially relevant for my study. Each in their own way, Rob Nixon and Elizabeth DeLoughrey (the latter often in collaboration with other scholars) critique traditional notions of place and place-attachment in environmental literary criticism and in the process have generated environmental theories of displacement that acknowledge the role of human and nonhuman mobilities in the production of places and the formation of postcolonial as well as transnational ecologies.

Rather than being viewed primarily as an individual experience or a particular perspective related to geographical movement, displacement has sometimes been discussed as a condition that the subject suffers either as a result of the legacies of colonialism or as a result of globalization.[4] Displacement in this sense is not, or not primarily, the result of human mobility. Instead, it is the result of living in a place that has either historically been affected by disruptive mobility regimes, such as colonization and settler colonialism, or in a place that is traversed by so many global flows of goods, peoples, and ideas that the very bases of place-attachment—meaningful political, social, cultural, and ecological relations—have been lost. In his influential study *Slow Violence and the Environmentalism of the Poor* (2011), Rob Nixon draws on this logic when he discusses what he calls "displacement in place" (17). Displacement here takes on the meaning of an environmental disenfranchisement linked to immobilization and experienced by those at the margins of society, whether for economic reasons or due to racial discrimination. According to Nixon, such "displacement in place" is a consequence of past and present acts of colonial violence and expresses itself in destructive human-nature relationships that cast "displaced" social groups as both victims of environmental injustice and as accessories to or even the primary perpetrators of environmental destruction (*Slow Violence* 17–22). While it is important to acknowledge such dynamics of "displacement without moving" (Nixon, *Slow Violence* 19), it is equally crucial to distinguish them from experiences of physical displacement linked to geographic mobility. One primary aim of this study is to explore the conceptually distinct, yet inter-linked phenomena of displacement with and without movement. Another is to investigate the varying effects that these displacements in place and between places have on human-nature relationships in the United States and, more specifically, the effects they have on the environmental imaginaries emerging in the works of contemporary American poets of migration.

More so than Nixon, Elizabeth DeLoughrey reflects on the environmental significance of displacement between places, that is, of displacement as a form of geographical and physical movement. In her writing on Caribbean and Pacific literatures and postcolonial as well as Indigenous ecologies, DeLoughrey repeatedly emphasizes that, as she and George B. Handley put it in their introduction to *Postcolonial Ecologies* (2011), "attachment to the land or localism itself is not an inherently ethical or ecological position" (6). Challenging environmental ideals of place-attachment and localism, many of DeLoughrey's publications interrogate how displace-

---

4   Displacement understood in this way bears a certain similarity with what John Tomlinson describes as "deterritorialization" (*Globalization and Culture* 9), that is, a condition affecting some places and peoples more than others, in which the "complex connectivity" that characterizes globalized modernity "weakens the ties of culture to place" in ways that underscore the "simultaneous penetration of local worlds by distant forces, and the dislodging of everyday meanings from their 'anchors' in the local environment" (Tomlinson 29).

ments and migrations of various kinds have affected and continue to affect the natural environment in the Caribbean and other (formerly) colonized island territories and how Caribbean literature in particular has been struggling to come to terms with the effects of "diaspora and transplantation" (DeLoughrey and Handley, "Introduction" 7). In her contribution to the *Routledge Companion to Anglophone Caribbean Literature* (2011), for instance, DeLoughrey points out that "Caribbean literature is deeply engaged with the history of human and plant diasporas, rendering a complex cultural ecology and a dialogic imagination" ("Ecocriticism" 266). This kind of engagement of literature with different "diasporas" is environmentally suggestive, she argues, because foregrounding these histories of displacement "calls attention to our very assumptions about what is a natural landscape" ("Ecocriticism" 266). Following DeLoughrey, I am exploring the complex cultural ecologies produced by diaspora and displacement in the Caribbean (Walcott), in the Pacific (Perez, Spahr), and in the continental United States (Spahr, Walcott, Ali, Adnan).

Due to the region's complex histories of displacement, I argue in drawing on DeLoughrey and her collaborators, Caribbean literature is prone to troubling received notions about human-nature relations. As a result, it generates environmental imaginaries that can provide insights applicable to other places, such as the United States. As I demonstrate in my study, Derek Walcott's poetry is a particularly salient example for the difficult yet ultimately productive translation processes that take place when Caribbean "postcolonial" environmental sensibilities are transposed onto U.S.-American geographies and into U.S.-American contexts. Linking issues of nature to questions of mobility in her scholarship about the Caribbean, which occasionally mentions Walcott, DeLoughrey raises questions that are pertinent for my reading of poems about landscapes, histories, and experiences of displacements in the settler-colonial United States. Which theories and concepts developed within the Caribbean postcolonial and environmental context can be productively transferred to the U.S. American context? Which ones cannot and why? In what ways would a "complex cultural ecology and a dialogic imagination" (DeLoughrey, "Ecocriticism" 266) concerned with U.S.-American landscapes and histories look different to one concerned with the Caribbean? How do images of "transplantation" and other textual strategies evoking human and "plant diasporas" change when they are transposed into literature focusing on the United States? My chapter on Walcott's long poem *Omeros* (1990), in which I trace the shift from a postcolonial to a transnational and ultimately planetary environmental imagination, addresses some of these questions.

Like many other ecocritics, I assume that humans turn to art in order to rethink their relationship to the more-than-human world, because "it is in art that the fantasies we have about nature take shape—and dissolve" (Morton, *Ecology* 1). In a similar fashion, I contend, we must examine the fantasies of mobility that take shape and dissolve in art—whether these fantasies involve notions of "[m]obility as progress, as freedom, as opportunity, and as modernity, [... or notions of] mobility as shiftlessness, as deviance, and as resistance" (Cresswell, *On the Move* 1–2). Indeed, as I argue here, the terms *nature* and *mobility*, especially when used in the plural, are ideally suited for a study focused on the art of poetry, precisely because of their semantic range. Poetry, as the modernist American poet Marianne Moore famously observed, is the art of creating "imaginary gardens with real toads / in them" ("Poetry"). Arguably "the most deliberately figurative of activities" (Knickerbocker 5), poetry does not stand at a distance to the world; rather, it foregrounds "how to figure forth the world and what kind of figures and formal devices best dramatize the complex relationships between the human and nonhuman" (Knickerbocker 16). It deals with the real as well as with the imagined, with the histories, lived experiences, and the observable features of the world as much as with abstractions, fantasies, mythologies, and metaphysics. What is more, it can capture the clashing spatial and temporal scales of the Anthropocene. As David Farrier argues in *Anthropocene Poetics: Deep Time, Sacrifice Zones, and Extinction* (2019):

> Poetry can compress vast acreages of meaning into a small compass or perform the kind of bold linkages that would take reams of academic argument to plot; it can widen the aperture of our gaze or deposit us on the brink of transformation. In short, it can model an Anthropogenic perspective in which our sense of relationship and proximity (and from this, our ethics) is stretched and tested against the Anthropocene's warping effects. (5)

When I thus speak about *nature* and *mobility*—or rather, *natures* and *mobilities*—in analyzing contemporary American poetry, I do so because both terms have material, social, political, cultural, historical, and symbolic or figurative dimensions; each can carry many different meanings in different contexts; and each encompass different scales, ranging from the microscopic to the planetary.

Drawing from theorizations of nature and mobility in the fields of ecocriticism and mobility studies, four main sets of questions provide the starting point of my study: first, which kinds of *places and nonhuman natures* figure prominently in contemporary American poetries of migration and what issues of identity, community, and belonging do they foreground? Second, which kinds of *histories of displacement and experiences of mobility* are particularly prominent in these texts and which questions do they raise about humans' relations to the more-than-human world? Third, which kinds of *poetic strategies* are employed by poems that deal with natural environments and human mobilities? And, fourth, what kinds of *environmental imaginaries* emerge in the process? In order to address these questions, I explore the complex evocations of non-human environments, natures, and places in contemporary American poetry and the ways in which the poets I have selected imagine meaningful human-nature relations in light of human mobility, migration, and displacement. I argue that the works of poetry I analyze produce *mobile environmental imaginaries* by engaging in a self-consciously *poetic fashioning* of human-nature relations in which all the material, social, cultural, as well as symbolic and figurative dimensions of nature and mobility come into play. It is this self-consciously poetic and environmentally suggestive fashioning of meaningful human-nature relations in light of different histories, experiences, and perspectives of mobility that I refer to as *ecopoetic place-making*.

Theorizing Ecopoetic Place-Making

The poetic works I discuss in my study engage in *place-making* from varying perspectives of mobility. Used primarily in the social sciences, anthropology, human geography, and urban planning, the term *place-making* refers to the act of creating culturally significant landscapes both for and by individuals and communities. As I analyze contemporary American poetries of migration, I am interested in how such acts of place-making in poetry and through poetry can become environmentally resonant. While there are many cultural practices that can be employed for place-making, poetic language and literature are a particularly effective tool for this purpose, as human-geographer Yi-Fu Tuan argues. In his essay "Language and the Making of Place" (1991), Tuan rejects the idea that places come into being because of "the material transformation of nature" (684). Instead, he suggests that practical activities of "speech" are an equally crucial "component of the total force that transforms nature into a human place" (Tuan, "Language" 685). Indeed, he urges scholars of place to take language seriously because it "enables us to understand [...] the *quality* (the personality or character) of place better, for that quality is imparted by, along with visual appearance and other factors, the metaphorical and symbolic powers of language" (694; emphasis original). Tuan here proposes what he calls a "narrative-descriptive approach" to "the process of place-making" (684). Building on Paul Ricoeur's phenomenology, Tuan explores how "individual words and, even more, sentences and larger units impart emotion and personality, and hence high visibility, to objects and places" (685). Although Tuan calls his approach to place-making "narrative-descriptive," he continuously stresses the importance of "language's metaphorical power" (685), indicating that works of poetry may be just as well, if not better suited for the project of place-making compared with everyday speech or narrative prose. Indeed, I would posit that prose narratives tend to have marked advantages when it comes to length and the portrayal of relationships over time. Poetry, by contrast, may be better suited for the purpose of place-making in cases where the many dimensions of N/nature and the multilayered histories of places—together with the multiple contexts and meanings of different forms of mobility—do not cohere into conventional forms of narrative. This may be the reason, then, why many of the poets I discuss combine narrative and poetic elements in their writing, such as when Spahr and

Adnan blur the boundaries of prose and poetry, when Perez integrates prose texts into his poetry or when Derek Walcott integrates poetic short forms into the long form of the epic. It may also be the reason for why all the works of poetry I discuss in this study exceed in some way or another the short form, whether because they consist of a book-length poem (Walcott), frequently make use of long poem sequences (Spahr, Adnan, Perez), or stem from a collection in which a significant number of the poems included cohere thematically (Ali). Contemporary American poetry about nature and mobility and concerned with practices of place-making tend toward longer forms, I suggest, to account for the multidimensional interrelations between different natures and mobilities as well as for the processual nature of place-making.

Often used in connection with concepts such as "place-attachment," "emplacement," or "sense of place," the term "place-making" began to appear more frequently in literary and cultural studies at the end of the first decade of the new millennium and under the influence of spatial and environmental criticism. In the introduction to her study *Migrant Sites: America, Place, and Diaspora Literatures* (2009), Dalia Kandiyoti, for example, draws attention to the "complexity of place-making" in the context of migration and suggests "translocality" as a lens through which to "view the production of place as a crossroads of practices and memories of multiple loci" (6). Following sociologists Hilary Cunningham and Josiah McC. Heyman, Kandiyoti views place-making as a cultural practice characterized by the "dual rubrics" of "[e]nclosure and movement" most poignantly manifested in borders and boundaries meant to allow or prevent particular forms of mobility (Kandiyoti 104; see also Cunningham and Heyman 295). Such a critical conceptualization of place-making is particularly useful for my analysis of Craig Santos Perez's poetry about Guam/Guåhan, which highlights moments of forced immobilization in the context of colonization and military occupation, and for my analysis of Spahr's poetry about Hawai'i, which repeatedly touches on matters of race-based exclusion and identity-based access to land.

More explicitly even than Kandiyoti, Sarah Jaquette Ray comments on the links between mobility and place-making in her study *The Ecological Other* (2013). Discussing issues of immigration and environmental pollution in connection to the disenfranchisement of Native American peoples in the U.S.-American Southwest, Ray draws on such ecocritics as Rob Nixon to argue that an uncritical celebration of "place-rootedness implicitly renders the *displaced* ecologically illegitimate" even as it "ignores the geopolitical conditions of their movement" (*The Ecological Other* 155; emphasis original). In order to find a way out of this impasse, Ray turns to the work of anthropologists Teresa M. Mares and Devon Peña, who provide an alternative to what Ray calls the "environmentalist fetishization of place" (*The Ecological Other* 156). Writing about environmental and food justice in the Southwest, Mares and Peña (2011) suggest that migrants engage in transnational forms of "place making" (199) in an effort to create viable links between places, personal identity, and their community even while remaining mobile. Where Mares and Peña consider the role of food cultivation and food culture for migrants' place-making, I return to Lawrence Buell's claim that "[s]tory and song are often vital to the retention of place-sense under such conditions [as exile, migration, and displacement]" (*The Future* 64). Indeed, like many scholars of ecopoetry have done before me (see, for example, Bate, Knickerbocker, Keller *Recomposing Ecopoetics*, or Ronda), I propose that "song" rather than "story," and more precisely, the relative complexity and opacity of poetry (see Milne, *Poetry Matters* 5; Keller *Thinking Poetry* 2; Rigby 5) rather than the relative linearity and transparency of (conventional) narrative prose, may be particularly well suited for the production of viable environmental imaginaries in our current moment in history and for imagining/theorizing more inclusive and mobile forms of place-sense and place-engagement in the face of displacement.

Following Karen Halttunen, I view "place-making as an ongoing and always contested process" ("Groundwork" 4) and analyze contemporary American poetry about nature and mobility as one particular manifestation of "the creative variety of cultural practices employed for place-making" (4). Insomuch as my study foregrounds processes of place-making in poetry, it resembles Jim Cocola's monograph *Places in the Making: A Cultural Geography of American Poetry* (2016), which identifies a "poetics centered upon more particular and situated engagements with actual places and spaces" and thus a poetic tradition that is centered on place(-making) as distinct from "related traditions including landscape poetry, nature poetry, and pastoral poetry" (xi). Like Cocola, I am interested in works of poetry that posit "place as a pivotal axis of identification," unfold "at the juncture of the proximate and the remote and establishing translocal, planetary, and cosmic connections," and in the process go "beyond epic and lyric modes" (xi). Where Cocola discusses a broad range of poets and poetic traditions across the Americas and from modernism to the present, at times in relation to issues of mobility (see especially the book's section on "Translocalities"), my study focuses specifically on late twentieth- and early twenty-first century migrant poets who evoke the complex layering of American places, the ways various kinds of human mobilities affect nonhuman environments, and the human-nature relationships as well as environmental imaginaries that emerge from the encounters of mobile subjects with the nonhuman world. What is more, where Cocola adopts a spatial or geocritical approach by advocating for "cultural geography as a crucial mode of inquiry" (Cocola xi), even as he occasionally touches on environmental issues, I approach my primary texts from a distinctly ecocritical perspective in an effort to carve out the social and environmental significance of practices of poetic place-making in the context of mobility.

When I speak of *poetic* place-making rather than merely of place-making, I do so to distinguish the broad spectrum of possible "cultural practices employed for place-making" (Halttunen, "Groundwork" 4) from literary and more narrowly poetic ones. I also do so to differentiate between the various *non-poetic* practices of place-making that can be *represented* in a poem from the practice of *poetic* place-making that the poem itself can *constitute*. By making these distinctions, I by no means intend to dismiss or belittle place-making activities such as gardening, hiking, taking a walk, or going bird watching, which are certainly well suited for many people, including migrants, who want or need to gain a better feeling and understanding of the place(s) they live in or move through. In fact, all of these activities appear frequently in the works of poets of migration. In particular, many of the migrant poets who write about the natural world consciously place themselves in a long line of American poets walking in nature, even as they complicate some of the racial, gendered, and class-based associations that come with the idea of the walking poet.[5] Evocations of non-poetic/non-literary place-making in poetry are interesting, because they can reveal the sexist, racist, classist, ageist, and ableist biases (more often intersectional than not) that make some forms of mobility and some cultural practices of place-making less accessible than others or outright dangerous for certain groups, such as when women hikers or Black birders experience harassment or even attacks, or when Indigenous people are kept away from their ancestral lands by private or government infrastructures of obstruction such as walls and fences. Problems of accessibility of a different kind become apparent in Etel Adnan's poetry, for example, when she alludes to the fact that her aging speaker is no longer able to climb the mountains or swim in the sea she so dearly loves and instead evokes the experience *in* poetry.

Again, the point is not to suggest that writing and publishing poetry are activities free of biases and exclusions. On the contrary, all the poets discussed in this study, but especially Craig Santos Perez, who writes about the occupied U.S. territory of Guam/Guåhan from an Indigenous perspective, and Juliana Spahr, who writes about Hawai'i from the perspective of a white continental settler, reflect in their poetry on who has access to certain places and who has the authority to write about certain histories of displacement in connection to certain kinds of environmental destruction. Still, it is one of my main arguments that practices of *poetic* place-making, that is, place-making by way of literary texts including but not limited to poetry, can be crucial under certain circumstances, circumstances that include different kinds of migration and forced displacement as well as cases of severe pollution and environmental destruction. Indeed, under circumstances that impede

---

5   Many of the most famous American writers and especially poets have written about walking in nature, including Henry David Thoreau, Walt Whitman, Emily Dickinson, John Muir, Wallace Stevens, Elizabeth Bishop, Theodore Roethke, and Gary Snyder. For a study on the concept of walking in American poetry, see, for example, Roger Gilbert's *Walks in the World: Representation and Experience in Modern American Poetry* (1991). For scholarly publications on the topic of walking in American literature and culture more broadly, see, among others, Michaela Keck's *Walking in the Wilderness: The Peripatetic Tradition in Nineteenth-Century American Literature and Painting* (2006) and *Peregrinations: Walking in American Literature* (2018) by Amy T. Hamilton.

meaningful human-nature relations, I argue, poetic place-making constitutes a viable alternative to other forms of place-making that require physical access to and close contact with particular natural environments plus one or several of the following: considerable financial means, leisure time, white(r) skin, the right passport, or a healthy (male) body.

Contemporary American poetries of migration frequently feature intertextual references to other works of literature invested in nature, mobility, and/or practices of place-making, a gesture that assigns literature a crucial role in the migrant's struggle for place-attachment without permanent emplacement. In my analysis, I thus often comment on instances of intertextuality, such as when Juliana Spahr evokes Walt Whitman, when Craig Santos Perez and Derek Walcott reference Charles Olson, or when Agha Shahid Ali's speaker quotes Emily Dickinson, Henry David Thoreau, or an ethno-botanical book about the Sonoran Desert. In all of these cases, the intertextual references highlight that reading (and writing) can help migrants, displaced peoples, and other mobile subjects to make sense of their relationships to places and to the more-than-human environments they encounter only in passing. Engaging with texts invested in nature, mobility, and (poetic) place-making allows mobile subjects to reflect critically on their own practices of (poetic) place-making. By foregrounding the potential and the limits of place-making in their works, their text can in turn help readers to imagine more inclusive notions of belonging, identity, and community and more sustainable relationships to the more-than-human world. At the same time, I argue, their texts help us to think through and develop more complex conceptualizations about what it means to live sustainable lives that not only account for and are enriched by the perspectives of migrants, exiles, refugees, and other displaced peoples but in fact depend on them for environmental insight.

Reading Contemporary American Ecopoetries of Migration

Discussing poets such as Derek Walcott, Agha Shahid Ali, or Etel Adnan under the rubric of "American poetry" is by no means the only or even necessarily the most obvious choice. I did not choose this classification because I want to make any claims about the poets' citizenship status or about their preferred or lived civic identities, all of which have been or could be debated with regard to most of the poets featured in this study. Instead, I deploy the designation "American poetry" because I focus on texts in the oeuvres of the chosen poets that prominently feature American places and American histories of displacement. The fact that I do so does not mean, though, that I disregard questions of identity and belonging. On the contrary, as my readings repeatedly make clear, the migrant poets whose works I analyze keep asking difficult questions about (place-based) identity, belonging, and community, especially where existing models are restrictive, exclusionary, or otherwise disruptive to the lives of marginalized individuals and communities.

Part of the work of re-imagination and revision undertaken by the poets analyzed in *Ecopoetic Place-Making* entails examining what positions migrants and displaced peoples occupy in the nation as well as in the national imagination, in particular where this position is connected to imaginaries of N/nature or place. Reading contemporary poetry about nature and mobility thus means re-examining longstanding narratives of the U.S. as "Nature's Nation" and as "a Nation of Immigrants," that is, narratives of nature as a primary location of Americanization and narratives of mobility as a central element of individual as well as collective identity formation.[6] It also means challenging those discourses that continue to imagine the West as a "virgin land," centuries of European settlement as an "errand into the wilderness," or the male settler colonial subject as an "American Adam" who is destined to (re-)discover the "New World" and lay claim to its bountiful resources.[7] Indeed, some of the works of poetry I discuss explicitly talk back to these and related settler-colonial nationali(ist) narratives, such as when Derek Walcott revisions the figure of the American Adam in the context of Westward Expansion and Native American Removal, or when Craig Santos Perez critiques notions of Manifest Destiny in the context of twentieth- and twenty-first-century U.S. militarist and imperialist actions in the Pacific.

---

6   For a discussion of the concept of "nature's nation," see Perry Miller's essay "The Romantic Dilemma" (1955), his influential study *Nature's Nation* (1967), and more recent publications such as Lloyd Willis's *Environmental Evasion: The Literary, Critical, and Cultural Politics of 'Nature's Nation'* (2011). For a conceptualization of the United States as a "nation of immigrants," see especially Oscar Handlin's *The Uprooted: The Epic Story of the Great Migrations that Made the American People* (1951).

7   Many of the cultural narratives these early Americanists identified were later challenged on the grounds of the histories and perspectives they omitted. The most famous revisionist critique published by representatives of the so-called Critical Myth and Symbol School (Paul *The Myths* 18) concerns Henry Nash Smith's *Virgin Land* (1950). While sensitive to issues of class, *Virgin Land* falls short in retrospective for not having reflected critically enough on the racist, sexist, and more broadly imperialist implications of the "collective representations" (vii) that the study discusses. In particular, as Smith himself later acknowledged, *Virgin Land* fails to adequately address the violence perpetrated against Native Americans throughout U.S. history and the gendered violence implicit in the myth of the "virgin land" (Smith "Symbol and Idea"). Richard Slotkin's *Regeneration Through Violence* (1973), one of the key texts of the Critical Myth and Symbol School, is concerned precisely with this history, highlighting the extent to which U.S.-American mythologies of nation-building have always depended on acts of extreme violence, especially against Indigenous peoples. In a similar corrective move, Annette Kolodny's highly influential study *The Lay of the Land* (1975) provides a feminist critique of the myth of the "virgin land" from the age of "discovery" onward, re-reading it as a fantasy of violent submission with highly problematic gendered connotations and environmental consequences.

Migrant poets such as Walcott, Ali, and Adnan are often either classified as postcolonial, transnational, diasporic or ethnic American poets and then analyzed according to the topics such a classification brings into focus. When discussing how their poetry addresses American natures and mobilities, the insights that these different critical perspectives provide are all worth considering, given how they foreground different understandings of human-place relations and mobility. I use the descriptive labels *migrant poets/poets of migration* because I want to argue that the poets I have selected approach questions of identity and belonging with a special sensibility resulting from their respective migratory experiences. While the result of their acts of ecopoetic place-making is anything but a secure sense of 'being American'—indeed one can claim that for Perez, Walcott, and Spahr, at least, ecopoetic place-making constitutes a way to resist or trouble such an idea—all five poets I discuss participate in ongoing debates about what "America," "being American," or writing "American poetry" means. In a more concrete sense, they also investigate where to draw the physical and symbolic borders of the territory known as the United States. Questions of geopolitics are particularly pertinent in the case of Craig Santos Perez, who writes about the unincorporated territory of Guam/Guåhan, a Pacific island occupied by the U.S. Military and, according to some, a colony of the United States (see, for example, Fojas, "Militarization," or Bevacqua and Bowman). In different yet related ways, questions of geopolitics are also relevant to Juliana Spahr's poetry about Hawai'i, and those passages in the poetry of Derek Walcott and Agha Shahid Ali where Native peoples appear, marking the United States as a settler-colonial space and neo-colonial empire. When I thus argue that the poets of migration I read in *Ecopoetic Place-Making* write "American" poetry, I do not do so to prevent questions that such a label raises about identity and belonging in the context of U.S. settler colonialism and imperialism but, on the contrary, to encourage them and, more even, to suggest that they are an inherent part of the issues addressed in contemporary poetries of migration.

For my study on nature and mobility in contemporary American poetry, I focus on poetries of migration, even though all the poets I read could also be classified more broadly as "poets of mobility." Yet, while such a framing would certainly be useful for other projects in the realm of poetry and mobility studies, it would be too broad for my purposes. Quite obviously, not all of the migrant poets I consider in *Ecopoetic Place-Making* are what one might conventionally refer to as "immigrant poets," a label that in the context of American studies is commonly used for literary works that feature movement across national borders with the intention of staying in the new place of residence. Such a narrower focus on immigrant poetry would of course be productive in other cases, but for my purposes it would be too limiting, not least because it would exclude Walcott and Adnan who kept moving internationally after first moving to the U.S. as well as Perez, who (despite his migrations between Guam/Guåhan, the continental United States, and Hawai'i) is of course anything but an 'immigrant.' What is more, the label "immigrant literature," just like the labels "ethnic" or "multiethnic" literature (Shankar & Srikanth 371), is still often used primarily in reference to texts by writers of color, particularly when it is applied to contemporary literature. Thus, using the label "immigrant poetry" could have given readers the impression that the works of non-POC poets with a migratory background are not of interest for the questions I am investigating in this study. This is not the case, however. Indeed, the poetry of Juliana Spahr offers very relevant insights, I show in this volume, as would have the poetry of Eavan Boland, who has repeatedly engaged in her poetry with the natural world and her own migration from Ireland to the United States. Focusing on poetries of migration rather than on immigrant poetry, then, allows me to read the works of Derek Walcott, Agha Shahid Ali, and Etel Adnan side by side with the works of Juliana Spahr and Craig Santos Perez. In order to make such juxtapositions productive, I insist in my analysis on the varying social, political, and cultural contexts in which migrations and other kinds of mobilities can take place. Moreover, I try to account for the complex ways in which these varying social, political, and cultural contexts of migration affect the environmental imaginaries of mobility produced in the texts.

Reading contemporary American poetries of migration requires grounding discussions of nature and mobility not only in specific historical contexts but also in theories that help to unpack the sexist, racist, and imperialist assumptions inherent in those U.S-American national narratives that have been used to make "America," to make some people "Americans" while denying this identity to others, and to make the literatures of some groups "American" literature, while questioning that label in the case of others. Simultaneously, reading contemporary American poetries of migration requires acknowledging that both "location" and "mobility" have always been central to the "postcolonial moments of US-American history and culture" (Paul, *Mapping Migration* 17), that is, to moments in literary and cultural production that highlight "the contested nature of this nationality and the postcolonial aspects that work internally as well as internationally to revise, modify, and differentiate the claims of 'American' literature" (17). I am interested in such "postcolonial moments" found in contemporary poetries of migration, poetries that frequently reflect on the United States' colonial past and its present status as a *post*-colony in relation to Europe, as a settler-colonial space in relation to Indigenous America, and as a (crumbling) neocolonial empire in relation to the various territories it occupies or controls in some other manner.

Due to the complexities that arise from the simultaneous reality of the United States as a post-colony, a settler-colony, and a neo-colonial empire as well as a nation of immigrants and a destination for transnational migrants, an analysis of contemporary American poetries of migration must, as Indigenous scholar Jodi A. Byrd insists in *The Transit of Empire* (2011), avoid the conflation of two separate, if concomitant regimes of oppression: colonization and racialization. Drawing from Byrd, who in turn draws from the late Afro-Caribbean poet Kamau Brathwaite, I thus distinguish between "settler, native, and arrivant" (xxx) in an effort to "reconceptualize space and history to make visible what imperialism and its resultant settler colonialisms and diasporas have sought to obscure" (Byrd xxx). Arrivants, as I define them here in building on, but also departing from definitions by Kamau Brathwaite, Sarah Dowling, and Jody Byrd, are racialized non-Indigenous individuals living in the United States who may or may not be part of the diaspora of a formerly colonized country.

In his acclaimed verse trilogy *The Arrivants: A New World Trilogy* (1973), Barbadian poet Kamau Brathwaite uses the term "arrivant" for people of African descent living in the Americas. Sarah Dowling follows this specific use in her study *Translingual Poetics: Writing Personhood under Settler Colonialism* (2018), when she distinguishes "the experiences of Indigenous peoples, diasporic communities, and arrivants" (6). In my study, however, I adopt Jodi Byrd's slightly broader use of the term, taking the designation "arrivants" to refer to all "those people forced into the Americas through the violence of European and Anglo-American colonialism and imperialism around the globe" (Byrd xix), including migrants of African (Walcott), Middle-Eastern (Adnan) and South Asian (Ali) descent, even as I carefully examine the specific conditions of mobility for each of the poets I discuss, noting how the poets themselves complicate the distinction between "forced" mobility versus "voluntary" mobility and mobility as a necessity versus mobility as a privilege. Following Byrd, I further contend that the United States is a modern settler-colonial empire that stands "on the verge of apocalyptic environmental collapse" (Byrd 3) not only because of a long history of colonial and racist violence, but because this violence against Natives, and as I would add arrivants, continues both in the United States and beyond its borders, accompanying and, arguably in many cases fueling, U.S. "global wars on terror, the environment, and livability" (Byrd xxxv). One of the weapons in these literal and figurative wars are, to modify Byrd for my purposes, "the language, grammar, and ontological categor[ies] of Indianness" (xxxv) and "Immigrantness" as well as the systems of knowledge and power hierarchies that sustain them. Challenging these grammars, categories, systems, and hierarchies through poetic language entails a revision of dominant settler-colonial and imperialist ideas about human-nature relations as much as a revision of traditional (poetic) language and form. The poets I analyze in this study attempt such revisions, whether they are settlers such as Juliana Spahr, Natives such as Craig Santos Perez, or arrivants such as Derek Walcott, Agha Shahid Ali, and Etel Adnan.

As the following five chapters demonstrate, this study is concerned not merely with contemporary poetries of migration but with contemporary *ecopoetries* of migration. In other words, *Ecopoetic Place-Making* reads contemporary American ecopoetries as poetries of migration (in the case of Perez and Spahr) and contemporary American poetries of migration as ecopoetries (in the case of Walcott, Ali, and Adnan) in order to explore the different *ecopoetics of mobility* that emerge in their works. In reading a body of works as diverse as the ones assembled here, I echo the broad definition of ecopoetry that Ann Fisher-Wirth and Laura-Gray Street employ in their introduction to *The Ecopoetry Anthology* (2013), where they initially define ecopoetry as poetry that "in some way is shaped by and responds specifically to […] the burgeoning environmental crisis" (xxviii) of the second half of the twentieth and first decades of the twenty-first century, but then include poetry published earlier as well. Fisher-Wirth and Street distinguish three types of ecopoetry: nature poetry, environmental poetry, and ecological poetry (xxviii–xxix). While their classification is by no means the only possible one, I find it useful to show how the poets I have chosen both fit and do not fit one of the more encompassing definitions of ecopoetry out there. Following Wendell Berry, for whom nature poetry "considers nature as subject matter and inspiration" (*A Continuous Harmony* 1), Fisher-Wirth and Street describe nature poetry as poetry that "often meditates on an encounter between the human subject and something in the other-than-human world that reveals an aspect of the meaning of life" (xxviii). By contrast, they define "environmental poetry" as poetry that is "propelled by and directly engaged with active and politicized environmentalism" (xxviii), and "ecological poetry" as poetry characterized by experimental form, self-reflexivity, and language-consciousness (xxix). Ecological poetry in Fisher-Wirth and Street's definition thus resembles what Angus Fletcher describes as the "environment-poem" (122), which is to say, a poem that functions as an ecological system of its own. Insofar as it can be described as "language-oriented" (Simpson ix), or, more accurately perhaps as "conceptually oriented" (Milne, *Poetry Matters* 8), "ecological poetry" in Fisher-Wirth and Street's sense can also be linked to the practice of ecopoetics as John Skinner defines it in his influential journal of the same name, that is, as an innovative form of environmentalist writing indebted to the avant-garde practices of the language poets as well as to "the system-aware writing of the 'New American' poetry" (Skinner, "Ecopoetics" 322–323) and thus to what Sarah Nolan describes as "unnatural ecopoetics" by which she means ecopoetry that uses "open and often extrapoetic forms and self-reflexive commentary on the failures of words to accurately express material reality in order to foreground naturecultures within the distinctly textual spaces created by the poem" (4). When I use the term *ecopoetics* in the following to suggest that each of the poets I analyze delineates his or her own particular ecopoetics of mobility, I deploy it in the more general sense of an environmentally-oriented or environmentally-suggestive poetics.

The works I analyze in *Ecopoetic Place-Making* encompass all three types of ecopoetry described by Fisher-Wirth and Street; at the same time, I suggest, they also challenge such categorizations and ultimately expand the boundaries of the genre. The work of Etel Adnan could be called "nature poetry" because it takes the nonhuman world as one of its key topics, reaches back to western and non-western mystic notions of N/nature and in doing so reflects on what it means to be in the world and physically within nature after having been displaced. At the same time, her contemplative poems are associative and impressionistic in ways that recall modernist language experiments more so than Romantic meditations and contemporary experiments in "contemplative ecopoetics" (Rigby 25) inspired by them. Similarly, the poems by Juliana Spahr and Craig Santos Perez may be classified as "environmental poetry" insomuch as both poets explicitly address environmental destruction as well as environmental injustice throughout their work and openly encourage the kinds of individual, communal, and political action necessary to protect nature. At the same time, some of their texts also qualify as "ecological poems" insofar as they evince a certain conceptual orientation and self-consciously construct poetic environments in and through experimental language that seek to undermine, each from their respective situated perspective, settler anthropocentrism along with the pervasive American ideology of "*settler* monolingualism" (Dowling 3; emphasis original).

Of the works I discuss in my study, the poetry of Walcott and Ali fits the label of ecopoetry least comfortably. While their texts can be read as postcolonial revisions of an Anglo-American (post-)Romantic tradition of nature poetry—that is to say, of the genres, forms, and imagery as well as of the perspectives on history, subjectivity, and artistic expression that this tradition is associated with—human-nature relations are not the primary focus of their poetry. Although Walcott and Ali occasionally hint at environmental destruction in their works, their poems are neither explicitly environmentalist (and thus "environmental poetry") nor legible as poetic environments evoked through experimental language (and thus "ecological poetry"). Still, I would argue, we *can* and *should* read their poetry as ecopoetry, because just like Adnan, Spahr, and Perez, Walcott and Ali examine human-nature relations from different, if less overt, perspectives of im/mobility and in doing so provide valuable insights for our current moment of global environmental crisis and mass-migration within and across national borders. In that sense, all the poets I read can be considered examples of "decolonial ecopoetics," as Kate Rigby outlines it in *Reclaiming Romanticism: Towards an Ecopoetics of Decolonization* (2020), namely an ecopoetics that holds the promise (in the case of Walcott, Ali, and Adnan) and actively enacts the limits and potentialities (in the case of Perez and Spahr) "for a decolonizing praxis, pitched against both human domination of nonhuman others and the domination of some humans by others, especially, in the case of settler nations, Indigenous and enslaved peoples by colonial powers" (Rigby 4).

Indebted to expressive as well as to innovative poetic traditions, the migrant poets I discuss in *Ecopoetic Place-Making* experiment with perspective and voice. They challenge the conventions of the traditional lyric without fully abandoning the perspectives of socially, culturally, and physically situated, yet also mobile speakers. Since lyrical poetry is often defined in reference to John Stuart Mill as poetry featuring a self "*overheard*" (1216; emphasis original) speaking to itself, the implication has sometimes been that lyrical poetry is poetry about a self overheard speaking to itself *about itself*. Contemporary ecopoetries of migration routinely question all these three "selves" and their relation to each other. Apart from challenging the authority and boundedness of the subject that speaks, contemporary American ecopoetries of migration frequently raise questions about which phenomena and whose experiences poetry can or should address and who should listen. In other words, the poets I read frequently evoke the problem of how to account for histories of violence that they have not been witness to or how to describe natural processes that cannot be perceived by human beings due to their spatial and/or temporal scale. As Alicia Ostriker notes in "Beyond Confession: The Poetics of Postmodern Witness" (2001), poets who attempt to act as poetic witnesses to the experiences and histories of others, including I would add nonhuman others, face a problem: "Formally, stylistically, what they represent is a crisis that is at once global and intimate: the simultaneous impossibility of objective witness and of subjective wholeness" (39). The struggle to write about and amidst a global yet intimate *environmental* crisis and the struggle to find a poetic language and form adequate to expressing both the global and intimate dimensions of a multitude of converging social, political, and environmental crises is at the heart of all the works discussed in this study.

Which genres, modes, poetic strategies, themes, and images are suited, then, for the challenge of writing about the intersecting issues of nature and mobility at a time of escalating environmental and mobility crises? As I suggest following poetry scholars Matthew Griffiths, and Jahan Ramazani, amongst others, many of the poetic qualities and strategies that enable ecopoetries of migration to deal with the conceptual complexities of climate change and environmental degradation on a global scale (Griffiths) as well as with the conceptual complexities of mobility in a globalized world (Ramazani) can be traced back to the innovations of modernist poetry in addition to those of Romantic poetry. In his study *The New Poetics of Climate Change* (2017), Griffiths articulates a number of challenges for thought and poetic practice that climate change poses and then reads the modernist poetries of T. S. Eliot, Wallace Stevens, Basil Buntin, and David Jones in order to explore the poetic qualities their poetry possesses and the strategies their works employ to respond to these challenges. According to Griffiths, these pertinent poetic qualities and strategies include:

> ironies of representation and a resistance to received ideas of 'Nature'; transnational or global scales, hybridization of natural change with cultural and social (anthropogenic) change and the breakdown of dualisms; a new problematics of environmental selfhood; language's vexed attempt to engage with the world and, reflexively, with its own materialism; and the expression of a troublesome environmental unconscious, which has been repressed by narratives of civilized progress. (Griffith 30)

While I have used different phrasings at times, some of the points mentioned here will sound familiar. The poets I read, too, engage critically with Romantic notions of mythic Nature; they too struggle to represent the unfathomable scales of the non-human; they too challenge the supposedly neat distinctions between the natural and the artificial, the human and the nonhuman, the urban and the rural; and their po-etries too investigate the possibilities and limits of the situated perspectives of em-bodied lyrical subjects. In addition, contemporary ecopoetries of migration rework established poetic genres; they challenge universalist, racist, capitalist, imperialist, and settler-colonial logics; last but not least, they put emphasis on memories and (informal) knowledges, and interrogate writerly authority, especially with regard to the mobile poet's ability to bear witness to the histories of others as well as to a non-human world experienced variously as familiar or alien, intimately close or unfath-omably vast, comforting or threatening, or all of these at once.

Like other recent studies of (world) poetry in English (see Hena or Suhr-Sytsma), Jahan Ramazani analyzes the works of poets from all kinds of cultural, ethnic, racial and migratory backgrounds. In his landmark study *A Transnational Poetics* (2009), for example, Ramazani explores the "new intergeographic spaces" (60) of Anglophone poetries, tracing the "circuits of poetic connection and dialogue across political and geographic borders and even hemispheres" (x-xi). Although Ramazani frequently mentions the migratory histories of the poets he reads and the ways human mo-bility figures in their works, he is generally more interested in "the cross-national mobility of modern and contemporary poetry" (*A Transnational Poetics* 23), that is to say, in instances of intertextuality, metaphorical border-crossing, and the transna-tional "travel" of genres, forms, and motives than in human mobility. He is also gen-erally more concerned with cultural mobility than with N/nature. Yet, in one of the chapters of his most recent books, *Poetry in a Global Age* (2020), Ramazani adopts an ecoglobalist perspective on modernist and postmodernist poetry, reading Wallace Stevens, A.R. Ammons, Jorie Graham, and Juliana Spahr, amongst others, as poets who try to "envision and formally represent 'the wholeness of the earth'" (158) and "[t]he temporality of the world's enmeshment" (167), while at the same time display-ing "exquisitely local phrases and textures and techniques" (161) and engaging "the micro-world of local experience" (175). Building on Ramazani's work, which reminds us that "poems reward attention to both their located and mobile qualities" (*Poetry in a Global Age* 10), I discuss how contemporary American poetries of migration em-ploy global, transnational, transregional, and translocal poetic forms, themes, and imagery in order to grapple with histories of place and displacement as well as with the lived experiences of human-nature encounters in light of migration. At the same time, I highlight the ethical, political, and poetic affordances of contemporary Amer-ican ecopoetries of migration that are neither fully ecolocalist nor fully ecoglobalist in orientation.

The Contours of this Study

The poetry collections I focus on in the different chapters of *Ecopoetic Place-Making* were published during the last decade of the twentieth century and the first two decades of the twenty-first century. In American studies, the terrorist attacks of September 11, 2001, are often taken as a historical event that produced a paradigm shift in the U.S.-American cultural imagination (see Hungerford; Banita 12–17; Pease "From Virgin Land to Ground Zero"), which is why one could reserve the label *contemporary poetry* for twenty-first-century poetry in a U.S.-American context. By including poetry collections from the 1990s, rather than only discussing twenty-first century works, as many studies on contemporary American poetry do (see Reed's *Nobody's Business*, Keller's *Recomposing Ecopoetics*, or Milne's *Poetry Matters*), I do not mean to disregard 9/11 as an epochal event that has profoundly affected cultural production in the United States. Indeed, the attacks and their aftermath are addressed in the works of most of the poets included in my study as well as in many other works that I could have included. When we look at the poetry of Juliana Spahr in comparison with the poetry of Meena Alexander and Ed Roberson, for example, an argument could be made about how witnessing the attacks of 9/11 not only instilled in some American poets a more acute sense of living in a world of multiple intimate and global crises but also reinforced the urge of writing about the complex interconnections of nature and mobility, including bodily natures and nonhuman mobilities. At the same time, the transnational orientation of many of the poets I discuss also cautions against an over-emphasis on a periodization based on American history only, even though 9/11 and the wars that followed it arguably had considerable political and ecological consequences across the globe in addition to claiming so many lives on site.

In a similar manner, the fact that I concentrate on poetry published from the 1990s onward does not mean that poems published before the 1990s cannot be read productively with regard to their treatment of issues of nature and mobility. Indeed, some of Derek Walcott's earlier collections prove otherwise, as does Robert Boschman's analysis of matters of ecology and westward expansion in the works of Anne Bradstreet, Elizabeth Bishop, and Amy Clampitt (*In the Way of Nature* 2009), Jim Cocola's discussion of place and mobility in the works of poets such as Allen Ginsberg and Kamau Brathwaite (*Places in the Making* 2016), Christine Gerhardt's scholarship on representations of nature and mobility in Walt Whitman and Emily Dickinson ("Imagining a Mobile Sense of Place"), Jahan Ramazani's discussion of Wallace Steven, A. R. Ammons, and Jorie Graham (*Poetry in a Global Age*), or my own work on Sharon Doubiago ("She Moves"). As will become apparent, I hope, whenever I discuss the ways in which Perez, Spahr, Walcott, Ali, and Adnan invoke literary precursors, poetry engaging in ecopoetic place-making from the 1990s onward has much in common with earlier traditions of American poetry concerned with environmental issues and issues of mobility.

All the works of poetry I discuss in *Ecopoetic Place-Making* and many of the earlier examples discussed by the scholars mentioned in the previous paragraph were published during an era sometimes referred to as the "Great Acceleration," a historical period following World War II that can be seen as ecologically, technologically, and economically distinct from previous eras due to rapidly accelerating growth and the attendant intensification of harm affecting the planet (Ronda 1–4). Much like the way Margaret Ronda argues for the poetries published from the 1950s onward that she analyzes in *Remainders: American Poetry at Nature's End* (2018), the ecopoetries of migration I am interested in, published from the 1990s onward, are attuned to "the planetary poiesis of global capitalism in the Great Acceleration" (Ronda 5) and to the "ongoing and intensifying processes that characterize natural-historical entanglements in this period" (13). Whether one considers Perez, Spahr, Walcott, Ali or Adnan, their works all engage—through experimentation with genre, voice, form, and poetic language—with the disjointed temporalities of a world in crisis, conceiving of "poetry as an aesthetic space for meditating on what remains" (Ronda 18) as well as on what may already be lost. Yet, the poems I read also distinguish themselves in significant ways from the longer tradition of American poetries of the Great Acceleration attuned to issues of nature and human mobility. They are frequently more critical in their treatment of U.S. imperialism and settler-colonialism and in their treatment of modern regimes of displacement, mobilization, and immobilization. They also differ in how they address longer histories of (localized) environmental degradation and injustice together with the contemporary effects of U.S. imperialism and settler-colonialism on the global environmental crisis, the scope of which came into focus for the broader public only toward the end of the twentieth century.[8]

---

8   From the perspective of environmental history, too, the decision to focus on literary texts written during the late 1980s and published from the early 1990s onward makes sense. Indeed, the late 1980s were marked by considerable social, political, and cultural change, both in terms of official government policies and in terms of changes concerning broader public awareness toward climate change as a global environmental crisis. Only one year after the stratospheric "ozone hole" was discovered in 1987, a discovery that caused considerable media attention, NASA climate specialist James Hansen testified at a U.S. congressional hearing about global warming on June 23, 1988, declaring that the persistent rise of global median temperatures could no longer be regarded as having entirely natural causes (Hansen "Statement"). While this was not the first time that leading climate scientists made such conclusions public—as a matter of fact, in 1986 Hansen himself had already testified at the U.S. Senate Committee on the Environment and Public Works—, Hansen's 1988 testimony certainly contributed to the transformation of the discourse on global warming from a scientific to a political and finally to a policy issue (See Bodansky "The History of the Global Climate Change Regime" 23–27).

The works I analyze do not merely respond to the accumulating social and environmental consequences of the Great Acceleration; they also respond more or less explicitly to what Lynn Keller calls the "self-conscious Anthropocene" (*Recomposing Ecopoetics* 2), that is, a "period of *changed recognition*, when the responsibility humans bear for the condition of the planet [...] is widely understood" (2; emphasis original). Keller dates the beginnings of the "self-conscious Anthropocene" to the year 2000 (*Recomposing Ecopoetics* 9), likely for the introduction of the term *Anthropocene* in print that year (see Crutzen and Stoermer) as well as for the symbolism this date holds as the dawn of the new millennium. As works by poets such as Derek Walcott demonstrate, however, the kind of (self-)conscious awareness of anthropogenic planetary change that Keller sees spreading in twenty-first-century American ecopoetry was already present at least a decade earlier in the writing of marginalized poets and specifically migrant poets from former colonies, that is to say, poets born and raised in places dramatically altered by human and nonhuman mobilities and disproportionally affected by environmental degradation and global environmental change. Even more, American ecopoetries of migration from the 1990s onward, I would argue, do not merely articulate the "changed recognition" (Keller, *Recomposing Ecopoetics* 2) that human beings have had a world-altering impact on local and global ecosystems ever since the beginning of the Anthropocene, whether one is inclined to date this epochal beginning back to the Great Acceleration, the industrial revolution, the colonization of the Americas, or a different point in human history. The American ecopoetries of migration I read also reflect on the altered politics, ethics, and poetics of place, mobility, self, and community that must accompany such a changed recognition, if it is to produce more ecological futures that are also more socially just.

Aside from the present introduction and a short conclusion, *Ecopoetic Place-Making* consists of five chapters, each focusing on the work of one poet. Chapter 1 analyzes passages from the first four volumes of Craig Santos Perez's ongoing series *from unincorporated territory* (2008, 2010, 2014, 2017, 2023). In turn, chapter 2 primarily concentrates on two collections that Juliana Spahr published in 2001 and 2011 respectively. I thus begin this study by reading two poets who have been widely recognized and discussed as ecopoets, but whose works reveal new depths when read with systematic attention to issues of mobility. In chapter 3, I discuss a book-length poem of migration by Derek Walcott, a poet whose decade-long career allows me to sketch a brief history of the different scholarly fields that my study draws and builds on. Analyzing Walcott's long-poem *Omeros* (1990) furthermore allows me to establish some of the key issues that emerge when one reads American poetries of migration as ecopoetries: these issues include, but are not limited to questions concerning genre, scale, and representability as well as questions concerning the limits of poetic witnessing and the ethics of poetic place-making. In some sense, then, my chapter on Walcott also represents a transition between a first part of *Ecopoetic Place-*

Making in which I discuss the work of two ecopoets as poetries of migration and a second part of my study in which I read the works of two migrant poets as ecopoetries. Specifically, chapter 4 of *Ecopoetic Place-Making* concentrates on Agha Shahid Ali's collection *A Nostalgist's Map of America* (1991), highlighting the role of memory for the production of environmental imaginaries informed by perspectives of mobility as well as the role of literature for the emergence of alternative forms of community and belonging in poetries about place and displacement. Last but not least, I analyze several of the late collections of Etel Adnan in chapter 5 of *Ecopoetic Place-Making*, showing how two different perspectives of im/mobility, or as I conceptualize it, post-mobility, inform her poetry about N/nature in ways similar to, yet also different from the works of the other poets in the study.

In my analysis of Craig Santos Perez's ongoing series *from unincorporated territory* (2008-ongoing) in chapter 1, I foreground the precariousness of place-based Indigenous knowledges in the context of colonization, environmental degradation, and CHamoru mass migration. Concentrating primarily on the first three volumes of his series, *[hacha]* (2008), *[saina]* (2010), and *[guma']* (2014) and including occasional references to the fourth volume *[lukao]* (2017), I outline how Perez frames CHamoru place-making on his native island of Guam/Guåhan as an epistemological and political project of decolonization that must be attentive to the inextricable link between cultural and environmental losses, while also addressing histories of immobilization and mass mobility. I first show how Perez's poems draw attention to the endangered ecologies of Guåhan by highlighting the continuities between historical practices of colonial enclosure and contemporary colonial practices of CHamoru immobilization. I then outline how Perez's collections reflect on the connection between precarious Indigenous genealogies and land-sky-ocean-based epistemologies as well as on resulting problems of environmental knowledge transmission in light of CHamoru mass migration. Finally, I demonstrate how Perez reaches beyond documentary modes in *from unincorporated territory* to highlight CHamoru environmental imaginaries of mobility and to formulate a participatory ecopoetics of mobility that engages his readers not only in what can be described as a decolonial project of ecopoetic place-making but also in a poetic experiment in critical environmental pedagogy.

In chapter 2, I read the poetry of Anglo-American settler poet Juliana Spahr arguing that it uses para-lyrical experimentations to investigate the limits of settler ecological agency in the context of global capitalism and U.S. imperialism. Focusing primarily on her collections *Fuck You—Aloha—I Love You* (2001) and *Well Then There Now* (2011), I examine how Spahr's experimental ecopoetry challenges notions of anthropocene subjectivity by drawing attention to how different scales of human and nonhuman mobility shape the ecosocial processes through which subjects and collectivities are constituted. In the first part of the chapter, I discuss poems set in the United States that emphasize issues of embodiment and "trans-corporeality"

(Alaimo) in the context of toxification, pointing to the need of rethinking of environmental ethics based on close contact with the more-than-human world. In the second part of the chapter, I demonstrate how Spahr's poems about Hawai'i render suspicious settler acts of ecopoetic place-making in the context of U.S. occupation of the archipelago by showing how continental migrants' desire for emplacement through an immersion in the nonhuman world of Hawai'i clashes with Indigenous rights of access to and control of the land. In the third part of the chapter, finally, I read poems set both in Hawai'i and the United States as poems that struggle, but ultimately do not claim to succeed in imagining forms of settler ecopoetic place-making that avoid the logic of settlement and exploitation.

Chapter 3 turns to the Afro-Caribbean poet Derek Walcott, arguing that his book-length poem *Omeros* (1990) can be read as a lyricized planetary epic that displays not only postcolonial and transnational, but also environmental sensibilities shaped by different perspectives of mobility. Starting with a discussion of the Caribbean passages, but focusing primarily on the understudied U.S.-American passages of *Omeros*, I show how Walcott's long poem combines epic with the short forms of travel poem, pastoral, elegy, and confessional lyric in order to draw attention in content and form to the discrepant scales of a world in crisis as well as to the challenges of representability these crises pose. Beginning with the passages of *Omeros* in which his narrator returns to the Caribbean, I demonstrate how the author's framing of his epic as a travel poem produces tensions between the postcolonial and the transnational sensibilities as well as between the localizing and globalizing tendencies in Walcott's planetary epic. These tensions, which shape the critical environmental imaginary of mobility that emerges in his text, I argue, result in part from the migrant poet's engagements with histories of place and displacement in the United States as well as from the problems of place-making that arise for an Afro-Caribbean migrant when he begins to write about place and displacement in the United States. Analyzing sections of *Omeros* set in the U.S. South that address the Transatlantic Slave Trade as well as Native American Removal, I explore how Walcott modifies the pastoral to counter what has been called "New World amnesia" (Handley). Reading sections that depict landscapes in the American West together with the history of Catherine Weldon, a white nineteenth-century immigrant woman who acted as secretary to the Lakota leader Sitting Bull, I discuss Walcott's use of the pastoral elegy for thinking through the ethics of bearing witness to histories of place and displacement that are not one's own. Last but not least, I show how Walcott employs a combination of confessional lyric and epic to dramatize the problems of representability that present themselves to a privileged postcolonial poet of color and migrant when he is confronted with the violent history and vast landscapes of what is now the United States.

In chapter 4, I read the collection *A Nostalgist's Map of America* (1991) by the Kashmiri-American poet Agha Shahid Ali, arguing that Ali does not sidestep or reject nostalgia in favor of memory as a seemingly more reliable and responsible basis for (eco)poetic place-making in the context of displacement. Instead, I suggest, Ali willfully reaches beyond the conventional limits imposed on migrants' place-memory and place-experience by integrating imagined histories and distant locales into his poetry about the Sonoran Desert and his speaker's movements between the U.S. Southwest and Northeast. In other words, Ali embraces reflective nostalgia as a place-conscious, and ultimately environmentally suggestive affect that is especially well suited for migrants who cannot depend on memories and experiences alone for ecopoetic place-making, but who must also rely on their own poetic imagination as well as the poetic imagination of others to build meaningful relationships to the places they pass through. As I posit in this chapter, Ali's nostalgic ecopoetics of mobility manifests in *A Nostalgist's Map of America* in two interrelated ways: first, in a translocal sense of place accompanied by evocations of mobile forms of place attachment; and second, in a "diasporic intimacy with the world" that depends both on a critical engagement with places and their histories and on a critical engagement with other works of literature and art invested in nature and mobility, including but not limited to the nature poetry of Emily Dickinson, the desert paintings of Georgia O'Keeffe, and the non-fiction of naturalist Gary Paul Nabhan. In embracing a translocal and mobile sense of place as well as the ultimately unfulfilled longing for a diasporic intimacy with the world, I lay bare in the last part of the chapter, *A Nostalgist's Map of America* gestures toward more mobile and inclusive forms of ecological citizenship, challenging exclusive notions of belonging and reductive conceptions of emplacement that over-emphasize long-term residency, personal experience, and first-hand knowledge as the basis of meaningful and environmentally significant place-attachment.

Chapter 5 entails an analysis of the poetry of Lebanese-American painter and writer Etel Adnan, whose poetry, I suggest, deals evocatively and provocatively with the temporal dimensions of human-nature relations in the context of two different yet ultimately related forms of "post-mobility." Focusing on her collections *There* (1997), *Seasons* (2008), *Sea and Fog* (2012), and *Night* (2016), I analyze how Adnan's poetry represents a migrant's relationship to the natural world of the Pacific Coast in the aftermath of migration on the one hand and in light of the reduced mobility that comes with old age on the other hand. Drawing on insights from queer ecocriticism, queer phenomenology, and queer theory more broadly, I argue that Etel Adnan's nature poetry produces a queering of environmental ethics in three related ways. First, the poet's emphasis on the disorienting effect of displacement and the resulting desire for reorientation through and toward nature results in a queering of traditional notions of dwelling. Second, her poetry suggests that ecological desire in the context of post-mobility, whether due to displacement or aging, must accommodate a queer erotogenic ethics based on touch as well as one based on the sensuality of thought. Third, I propose, that an experimental ecopoetry that continues to disorient its readers, while simultaneously reorienting them toward the natural world as it explores approaching death as well as environmental apocalypse, may be a useful tool not only to imagine queerer and more ecological futures but also to enact them in the present.

In my conclusion, finally, I provide a short summary of the different environmental imaginaries of migration and the different ecopoetics of mobility that emerge in contemporary American poetry about nature and mobility. Contemporary American ecopoetries of migration along with contemporary American ecopoetries of mobility more broadly, I emphasize in closing, challenge settler-colonial nationalist, racist, and otherwise exclusionary models of belonging on which traditional understandings of environmentally-conscious living and environmentality—in the sense of the institutionalized and non-institutionalized organization of environmental governance—are based. At the same time, they challenge imperialist, settler-colonial, and neocolonial forms of place-making, whether in poetry or through other practices, pointing to the ways in which contemporary mobilities and the place-making they engender remain enmeshed with violent systems invested in regulation human-nature relations as well as human and nonhuman mobilities. At the same time, I suggest, the analysis of ecopoetries of migration raises important questions about environmental cultures of mobility more broadly conceived, whether in the United States or beyond. How might the analysis of such environmental cultures of mobility help us to rethink notions of subjectivity and community, belonging and identity in light of our current moment of converging environmental and mobility crises? How can they help us to rethink traditional notions of place and emplacement, place-attachment, and sustainability in order to accommodate lives and cultures on the move? What could be the function of history, memory, and the imagination in forms of cultural expressed informed by mobile environmental imaginaries? What would be the place of ethics, politics, and poetics in these cultural works? And, last but not least, what place might literature and the arts hold in environmental cultures of mobility as well as in the scholarship exploring them? The answers to these questions are complex and sometimes elusive. Yet, they must be asked, I contend, in order for us to begin to make sense of a world in which both the most intimate forms of human-nature engagements and the most common practices of mobility can come to signify freedom or oppression, life or death, a risk of self-destruction or a chance at survival.

1. Decolonizing Environmental Pedagogy: Rerouted Knowledges and Participatory Ecopoetics in the Poetry of Craig Santos Perez

Born on the northwestern Pacific island of Guam/Guåhan, raised in California, and currently residing on the island of Oʻahu, Hawaiʻi, the CHamoru poet, scholar, and activist Craig Santos Perez writes about his native island and culture from a perspective of migration. Widely acclaimed and frequently discussed both by ecocritics interested in Indigenous literatures and by scholars working in transpacific studies and the blue humanities who emphasize "concepts of fluidity, flow, routes, and mobility" (DeLoughrey, "Toward a Critical Ocean Studies" 22), Perez explores Indigenous practices of place-making as well as creative modes of resistance against settler acts of land-taking that threaten his native island of Guam/Guåhan. Perez's ongoing series of poetry collections, *from unincorporated territory* (2008-ongoing), makes visible historical as well as contemporary acts of colonial violence and environmental devastation in the Pacific. At the same time, it imagines poetry as a tool of resistance against the ongoing violation of Pacific Islanders' rights to sovereignty, communal well-being, and environmental as well as mobility justice. Building on the insights of a number of scholars who have written about Perez's work, I show in this chapter how his poetry seeks to educate his readers and sensitize them toward the harmful impact of military invasion and colonial enclosure on both Guåhan's natural environment and CHamoru relationships to the nonhuman world, while also re-articulating CHamoru identity and cultural production as both place-based and mobile. Highly attentive to various kinds of im/mobility and invested in producing a new kind of mobile environmental imaginary for the purpose of CHamoru cultural restoration, Perez's first four collections explore how the environmental knowledges derived from CHamoru cultural practices have been made precarious by ecological devastation and CHamoru immobilization, on the one hand, and by continental migration and the resulting disruption of CHamoru genealogies of knowledge, on the other hand. As I argue, Perez's poetry responds to this devastation and disruption with a participatory ecopoetics that promotes poetry as a means of mobile CHamoru place-making and community formation and as a means of environmental pedagogy that seeks to engage the broadest audience possible in an Indigenous-led collective project of decolonization.

Craig Santos Perez: A CHamoru Poet Writing
from Unincorporated Territory

Perez writes both in response to a long history of colonization and ecological degradation in Micronesia and under the compounding pressures of a new era of U.S.-led "[t]ransoceanic militarism" (DeLoughrey, "Critical Ocean Studies" 23) in the Indo-Pacific that perpetuates the disenfranchisement of Indigenous Pacific Islanders such as the CHamoru. Perez's poems thus simultaneously document and enact, for the specific geopolitical and environmental context of Guåhan, what Anishinaabe writer Gerald Vizenor calls "native survivance" (Vizenor 1; see also Lai 2), that is, a political as well as cultural struggle against the erasure of Indigenous presences that acknowledges structures of (neo-)colonial domination while renouncing the paralyzing effects of victimization. Put differently, Perez's poems perform what Tongan scholar Epeli Hau'ofa has called "a spirit of creative originality" (Hau'ofa, "Our Place Within" 85; see also Jansen 5) that critiques and challenges these structures of domination. Evoking the legacies of Spanish colonization and Japanese occupation as well as Guåhan's current political status as an unincorporated U.S. territory, Perez's poetry denounces ongoing CHamoru territorial dispossession as well as the cultural and environmental devastation it has caused on the island. More specifically, Perez links the ecological devastation of the island and the larger ecosystem of the Marianas to the loss of Indigenous cultural practices and knowledges as well as to varying frames of mobility and immobilization that have disrupted and continue to disrupt CHamoru genealogies and knowledges.

Perez's ecopoetry of migration bespeaks a desire for a meaningful engagement with the natural world in the context of colonization and militarization that cannot be reduced to a simple desire for emplacement in the sense of rootedness. Rather, his experimental and stylistically varied ecopoetry of mobility depends in crucial ways on a critical investigation of those histories and experiences of displacement that inform CHamoru identity and culture in the twenty-first century. As I show by reading the first four volumes of his series *from unincorporated territory* ([hacha] 2008, [saina] 2010, [guma'] 2014, [lukao] 2017), Perez's poems sound out the possibilities and limits of Indigenous knowledge production and transmission in the context of occupation and ecological crisis by evoking alternative epistemologies and genealogies of knowledge. As his work showcases, poetry as a means of record keeping and of developing a counter-hegemonic vocabulary of resistance against the exploitation of Indigenous peoples and homelands plays a crucial role in this endeavor. By writing a multi-voiced poetry that combines "mobile visual forms" and "lyrical lines" (Knighton 343) with quotations from and references to a great variety of source texts, Perez foregrounds the particular perspective on human-nature relationships afforded to a CHamoru migrant and poet who writes about the contested social, political, cultural, and environmental territory of Guam/Guåhan. In this chapter, I follow Perez in using the name *Guåhan* to refer to the geographical place and politically contested territory officially known as Guam, except when a distinction between the two names helps to clarify an argument about the occupied status of the island. Similarly, I use the self-chosen term *CHamoru/s* for the Indigenous people of Guam/Guåhan, instead of the official designation *Chamorro*.[1]

The western Pacific island of Guam/Guåhan is positioned at the heart of Oceania but at the fringes of what Paul Lai has so aptly called the "Discontiguous States of America" (3). Lai speaks of the "Discontiguous States of America" in order to foreground "the imperial topography of the United States" as well as "Native American reservation spaces within the boundaries of the contiguous states, offshore territories in the Caribbean and Pacific Oceans (including Guantánamo Bay, Cuba), and the two outlying states of Alaska and Hawai'i" (3). Guam/Guåhan is the largest and southernmost island of the Marianas archipelago, which in turn lies at the eastern rim of the Philippine Sea. Claimed by Magellan for the Spanish Crown in the sixteenth century and colonized by Spanish missionaries during the seventeenth century, Guåhan was ceded by Spain to the United States after the Spanish-American War of 1898. Having been turned into a dependent territory of the United States without prospects of full statehood as a result of the Insular Cases of 1901, the island remained under U.S. naval control until it was captured by the Japanese during WWII. After Guåhan was retaken by the United States in 1944, the *Guam Organic Act* (48 U.S.C. § 1421 *et seq.*) of 1950 formally turned Guåhan into an "unincorporated, *organized* territory" (Perez, *[hacha]* 8; emphasis added), granting its inhabitants U.S. citizenship and a certain degree of self-governance without, however, granting them full constitutional rights, thus ultimately perpetuating the island's colonial status. To this day, Guam/Guåhan and its Indigenous population, the CHamoru, retain a liminal political position that has allowed the U.S. government to exploit the island for military purposes (Perez, *Navigating CHamoru Poetry* 9). Local activist groups, such as We are Guåhan, continue to protest military buildup, not least because of its projected disastrous environmental impact on the island. In 2010, the acting governor of Guåhan, Felix Perez Camacho, introduced a bill to change the island's name to "Guåhan," a name signifying "place of resources" (Guam Legislature 1) in CHamoru and meant to "instill indigenous ownership" (2). Since the change was

---

1   As Craig Santos Perez outlines, the doubly-capitalized spelling "CHamoru" is to be preferred over the older spelling "Chamoru," because the letters CH are considered one character in the CHamoru alphabet (*Navigating CHamoru Poetry* 10). In quotations from primary and secondary sources, I leave the terms and spellings used by the respective authors.

never officially recognized by the U.S. government, however, the political project of renaming the island has been stuck in a legal limbo, a situation tragically befitting its unincorporated yet organized (read occupied) status.

Taking the contested status of his native island as a central theme and originally envisioned as a twelve-book project (Perez qtd. in Schlund-Vials 57), Perez's ongoing book series *from unincorporated territory* consists, as of date, of five thematically and formally linked volumes of poetry. The CHamoru subtitles of the first four collections point to important themes of the series and, as Erin Suzuki remarks, to each book's main "organizing principle" (182): the first volume, *[hacha]* (2008), is named after the CHamoru word for 'one,' expressing Perez's "interest in origins and sourcings" (Suzuki 182); the second volume, *[saina]* (2010), takes as its title the CHamoru word for 'ancestor,' 'elder,' or 'spirit,' but also refers to a CHamoru outrigger canoe built as part of a cultural revival project, pointing to "reflections on navigation, the erasures and gaps in knowledge created out of the experience of colonialism, and Perez's personal experience of diaspora" (Suzuki 182); the title of the third volume, *[guma']* (2014), translates as 'house' or 'home,' which brings to mind not only "how the concept of home itself gets deconstructed and reconstructed across a number of diasporic sites" (Suzuki 182), but also the endangered ecosystem of Guåhan and the so-called *guma' uritao* or 'men's house,' a traditional place of learning for young CHamoru men (Rogers 34); the fourth volume is called *[lukao]* (2017), which means 'procession' or 'wandering around,' alluding to the succession of generations as well as, once more, to CHamoru experiences of displacement and migration; the title of an upcoming fifth volume *[åmot]* (2023), finally, names herbs or medicine and thus gestures both to CHamoru practices of healing with local (and imported) plants and to poetry as a means of healing a community severely impacted by colonization and military occupation. Before *[åmot]*, Perez published a collection of poems, *Habitat Threshold* (2020), that stands independently from his ongoing series, even as it remains thematically connected to *from unincorporated territory*. Like some poems in *[lukao]*, *Habitat Threshold* shifts the primary focus away from Guåhan and toward Hawai'i, where Perez moved to take up a teaching position and where his two daughters were born. It is due to this shift in *[lukao]* that I concentrate on the first four and primarily on the first three collections in my analysis. I use the first edition of *[hacha]*, published with Tinfish Press, rather than the partly revised edition republished with Omnidawn, not because I fetishize a supposed original version of the collection over the revised one, but because some of my readings reference visual aspects of Perez's poems that were modified as part of the switch from the square format of the first edition of *[hacha]* to the Din A5 format of the revised edition.

The first four collections of *from unincorporated territory* consist of several poem sequences whose titles—"tidelands," "(sub)aerial roots," "achiote," "ocean views" or "the micronesian kingfisher *[I sihek]*"—frequently reference island geographies or natural phenomena. The individual sections of these sequences do not form self-contained wholes; they are not grouped in each volume by sequence or contained within one volume only. Rather, the individual sections, or installments, are dispersed throughout the books in which they appear. Even more, some sequences spill from one book into the next, appearing in two or more collections. Parts of the sequence "aerial roots"/ "(sub)aerial roots," for example, can be found in the first two volumes of *from unincorporated territory*, while sections of "tidelands" are included in the first three volumes of the series and individual installments of "organic acts" appear in the second as well as the fourth volume, pointing both to ecological entanglements and to the historical entanglement of Indigenous and foreign cultures on Guåhan and in the Pacific at large. When viewed as a project of place-making in the context of im/mobility, *from unincorporated territory* can be read not only as a project of revitalizing Indigenous environmental knowledges from a perspective of displacement, but also as an experiment in ecopoetics that tries to reconfigure what is known about small island ecologies and, more specifically, how Indigenous epistemologies and cultural practices, including poetry, come to matter in the production and transmission of knowledges about small island ecologies that are shaped by all kinds of human and nonhuman mobilities.

From a Cartographic to a Transoceanic Imaginary of Place

As a number of scholars have noted, references to the politics of cartography play a central role in *from unincorporated territory* (see Hsu, Cocola, Heim "Locating Guam," Lai, Schlund-Vials). From its first pages onward, Perez's series *from unincorporated territory* repeatedly uses maps, or "poemap[s]" (Perez, *[lukao]* 9), to engage critically with Guåhan's past and current status as a contested political and cultural territory that is defined by human mobility. The first installment of the sequence "lisiensan ga'lago" in *[hacha]*, whose CHamoru title means "dog tag" and refers to the stripes of cloth that CHamorus had to wear as markers of identification during the Japanese occupation of WWII (Lai 12), presents the conflicting cartographic imaginaries of Guåhan promoted by the island's varying occupying forces as well as a CHamoru counter-perspective to these colonial projections. The first half of this installment reads:

> "goaam" ~
>   "goam" ~
>
> "islas de las velas latinas"
>   (of lateen sails ~

"guan" ∼   "guana" ∼

"isles de los ladrones"
(of the thieves ∼ "Guåhan" ∼ "guajan" ∼ "islas marianas"
(after the spanish queen ∼   "bahan" ∼

"guhan" ∼   "guacan" ∼   "isla de san juan" ∼ "guaon"

"y guan"   ∼   "omiya jima" ∼ "guam"

"the first province of the great ocean" ∼
([hacha] 15)

The visually striking composition of the section's text mainly consists of exonyms for Guåhan and the Marianas, that is, historical names for the island and the larger archipelago used on colonial maps and in travel accounts by outsiders rather than its Indigenous inhabitants. Among the quoted names are several that mark relations of possession, such as the Spanish name "islas marianas" [hacha 15] which claims the islands for Spanish Queen Mariana of Austria (1634–1696), or the byname "the first province of the great ocean" (15) given to the Marianas by the Russian explorer Otto von Kotzebue at the beginning of the nineteenth century (Rogers 1). Other exonyms express the ideological distortions of colonial cartography, such as the two Spanish names going back to Magellan. Magellan first baptized the Marianas "islas de las velas latinas" ([hacha] 15), a designation that acknowledged local seafaring traditions. Later, he renamed the island chain "isles de los ladrones" (15), islands "of the thieves" (15), after a group of CHamoru used their agile sailboats to steal a rowboat from Magellan's ship the *Trinidad* (Rogers 9). As the opening poem of [hacha] suggests, the act of re-naming a geographical place betrays the colonizers' will and power to control the knowledges that circulate about a particular locale along with the place itself.[2]

---

2   For a more detailed discussion of the politics of the spatial practice of colonial map-making, see Mahshid Mayar's *Citizens and Rulers of the World: The American Child and the Cartographic Pedagogies of Empire* (2022), which argues, amongst other things, that "[r]enaming has long been adopted as a potentially tentative and revocable yet irrefutably violent project of imperial appropriation and colonial reclamation of space [...and that] as such, it both facilitates and justifies the spatial and cultural advances made by the colonizer" (104). Significantly, too, Mayar discusses the long-term consequences of such a seemingly abstracted act of cartographic renaming on both the colonized and the environment they inhabit: "The act of renaming alienates the colonized not only from their past and present, their language and culture, but also from their right to protest the depletion of the limited natural resources the colonized spaces have in store, the destructive impact of such depletion on Indigenous ways of life, and the ensuing ecological crises that will assume global dimensions in the decades and centuries to come" (104).

Renaming is anything but innocent and can be used to establish and maintain relations of domination vis-à-vis the people and the land, the first installment of "lisensian ga'lago" displayed above confirms. In the case of Guåhan, it enabled what Michael Lujan Bevacqua refers to as Guåhan's "banal coloniality" (33), that is, the seemingly casual way in which the island has been subjected, and continues to be subjected, to colonization and militarization (See Heim; "Locating Guam" 187). Taken from Spanish, Japanese, and English sources, the place names in the quoted excerpt provide a linguistic record of the territorial conflicts and imperialist discourses that determined the island's geopolitical and cultural position after Magellan's voyages first put the Marianas on European maps. Exemplifying what Jim Cocola has called Perez's "cartographic poetics" (188), the different designations in this particular poemap form the shape of Guåhan, albeit one turned by 90-degree counter-clockwise in comparison to common Euro-American representations of the island on world maps, putting the counter-hegemonic perspective of Perez's collections on display. The pivotal point of this cartogram—and the only capitalized word on the page in the original edition of [hacha]—is "Guåhan," the CHamoru name for the island. Placed roughly at the form's center, this endonym challenges the colonial discourses associated with the exonyms on the page's peripheries and thus gestures toward the CHamorus' ongoing struggle for sovereignty.

The poem's visualization of Guåhan's discursive over-determination by foreign powers in the form of a map counters the figurative "geographic absence" ([hacha] 16) of Guåhan in the collective memory of its various occupying nations (Schlund-Vials 46). It exemplifies what Cathy J. Schlund-Vials calls the "cartographic pedagogies" (46) of Perez's poetry, which make visible "the role distance plays in the making of U.S. imperialism while at the same time unmasking the absented registers of American empire" (46). In the preface to [hacha], Perez too addresses "Guåhan's marginality to discourses of US nationalism and Western historiography" (Hsu 283), here by pointing to Robert Duncan's 1968 poem "Uprising: Passages 25" as "one of the few poems in American poetry that mentions Guam" (Perez, [hacha] 11). Duncan's anti-war poem begins "with planes roaring out *from Guam* over Asia" (Duncan 154; emphasis added) before launching into a pointed critique of U.S. imperialism and militarism, albeit one that centers a (continental) American perspective, even though it decries the "holocaust of burning/ Indians, trees and grasslands" (155). It is in part in response to Duncan's poem, in which "'Guam' only manages to signify a strategically positioned military base" (Perez, [hacha] 11), that Perez chose the title for his series *from unincorporated territory*. Indeed, every section in the series begins with the word *from* or its CHamoru equivalence *ginen*, indicating Perez's avoidance of "the closure of a completion" (Perez, "The Page" n. p.) as well as the complex relationship of the individual sections to the longer sequences they are excerpted *from* (Perez, [hacha] 12). What is more, the repetition of *from/ginen* points both to the place-based nature of Perez's poetry and the fact that he is writing about the contested geographi-

cal and cultural territory of Guåhan "'from' the diasporic condition" (Cocola 186) of a
CHamoru migrant moving first to California and then to Hawaiʻi.[3]

While the first half of the "lisiensan gaʻlago" section just discussed demonstrates
how Perez's poetry challenges colonial and imperial knowledges that reduce Guåhan
to a strategic site of military and economic exchanges, the second half of the same
installment (displayed in both editions of *[hacha]* on the next page but marked as
a new installment of "lisiensan gaʻlago" in the revised edition) underlines how such
acts of epistemological flattening need to be upset by counter-hegemonic perspectives. Here and elsewhere in the series, these counter-hegemonic perspectives are,
at least in part, perspectives shaped by Indigenous environmental knowledges that
are evoked in poetry:

> geographic absence   ~   "the old cencus records show"
> because who can stand on the
>   reef
>
> and name that
>   below water   or sky
>
> imagined territory ~
>   "a Spanish baptismal name and" burnt villages   archipelago of
>   "chamoru last names drawn
>
>   from the lexicon of everyday language" ~ bone carved word
>   ~ "it is possible they changed
>   their last names throughout their lives" ~ remade : sovereign
>
> ([hacha] 16)

Simultaneously experimental and lyrical, fragmented and highly figurative, the
above passage expresses a place of many dimensions. Instead of looking at the

---

3   Instead of quoting the titles of the individual installments as "*from* tidelands" or "*ginen* or-
     ganic acts," I refer to them as parts of an abstract larger sequence ("tidelands," "organic acts").
     While the geographical connotation of the title component *from/ginen* gets obscured by this
     choice, Perez's variable use of *from/ginen* as title components for the individual sections in
     some sequence makes it impossible to refer uniformly to an entire sequence. In effect, it
     would neither be accurate to speak of the sequence "*from* tidelands" nor of the sequence
     "*ginen* organic acts." Similarly, it would be somewhat illogical to speak of a section of "*gi-
     nen* organic acts." In the first edition of *from unincorporated territory: [hacha]* (2008), which
     I quote from in this chapter, the titles of the individual installments are capitalized ("*from*
     TIDELANDS"), while they are in lowercase in all subsequent collections ("*from* tidelands"),
     including in the re-issued version of *[hacha]* (2017). To avoid unnecessary confusion, I use low-
     ercase for all section titles mentioned.

island from above and from the distance implied by colonial maps, the poem's speaker imagines the perspective of someone standing on a "reef," that is, on the threshold between land and the open ocean. From the vantage point provided by such a liminal positioning, the speaker proposes, one might be able to "name that [...] imagined territory." One might also familiarize oneself with all that is "below water or sky" and thus be "remade : sovereign" of the very terrain that was taken from the CHamoru in the process of colonization. Instead of flattening the contested territory of Guåhan through a colonial cartographic imagination, Perez endeavors here to chart the island's historical and environmental depths with his poetry. What is more, he refutes the colonialist idea of Guam as one small, isolated island among other small and isolated "islands in a far sea" (Hao'ofa, "Our Sea of Islands" 152), instead re-establishing Guåhan's cultural position within an interconnected "sea of islands" (152).

Rather than presenting Guåhan as a place of absence that invites colonial fantasies and imperial projections, *from unincorporated territory* evokes the island as a multidimensional place that is characterized by cultural richness and a strikingly beautiful, if endangered, natural world. The island ecologies evoked in Perez's poetry by far surpass any territory that could be measured by quantifiable data or by what "the old census records show" (*[hacha]* 16). Instead, his poetic work suggests that Guåhan is worthy of a caring attention that celebrates it as an Indigenous homeland rich in cultural traditions and natural resources and in need of critical attention that accounts for the complexities and contradictions resulting from its status as an occupied U.S. territory. Indeed, Perez's entire series can be read as a project of ecopoetic place-making that attempts to make sense of Guåhan as an increasingly degraded cultural and natural environment as well as of the possibilities of environmental and cultural restoration that a poetics of caring and critical attention like his own may help to engender. What emerges in Perez's poems in response to this degradation and as a result of his poetic project of restorative place-making is a "transoceanic" sense of place that draws from Pacific Islander place-based knowledges and practices, while also acknowledging the challenges that colonial histories of displacement and the ongoing U.S. occupation pose for twenty-first-century CHamoru environmental imaginaries.[4]

Perez's collections conceive of places as at-once lived-and-imagined spaces that encompass the land, the sky, and the sea and are shaped by various perspectives

---

4   For discussions of the decolonial dimensions of figurations of the "transoceanic," see for example Elizabeth DeLoughrey's influential discussion in *Routes and Routes* (2007) of a "transoceanic imaginary" (especially 20–30), developed, amongst others, from Derek Walcott's idea that "the sea is history" (4).

of mobility.[5] The sense of land-sky-ocean evoked in *from unincorporated territory* relies on what the poet himself calls "an oceanic préterrain" (*[saina]* 63). Perez borrows the notion of the "oceanic" from the writings of Tongan social anthropologist Epeli Hau'ofa, because it draws attention to "the deeper geography and mythology" of "an oceania, préoceania, and transoceania surrounding islands, below the waves, and in the sky" (*[saina]* 63). Perez proposes the concept of the "oceanic préterrain," as several scholars have noted, because his poetry is very much indebted to a "field" or "terrain" in both ethnographic and poetic terms.[6] The concept also resonates with his poetic work in environmental terms, I would add, insofar as it gestures toward the specific (trans)oceanic culture *and* environment that are at the center of his writing. Perez's insistence on the "oceanic préterrain" thus not only indicates how his poetry "imagines a larger oceanic world for Guam" (Lai 5); it also responds to the geopolitical and environmental problems of Guåhan with "new configurations of space that emphasize oceanic as well as terrestrial space" and, in doing so, "foregrounds indigenous and hybrid modes of perception and practice" (Hsu 297). For my analysis, I am especially interested in the ecological implications of Perez's poetics of the "oceanic préterrain" and in moments where the "forces that exist within and beyond the [traditional] ethnographic frame of the 'field'" (Perez, *[saina]* 63) that interest Perez are connected to human mobility and displacement. As I proposed here, Perez's explorations of Guåhan's oceanic préterrain are inextricably linked to a project of ecopoetic place-making that seeks to harmonize traditional CHamoru place-based imaginaries with the lived realities of intensifying environmental degradation and changing CHamoru cultures of mobility.

Perez's poetry can be called "place-based" and "mobile" in that it foregrounds both the island's natural environment and a long history of CHamoru continental migration.[7] Migration constitutes a considerable challenge for CHamoru culture,

---

5   Drawing from Epeli Hau'ofa's influential anti-colonial reconceptualization of the Pacific as "a sea of islands," Vicente Diaz suggests that Australasian seafaring cultures such as the CHamoru rely on an "archipelagic way of apprehending self and space" (91) that depends in crucial ways on mobility. Taking an oceanic (Hau'ofa) or archipelagic (Diaz) approach to small island cultures and ecologies, both scholars insist, entails considering the sea not as empty space but as an extension of the islands and cultures it connects.

6   As J. Michael Martinez points out, Perez's notion of "préterrain" is highly conscious of the hierarchies and power dynamics in the kind of ethnographic research that Peter Pels and Oscar Salemink discuss in their work. Pels and Salemink, Martinez notes, "employ the préterrain as the apparatus whereby the fieldwork process is exposed as performing a colonial mediation upon the represented subject" (Martinez 332). As Martinez observes, Perez further "complicates this dialectic of the préterrain by echoing it against Charles Olson's field poetics" (332–333), which demands of poetry "full attentiveness to the range of objects (language, syntax and semantics, meter, space, and so on) operating in the field composition" (333).

7   As Faye F. Untalan explains, CHamoru migration to the continental United States started in the early 1900s when a small number of young CHamoru men, known as *"Balloneros,"*

not least because the departure of entire families from Guåhan puts to the test local communities as well as cultural frames of reference. Despite the fact that contemporary CHamoru mass migration to the West Coast of the United States continues a long tradition of Pacific Islander transoceanic mobility (Perez, *Navigating CHamoru Poetry* 110), it calls for a revision of CHamoru cultural identity shaped by colonization. While CHamoru identity continues to depend on people's relationship to the specific (cultural) geographies of Guåhan, displacement has to be acknowledged as a key factor as well. After all, as Perez reminds us in *Navigating CHamoru Poetry* (2021), "[t]oday, more CHamorus live in the diaspora than in the Mariana Islands" (113). If there are indeed no traditional narratives of migration in CHamoru oral literature, as Perez suggests in a section of "(sub)aerial roots" (*[guma']* 17) in drawing from Robert Tenorio Torres, *from unincorporated territory* may be read as an attempt to produce a more mobile cultural and environmental imaginary for those CHamorus who live in diaspora as well as those left on the island. It is important to note that this new mobile cultural and environmental imaginary draws on Pacific Islander traditions of seafaring and evocations of such traditions in Pacific literature (see Heim 186–87, Hsu 300). Yet, in analyzing them one must heed the difference between contemporary transoceanic migrations and (pre-)colonial/ recovered forms of transoceanic and circum-insular travel, especially when it comes to their vastly different effects on place-based cultural practices and environmental knowledges.

When considered as a poetic project of CHamoru place-making that demands a critical engagement with Indigenous histories of im/mobility, the four volumes of *from unincorporated territory* enable an investigation into the ways in which cultural and environmental losses are inextricably entangled with displacement on Guåhan. The environmental imaginary of mobility that emerges from these collections depends on three interconnected themes: the CHamoru as an a historically mobile and forcibly immobilized people, present-day effects of CHamoru mass migration and environmental degradation, and problems that arise from these histories of displacement and current realities of mobility for intergenerational knowledge production and transmission. In the remainder of the chapter, I first engage with the

---

signed on as crew on U.S. whaling ships. The first CHamoru families began to migrate to the continental United States after WWII, when many CHamoru men entered military service. CHamoru mass migration to the mainland began, however, with Typhoon Karen, in 1960, a catastrophic event that Craig Santos Perez also mentions in his poetry. This trend has continued as growing numbers of young CHamoru left Guåhan to go to college from the 1970s onward. In 1980, 47,690 Guamanians (the census does not distinguish between CHamorus and non-Indigenous inhabitants of Guåhan) were living on Guåhan, while 30,695 were living in the continental United States. Twenty years later, there were 61,922 CHamorus on Guåhan versus 58,240 on the mainland. And finally, according to the 2010 census, around 45,000 CHamorus were counted in California alone, the state which has historically been the main destination of CHamoru migrants (Perez, *Navigating CHamoru Poetry* 112).

ways Perez's poems draw attention to the connection between Guåhan's endangered ecologies and the precariousness of Indigenous cultural practices in the context of colonial enclosure and CHamoru immobilization. I then outline how Perez's poetry reflects on the precariousness of CHamoru genealogies and knowledges in relation to environmental degradation and CHamoru mass migration. Finally, I demonstrate how *from unincorporated territory* uses the documentary mode to reach out to non-CHamoru audiences in an effort to promote a deeper understanding of CHamoru history and culture as well as greater awareness about the political and environmental challenges Guåhan faces due to its colonial history and ongoing U.S. occupation. As I argue, Perez formulates a participatory ecopoetics that does not merely present readers with a CHamoru project of ecopoetic place-making, but actively engages them in a project of decolonial environmental pedagogy.

Endangered Ecologies, Colonial Enclosure, and CHamoru Immobilization

Following several centuries of colonial occupation, Guåhan's island ecologies continue to be devastated by the ongoing military buildup on the island as well as a growing tourist industry.[8] The richly figurative "tidelands" sequence in *[hacha]* highlights the longer histories of environmental loss, further aggravated by these contemporary developments. Divided, up until now, into eighteen similarly structured sections, the "tidelands" sequence revolves around eighteen CHamoru nouns that relate to the nonhuman world and organize the sections thematically. All except one of these nouns are translated into English at the end of their respective section, a fact that draws attention to these translations as glossaries to a poetic exploration of a distinctly *CHamoru* environmental imaginary. Amongst others, the natural phenomena evoked in "tidelands" include *"[tano : land, soil, earth, ground]," "[tasi : sea, ocean]," "[cha'guan : grass]," "[manglo' : wind]," and "[langet : sky, heaven]"* (*[hacha]* 25, 26, 42, 48, 62; emphasis original). Significantly, in the ninth "tidelands" section of *[hacha]*, no translation is provided for the word "tinaitai," the CHamoru word for 'tree,' an omission that hints at the loss of significant parts of Guåhan's tree population under Spanish and Japanese rule. Relatedly, this omission can be read

---

8   For more information on the projected consequences of the current military buildup on Guåhan, see the Draft Environmental Impact Statement (DEIS) "Guam and Commonwealth of the Northern Mariana Islands Military Relocation," published in July 2010 by the Department of the U.S. Navy on behalf of the Department of Defense. The statement consists of nine volumes detailing the proposed actions (such as the construction of a deep-draft wharf in Apra Harbor to allow nuclear-powered aircraft carriers to anchor in Guåhan) and their likely environmental effects, with a tenth volume documenting public comments on the Draft EIS. In the sequence "fatal impact statements" from *[guma']*, Perez invokes, and at times quotes from, these comments.

as an allusion to the significance of Banyan trees in pre-Christian CHamoru culture and thus to the loss of ancestral traditions as a result of colonization. Whether they are translated or not, the CHamoru terms inserted into the poems and the poems that environ them gesture beyond place as a mere geopolitical territory or site of natural resources and toward endangered small island ecologies as places of cultural significance saturated with meaning.

The fourth section of "tidelands," organized around "[cha'guan : grass]" (Perez, [hacha] 42; emphasis original), explicitly links histories of foreign occupation and environmental devastation to the ongoing CHamoru struggle for sovereignty and control of ancestral lands. The section reads:

this
chained ground—"does not constitute a
            navigational hazard" but delves
"one witness"—"of different flags"

[cha'guan]

in dull ashes shining

                              ~
                    [cha'guan : grass]
                              ~
                                        ([hacha] 42; emphasis original)

Using the language of conquest and enslavement, the above section points toward the mechanisms of colonization that have turned the island into "chained ground." Rejecting use-oriented discourses according to which the reefs and shallows surrounding the island "constitute a / navigational hazard," discourses that justify foreign management and destruction of Guåhan's natural environments, the speaker foregrounds a different notion of tidelands, one that recalls theorizations of "tidalectics." An idea originating with Caribbean poet Kamau Brathwaite and taken up by various scholars of Pacific literature, "tidalectics" describes "a dynamic model of geography" that can "elucidate island history and cultural production" by providing a "framework for exploring the complex and shifting entanglement between sea and land, diaspora and indigeneity, and routes and roots" (DeLoughrey, *Routes and Roots* 2). A liminal space perched between ocean and land, the tidelands in Perez's poems resist colonial control and act as "one witness" (Perez, [hacha] 42) to centuries of violent conquest as well as Indigenous survival.

Among the different foreign powers who planted their "flags" (Perez, [hacha] 42) on Guåhan were Spanish missionaries who burnt villages, canoes, and fruit trees to break CHamoru resistance ([hacha] 16, 37; Rogers 54–58), the Japanese who implemented "forced agricultural and military labor in order to teach the CHamorus the Japanese spirit of 'hard work and devotion'" (Perez, *Navigating CHamoru Poetry* 13), and, eventually, U.S.-American military forces who bulldozed and burned down vast areas of *ifit* trees during WWII in an effort to defeat the Japanese (Perez, *[hacha]* 65, 77; Rogers 177, 184). These strategic acts of environmental destruction would have left only "[cha'guan : grass]/ [...] in dull ashes shining" (*[hacha]* 42; emphasis original), as the excerpt notes, crystallizing Perez's portrayal of how Guåhan's island ecologies have been disrupted and permanently changed by invading forces ever since the arrival of the first Europeans on the island.

Zooming in on the destructive effects of U.S. military invasion on the island, the seventh section of "tidelands" presents the U.S.-American expansion into the Pacific and the current military buildup in the Pacific as a continuation of the American rhetoric of "manifest" destiny in the "republic['s]" relentless movement "west" (*[hacha]* 48). By evoking the dual genocidal and ecocidal logic inherent in the nineteenth-century American search for new territories, Perez critiques the false ideal of an agrarian democracy predicated on Native American removal ("fields of arable light," 48). Section eight of "tidelands" further explores what Perez views as parallels between histories of colonization and the devastating environmental consequences of the contemporary U.S. military buildup and mass tourism on Guåhan's after WWII:

> knells
> "scaffold the course of submission"
>   made landfill—"this bridge over salt"
> gardens—"dead fish occupying" the
>
> [saddok]
>
> of advent—"harvesting"
>
>   ~
>   *[saddok : river]*
>   ~

([hacha] 50; emphasis original)

Death bells ("knells") are ringing for Guåhan's mudflats, coral reefs, and rivers, which have been "made landfill" in the "course of submission" of the island, the poem showcases. Playing with connotation and consonance, the phrase "[saddok] / of advent 'harvesting'" ascribes the ecological devastation alluded to in the excerpt to the arrival ("advent") of masses of people from abroad (river "of advent" 50), as a result of advertising ("advent—'harvesting'"). What the poem denounces here, and what Perez explores in more detail in the sequence "all with ocean views" (*[saina]*;

see Jansen 16–17), are the ecological effects of what *Kānaka Maoli scholar* Teresia Teaiwa calls "militourism" ("Reading" 251), that is, a "phenomenon by which military or paramilitary force ensures the smooth running of a tourist industry, and that same tourist industry masks the military force behind it" (251).

Despite the dramatic impact that three centuries of foreign occupation have had on Guåhan's ecosystem, the "tidelands" sequence of *[guma']* suggests, the island may presently be facing its greatest challenge yet. The reason is the environmental degradation associated with current plans of a "mega-buildup" that would entail "the creation of a deep-draft wharf in Apra Harbor for nuclear-powered aircraft carriers" (Perez, *Navigating CHamoru Poetry* 59). After pointing to the fact that the bay had served as "fishing/ grounds" (Perez, *[guma']* 41) for islands' precolonial Indigenous inhabitants, as a transfer site for Spanish colonial traders, and as a "naval / coaling station" (41) under U.S. rule after the American-Spanish War, the poem turns to the bay's current use as a military harbor and the "proposed/ dredging" (41) intended to make the harbor accessible to even bigger military and commercial vessels. This dredging ("veils of sediment / and silt will / plume / smolder and // shield all / light" 41–42) will be even more harmful to the local environment than the many strategic fires started on the island by former occupying forces or previous buildup in the Apra Bay. As government reports confirm, inner Apra Harbor is a particularly damning example of the disastrous levels of pollution that U.S. military presence and mass tourism have caused on the island over the past century (Perez, *Navigating CHamoru Poetry* 59–60). As military and commercial traffic increased in the bay, Apra Harbor turned into a pivot for "fuel transfer; nuclear and conventional weapon transfer; fishing, recreational and tourist ship support and import of all kinds of commercial and construction cargoes" (GEPA 3), producing "some of the most polluted harbor sediments in the world" (4). Dredging these sediments, the "tidelands" sequence of *[guma']* warns, will leave "coral weaves dead" and cause "permanent/ loss" (42) of ocean habitats that cannot be redressed by governmental mitigation efforts consisting of plans to "build / an artificial reef" out of "concrete / debris and plastic / pipes" (43).[9] Selecting one of the island's most iconic endangered marine animals as an example, "tidelands" warns that sea turtles will suffer from the infringement

---

9   Current research on the ecological importance of coral reefs highlights the crucial role they play in sustaining oceanic species diversity as well as hundreds of millions of people worldwide (see Rinkevich). At the same time, scholars stress that roughly forty percent of the global coral-reef system has been destroyed over the past four decades, a process that is projected to accelerate in the future. As a consequence, instead of attempting conservation, environmentalists aiming to protect coral reefs throughout the world are increasingly turning toward ecological restoration efforts. One of the most promising restoration methods today is the so-called "gardening concept," which rejects the kind of artificial rebuilding referred to in Perez's text or earlier controversial approaches such as "assisted colonization" (the transplantation of harvested coral colonies from one place to another) and instead relies on nursery-

on their habitat not only due to pollution, but also because they "use natural light /
cues / to navigate" (*[guma']* 42; emphasis added). The use of the word *navigate* in this
passage points beyond the nonhuman world and toward human activities in Apra
Harbor. Specifically, it points to traditional practices of fishing and "pacific island
navigation" (*[saina]*14), that is, to those CHamoru place-based cultural practices that
colonization and current military buildup have been disrupting for centuries now.

As a number of scholars have noted, Perez repeatedly uses endangered species to
link environmental destruction to matters of environmental injustice (Lai 6, Cocola
189). The sequence "the micronesian kingfisher *[i sihek]*" for instance evokes parallels between endangered animal species and Guåhan's Indigenous population, while
also expressing the tensions that arise from colonial practices of enclosure and immobilization that have shaped Guåhan since the earliest days of the island's colonization.[10] A local endemic bird species, the Micronesian kingfisher became extinct
during the 1980s after an American cargo ship accidentally introduced the brown
tree snake to Guåhan shortly after WWII (see Colvin et al.; Rogers 261–62). Jim Cocola reads the kingfisher as a "symbol and symptom of Guam's vulnerability under
U.S. rule" (189) and Anne Mai Yee Jansen suggests that Perez's kingfisher sequence
"maps parallels between the natural world and the effects of militarization and oppression" (11). As the sequence "the micronesian kingfisher *[i sihek]*" emphasizes as
well, the tragic tale of the endemic bird did not end with the arrival of the brown
tree snake on Guam. Indeed, much of the evocative power of Perez's kingfisher poems depends on the survival, or perhaps more accurately, the curious *afterlife* of the
bird in captivity, which raises pertinent questions about the survival of Guåhan's endangered ecologies and CHamoru place-based cultural practices under conditions
of colonial enclosure.

The first section of "the micronesian kingfisher *[i sihek]*" begins with a brief account of how the last twenty-nine surviving Micronesian kingfishers were taken to
U.S.-American zoos to save the species from extinction. This history is followed by,
and partly interspersed with, detailed instructions on how to build an artificial nest-
ing place that will coax Micronesian kingfishers into breeding in captivity. Mixing
technical and poetic language, the text evokes both scientific reports and Charles

---

farmed coral that is grown outside the reef and later integrated into the reef in need of reconstruction (Rinkevich 29).

10   Describing the practice of fencing in a certain piece of land as well as the land that has been
fenced in, the term *enclosure* is historically associated with the privatization of the commons
on the British Isles, from where the practice spread throughout the British colonies, including the United States. For a detailed history of the ideology of enclosure and the resulting assumptions about how land rights affected settler-colonial relations in North America, see Allan Greer's article "Commons and Enclosure in the Colonization of North America" (2012). For
a discussion of "enclosure" from ecocritical and postcolonial perspectives, see, for instance,
Robert P. Marzec's *An Ecological and Postcolonial Study of Literature* (2007).

Olson's subtly environmental anti-imperialist poem "The Kingfishers" ("what does not change / is" and "is born and fed"; see Cocola 189). By bringing together these seemingly contrary references, the poem presents a critique of initiatives such as the Guam Bird Rescue Project, an American-led conservation project that was started in 1983 by Larry C. Shelton, who, at the time, was Curator of Birds at both the Houston and the Philadelphia Zoo. Even while acknowledging that non-CHamoru rescue efforts saved the Micronesian kingfisher from extinction by raising individual birds in captivity, Perez presents continental conservation projects as a continuation of the same imperialist logics that ravaged the island's ecosystem and pushed the birds as well as CHamoru culture to the brink of extinction. The analogy between the birds and the CHamoru suggests that Guåhan's Indigenous people too are living under precarious conditions of containment or "enclosure" ([guma'] 31), conditions acerbated by environmental degradation and ongoing U.S. land seizures.

Forced immobilization and relocation by colonizing forces have not only meant an infringement on Indigenous land rights, they have also meant a disruption of Indigenous place-and-ocean based practices. As the last section of "the micronesian kingfisher [i sihek]" stresses, colonial enclosure has harmed Guåhan's nonhuman world and CHamoru culture in ways that not only affects life on the island in the present, it will also have harrowing effects for the island's future:

—of trespass—[i sihek]

when land is
caged [we]

—of theft—[i sihek]

are caged within
[our] disappearance
[...]
invasion is
a continuous chain of
immeasurable destructive
events in time—

is death of [i sihek]
origins—
is a stillborn [i sihek]
future—is the ending of

> all nests this
> choked thing [we] *[i sihek]*
>
> ([*guma'*] 71; emphasis original)

Due to centuries of "invasion," "trespass," and "theft" of ancestral lands, the CHamoru are "caged within/ [their] disappearance," that, is threatened by cultural extinction. Immobilized literally and figuratively by the material and non-material constraints imposed on their everyday lives, including their engagements with the natural environment, CHamorus are confronted not only by the threat of a "stillborn [...] future" but also by the threat of an "ending of/ all nests," that is to say, the very survival of Guåhan's endangered ecosystem on which many of their cultural practices depend.

In order to prevent further destruction of CHamoru ancestral lands, culture, and community, present and future generations cannot rely on half-hearted preservation measures undertaken by the U.S. government (such as the construction of artificial reefs or the breeding of Micronesian kingfishers in captivity). Rather, the end of the "the micronesian kingfisher *[i sihek]*" sequence of [*guma'*] insists, CHamorus themselves have to begin to act and fight for the survival of Guåhan's nonhuman world and, in consequence, the cultural practices it has sustained. In light of the island's increasing militarization ("as weapons / mount"; Perez [*guma'*] 72), the poem implores, the Indigenous people of Guåhan have to "rise / above fences" and "risk / being Chamoru" (72). They have to contest colonial practices of enclosure and to participate in community efforts to keep Indigenous knowledges and place-based practices alive. Poetry emerges as a crucial tool in this project, especially for CHamorus living in diaspora. Indeed, as the sequence "island of no birdsong" from Perez's most recent collection *[lukao]* maintains, what makes the situation of CHamorus similar to that of the Micronesian kingfishers is not only that both have suffered from the environmental impact of U.S. occupation or that both are surviving but not thriving under conditions of colonial enclosure; rather, it is also that many CHamorus do not live on their native island but in the continental United States:

> fanhasso : *remember* studying native birds of guam in school //
> "the micronesian kingfisher, or sihek, can see into the water" \\
> "added to the endangered species list in 1984" // "the last wild
> birds were captured and transferred to American zoos for captive
> breeding" \\vocabulary test : "invasive, colonize, extirpate,
> extinct" // 44, 000 chamorros now live in california \\ 15,000 in
> Washington // what does not change \\st gail, tayuyute [ham] :
> *pray for [us]*
>
> ([*lukao*] 22; emphasis original)

Emphasizing the resonances of the story of the Micronesian kingfisher with the relatively recent phenomenon of Chamoru mass migration, this passage evokes two
different scenarios of knowledge transmission: the "vocabulary test" of conventional
schooling and, on a meta-level, the "vocabulary test" on the U.S. language of imperialism that Perez's poetry administers to its reader. If Guåhan is, as the sequence's
title suggests, an "island of no birdsong," it must remain an island of song in order
to ensure cultural and environmental survival and, even more, work toward cultural
and environmental flourishing.

Exploring poetry not only as a means to help along such cultural and environmental flourishing, but also as a means of place-making in the context of displacement, the first section of the sequence "sourcings" from the collection *[saina]* brings
together Indigenous as well as non-Indigenous poetic traditions:

'*[hanom] [hanom] [hanom]*'

∼

what echoes across waters :
taotaomo'na –
   from 'taotao' ['people'] *ginen* 'mo'na' ['precede'] –
'people of before' 'before time ancestors' 'ancient people' 'people before
recorded time' etc

     while my ancestors did live breathe love die *before*
     contact *before*
     colonialism *before*
     history
taotaomo'na also exists
     in time *in*
     our histories remembered forgotten
     in our bodies homes words *in*
     every breath '*in*

relation to my own body by wave of the page' and [we]
will continue *after in*
   all *afters*

               (*[saina]* 13; emphasis original)

The first line of the quoted passage repeats the penultimate line of *[hacha]*, formally
connecting the first and second collection of the series, emphasizing Perez's long-
term investment in his poetry and the cultural work he intends his poetry to ac-
complish. The CHamoru refrain "*[hanom] [hanom] [hanom]*" ('water – water – water'),
establishes a literary genealogy that links Perez's books of poetry to the CHamoru
oral tradition of *kåntan chamorrita*, "a call-and-response, extemporaneous, commu-

nal oral poetry that was displaced and suppressed by colonial forces" (Perez, *Navigating CHamoru Poetry* 131). The line has also been read as a reference to—and hence a response to the call for peace and new insight made in—the ending of T. S. Eliot's *The Waste Land* (Cocola 192). As a poetic project that mixes and carries forward different poetic traditions, including Pacific Islander and Euro-American ones, and as a text that frequently addresses matters of nature and mobility, *from unincorporated territory* can be read as a meditation on the importance of tradition in times of cultural crisis and environmental devastation. It may also be read as a commentary on the fact that CHamoru cultural traditions and the Anglo-American cultural traditions do have things, such as a spiritual-philosophical concern with water as a source of life, in common and may be combined productively, if the hegemonic impulse of the latter and its tendency to erase Pacific Islander knowledges and practices is overcome.

Perez claims his position as heir to the American poetic tradition from a perspective of migration without turning his back on CHamoru cultural practices. It is in this conflicted cultural territory and as a response to the threat that Guåhan's culture and environment are facing that poetry emerges as a particularly useful tool of environmental knowledge production and transmission that can resist imperial logics of homogenization through openness and ambiguity. The second part of the "sourcings" section quoted above explicitly reaches back to the "ancient people" who lived "*before* / contact" and "*before* / colonialism" (*[saina]* 13; emphasis original). The excerpt begins with a homage to the "taotaomo'na" (13), the ancestors, and thus to a meaningful, common past; it ends by directing the reader's attention toward a present and future in which CHamoru culture, traditions, and "histories"—while still facing the danger of being "forgotten"—can survive "*in* our bodies homes words" (13; emphasis original). The enumeration "bodies homes words" evokes a triangulation of the material self, the natural environment, and the poetic language (Martinez 336). Specifically, the above excerpt proposes that ancestral CHamoru histories, and, as I would add, place-based practices and the environmental knowledges associated with them, will live on "*in* / every breath" and "*in* / relation to *[the poet's] own body by wave of the page*" (Perez, *[saina]* 13; emphasis original).

By making the physical as well as the cultural conditions of the tradition/ transmission of contested histories and precarious knowledges a key concern of his poetry, Perez's poems interrogate both Indigenous and hegemonic American epistemologies (Martinez 338). In and through poetry that expresses the embodied perspectives and affective dimensions of a life lived on the move that still remains deeply connected with Guåhan's endangered oceanic préterrain, Perez emphasizes that the histories and knowledges of the "people of before" may again "echoe[/] across waters" and reach even those CHamoru living in diaspora far from Guåhan. Even though it is implied in "sourcings" that these echoes risk fading away or being distorted, the poem insists that they will reach other shores, if necessary, after being rerouted in one way or another. This is an important point repeatedly addressed throughout *from unincorporated territory*, as Perez writes from a perspective of migration about the precariousness of human and nonhuman life on his native island of Guåhan and the precariousness of CHamoru place-based knowledges and practices.

Precarious Genealogies, Rerouted Knowledges, and CHamoru Mobility

References to ancestral figures and lines of descent are omnipresent in *from unincorporated territory*. They often appear in connection to evocations of (disrupted) human-nature relations and (family histories of) mobility. Perez's second collection *[saina]* is dedicated in its entirety to various "elders." The volume's focus on CHamoru genealogies and ancestral knowledges is not only indicated by its title but also implicit in the question that prefaces each of the volume's five parts. The sentence *"gue'la yan gue'lo, kao siña malufan yo?"* (*[saina]* 12, 38, 61, 85, 109; emphasis original) translates as "grandmother and grandfather, may I enter?" and is said to have been used by pre-colonial CHamorus to ask banyan trees—alternatively believed to house ancestral or malevolent spirits—for permission before entering unfamiliar parts of the jungle (Perez, *Navigating CHamoru Poetry* 41). This prefacing to the different parts of *[saina]* not only conjures up a deep veneration for both ancestors and the natural world, it also serves as a poetic refrain that relates Perez's own poetry back to nature-oriented CHamoru cultural and spiritual practices. In his collections, Perez most frequently evokes Guåhan's jungles in relation to the island's occupation by the Japanese, a time when thousands of CHamoru men, women, children, and elders were forcibly marched to poorly equipped prison camps at the interior of the island (see Rogers 167–68), an ordeal that some of them did not survive (Rogers 178–9). These violent acts of forced CHamoru relocation, which recall the forced resettlement of CHamorus under the Spanish (Perez, *Navigating CHamoru Poetry* 12, 104), and their imprisonment in places ill-suited to inhabitation not only demonstrates the Japanese's disregard for their captives' physical well-being, in particular that of the children and elders; they are further symptomatic of the invaders' disregard for Indigenous environmental knowledges and, more broadly, for established CHamoru ways of relating to the natural world.

CHamoru genealogies and environmental epistemologies are not only depicted as closely linked in Perez's poetry; they are also highly precarious. In the "organic acts" sequence of *[saina]* the resulting layering of meanings is particularly complex. On the one hand, it points to the establishment of the first Spanish mission (*[saina]* 24, 49) and the condemnation proceedings brought on by the *Guam Organic Act* of 1950 (*[saina]* 26, 31), the federal law that codified U.S. land seizure and CHamoru dispossession. On the other hand, "organic acts" tells the story of the speaker's grandmother, who left Guåhan to be with her relatives, and suffers from an aggressive degenerative disease (*[saina]* 54, 71, 75) as well as from painful longing for her place of birth. Throughout "organic acts," Perez uses CHamoru myths that evoke human-nature relations to associate the speaker's grandmother closely with the island. Guåhan is accordingly framed both as a place CHamoru lineages point back to, even in the context of migration, and as a place whose environment is in decline due to U.S. land grabbing and the resulting environmental deterioration. As "organic acts" outlines, both the poet's grandmother and her native island are about to undergo invasive procedures: the grandmother is waiting for surgery, while the island is about to witness the realization of a number of large-scale military construction projects. But whereas an operation may improve the grandmother's condition at least temporarily, even though the poem itself only speaks of her fearful resignation, the "tunneling" (*[saina]* 76) of the island for the benefit of military development is guaranteed to cause more environmental destruction. Although it is not clear whether the grandmother's illness is merely the consequence of old age or whether it results from environmental factors, her identification in the poem with Guåhan's geography and precarious natural world points to the latter, as does Perez's commentary on the detrimental effects of pollution on CHamoru health in other parts of *[saina]*.

What is more, the grandmother's fate as a CHamoru migrant who is unable to return to her place of birth because her body is failing her, and the possible collapse of Guåhan's ecosystem are interwoven in "organic acts" by way of the CHamoru myth of "I guihan dånkgolo" (Perez, *[saina]* 26). In the CHamoru legend of *I guihan dånkgolo*, a giant fish is gnawing at the island's foundation (*[saina]* 26–29), paralleling the way in which military buildup, touristic development, and climate change are increasingly compromising Guåhan's natural environment. As Perez puts it in one of the sections of "organic acts" that comments through ellipsis on the erosion of CHamoru lands and language: "[we] afraid/ be no earth" (*[saina]* 33), only to add in a later one: "*if this goes on/ [we] will fall to pieces*" (*[saina]* 76; emphasis original). The bracketed "[we]" in both quotations identifies the island with its people, conjuring a community united by a special relationship to and responsibility for the land as well as a community and a culture that has come under threat. The implicit threat here, articulated in the legend via an island about to be broken apart by a giant sea monster, is not only further loss of land and culture, however, but also mass migration which has literally split the CHamoru population in two: as it was pointed out before, barely one half of CHamorus still lives on Guåhan, while more than half reside in the continental United States (Perez, *Navigating CHamoru Poetry* 113).

According to the version of the story the speaker's grandmother tells her grandson, a story she believes to have heard from "[her] mom [his] great grandma" (29), *I guihan dånkgolo* was defeated by the Virgin Mary (Perez, *[saina]* 26–29). In an alternative version of the same legend presented by the grown-up speaker later in the sequence, the giant fish is instead caught by a group of young CHamoru women who braid their hair into a net using traditional CHamoru weaving techniques in order to catch the fish (*[saina]* 55, 75). Significantly, the grandson's version locates the power of protecting the island not with a Christian Saint, but with the CHamoru and specifically in women's bodies, implying that the large-scale efforts necessary to save Guåhan will have to involve communal action rather than interventions by non-Indigenous entities or the U.S. government. In juxtaposing the mythical CHamoru maidens' hair with the grandmother's hair loss, "organic acts" gestures toward the loss of culture and strength that comes with the loss of elders and shifts the responsibility for protecting the island and the CHamoru community to the younger generations. This shift is significant, because on a more abstract level, the two competing versions of "I guihan dånkgolo" highlight not only the precarious nature of cultural knowledges transmitted from generation to generation in CHamoru families but also the fact that even Indigenous knowledges transformed by colonial influences—here knowledges rerouted by Christianity—may be useful in some instances for drawing attention to the geopolitical and environmental threats the island faces in the twenty-first century.

How the preservation of precarious Indigenous place-based practices and knowledges is made difficult by both CHamoru immobilization and migration is addressed in the "ta(la)ya" sections of *[hacha]*. In one of the passages in question, the speaker's grandfather teaches his grandson how to recognize the location of fish in the ocean by studying the water's surface and how to weave the traditional CHamoru fishing net, the *talaya*, which in the poem, as Paul Lai notes, "embodies the transmission of Indigenous practices" (8). As the text stresses, the grandfather did not learn these skills from his own father, as one might suspect, but from a group of "minor offense prisoners" (Perez, *[hacha]* 32) living at a prison farm on Guåhan, where the grandfather's father worked as a guard. According to the poem, the poet's grandfather regularly met with the prisoners, while they sat "in their barracks at night [...] and talked and wove the [thread : nasa]" (32). This unconventional moment of intergenerational learning occurs in the context of imprisonment as a prime instance of institutionally enforced CHamoru immobilization. The successful transmission of Indigenous knowledges from one generation to the next under such adverse conditions can be read, if not as an act of active resistance against colonial oppression, then at least as an example of how colonized Indigenous peoples like the CHamoru have always found ways to circumvent measures intended to suppress their culture by passing on precarious knowledges, if necessary through alternative genealogical routes—a dynamic that lies at the heart of Perez's poems.

In contrast to the informal lessons the speaker's grandfather received at the prison farm during his childhood on Guåhan, the conversation between grandfather and grandson also described in the same "ta(la)ya" section takes place in the continental United States, and thus in the urban context of the CHamoru diaspora, far away from the two men's native island. It also occurs far away from any place where the grandfather's traditional place-based knowledge about fishing and net-weaving would possess any obvious practical function:

threads suspended from ceiling hooks

~

[my grandfather] points to the ceiling of his small apartment in fairfield california

"you hold the nicho like this" he says "and the nasa around your finger like this"— his hand of

ghost   knot

tight   weave and pull   cross-

"like this"   he says ~
[…]
his hands begin to cramp
he looks at them, surprised they are empty [taya]
he looks at the empty ceiling   "you have to imagine" he says
([hacha] 31–32)

Like the scene in the prison camp, this scene too highlights the irregularities imposed on CHamoru lines of knowledge transmission. This time, the interruption is caused by migration. Living far from Guåhan and removed from CHamoru fishing grounds, the grandfather appears as a "ghost" of a long-gone past who stiffly demonstrates an almost forgotten skill but ultimately cannot fully succeed in his demonstrations, because they occur out of context. Yet, in the end, the poem seems to offer a glimmer of hope. By establishing a correlation between the act of net-weaving and the act of poetry writing, the poem submits that the speaker will honor the ancestral traditions his grandfather struggles to pass on to him with his very own kind of imaginary net-weaving, one that can be practiced in a meaningful way from a position of migration: he will "imagine," writing environmentally attuned poetry that both investigates the historical, material, and metaphorical "threats" and connects an Indigenous migratory subject such as the speaker to the traditions, cultural practices, and environmental imaginaries of his ancestors, even in the context of mobility.

It is significant for my reading that Perez chooses the practice of net-weaving for this poem in which the transmission of knowledges about Guåhan's natural world is so central a theme. It is also significant that the sequence about net-weaving is called "ta(la)ya." In Perez's spelling, which brackets the middle-syllable, the title of the sequence is itself a chain of interrelated CHamoru words ta 'our,' taya 'empty,' and talaya 'throwing net' (Jansen 26, n. 17), forming the phrase 'our empty throwing net.' The poem's title can thus be said to reference the depletion of CHamoru fishing grounds as a result of industrial fishing and pollution. At the same time, it alludes to the challenges of knowledge preservation in an endangered culture and environment. The title captures this double threat/d and the speaker's response to it with an economy that only poetic language is suited for. Using a single word with an altered spelling, the poem calls attention to the literal and the metaphorical empty throwing nets of Guåhan, that is, to the imminent loss of CHamoru culture and to the ongoing degradation of the unique natural environment that shapes and sustains it. Yet, the poem, like the collections as a whole, does not simply meditate on an endangered local environment. Because Perez highlights not only his CHamoru roots but all kinds of transpacific networks in his poetry—networks woven through the migration routes of his people, the itineraries of invasive species such as the brown tree snake, the travels of plants such as the *achiote* or the mobility of toxins and viruses.[11]

All four collections of *from unincorporated territory* published so far contain passages that explore precarious CHamoru genealogies and disrupted environmental knowledges in relation to different forms of mobility. Perhaps the most fascinating passages in this regard are those sequences from *[hacha]* and *[saina]* that deal with the so-called "flying proas," the legendary CHamoru sailing vessels, the largest of which were called "sakman" (Perez, *Navigating CHamoru Poetry* 103). As Hsuan L. Hsu notes, Perez uses the image of the *sakman* in order to address "the uneven regimes of mobility, housing, and environmental well-being imposed upon Guam" (300). Environmental knowledge production and transmission too are crucially affected by these uneven regimes of mobility. As Perez explains in one of the "sourcings" sections of *[saina]*, larger outrigger canoes allowed the precolonial peoples of the Mariana islands to travel the open ocean, a practice the Spanish colonizers eradicated by destroying all existing canoes and by prohibiting the construction of new ones (*[saina]* 14–15; see also Denoon 249; and Perez, *Navigating CHamoru Poetry* 104). By the nineteenth century, this particular Pacific Islander tradition of boat building had been lost to the CHamoru, together with much of the ancestral knowledge concerning open-ocean navigation. After this significant part of CHamoru culture had been suppressed for more than 200 years, the first modern-day *sakman* was built between 2007 and 2008 and let to water a year later by the Pacific Islander heritage organization *TASI* (*[saina]* 14–15).[12] Because no CHamoru had constructed a full-sized *sak-*

---

11   For evocations of the movements and conflicted cultural meanings of the achiote plant, see the "from achiote" section of *[hacha]*, (17–20) Similar to this section, the sequence "understory" from *[lukao]*) and the "ta(la)ya" sequence of *[hacha]* too can be read as a warning about how the cultural and environmental losses on Guåhan may come to affect larger networks and relations, that is, not only local but in fact global ecosystems.

12   The acronym *TASI* stands for *Traditions About Seafaring Islands*, but also "means 'ocean' or 'sea'" in CHamoru, as Perez explains in the first "sourcings" section of *[saina]* (14). Next to *TASI*, there is also the organization *TASA* (*Traditions Affirming our Seafaring Ancestry*), which Perez refers to

man in centuries, *TASI* had to enlist the help of a non-CHamoru canoe builder from the island of "polowat [in the federated states of Micronesia" (*[saina]* 15; *Navigating CHamoru Poetry* 127–28) to complete the task. As Perez points out in his *sakman* poems, this master canoe builder by the name of Manny Sikau relied for his work on descriptions and drawings taken from historical colonial documents (*[saina]* 14–15), the only detailed source on *sakman* design still available (*Navigating CHamoru Poetry* 106). By stressing this ironic circumstance, the text foregrounds how, as a result of disruptive colonial histories that have eroded and erased CHamoru histories and stories, non-linear genealogies of knowledge are crucial in sustaining CHamoru culture today. It also speaks to the value of such non-linear genealogies in places such as Guåhan, where knowledge preservation remains a crucial project that cannot rely, at least not exclusively, on traditional methods and modes of transmission.

Once completed, the reconstructed CHamoru outrigger canoe was baptized "Saina" (*[saina]* 14), that is, 'ancestor' or 'elder,' a fact that points directly to the collection's main theme. Throughout *[saina]*, Perez's words show great interest in the *sakman* Saina, in the revitalized CHamoru culture of transoceanic mobility it represents and in the rerouted environmental knowledges connected to the tradition of open-ocean sailing that the mention of the famous outrigger canoe recalls. As he notes in the first "sourcings" section of the collection:

> [the] art of traditional pacific island navigation […] includes the geographic knowledge of the locations and inter-relationships of islands, the physics of wind and wave processes, the astronomical alignments and seasonality that provide orientation, as well as the subtle human interpretations of all of these phenomena.
>
> (Perez, *[saina]* 14)

Without modern instruments and navigation technologies, Chamoru seafarers depended entirely on an intimate knowledge of their environment and various natural phenomena for sailing the open ocean. Especially the sequence "aerial roots" in the same volume expresses the speaker's admiration for "traditional pacific island navigation":

[hila': tongue : once fly
    oceania free in
'galaide' 'duduli' 'dudings' 'lelek' 'ladyak' 'sakman'
    hunggan hunggan hunggan magahet

    until fires anchored   *without bow or stern*
    in reef in-   *lateen sail of*

---

in the collection *[guma']* (40). Like *TASI*, the Guam-based organization *TASA* has as its mission to preserve the cultural heritage of the Mariana Islands.

sular words

[**pachot** : 'tasi' dreams'
'tasi' hands carved
and cast
keel

finely woven
pandamus matting
outrigger balancing
does not rely on force
but on ability
to draw water

[...]

[**lengguahi** : bowsprits cut planks cut
   fitted to form
   hull—

[**bos** : **voice** : teach me
to read the currents

skin friction and
wave drag
to fly'
([*saina*] 20–21, emphases original)

The speaker here celebrates CHamoru mobility and the traditional knowledge of open ocean navigation; he links it with his family's migratory history, which is recounted in a longer prose passage omitted from the above excerpt. The poem opens with an ancestral CHamoru chant that emphasizes the truthfulness of the account that is to follow. At the same time, the beginning evokes a much larger Austronesian tradition of seafaring chants, that is, the practice of using songs as a "mnemonic map for travel" (Diaz, "No Island" 92) referencing the landmarks and natural phenomena encountered on the way.[13] In the passage just quoted, the speaker juxtaposes a description of the different types of CHamoru outrigger canoes with phrases that evoke the "'tasi' dreams" of an "oceania free" of "fires anchored/ in reef" (Perez, [*saina*] 20), an image linked to Spanish attempts at securing what they considered the island's hazardous coastal waters through signal fire. This supposedly preventive strategy once again directs attention to the colonizers' dismissal of the precolonial place-and-ocean-based knowledges of the CHamoru, who, thanks to navigating

---

13   For a more detailed account of how Pacific Islanders used chants to remember and pass on information about ocean currents, astronomical constellations, characteristic wave patterns and winds, the distribution of certain marine animals and plants, and other natural indicators to navigate the open ocean, see, for example, Vicente M. Diaz's article "No Island Is an Island" (2015). Diaz discusses Indigenous technologies of travel and practices of narratological mapping, arguing that they can help to "challenge prevailing assumptions that underwrite conventional apprehensions of land, indeed, of place and space" (90–91) and urge us to rethink "the underlying terms and assumptions about indigenous subjectivity and locality" (102).

them for generations, would have been familiar with the reefs and shallows around their island.

Aside from honoring an ancestral Indigenous cartographic practice, Perez's evocation of seafaring chants points to a longer Indigenous tradition of ecopoetic place-making in the context of mobility that his poetry hopes to continue. At the end of the passage quoted above, the speaker begs an unidentified addressee – maybe his grandfather, another elder, the *sakman* Saina, or even the ocean itself – to "teach [him] / to read the currents" and, if one reads across the gap in the middle of the page, also *"to fly"* (Perez, *[saina]* 21). By juxtaposing text fragments that can be read either separately from each other or in varying combinations and by stressing the "in-/sular" CHamoru words *hila, pachot, lengguahi,* and *bos* (20–21; 'tongue,' 'mouth,' 'language,' and 'voice'), this section of "aerial roots" connects the ancestral art of seafaring to the art of poetry, that is, to the art of producing carefully crafted language "fitted to form" (21) just like the individual parts of a *sakman*. By making this connection between seafaring and writing, the text imagines culturally conscious and environmentally oriented poetry as a continuation of the ancestral CHamoru tradition of open ocean navigation, and thus as an act of resistance. Like in the "ta(la)ya" sequence discussed earlier, the poet's efforts at celebrating traditional Pacific island navigation in "aerial roots" are hindered here not only by colonial erasures, but also by his family's migration history. Living in California, the speaker cannot actually feel the *"skin friction and / wave drag"* produced by a CHamoru *sakman*, or a similar outrigger canoe, as it is sailing the open ocean. He can only imagine the experience. Be it traditional open ocean navigation based on currents, winds, and the location of reefs, the practice of fishing with a *talaya* in Guåhan's rivers and bays, or the act of writing environmentally suggestive poetry about the island, many CHamoru cultural practices depend on an intimate knowledge of natural phenomena and complex ecological systems. If these ecological systems change too drastically, or are destroyed, so are century-old place-based practices and knowledges, knowledges that are not only important for the survival of Indigenous cultures and lifeways in the Pacific but that may be able to teach valuable lessons about more sustainable ways of living near and with the ocean to humanity at large.

Participatory Ecopoetics and Decolonial Environmental Pedagogy

Preoccupied with themes of knowledge production, transmission, and recovery, Perez's poetry constantly confronts readers with their own knowledge gaps regarding the history of colonization and U.S. imperialism in the Pacific. At the same time, the countless quotations from diverse sources in his texts—among them colonial histories, political documents, newspaper articles, activist websites, personal accounts, and works of poetry—highlight the need to consider multiple perspectives when trying to close these gaps. The poets alluded to in *from unincorporated territory*, for instance, include Walt Whitman, the American modernists Gertrude Stein and Charles Olson, the Jamaican American Modernist poet Claude McKay, the American post-war poets Robert Duncan and George Oppen, the Asian American poets Theresa Hak Yung Cha and Myung Mi Kim, Caribbean poet Derek Walcott, Pacific Islander poets such as Haunani-Kay Trask (Native Hawaiian/ Kanaka Maoli) as well as Native American poets such as Joy Harjo (Mvskoke). In his references to Cha and Kim, as Jim Cocola suggests, Perez "thinks their transpacific displacements in connection with his own diasporic trajectory" and in doing so arrives at "more elusive, evocative, and extensive networks of places that help make up the larger planet" (198). A similar argument can be made for many of the other poets mentioned. In other cases, such as in the case of Duncan or Olson, the intertextual references constitute a "writing back to" in addition to a "writing with or toward."

Many of Perez's poems can be understood as didactic in that they try to educate readers by presenting information and commentary on the history, cultural contexts, and current political situation of the CHamoru. Yet, the collections also prominently feature poems that make readers assume a more active role in their own learning process, inviting them to reflect on their own position in relation to the power inequalities, histories of oppression, and competing epistemological traditions explored in the texts. What is at work in these sections can be called a *participatory ecopoetics* that experiments with documentary modes to foster anti-colonial and anti-imperialist critique as well as a more complex understanding of human-nature relations that acknowledges perspectives of mobility. Ultimately, I argue, Perez's participatory ecopoetics stands in the service of a decolonial environmental pedagogy that demands of readers to take responsibility for their own knowledge acquisition and encourages them to understand the reading of poetry as a process of questioning, negotiating, and re-contextualizing information from a vast variety of sources, while also urging them to develop a deep-rooted emotional investment in the matters of social and environmental justice presented.

from unincorporated territory harkens back to a documentary tradition that has characterized American poetry for over a century now (Cocola 109, Suzuki 175). First fully developed in the United States in the socialist poetry of the modernist period, poetry in the documentary tradition is characterized by poets' desire to testify to the injustices of their times, while remaining respectful to the perspectives and voices of the victims of violence (see Metres, "From Reznikoff to the Public Enemy" n. p.). Documentary poetry is interested in "the linguistic authenticity of the oppressed" as well as "in their capacity to tell the truth about themselves, and, as such, about us, their oppressors" (Earl n. p.). In comparison to lyrical or narrative forms, documentary poetry is more information driven and often employs collaging techniques, producing works that consist either entirely or in significant parts of re-arranged quotations from official documents and victims' testimonies. Thanks to this practice of sampling and rearranging, poetry in the documentary tradition "raises complex issues of voice" (Swensen 55). Poets invested in the documentary mode are driven by the urge to speak for those who have suffered injustices, while at the same time struggling to avoid "appropriating the experience or voice of another" (Swensen 55). Frequently writing in this mode, Perez combines personal and family experiences with the voices and stories of others, while also addressing the relative privilege and the particular challenges that follow from writing about Guåhan as a highly educated member of the CHamoru diaspora. Rather than using the documentary mode to compensate for a lack of personal experience, Perez employs it to interrogate the gap between experience and knowledge, processes of knowledge production and transmission as well as the complex interplay of discourses of oppression and empowerment that disrupt or reroute these processes.

According to Philip Metres, documentary poetry is "fundamentally concerned with cultivating historicity" and is inclined toward "the pedagogical or didactic" (Metres and Nowak 10). In the same conversation, Mark Nowak describes documentary poetry as "a poetic version of critical pedagogy" (Metres and Nowak 11). It is this critical pedagogical dimension of Perez's poetry that I want to explore in relation to his joint treatment of environmental issues and questions of mobility. In Perez's poetry the documentary impulse comes to the fore in sequences such as "organic acts," which quotes extensively from historical and legal sources addressing the occupation of Chamoru territory by different foreign powers (*[saina]* 26, 31–33, 49, 50 77–78), or in the "fatal impact statements" sections from *[guma']*, which sample online comments on the 2009 Draft Environmental Impact Statement (DEIS). The ecological devastation of the island following from U.S. military buildup is also addressed in documentary passages in the "tidelands" sections of *[saina]*, where each section is accompanied by a visibly crossed-out footnote quoting Perez's 2008 speech before the UN Special Political and Decolonization Committee, in which the poet-activist detailed the dramatic effects of pollution on the people, the wildlife, and the ecosystem of Guåhan (Knighton 344; Heim, "How (Not) to Globalize Oceania" 138).

Throughout *from unincorporated territory*, documentary passages provide evidence for the endangerment and exploitation of CHamoru lives and lands, portraying them as interlinked issues of social and environmental justice that affect individuals and the community alike. Presented with carefully arranged materials and more traditionally lyrical passages, Perez's readers are not only tasked with piecing together relevant background information, they are also encouraged to examine their own relationship to and—especially in the case of non-Indigenous readers from settler nations—their tacit, often unchecked, complicity with the structures of oppression and exploitation addressed in the collections. As Perez's work testifies, poetry in the documentary mode is never purely informational. Instead, language becomes "performative, making it an action with the potential for real effect in the world" (Swensen 57), an effect that will in turn "be another action, this time on the part of the reader" (57). The performativity of poetic language described here, its potential to call for not only a change of consciousness but also a change of conduct and indeed of collective action, is crucial to Perez's work. Indeed, as Otto Heim suggests, Perez pushes his readers toward "an active participation in his [poetic] project" in order to "realize a sense of political community" (Heim, "Locating Guam" 189). Precisely where his poems presuppose action and community formation on the part of his readers, Perez's poems most fully exhibit his participatory ecopoetics.

The fact that "Perez's poetry frequently performs the dual work of educating and critiquing" (Jansen 6) links it to a longer history of politically-minded Indigenous literary production. It also links it to what Anne Mai Yee Jansen describes within the context of Oceanic literary studies as an "affinity poetics" that seeks to "engage hearts and minds toward antihegemonic theory and praxis" (21) by "creating [a] sense of solidarity across identities and across distance for the purpose of advancing a decolonizing agenda" (8). At the same time, Perez's ecopoetry of mobility also builds on the poetic innovations of an (Anglo-)American experimental tradition most visible in his work in the many references to the Black Mountain poet Charles Olson. Perez does not only include intertextual allusions to one of Olson's poems in the "the micronesian kingfisher [i sihek]" sequence of [guma'], the "stations of crossing" sequence of [hacha] (54) or the "island of no birdsong" sequence of [lukao] (38), he also references Olson's poetological reflections. In the same metapoetic "sourcings" section in which he presents his own theorizations of a poetics of the oceanic préterrain, Perez discusses Olson's programmatic "essay 'projective verse'" as well as the poet's theory of "FIELD COMPOSITION" ([saina] 63; emphasis original). In mentioning Olson's poetological work, Perez's establishes an explicit (meta)poetic genealogy that, amongst other things, speaks directly to what I describe as his participatory ecopoetics.

In *Paratextual Communities: American Avant-garde Poetry Since 1950* (2001), Susan Vanderborg argues that Olson's "elliptical, open-ended field composition of archival references, anecdotes, and mythic fragments"—a description that fits Perez's poetry just as well as Olson's—"emphasized the participation of both author and audience in 'istorin,' an active process of investigating local events and cultural documents on one's own rather than accepting an authorized version of history" (Vanderborg 23). In enlisting readers in such a project of "finding it out on their own," Vanderborg suggests, Olson proposed a "participatory poetics" (Vanderborg 23). Perez too challenges readers to question "authorized version[s] of history" and invites them to participate in an "active process" of investigating a variety of events and documents, be they U.S. executive orders, newspaper articles, websites, scholarly publications, as well as other works of poetry. Invested in the transoceanic and environmental dimensions of "local events" and in the hegemonic as well as the counterhegemonic dimensions of "cultural documents," Perez puts his participatory *eco*poetics at the service of a decolonial environmental pedagogy that seeks to involve readers from a variety of backgrounds and with a broad range of prior knowledges about the history and current situation of Guåhan, while at the same time keeping precarious Indigenous genealogies and epistemologies in view.

One way in which Perez's participatory ecopoetics expresses a critique of the destructive knowledge regimes of colonialism and imperialism is through the use of multilingualism. Poem sequences like "lisiensan ga'lago" and "tidelands" from [hacha] are full of phrases in CHamou, many of which remain untranslated, marking Perez as a poet who is, as Jim Cocola describes it, "uneasily Anglophone" and "resolutely polyglot" in his writing practices (175–76). As Juliana Spahr notes in a scholarly article on "Multilingualism in Contemporary American Poetry" (that also mentions Perez), the use of multiple languages is a strategy that enables "a questioning investigation of what it means to be a writer in English when English is a global and imperial language" (1125). Precisely such a "questioning investigation" occurs in poems such as one of the "aerial roots" sections from [saina], which reflects on the limits of poetic language as a means to keep record of traditional cultural and environmental knowledges threatened by colonial violence and U.S. imperialism by representing both poetry and traditional CHamoru open ocean sailing as embodied practices. The second section of "aerial roots" reads as follows:

[**gofes : lung** : if breath
            is our commonwealth

            if we are evidence of
    what words bury [**apuya'**:   "sakman"   i say
            it say it
            navigates the air—

            after measured and form   disassembled   to sand

        —sanding—sanding—sanding—

is remembered the first time i paddled—freshman year at chief gadao academy
[...]

        [**pecho** : prayers flay

            wood treated

                                        to strengthen—
hunggan hunggan hunggan magahet

```
                                     signs
                                     of crossing—

         'mast' 'yard' 'boom' 'sail' 'rigging'—

[patnitos : they can't bury light
                        even if they burn
                                          our word for light—
                        even if we have
                               no nation—
                                          ([saina] 34–35, emphases original)
```

Visually evocative of waves, this passage seems to underline the precariousness of isolated CHamoru words in a predominantly English poem. Using the CHamoru words for 'lung', 'navel,' 'chest,' and 'heart,' the poem conjures the physical exertions of rowing, while also drawing attention to the fact that language is anchored in the body by way of breath. Breath, in Perez's poem, is described as "our commonwealth," that is, as a constitutive element of a global ecological community of shared interests, also in political terms. Although the poem seems to conceive of cultural practices such as traditional open ocean sailing as a means to resist forces of oppression and colonial enclosure, it also highlights the extent to which CHamoru culture and communities remain precarious both as a result of Guåhan's colonial history ("they can't bury light / even if they burn / our word for light") and the island's ongoing status as an occupied territory ("even if we have / no nation"). Celebrating poetic language as a tool of resistance ("if we are evidence of / what words bury [apuya': 'sakman' I say / it say it / navigates the air"), the text links the act of speaking to TASI's attempts at rebuilding the CHamoru "sakman" Saina. By including CHamoru words and by using highly fragmented, figural, and frequently meta-poetic language to familiarize readers with TASI's work and the larger struggle it represents, Perez's poem resists facile consumption. Instead, it encourages a critical examination of the conditions and pressures—whether linguistic, socio-political, cultural, or indeed ecological—under which poems like the second section of "aerial roots" quoted above are being produced as carrier of precarious Indigenous *and* migrant knowledges.

In order to uncover the many layers of meaning in poems such as "aerial roots," readers who are unfamiliar with the CHamoru language either have to consult a CHamoru dictionary or turn to other passages in Perez's collections in which the same words appear together with a translation or in a context that hints at their meaning. Paul Lai has commented on this activating effect of Perez's poetry. When discussing the prevalence of what he calls "deictic lines and pages" (13–14) in *from unincorporated territory*, Lai points to passages that encourage readers to jump back and forth between the different sections or volumes of the series as well as to passages that invite readers to consult sources outside the pages of his books. One of the most striking moments of paratextual deixis occurs in a section of "Lisiensan Ga'lago" from *[hacha]* (Lai 14). The section in question lists the URLs of three websites dedicated to the decolonization of Guåhan and appeals to readers to "please visit" (*[hacha]* 83) these websites for further information on different social and environmental justice initiatives led by CHamoru and non-CHamoru activists from Guåhan. On the same page, Perez presents a language puzzle without an obvious solution that raises questions about the linkages between poetry, the body, natural environments, and U.S. militarism. In order to solve the puzzle of Perez's poems, readers of *from unincorporated territory* have to participate actively in their own education about political, cultural, and environmental issues in Guåhan, whether by following the alternative trajectories of knowledge presented in the collections, searching for translation clues in the pages of Perez's collections or by researching background information for some of the more fragmented and hermetic passages of his poems.

Much like the "aerial roots" sequences, the section "*ginen* tidelands [latte stone park] [hagåtña, Guåhan]" in *[guma']* explores the potential of poetry as a means of (teaching modes of) resistance. More explicitly than the sequence "aerials roots," "tidelands" presents poetry as one of the most effective archives of Indigenous knowledge and means of knowledge transfer available to colonized, dispossessed, and displaced peoples such as the CHamoru. It offers readers a lesson about a key element of traditional CHamoru architecture, the so-called "latte stones," many of which, the text laments, were "removed from [the island] / to museums" (*[guma']* 16; emphasis original) during colonial rule. The poem first elaborates on how to "carve/ limestone" and "outline forms" at the "quarry;" then, the text relates how the speaker's father taught him to "make rope" from "coconut/ fibers" (*[guma']* 14–16). By reflecting on the traditional CHamoru crafts of stonecutting and ropemaking together, the poem proposes that the speaker must right the fallen latte stones ("pull, son" 15) and thus, metaphorically, keep alive the cultural practices and practical knowledges of his ancestors. In the poem itself, this responsibility is passed on from one generation to the next. At the same time, the mode of transmission in the poem switches from instruction by example and emulation to instruction by poetic language and interpretative work.

In contrast to his father, the speaker's choice of craft is not rope-making but poetry-making. Poetry, and especially one that predominantly uses the colonizer's language, English, certainly operates under different premises than the more obviously place-bound cultural practices of latte-stone building and the kinds of net-weaving and ropemaking associated with traditional CHamoru forms of fishing and sailing. Yet, when poetry pays careful attention to the specific environmental challenges and the history of a place and its community, including histories of forced and voluntary mobility, while simultaneously reaching across ethnic and cultural borders, as Perez's poems do, when it is both nature-oriented and mobile, then poetry can help to disseminate precarious knowledges about endangered environments and even gesture toward embodied experiences where those knowledges and experiences might otherwise be lost to the violence of history. Reading Perez's poetry and doing the necessary work of contextualization and cross-reading that it demands means responding to the rallying call of Perez's participatory ecopoetics. It means accepting the invitation *"to sing / forward* [...and] *to / sing past* [...] with [our]/ entire breath"* (*[guma']* 15; emphasis original) as in the ancestral CHamoru "communal poetic form / [of] kåntan chamorrita (which translates as *to sing both forwards and/ backwards*)" (*[lukao]* 19; emphasis original). What is at stake in this rearticulated version of the chant that *from unincorporated territory* represents is nothing short of the survival of CHamoru cultural practices and environmental knowledges and, with them, the survival of the transoceanic terrains on which these practices and knowledges depend.

Like the juxtaposition of reflections on the function of poetry with latte-stone carving and rope making in the "tidelands" sequence, the comparison of the role of poetry in the CHamoru struggle for cultural and ecological survival with the speaker's memories of rowing lessons in the "aerial roots" sections from *[saina]* draws attention to the precariousness of traditional CHamoru environmental knowledges. More so than the former, the latter turn not only to the past, but also to the future. As a later section of "aerial roots" notes, the ultimate goal of these rowing lessons was for the students to take the canoe out onto the open ocean: *"—we paddle—the current—our bodies aligned—row /—in the apparent wind—past the breakwater—past the reef"* (*[saina]* 105; emphasis original). The mention of the *"reef"* in these lines is significant, because it brings to mind all the other passages in Perez's collections that denounce the ongoing destruction of Guåhan's ecosystem by U.S. military buildup; it is also significant because it once more evokes a liminal position from which to indict acts of colonial violence. Contemplating ecological devastation as well as colonial violence, the following passage from "aerial roots" puts particular emphasis on how the U.S. military's careless handling of Guåhan's natural resources will affect many generations to come:

> **[attadok** : one second of damage
>   to coral can take centuries to repair—
>   saina,
>   does time sail in straight lines

> *is said [chief] gadao's broken half [of the canoe] struck the reef near asgadsa bay and became asgadsa island—* [...]

> (*[saina]* 94, emphases original)

The destruction of the reef for the sake of short-term political and economic advantages, the poem suggests, is not only wasteful and irresponsible from an environmental perspective, it also reveals the decision makers' complete disregard for the cultural significance Guåhan's reefs hold for the CHamoru, as implied through the mention of a CHamoru creation myth in the passages in italics. Facing the threat of permanent cultural and environmental loss, and thus an uncertain future for his people, the poem's speaker seems to call to the elders for guidance. However, because genealogies of knowledge have been violently interrupted, as the allusion to the *sakman* "saina" emphasizes, the most immediate response to this call for help comes not from an elder. Instead, Perez's poem has to arrive at its own answers as the ambiguous lack of punctuation in the above passage implies. It is poetry, then, and more specifically the participatory ecopoetics of *from unincorporated territory* that becomes a means of environmental and decolonial awareness-raising, engaging CHamoru readers as well as readers outside the CHamoru community through active reading practices that turn them from uncritical consumers of knowledge into critical and caring interrogators of dominant epistemologies and self-aware actors in the circulation of precarious knowledges.

The more fragmented, figurative, and allusive poems in Perez's collections rely on the potential of experimental poetry to produce critical, self-aware, and active readers (Retallack and Spahr 3). The sequence "preterrain" from the collection *[saina]* is especially interesting in this regard, because it reflects on questions of knowledge production, preservation, and transmission in the context of environmental and cultural catastrophe, while also thinking about the possibilities and limits of poetry as a substitute for bodily experience. The first section of "preterrain" in the collection begins as follows:

[we] reach the unwritten point of arrival
learn 'body

language' is more than a 'litany
        of signs' each sound turns to us

returns to 'salt-
water'
because names are preparatory

name everything
"saina"
     the root

                                                                  ([saina] 18)

Initially, one might read this passage as a celebration of that which is "unwritten," which is to say of an immediate bodily experience of the natural world conceived of as a primordial return "to 'salt-/water'" and thus to a place before language. However, the poem counters such a surface reading by emphasizing that language is not what must be left behind, but what prepares any such "arrival." "[B]ecause names are preparatory," the speaker urges the reader to "name everything / 'saina' / the root" and thus to engage in a performative speech act that produces feelings of kinship and respect rather than relations of ownership and control as in the map of names discussed at the beginning of this chapter. The poem acknowledges that "'body / language' is more than a 'litany / of signs'" and suggests that the poet must "learn" how to use poetic language to communicate experiences of embodiment and emplacement that conventional language fails to express. The "unwritten point of arrival" of embodied and emplaced experiences is not the endpoint of Perez's poem, then. While "each sound turns to us," which is to say, while sound—in particular of poetic language—makes everyone reading in solidary aware of their respective body by way of breath, this awareness becomes the basis for a poetry that is concerned both with the struggles of different individuals and with the collective struggles that are larger than the individual:

> i want to say *belief is almost flesh because flesh holds song*
> each memory of
> what our house was in what
>
>   is never lost
>
> ([saina] 18; emphasis original)

The embodied and embedded, thinking and caring subject is central to Perez's participatory ecopoetics insomuch as *"flesh holds song."* Accompanied by other voices, it is such an embodied and embedded subject, which in Perez's case speaks from a perspective of migration but may also be speaking from a different cultural position, that can hope to preserve "each memory of / what our house was." Imagined as "song," which is to say as a cultural practice that must be enacted to develop its full potential, whether individually or communally, but that can also travel in its written form to be taken up by people elsewhere if circumstances require it, poetry is tasked here with archiving at least some of the cultural and environmental knowledges that would otherwise be lost to the CHamoru, along with the intellectual and affective lessons they may be able to teach to non-CHamorus.

Of course, poetry is not always "what / is never lost," as the speaker must eventually admit, even if he likes to pretend otherwise. Many sections of "preterrain" thus appear torn between a belief in the power of poetic language and the recognition that a poetry of place too is precarious insofar as it depends, like so many CHamoru cultural practices and knowledges evoked in Perez's collections, on a precarious natural environment:

> [we] watch the tide
> at poise the tide wounding
>
> a song
>
> that becomes less and less forgiving
> i imagine 'surfacing'
> where lines end
> 'tell even us' what does 'driftwood' know about geography
>
> that [we] have never learned

([saina] 57)

In this excerpt, like in several others in *from unincorporated territory*, Perez evokes a sense of place that calls for deep immersion and intimate engagement with the natural world, exactly because doing so can teach lessons "[we] have never learned" but that readers might learn in the future. This immersion and engagement—this place-making—is figured once again as the liminal space marked by "the tide / at poise," while also calling for a mobile perspective on "geography," figured here as the "knowledge of driftwood," an image that recalls the ancestors associated with banyan trees and open ocean travel throughout *from unincorporated territory* as well as CHamoru histories of displacement and contemporary CHamoru cultures of migration.

More so than in other poems, the different sections of "preterrain" foreground poetic language as the material that allows for a deep immersion and intimate engagement in the context of displacement, even if the "song" that emerges "becomes less and less forgiving" ([saina] 57). As Perez writes elsewhere in the poem sequence: "i don't know if i can say *our language / will survive here*" ([saina] 36; emphasis original). Given the dramatic degree of cultural and environmental loss on Guåhan, poetry seems to hold the possibility that "language" might survive elsewhere, geographically outside Guåhan and imaginatively within the poem. The "language" evoked here does not only stand for the CHamoru language but also for other forms of mobile place-making and community formation that evoke embodied experiences along with environmental knowledges. Through ecopoetic place-making, embodied experiences and environmental knowledges that have been made precarious by colonial violence, displacement, and environmental degradation can be transmitted to future generations along with an appeal to care and a call for (collective) action. Because of the genealogies that Perez's poetry traces and the alternative genealogies it constructs, readers in the continental United States or elsewhere in the world too are able to come to learn about Guåhan's endangered natural environments and CHamoru cultural practices and, in so doing, enter a place of learning and critical self-examination of the poet's design, or, as Perez's puts it, a "place called 'voice'":

> return
>
> it is true that you can live with thirst
>   and still die from drowning only to have words
> become as material as our needs
>   i want to ask you *is it still possible to hear our paper skin opening* [we]
> carry our stories overseas to the place called 'voice'
>   and call
>
>   to know our allowance of water
>   (*[saina]* 126; emphasis original)

2. Situating Ecological Agency: Anthropocene Subjectivity and Settler Place-Making in the Poetry of Juliana Spahr

Juliana Spahr is an Anglo-American writer, literary scholar, and the author of several collections of poems, scholarly essays, and mixted-genre pieces.[1] Like most American poets who are also academics, Spahr has lived in many different places in the United States, including Applachian Ohio, the Hawaiian island of Oʻahu, and the urban centers of Buffalo, New York City, and Oakland.[2] Instead of leading a life on the move detached from place, the short biography on the dustjacket of her poetic memoir *The Transformation* (2007) informs readers, Spahr "has absorbed, participated in, and been transformed by the politics and ecologies" of each of "the many places she

---

1   Spahr has published numerous individual poems, poetic essays, and chapbooks that later reappeared in collections distributed by different presses. In these collections, several of which are mixed-genre works, Spahr touches on a wide range of issues, including environmental ones: she reflects on the challenges of producing art in a post-Cold-War nuclear age (*Nuclear* 1991); evokes the absurdities of life in a world shaped and distorted by the mass media (*Response* 1996); comments on the aftereffects of 9/11 and the U.S. invasion of Iraq (*This Connection of Everyone With Lungs* 2005); engages with the social, cultural, and environmental effects of U.S. colonization in Hawaiʻi and the global politics of climate change (*Fuck You–Aloha–I Love You* 2001, *The Transformation* 2007, *Well Then There Now* 2011); examines the ecologies, histories, meanings, and functions of a small urban plot of land (*An Army of Lovers* 2013, written with David Buuk); and considers the ethical implications of choosing either writing or marching in protest of corporate exploitation and state violence (*That Winter the Wolf Came* 2015).

2   Juliana Spahr was born in Chillicothe, a small town located in the rural Southeast of Ohio also known as Appalachian Ohio. After attending Bard College on a stipend and receiving a Ph.D. from the State University of New York at Buffalo in 1996, Spahr spent several years teaching at the University of Hawaiʻi at Mānoa. Only months before the events of 9/11, she moved to New York City, where she witnessed the collapse of the World Trade Center and the traumatic aftereffects of the terroristic attacks on the city's inhabitants. After moving back and forth between Hawaiʻi and New York for several years, Spahr took up an academic position at Mills College in Oakland, California, in 2003, where she continues to teach courses in literary studies as well as creative writing.

has lived in." While such a statement must of course be taken with the necessary caution, it is undeniable that place-based poems have been a central feature of Spahr's poetic work throughout her career, as has been the decidedly mobile perspective of an American settler poet and academic migrant. In the following, I focus on selected poems Spahr wrote after and in response to her move to Hawai'i. It is in these texts, I contend, that Spahr's poetry examines how human and nonhuman mobilities of varying scales—from the movement of chemicals between bodies and ecosystems to the large-scale migrations of peoples, plants, and animals—shape human-nature relations. Foregrounding these different scales of mobility and the conflicted human-nature and human-human relations that result from them, I demonstrate in this chapter, raises pertinent questions about settler place-making in the context of global capitalism and U.S. imperialism.

Spahr is well-known as a poet of collectivity and entanglement whose work addresses the complex connections between environmental degradation, climate change, militarism, capitalism, and imperialism (see Arigo, Ergin, Ronda). She is also known as an experimental ecopoet who has emphatically rejected traditional nature poetry along with the traditional lyric and, instead, embraced ecopoetics as a more self-reflective and politically engaged form of writing (see Carr, Chisholm, Luger). Exploring notions of "dis/connection, complicity, and accountability" (Ergin 8) along with the personal and social effects of living in a world of multiple crises, Spahr's poetry frequently deals with the quandaries of cultural positioning, social privilege, and political responsibility that arise when a highly educated, white settler poet from a working-class background, such as herself, moves between and writes about places as different from each other as rural Southeastern Ohio, Hawai'i, New York City, and the San Francisco Bay Area. Focusing on issues of nature and mobility in Spahr's poetry draws attention to the complex ecosocial conditions that shape anthropocene subjectivity and matters of ecological agency, two issues that have generated considerable debate in ecocriticism and the environmental humanities in recent years (see Bennett *Vibrant Matter*, Latour, Alaimo, Iovino and Oppermann). Rather than merely highlighting nonhuman agencies or flattening hierarchies between human and nonhuman agencies, Spahr's ecopoetics of mobility—or rather, her ecopoetics of multi-scalar mobilities—explores the cultural and political conflicts as well as the emotional and cognitive contradictions produced by life in the Anthropocene for the more privileged demographic segments in the United States. Because I am interested in poetic place-making as well as ecological agency, I highlight moments in Spahr's poetry in which entanglement as an unavoidable fact of life in the Anthropocene is juxtaposed with notions of entanglement as an effect of (ecopoetic) place-making. Analyzing Spahr's poems about Appalachia and Hawai'i, I begin by demonstrating how Spahr employs para-lyrical experimentations to present anthropocene subjectivity as embodied and located. Considering different scales of human and nonhuman mobility in connection to the highly differentiated ecological agencies of embodied and located anthropocene subjects in Spahr's poetry, I argue, points to the importance of situated perspectives in poetries of mobility. It also points to the fact that acts of (ecopoetic) place-making can become ethically fraught when they are represented as or conflated with conditions of material-discursive entanglement, not only but especially in cases where the migrants engaging in place-making are also settlers.

Embodied Anthropocene Subjectivity and Para-Lyrical Experimentations

Spahr's poems frequently evoke different scales of place, stretching from the home or neighborhood and regions of varying expanse to the entire planet (Keller *Recomposing Ecopoetics* 32). They also consider different scales of mobility, ranging from the "little mobilities" of chemical exchanges on the molecular level to the "'big mobilities' of people's mass movements across long distances all around the globe" (Adey, *Mobility* 7, 10). The most well-known example for Spahr's treatment of little mobilities on a global scale is probably her "Poem Written after September 11, 2001" from the collection *This Connection with Everyone with Lungs* (2005). Often discussed by scholars interested in ecopoetry and ecopoetics (see Keller *Recomposing Ecopoetics*, Milne "Dearly Beloveds," Ronda), "Poem Written after September 11, 2001" imagines how residues of the buildings destroyed during the 9/11 attacks such as "titanium and nickel" circulate around the globe, "mixing inside of everyone" with more common organic materials such as "suspended dust spores and bacteria" (Spahr, *This Connection* 9–10). The "connection of everyone with/ lungs" that the poem conjures is "lovely" (Spahr, *This Connection* 10) because it is suggestive of a temporary global community, although its members are separated by borders, degrees of privilege, and species boundaries. At the same time, though, it is also "doomed" (10) because the air circulating between the individual members of this imaginary collectivity carries the hazardous micro-particles coming from the fallen towers. What I explore in my reading of Spahr, amongst other things, is which tensions arise in her poetry, when we consider the mobility of people along with the mobility of substances, acknowledging the fact that not "everyone" is exposed to environmental harms in the same manner, not least because of class-based and racialized mobility regimes.

In "Poem Written after September 11, 2001" as in many others of Spahr's poems, the vulnerable bodies of individual subjects constitute an important if contested point of reference. Indeed, it is this vulnerability of bodies that raises questions in Spahr's work about the boundaries of what Stacy Alaimo refers to as the "anthropocene subject" (*Exposed* 144), that is, a subject that must be viewed "as immersed and enmeshed in the world" (157). Although the anthropocene subject, Alaimo contends, is commonly imagined "en masse" and hence as part of "a safely abstracted force" (*Exposed* 167), one should consider it also, if not more importantly so, in terms of "a fleshy posthumanist vulnerability that denies the possibility of any living creature existing in a state of separation from its environs" (167). Spahr's poetry frequently evokes this same vulnerable fleshiness of bodies along with anthropocene subjects who yearn toward, but are also troubled by the material realities of being entangled with their environs and an existence "en masse."

A case in point for what one might call with Kate Rigby Spahr's "affective ecopoetics" (18), that is to say, a way of writing that turns the subject's "attention back upon the self in its trans-corporeal responsiveness to its environs" (18), is Spahr's poem "Tradition" from *That Winter the Wolf Came* (2015). "Tradition" uses experimental language to suggest how the small-scale mobilities of substances accentuate the vulnerability of the embodied anthropocene subject. "Tradition" begins with a gesture of tender bodily contact that evolves into a meditation on the material dimensions of social relations in the context of anthropocene toxification:

> I hold out my hand.
> I hand over
> and I pass on.
> I hold out my hand.
> I hold out my hand.
> I hand over
> And I pass on.
> [...]
> This hand over
> and this pass on.
> This part of me and this not really me.
> This me and engine oil additive.
> This me and not really me and engine oil additive.
> Back and forth.

(*That Winter* 53)

Repeating a limited set of phrases with slight variation, the poem's beginning describes both intimate human-human interactions and the resulting transmission of petrochemical substances from one person to another. The hand that touches things as well as other bodies takes center-stage here because it is the vehicle for the "engine oil additive" and other substances that pose a substantial health risk to individuals repeatedly exposed to them. The text's repetitive structure and its repeated use of phrases without grammatical subjects foreground the concrete material and social effects of unconscious everyday bodily gestures and chemical processes rather than the intentional actions and thought processes of a sovereign subject. Contesting humanist ideas of bounded, fully rational, and disembodied subjectivity, "Tradition" sounds a warning about the dangers of petrochemical pollution as one of the less visible environmental problems in the Anthropocene, drawing attention to what

Alaimo describes as the far-reaching "traffic in toxins" that "may render it nearly impossible for humans to imagine that our own well-being is disconnected from that of the rest of the planet" (*Bodily Natures* 18). What is more, "Tradition" experiments with lyrical poetry to challenge the humanist idea of independent and individualized subjectivity: while it initially seems to project such an individualized subject through the repeated use of the pronoun "I," it eventually abandons that I and instead draws attention to shifting bodily constellations in which the "I," the "you," and later an ambiguous "we" exist in relation as well as in tension with each other.

"Tradition" is not just a poem about one singular vulnerable and fleshy body. It is also a poem about nursing, an intimate physical and social act during which toxins travel from the mother's body to that of the child, "this other thing that once was [her], this not really [her]" (53).[3] Evoking a caring, quasi-symbiotic relationship but also a potentially harmful one, the poem presents a long list of "chemicals commonly found in breast milk" (*That Winter* 87), including "refractive index testing oils and wood preservatives," "pesticide extenders," "dedusting agents," and "hydraulic fluid" (*That Winter* 54). Reinforcing the list's shock effect, "Tradition" weaves the names of the chemicals into a description of breastfeeding that taunts the romanticized depictions of the nonhuman world as a source of bodily and spiritual regeneration. Instead of offering the "cup" of life to her child or the "nectar" (54) of the gods that promises immortality or at least a long and healthy life, the speaker passes on to her infant a disturbing cocktail of industrial poisons and thus the burden of toxification that she herself has been forced to bear. The chemicals recorded in the text, the poem insists, are frighteningly mobile. Their movement from body to body is proof of the porosity of the boundaries between human bodies and their environs, while also being suggestive of an intimate connection between embodied anthropocene subjects that points to the sociopolitical dimensions of embodiment in our contemporary petrochemical age brought on by global capitalism.

"Poem" and "Tradition" reflect each in their own way on shared experiences of environmental vulnerability as a source of and community-formation. Both poems thus explore the social, political, and cultural dimensions of "trans-corporeal" exchanges. Stacy Alaimo coined the term "trans-corporeality" in her influential study

---

3   Spahr references scientific studies that address the transmission of toxic substances during breast-feeding in an endnote to the poem. Stacy Alaimo too notes the considerable threat that toxic traffic poses, amongst many other things, to "children's health and welfare" (Alaimo, *Bodily Natures* 18). For a detailed discussion of the dangers of POPs (persistent organic pollutants)—toxic, fat-soluble and semi-volatile chemical substances which enter the food-chain when pesticides such as DDT, the class of industrial oils called PCBs, or dioxins are released as a result of waste incineration and come in contact with the environment, amass in the human body, and are then passed on from mother to child—see Sandra Steingraber's *Having Faith: An Ecologist's Journey to Motherhood* (137–45).

Bodily Natures: Science, Environment, and the Material Self (2010) to point to "the interconnections, interchanges, and transits between human bodies and nonhuman natures" (2) and to re-conceptualize the body as a "literal contact zone [...] in which the human is always intermeshed with the more-than-human world" (2). Trans-corporeality, according to Alaimo, "opens up a mobile space that acknowledges the often unpredictable and unwanted actions of human bodies, nonhuman creatures, ecological systems, chemical agents, and other actors" (*Bodily Natures* 2). Analyzing how such mobile spaces are evoked in and at least partly generated by scientific discourse, literary texts, and popular culture, Alaimo calls for a "trans-corporeal ethics" that requires us to "find ways of navigating through the simultaneously material, economic, and cultural systems that are so harmful to the living world and yet so difficult to contest and transform" (*Bodily Natures* 18). Because "trans-corporeality denies the human subject the sovereign, central position" (*Bodily Natures* 16), Alaimo notes, it produces conditions in which "ethical considerations and practices must emerge from a more uncomfortable and perplexing place where the 'human' is always already part of an active, often unpredictable, material world" (16–17). Juliana Spahr's poems about small mobilities focus on such an "active, often unpredictable, material world." What is more, Spahr's experimentation with poetic language and form can be understood as an attempt to articulate the "uncomfortable and perplexing" repositioning of the humanist subject in relation to a more-than-human world with which anthropocene subjects are always already intimately entangled, even if the effects of that entanglement greatly vary depending on the individual subject's social position and geographical-physical location.

As Alaimo's discussion of ethics highlights, the repositioning of anthropocene subjectivity does not relieve human beings—and particularly those in positions of privilege—of their responsibility to act against the environmental harm caused by governments and corporations. The "the intimate multitudes" (Ergin 101) evoked in "Poem Written after September 11, 2001" holds the potential for such an action, as do what one might describe as the "material sympathies" (Bennett, "Material Sympathies" 239) evoked in "Tradition" through allusions to the last stanza of Walt Whitman's "Song of the Open Road" (1856): "Camerado, I give you my hand!/ I give you my love more precious than money, [...] will you come travel with me?" (Whitman 307). Indeed, in agreement with what Dianne Chisholm observes about Spahr's collection *This Connection of Everyone with Lungs*, "Tradition" revises Whitman's logic of "democratic affection" (Folsom and Price, n. p.) for our contemporary age, in which vulnerable embodied subjects are called upon to form insurrectional political collectivities. Indeed, while "Tradition" initially focuses on the close relationship between a mother and her child ("this not really me"; Spahr, *That Winter* 56), the group of people to whom toxins are passed on in the poem gradually becomes much larger. In the end, the poem includes everyone, even "those of you who are *not really me* at all" (*That Winter* 56; emphasis added), a choice of words that suggests that although everyone is being exposed to the toxic substances the poem lists, the risk is considerably higher for those less privileged.

"Tradition" affirms and simultaneously casts doubt at the hope that poetry might be able to help forge alliances across differences and lead to truly collective political action at the very moment in which the poem extends its address to a wider audience: "I'd like to think we had agreed upon this together, / that we had a tradition, / that we agreed *these things explained us to us*" (*That Winter* 55; emphasis added). The responsibility of the (privileged) poet to the larger community, the poem suggests, is to continue a poetic "tradition" invested in inspiring democratic sympathies and collective political action. What such an approach to poetry cannot easily solve, however, is what happens, when "we" do not "agree" on a shared "tradition" that "explain[s] us to us" or when the available traditions are in fact harmful because they promote structures of oppression, exclusion, and exploitation, a problem I come back to in my reading of Spahr's poetry about Hawai'i. My primary interest here lies not so much in the moments in Spahr's poetry in which breathing the same air, coming in contact with the same toxins, or, more generally, being together in the same place translate into some form of material sympathy or ecological affection, but in those moments when such processes are called into question in ways that are, to circle back to Alaimo, uncomfortable and perplexing.

One way in which Spahr's poetry challenges the sovereign humanist subject in her poetry is by challenging the self as presupposed and projected by conventional lyrical poetry. If Spahr thus revises Whitman's expansive political lyric (Altieri 134), she also engages with the experimental poetics and leftist politics of an avant-gardist tradition represented by such poets as Ron Silliman or Charles Bernstein. This is why scholars have sometimes described Spahr as a representative of a second generation of Language poets (Spencer-Regan 16–17), or, as Lynn Keller would have it, as a representative of a "post-language generation" who readily avows her debts to her predecessors without feeling "bound to the practices of her Language mentors" ("Post-Language Lyric" 75). Indeed, while Spahr affirms her investment in "an avant-garde practice" that can be traced back to high modernist experimentations with "fragmentation, quotation, disruption, disjunction, [and] agrammatical syntax" (*The Transformation* 49), her poetry is referential and politically engaged in different ways than traditional Language poetry. Influenced by the formal innovations of poets such as Joan Retallack and Lyn Hejinian, Spahr embraces a complex, community- and system-oriented lyricism that tries to de-center the authoritative lyrical subject (see Spahr "Resignifying Autobiography"). Indeed, although some of Spahr's poems omit first-person pronouns, many others retain a more or less fragmented "I," or go back and forth between an explicitly relational "I" and a highly ambiguous "we." In other words, Spahr does not fully abandon the lyric; she employs an experimental political lyric.

Spahr relies on variations of lyric out of "a sense of political urgency" (Keller, "Post-Language Lyric" 83), while also struggling with the limits of the genre in connection to what she perceives as poetry's responsibility to engage critically with history and contemporary systems of oppression. Both Heather Milne and Moberly Luger comment on Spahr's investment in writing a socially responsible and politicized lyric. Analyzing themes of connectivity in *This Connection of Everyone with Lungs*, Milne posits that Spahr "engages the potential of the political lyric to advance a poetics of global intimacy" ("Dearly Beloveds" 203) as well as to evoke a "spatial poetics that connects body to world" ("Dearly Beloveds" 206). Luger, who also reads *This Connection*, finds in Spahr's lyric experimentations a "new poetics of witness" (176) based on distance, liminality, and a logic of "circulation" (183). While I agree that it is crucial to examine precisely how Spahr's poetry connects "bod[ies] to world" and also see her desire to bear witness to social and environmental injustices operating in many of her collections, questions of intimacy and distance play out differently in her more emphatically deterritorialized poems than in her more explicitly place-based poems about Appalachia and Hawai'i. Apart from exploring the political consequences of the material entanglements of embodied subjects with the world and each other, these poems respond to the challenge of expressing in and through poetry the situated perspectives of mobile subjects along with the differentiated agencies that come with different social positions.

In an analysis of "Poem Written after September 11, 2001," Dianne Chisholm suggest that Spahr conceives of social responsibility and collective political agency in relation to a "cosmic bodies politic" (144). Chisholm borrows the phrase "bodies politic" from the materialist philosopher John Protevi, who in turn employs it to emphasize that the social collectivity commonly referred to as the "body politic" is constituted not by abstracted political subjects but by highly diverse, embodied subjects. As a complex, hierarchically ordered structure, Protevi's "bodies politic" is determined by processes that are not subject-directed, but instead go "above, below, and alongside the subject" (4), highlighting how "our bodies, minds, and social settings" (xi) are imbricated with each other in ways that are politically significant. Rather than viewing subjects as self-contained entities, Protevi's materialist understanding of sociopolitical relations aims to capture "the emergent—that is, the embodied/ embedded/ extended—character of subjectivity" (xii). It acknowledges that subjects are produced discursively by cognitive processes smaller than the self as well as by sociocultural forces that lie far beyond it (22). At the same time, it acknowledges that subjects are constituted materially through their "ecosocial embeddedness" (Protevi 22) in the world as well as through biochemical processes that affect both physical environments and the bodies these environments hold. When I thus suggest, then, that Spahr uses *para*-lyrical experimentations in order to evoke embodied anthropocene subjectivities, I mean to emphasize that she goes "above, below and alongside" (Protevi 4) the "rational cognitive subject" (Protevi 3) as well as the traditional lyrical subject in her poetry about nature and mobility and in doing so questions notions of ecological agency.

Located Poetry, Ecological Agency, and Place-Making

As the dustjacket of *Well Then There Now* (2011) suggests, Spahr's poetry is informed by an "investigative poetics," a phrase that carries two different, yet ultimately complementary meanings. On the one hand, it implies an impulse in poetry toward the kind of journalistic-scholarly detective work that is also a key feature of documentary poetry, a popular mode in contemporary ecopoetry that I discuss in more detail in the chapter on Craig Santos Perez. On the other hand, the phrase "investigative poetics" refers to a long-standing American tradition of non-descriptive, non-expressive experimental poetry that "operate[s] in the interrogative, with epistemological curiosity and ethical concern" and uses language as an instrument for "investigative engagement" (Retallack, "What is Experimental Poetry" n. p.). This second kind of "investigative poetics" resonates with the idea of ecopoetics as an experimental creative-inquisitive practice, an understanding promoted, among others, by Jonathan Skinner, the founder and editor of the journal *ecopoetics* (2001–2005). In his introduction to the first issue of *ecopoetics* (2001), Skinner criticized the environmental movement for taking largely conventional approaches to literature, culture, and art and for having "protected a fairly received notion of 'eco' from the proddings and complications, and enrichments, of an investigative poetics" ("Editor's Statement," paragr. 1.7). Juliana Spahr's poetry combines these two strands of investigative poetics: it not only documents and enquires into matters of social and environmental injustice, it also prods, complicates, and enriches readers' understanding of their own and others' experiences of the world through experimental language and form.

An investigative poetics also informs what Joan Retallack and Spahr in their joint introduction to an edited collection on *Poetry & Pedagogy* (2006) describe as "located poetries" (5). When Retallack and Spahr use the phrase "located poetries," what they mean is poetry that employs "investigative or critical modes that take environmental, ecological, social, and/or political awareness into their framework" (6), or more succinctly, poetry "that is less about the self and more about the world" (6). In Spahr's own work, this shift of attention from the self to the world—or rather, from the self to the entanglement of self and world—produces tensions: while her poetry often avoids evoking the traditional humanist subject by going above, below, and alongside the lyrical I, Spahr also frequently demonstrates a preoccupation with her own ecosocial position and the exploitative relations that privileged subjects like herself enter into with other human beings and the nonhuman world. Spahr writes "located poetry" insofar as her poetry is often keenly invested in specific places as well as in the perspective that the resulting ecosocial embeddedness produces. This does not

mean, however, that Spahr's located poems are localist or "local poems" in any traditional sense (see Ramazani, *Poetry in a Global Age* 51–55). Indeed, Spahr's poetry
documents the ecological specificity of places, while at the same time prodding and
complicating ideas of the local by investigating how multiscalar human and nonhuman mobilities shape the ecosystems in different places along with the differentiated ecological agencies of the more or less mobile subjects who are embedded in
these ecosystems.

Questions of agency have been a central matter of debate in the environmental
humanities at least since Paul J. Crutzen's and Eugene F. Stoermer's concept of the
Anthropocene and new materialist ideas inspired by such thinkers as Karen Barad,
Elizabeth Grosz, and Jane Bennett began to circulate more widely in the field along
with other posthumanist theorizations aimed at decentering the humanist subject.
As Gabriele Dürbeck, Caroline Schaumann, and Heather I. Sullivan note, the idea of
an "epoch of accelerated and global human impact throughout the Earth's biosphere
[…] poses many challenges to the humanities, particularly in terms of human and
non-human agency" (118). Thinking about agency in the Anthropocene, they contend, confronts scholars with the paradoxical fact that "human agency is now […]
equivalent to a geological force" while "the sum of countless human activities lacks
any characteristics of a coordinated collective action" (118–19). What is more, it forces
us to reckon with the new materialist idea that agency is "always part of larger cultural and material flows, exchanges, and interactions" (119). Describing such flows,
Jane Bennett draws on Bruno Latour theorizations of "a more *distributive* agency"
(Bennett, *Vibrant Matter* ix; emphasis original) to describe "the material agency or
effectivity of nonhuman or not-quite-human things" (Bennett, *Vibrant Matter* ix) in
ways that acknowledge the "vital force" of "[e]ach member and proto-member of the
assemblage" (24). While I am interested in explorations of nonhuman agencies in
Spahr's poems about small mobilities, I am even more interested in how Spahr nego-
tiates differently distributed human and nonhuman agencies in light of multiscalar
mobilities. Because my analysis centers on the question of how mobile subjects can
forge more meaningful and less harmful relationships with the nonhuman world, I
concentrate on ecological agency rather than agency more generally. In doing so, I
also try to be attentive to the complications that arise when one considers matters
of ecological agency in Spahr's located poems about Appalachia versus her poems
about Hawai'i. These complications include the "difficulties of reconciling an awareness of different kinds of ecological agency, inflected by socioeconomic inequality
and political oppression as well as by divergent historical memories, social structures, and cultural practices" (Heise, "Introduction" 4).

The poem "Gentle Now, Don't Add to Heartache" from the collection *Well Then
There Now* (2011) is one of Spahr's place-based poems that investigates the socio-eco-
logical conditions that determine whether more *or* less mobile subjects are more *or*
less vulnerable to environmental harm and have more *or* less ecological agency. In

contrast to poems such as "Poem Written After September 9/11, 2001" or "Tradition," "Gentle Now" can be precisely located geographically based on information in the text. While the poem is preceded by a drawn map and coordinates that point to Oakland as its place of composition, the geographical details in the text identify it as one of two poems from *Well Then There Now* set in Appalachian Ohio. The discrepancy between the expository map and the poem's content, together with the fact that "Gentle Now" is positioned at the end of the collection after several poems concerned with the speakers' life in Hawaiʻi, allow for a reading of the poem as a poem of work-related migration. As the poem explores changing human-nature relations in a context of toxification in which prolonged physical contact with and long-term embeddedness in a particular environment constitutes a risk to one's well-being that some can avoid more easily than others, it also examines questions of place-making in the context of social and geographical mobility.

"Gentle Now" begins by drawing attention to the biological fact that human beings are enmeshed in the "world without" (*Well Then* 124) from the moment they "come into the world" and "breathe in it" (124). "*We* come into the world" (24; emphasis added), the poem asserts, using a universal first-person plural, only to then imply that life for some is characterized by constant movement between different, more or less damaged environments. Having "move[d] between the brown and/ the blue and the green of it" (124), the poem's plural speakers remember a time when they stood "at the edge of a stream" that "flowed/ down a hill into the Scioto that then flowed into the Ohio that then/ flowed into the Mississippi that then flowed into the Gulf of Mexico" (*Well Then* 124). By focusing on a place for which a mobile body of water is of central importance, "Gentle Now" indicates that even seemingly local places are always intricately connected to larger ecosystems. In reference to Appalachian Ohio and the larger bioregion it is part of, this insistence on the interconnectedness of ecosystems has important implications, because Appalachia is a "unique place where one of the highest biodiversity levels in the world overlaps geographically with some of the most destructive land use practices in the world" (Curry qtd. in Payne n. p.). Spahr's poem "Gentle Now" documents the diminishing biodiversity of Appalachian Ohio caused by the local "chemical/ factory and [...] paper mill and [...] atomic waste disposal plant" (*Well Then* 132). What is more, it emphasizes that the pollution that harms biodiversity in the region is also a threat to human beings, especially those who cannot avoid being exposed to the region's polluted environment.

Rather than only employing the river as a metaphor of origin or (re)birth, "Gentle Now" portrays it as a complex ecosystem teaming with life. Using the kind of sprawling catalogues Spahr is known for (Keller, "Post-Language Lyric" 78), the poem names over one hundred local species, including many that have been extinct or are at acute risk of becoming extinct. In mentioning all of these disappeared and vulnerable species, the poem resists what Ursula K. Heise describes as the "'proxy logic' of discourses about endangered species and biodiversity" (*Imagining Extinction* 23), that is, the tendency to choose one exemplary species as representative for all the endangered species in a particular environment. In "Gentle Now," it is not charismatic megafauna that captures the speakers' loving attention, but Appalachian creaturely life on a much smaller scale:

> We immersed ourselves in the shallow stream. We lied down on the
> rocks on our narrow pillow stone and let the water pass over us and
> our heart was bathed in glochida and other things that attach to the
> flesh.
> And as we did this we sang.
> We sang gentle now.
> Gentle now clubshell,
> don't add to heartache.
> Gentle now warmouth, mayfly nymph,
> don't add to heartache.
> Gentle now willow, freshwater drum, ohio pigtoe,
> don't add to heartache.

(*Well Then* 128)

Having undergone a form of baptism in nature, the poem's speakers become emotionally attached to "the shallow stream" that extends not only to endangered creatures such as the "clubshell," but also to parasites such as the "glochida and other things that attach to the/flesh" (128). The speakers' affection for the stream is not portrayed as an automatic consequence of having been born in the stream's vicinity, as the poem's beginning implies. Rather, their affection is the effect of prolonged physical contact as well as sustained intellectual engagement with the local ecosystem. What is more, the speakers' place-attachment depends on the kind of "re-enchantment" of human-nature relations ("We sang gentle now") that materialist ecocriticism has long been interested in.[4] In other words, the speakers' intimate rela-

---

4   As Jane Bennett notes in *Vibrant Matter*, "the figure of enchantment" (xii) is useful not only because "moments of sensuous enchantment with the everyday world—with nature but also with commodities and other cultural products—might augment the motivational energy needed to move selves from the endorsement of ethical principles to the actual practice of ethical behaviors" (xi), but because it "points in two directions: the first toward the humans who *feel* enchanted and whose agentic capacities may be thereby strengthened, and the second toward the agency of the things that *produce* (helpful, harmful) effects in human and other bodies" (*Vibrant Matter* xii; emphasis original). "[M]aterialist ecocriticism," Serpil Oppermann contents, "enhances the postmodern concept of reenchantment" by proposing that "agentic materiality generat[es] meanings and stories in which both microscopic and macroscopic and even cosmic bodies display eloquence" and that "these material agencies are self-

tionship to the stream depends on physical exposure, intellectual engagement, and poetic place-making.

Initially, "Gentle Now" using poetic language reminiscent of both love poetry, Indigenous chant, and traditional nature writing to describe a state of blissful immersion:[5]

> We loved the stream.
> And we were of the stream.
> And we couldn't help this love because we arrived at the bank of the
> stream and began breathing and the stream was various and full of
> information and it changed our bodies with its rotten with its cold
> with its clean with its mucky with fallen leaves with its things that
> bite the edges of the skin [...]

(Well Then 125)

With the help of carefully placed line breaks, Spahr emphasizes that the speakers' "love" of the stream is the result of physical immersion as well as of cognitive engagement. Pointing to how "the stream [...] changed [the speaker's] bodies" as soon as they "arrived at the bank of the / stream and began breathing," this passage imagines human-nature relations as trans-corporeal on the molecular level. For the speakers, engaging with the nonhuman world in this place means letting the "things" populating the stream "bite the edges of [their] skin" (125). It also means being attentive to nature. Indeed, as the poem progresses, the speakers revise the notion that "[their] hearts took on new shapes, new shapes every day" simply because "[they] went to / the stream every day" (Well Then 127), instead suggesting that they actively "shaped [their] hearts into the water willow and into the eggs / spawned in the water willow" (Well Then 128). In the same measure as the speaker's attentiveness to nature increases, the poem's tone changes from an exuberant celebration of the small stream's aliveness to a more mournful tone, a gradual shift foreshadowed by the references to the "rotten" and the "cold" in the passage just quoted. In the second half of the

---

representational, interlocked with human social practices, and compounded of each other" ("From Ecological Postmodernism to Material Ecocriticism" 28).

5   Meliz Ergin links the chant-like quality of "Gentle Now" to Spahr's encounter with Pacific literatures and specifically with "nature poetry composed by islanders" (92). Listing texts that inspired "Gentle Now" preceding the first poem in the collection, Spahr herself credits "a writing workshop at Goddard College in the winter residency of 2004" and "a hypnotherapy session with Michelle Ritterman" (Well Then 7) as well as several books that illustrate the range of Spahr's readerly interests: A Guide to Ohio Streams, a text published by the Ohio Chapter of the American Fisheries Society; the anthology of Indigenous songs, chants, and poems The Path of the Rainbow: The Book of Indian Poems (1918), the scholarly monograph Dangerous Voices: Women's Laments and Greek Literature (1991) by Gail Holst-Warhaft and, as a source for the poem's central phrase, Stations of Desire: Love Elegies from Ibn Arabi and New Poems (2008).

poem, "Gentle Now" turns into a "species elegy" (Heise, *Imagining Extinction* 32), albeit an unusual one, insofar as it uses the "enumerative logic" (59) of lists to expresses
collective rather than "individual mourning" (*Imagining Extinction* 61).[6]

"Gentle Now" explores regional biodiversity loss together with what is at stake
for human beings when they make themselves vulnerable to damaged environments, or, as is more often the case, when they have but little choice to be in close
contact with these environments. Moving from a gentle but enthusiastic love song
to a "lament for whoever lost her elephant ear lost her/ mountain madtom/ and
whoever lost her butterfly" (*Well Then* 131), the poem begins to list the chemicals
that pollute the stream ("chloride, magnesium, sulfate [...] nitrate, aluminum, suspended solids, zinc, phosphorus, fertilizers" and "pieces of plastic [...] travel through
/ the stream," 131). Combining scientific data with highly figurative language, Spahr
engages what Lawrence Buell calls "toxic discourse" ("Toxic Discourse"), exposing
species loss and expressing concern for the well-being of the human as well as the
nonhuman inhabitants of the region. Indeed, while the speakers of "Gentle Now"
are people on the move who have options when it comes to which environments
they want to immerse themselves in, the poem also points a different demographic:
the less mobile working-class inhabitants of Greater Appalachia, a segment of the
U.S. population that is disproportionately affected by the kind of environmental
disenfranchisement that Rob Nixon describes as "displacement in place" (*Slow
Violence* 17). Displacement in place, as Nixon defines it, not only expresses itself in
an emotional alienation from nature; it also expresses itself in mutually destructive
human-nature relationships, insofar as marginalized social groups are often victims of environmental injustice as much as the inadvertent agents of environmental
destruction (*Slow Violence* 17–22). Spahr implies as much in "Gentle Now," when she
switches from a plural to a singular speaker in section five of the poem, a speaker
who, after having spent her childhood in nature, joins the local workforce, becoming
part of and profiting from the very same industries that harm the region's natural
environment and its human population:

---

6   Whereas lists of endangered species in literature usually point to a "confrontation with global
     loss" (Heise, *Imagining Extinction* 61), the catalogue of species in "Gentle Now" sheds light first
     and foremost on regional biodiversity loss. At the same time, it is implied that the great dying
     chronicled in the poem should be of concern for people on site as well as for people elsewhere,
     not only because the pollution that causes species loss cannot be geographically contained,
     but also because (seemingly) localized biodiversity loss prefigures what will eventually hap-
     pen in places that, as of yet, seem untouched by environmental degradation, a point under-
     lined in another poem from *Well Then There Now*, "Unnamed Dragonfly Species."

Ensnared, bewildered, I turned to each other and from the stream.
I turned to each other and I began to work for the chemical
factory and I began to work for the paper mill and I began to work
for the atomic waste disposal plant and I began to work at
keeping men in jail.
[...]
I replaced what I knew of the stream with Lifestream Total
Cholesterol Test Packets, with Snuggle Emerald Stream Fabric
Softener Dryer Sheets, with Tisserand Aromatherapy Aroma-
Stream Cartridges, with Filter Stream Dust Tamer, and Streamzap PC
Remote Control, Acid Stream Launcher, and Viral Data Stream.

(*Well Then* 132–33)

While Spahr does not deny people's active involvement in the activities that destroy the places they inhabit, whether by occupation or consumer choices, the play with pronouns in this section suggests that individualizing responsibility for environmental harm caused by corporations creates an incomplete picture. Indeed, I would argue, Spahr questions neoliberal notions of ecological agency by showing how industrial capitalism and consumer culture force workers to participate in the production of the very substances that harm them, their communities, their immediate living environments, and, due to the longevity and mobility of many industrially produced toxins, ultimately the entire local, regional, and global ecosystem.

Instead of unequivocally promoting an environmental ethics of proximity, then, "Gentle Now" ultimately asks how exactly people are to love nature in the places they inhabit or revisit, if these places are toxic and the very behavior that is commonly believed to strengthen humans' emotional attachment to place, namely intimate, long-term engagement with it, poses a serious health risk. One option, the poem suggests, is song or poetry. Although "Gentle Now" ends with the speaker's assertion that she "did not sing" (*Well Then* 133) when she first moved away from her place of origin, the poem's retrospective perspective indicates that she eventually began to do so. Her song, the poem in Spahr's collection, draws attention to biodiversity loss and environmental degradation in Appalachian Ohio as well as to the frightful mobility of pollutants. It also implies that less mobile working-class communities are at a disadvantage compared to more socially and geographically mobile individuals, when it comes to avoiding exposure to toxic environments. One thing that subjects with more mobility privilege and more ecological agency can do, the poem implies, is care enough about the places and communities they leave behind and to help expose instances of environmental injustice along with those larger social and economic structures that cause them. Even though their perspective on the more-than-human world is decidedly different from that of less mobile working-class people in Appalachian Ohio, the migrant speakers who have been doubly alienated from their place of origin have one thing in common with the working-class people that have stayed put: for both groups, a less destructive relationship to the nonhuman world in Appalachian Ohio is not a given. It is not an automatic result of material-discursive entanglements. It must be arrived at and worked for. Because immersion in nature of the kind the speakers imagine at the beginning of the poem may no longer be a viable option, one alternative that remains is engaging with located poetry as a practice of attention and care. Modelling such a practice of attention and care, "Gentle Now" explores environmental degradation, species loss as well as questions of "ecological agency, inflected by socioeconomic inequality," to circle back to Ursula Heise's caution quoted earlier. While the speakers of "Gentle Now" confidently turn to song as an alternative means of place-making in relation to Appalachian Ohio, their place of origin, the same strategy causes problems, where ecopoetic place-making in Hawai'i is concerned.

Dis/Located Poetry, Settler Ecological Agency, and Place-Taking

In their preface to the *Ecopoetry Anthology* (2013), Anne Fisher-Wirth and Laura-Gray Street use a quote from Juliana Spahr's poem "Things of Each Possible Relation" to illustrate the difference between traditional nature poetry and environmental(ist) poetry. The quote taken from Spahr, which appears in slightly different versions in several of her writings, criticizes nature poetry for its tendency "to show the beautiful bird but not so often the bulldozer off to the side that [is] about to destroy the bird's habitat" (Spahr qtd. in Fisher-Wirth and Street xxviii-xxix).[7] Spahr's image of the bird and the bulldozer is simple and evocative, which is probably why it is routinely mentioned by scholars who address Spahr's ecopoetics. Contextualizing Spahr's statement as one made about human-nature relations in Hawai'i specifically, Christopher Arigo discusses a talk in which Spahr admitted to having long held the opinion "that nature poetry was the most immoral of poetries because it showed the bird, often a bird that like them had arrived from afar, and not the bulldozer" (Spahr qtd. in Arigo 4). Rather than merely rejecting traditional nature poetry as "immoral" for its failure to address environmental destruction, Arigo argues, Spahr used the image of the bird and the bulldozer in her talk to demand an "anti-colonial poetry" that acknowledges both "ecological and sociopolitical colonization" (4). Or,

---

7   It is not clear which version of "Things of Each Possible Relation" Anne Fisher-Wirth refers to in her preface, since the introduction does not specify the source. In any case, the version of the poem included in the collection *Well Then There Now* (2011) has a slightly different wording: "But I was more suspicious of/ nature poetry because even when it got the birds and the plants and/ the animals right it tended to show the beautiful bird but not so often/ the bulldozer off to the side that was destroying the bird's habitat" (*Well Then* 69).

as Jim Cocola phrases it when he takes up the bird-and-bulldozer image in his discussion of Spahr's *The Transformation*, the poet aims for a "poetry of place making" that insists not merely on a discussion of bird and bulldozer, but on "the who, what, when, where, why, and how of bird and bulldozer alike" (Cocola 184). While those questions are worth asking in relation to poetry written about all kinds of places, most of the iterations of the bird-and-bulldozer image to be found in Spahr's own writing makes it clear that she began to think about place-based poetry differently as a result to her work-related move to Hawai'i and in light of the specific sociopolitical and environmental conditions she encountered there, conditions determined in crucial ways by Hawaii's political status as a colonized, or as some hold, an occupied place.

The Hawaiian archipelago consists of 137 volcanic islands, atolls, and islets located in the northern Pacific Ocean and thus belongs to the Polynesia subregion of Oceania. With the exception of Midway Atoll, one atoll belonging to the mostly uninhabited Northern Hawaiian Islands, the Hawaiian island chain forms the U.S. state of Hawaii.[8] Hawaii only became a state in 1959, a little over 60 years after the sovereign Kingdom of Hawai'i had been taken over by the United States, a political move that must be viewed either as an act of colonization that ended Indigenous sovereignty over the archipelago or an act of occupation that occurred and continues despite the *de facto* persistence of Indigenous sovereignty. Even before the United States occupied Hawai'i, Indigenous control of the island chain had been challenged by foreigners. British explorer James Cook had arrived on the archipelago in 1778 and was soon followed by traders, missionaries, planter colonists, and immigrant workers from the continental United States, Western Europe, and East Asia. The influx of explorers, traders, whalers, and missionaries as well as foreign immigration to, and settlement on, Hawai'i led to a dramatic decline in the local Indigenous population: it is estimated that the number of Kanaka Maoli on the archipelago decreased from between 500 000 to 800 000 at first contact to only 40 000 at U.S. annexation in 1898 (Jonathan Osorio 10–11). As both Jonathan Kay Kamakawiwo'ole Osorio and Haunani Kay Trask note, this massive decline in the number of Native Hawaiians weakened the traditional land tenure system on which pre-contact Hawaiian society had depended, resulting in the continual expansion of foreign influence on the islands and in a general reorganization of social, political, and religious life (Jonathan Osorio

---

8   The U.S. state of Hawaii derives its name from the island of Hawai'i, the largest of the eight major islands in the archipelago. People use both *Hawai'i* and the simplified *Hawaii* to refer either to the state or the archipelago as a whole, but for the sake of clarity and because the Americanized spelling is linked to U.S. control of the island chain, I will use *Hawaii* or *the state of Hawaii* when I mean the U.S. state, *Hawai'i* or the phrase *the Hawaiian archipelago/ island chain* when I mean the geographical place in contrast to (but due to the current political situation never truly independent of) the state, and *the island of Hawai'i* when I mean the Big Island specifically.

44–45, Trask 3–4). In response to this "population collapse" (Trask 6), under pressure from influential missionaries, and threatened by the private land claims of non-Native inhabitants of Hawai'i, local Kanaka officials formed the Board of Commissioners to Quiet Land Titles, an attempt at maintaining Indigenous control over the land that instead set in motion the large-scale privatization, division, and dispossession of Native-owned lands in Hawai'i (Jonathan Osorio 45–46, Trask 6–7). The resulting disruption of century-old land-and-sea-based Indigenous practices had disastrous consequences for Native Hawaiians, Native Hawaiian culture, and the local ecosystem, consequences that are still felt today as U.S. occupation and conflicts over land rights continue.

Despite constant infringements on Native sovereignty by foreign settlers and continental American settlers in particular, Hawai'i remained an internationally recognized independent Kingdom until 1893, when a powerful group consisting mainly of white American businessmen, politicians, and plantation owners, who had formed the so-called "Hawaiian League" in 1887, deposed the reigning Kanaka monarch, Queen Lili'uokalani, with a coup supported by U.S. state officials (See Jonathan Osorio 235–49). Five years later, in 1898, the United States officially annexed the short-lived Republic of Hawai'i, a fact that has caused ongoing social, political, and cultural conflict on the archipelago, as Kanaka Maoli groups continue to fight for (the recognition of) Hawaiian sovereignty and restitution of Aboriginal lands (See Trask 92–97). Frequently, this fight has made use of notions of *aloha 'āina*, an ethics and politics of "love of the land" that, as Kanaka poet and scholar Jamaica Heolimeleikalani Osorio explains, has complex social, cultural, and spiritual dimensions and relies in important ways on story, song, and poetry as forms of community-oriented political practice (1–2). It is perhaps not surprising, then, that at least since the Hawaiian Sovereignty Movement of the 1990s, but arguably already since the Hawaiian Renaissance of the 1970s, the fight for political and cultural sovereignty on Hawai'i has prominently involved Native poets whose works frequently combine a particular Native Hawaiian form of ethnic nationalism with concerns for the environment.[9] It is in this context of social, political, and cultural

---

9   One particularly vocal advocate for Native sovereignty was the late Haunani-Kay Trask (1949–2021), a Kanaka activist, poet scholar, and staunch Hawaiian Nationalist. Originally a professor at the American studies department, Trask became a key figure in establishing Hawaiian Studies as a discipline. She was also the founding director of Kamakakūokalani Center for Hawaiian Studies at the University of Hawai'i at Mānoa, where she continued to work and teach until her retirement in 2010, which is to say that she was still active when Spahr joined the university's English department in 1997. In her poetry, which includes the collections *Light in the Crevice Never Seen* (1994) and *Night is a Shark* (2002), Trask wrote about the strain put on the relationship between Native Hawaiian communities and the land by U.S. occupation. Trask not only used her poetry to call into question the actions and legitimacy of the U.S. government, though, she also leveled heavy criticism at all foreigners on Hawai'i and

conflict and with increasing awareness of her own problematic position as a white continental American university instructor and *haole* poet in Hawai'i that Spahr has written about human-nature relations on O'ahu, pointing to settler place-making as a form of place-taking and to the political and ethically suspicious dimensions of environmental imaginaries of mobility formed in the context of the ongoing U.S. occupation of Hawai'i.

If one closely examines the bird-and-bulldozer passages in Spahr's writing with an eye to questions of mobility, it becomes apparent that this image does not only evoke the detrimental effects of environmental destruction and colonization. Indeed, when Spahr specifies in her talk about anti-colonial (eco)poetry that the bird, whose habitat the bulldozer encroaches upon, is "often a bird that *like them* had arrived from afar" (Spahr qtd. in Arigo 4; emphasis added), she specifically highlights the effects of both human and nonhuman mobilities on the local ecosystem. When Spahr compares human and bird mobility here, the question arises in how far these mobilities are similar and in how far they are different. While both kinds of mobility are shaped by colonization/occupation, they cannot be viewed in equal measure as colonizing practices, even if we employ a broad understanding of colonialism, as scholars such as Max Liboiron do. When Liboiron (Red River Métis/Michif) suggests that "colonialism" is not "a monolithic structure with roots exclusively in historical *bad action*" but, rather, "a set of contemporary and evolving land relations that can be maintained by *good intentions* and even *good deeds*" (6; emphasis added), the Indigenous scholar makes the important point that intention is not what distinguishes colonial practices from anti-colonial ones. At the same time, settler agency in the sense of the heightened potential of settlers to impact the world through their actions and settler ecological agency in the sense of settlers' heightened potential to impact the environment as well as other peoples' relationships to nature, remains an undeniable fact. It is especially acute in places such as Hawai'i, where the harm on the more-than-human world caused by settler activities, Spahr's poem indicates, is as omnipresent as the destruction wrought by bulldozers.

The identity of the "migratory" human beings who arrive "from afar"—human beings who are like migratory birds but perhaps more importantly *unlike* them because they possess an ecological agency heightened by the sociopolitical status of Hawai'i that birds do not—is revealed in the bird-and-bulldozer passage included

---

especially at those who exploit Hawaiian culture and natural resources for personal or corporate profit. Her criticism also centered on colonial education and specifically on the role of haole scholars and instructors at the University of Hawai'i, that is to say, positions like Spahr's. Not least due to the lasting influence of Trask's on Native Hawaiian poetry and politics, a new generation of politically engaged Native Hawaiian poet scholars has emerged in recent years, one of them Jamaica Heolimeleikalani Osorio.

in *Well Then There Now* (2011). The relevant passage appears in a short poetic commentary that concludes Spahr's poem sequence "Things of Each Possible Relation
Hashing Against One Another." The passage in question reads as follows:

> *Shortly after I moved to Hawai'i I began to loudly and hubristically*
> *proclaim whenever I could that nature poetry was immoral. There*
> *is o lot of nature poetry about Hawai'i. Much of it is written by those*
> *who vacation here and it is often full of errors. Rob Wilson calls these*
> *poems 747 poems. These poems often show up in the* New Yorker *or*
> *various other establishment journals. But I was more suspicious of*
> *nature poetry because even when it got the birds and the plants and*
> *the animals right it tended to show the beautiful bird but not so often*
> *the bulldozer off to the side that was destroying the bird's habitat. And*
> *it wasn't talking about how the bird, often a bird which had arrived*
> *recently from somewhere else, interacted with and changed the larger*
> *system of this small part of the world we live in and on.*   (69; emphasis original)

Hinting at how nature, mobility, and poetry as a means of place-making are brought
together in her work, Spahr's commentary avers that the poet changed her attitude
toward nature poetry after moving to Hawai'i and after reading what Pacific studies scholar and poet Rob Wilsons calls "747 poems," that is to say, poems written by
(American) tourists and continental migrants with only cursory knowledge of the local environment, history, and culture (Wilson ix, fn. 4). While Spahr also sometimes
raises the question whether ongoing continental American migration to and settlement on Hawai'i can ever be defensible, the passage quoted above implies that she
sees a qualitative difference between the way many tourists interact with the natural environment of the archipelago and the way migrants may engage with it, if they
make an effort to learn about their new place of residence, something Spahr tried to
do by reading extensively about the archipelago's natural environment and taking
an ethnobotany course (*Well Then* 51; see also Keller, *Recomposing Ecopoetics* 191). As
her own activities suggest, the difference between tourists' engagement with place
and (some) continental migrants' engagement with place is one that results from a
different quality of place-making for which a different perspective on the natural
world is key.

   As "Things of Each Possible Relation" suggests, people "who vacation" on the
archipelago are at least indirectly responsible for the considerable infrastructural
development that threatens local ecosystems. "Things" emphasizes that some kinds
of mobility cause destruction of "habitat[s]" (69), while other kinds of mobility
have been crucial in creating or sustaining those same habitats in their current
form. Even seemingly self-contained ecosystems, the quoted passages stresses in
accordance with what scholars focusing on island ecologies have long recognized
(DeLoughrey, "Island Ecologies" 298), have always been open to certain forms of

human, plant, and animal migrations, resulting in environmental change of varying scale and consequence. In denying this fact in favor of a romanticized depiction of Hawai'i as an untouched "island paradise" (Wilson 80), many continental poets writing about the archipelago, Spahr insists, have promoted colonial fantasies that erase the ongoing effects of colonization/occupation and environmental degradation on the island chain. One way to trouble these fantasies is to examine more closely how different kinds of mobility affect "the larger system of this small part of the world" (*Well Then* 69) and how some of them do more harm than others, whether socially, politically, culturally, or ecologically.

When Spahr writes about human-place relations in Hawai'i —just as when she writes about Appalachian Ohio, New York City, or the Bay Area—her poetry often explores what it means to have a body while being in a particular place and moving between different physical environments. Specifically, Spahr explores the complicated situated perspectives that arise from the experience of feeling simultaneously dislocated and ecologically embedded. In her influential essay "Situated Knowledges: The Science Question in Feminism and the Privilege of Partial Perspective" (1991), Donna Haraway points to the politics and epistemologies of embodiment and embeddedness, calling for "politics and epistemologies of location, positioning, and situating, where partiality and not universality is the condition of being heard to make rational knowledge claims" (195). As Haraway elaborates, such politics and epistemologies of location require privileging "the view from a body, always a complex, contradictory, structuring and structured body, versus the view from above, from nowhere, from simplicity" ("Situated Knowledges" 195). However, emphasizing situatedness and situated perspectives, Haraway continues to insist in later publications, does not simply mean acknowledging "what your identifying marks are and literally where you are" (*How Like a Leaf* 72), nor does it mean "only to be in one place" (72). Rather, it means "to get at the multiple modes of embedding that are about both place and space" (72), that is to say, at the ecological and the social, the material and the discursive dimensions of human beings' embeddedness in what Haraway so aptly describes as "naturecultures" (*The Companion Species Manifesto* 1). Situatedness in this sense does not rule out mobility, nor does it imply a simplistic understanding of emplacement. Instead, situatedness, as I understand it here, is the material-discursive fact of the anthropocene subject's ecosocial embeddedness enriched by an awareness of how the social, political, and cultural dimensions of embodiment differ depending on a person's social and geographical location. While this definition of course shows certain similarities with Indigenous conceptualizations of multispecies relationality and human embeddedness in a more-than-human world, including ones that precede Haraway's reflections, I draw from Haraway's non-Indigenous feminist standpoint theory to describe Spahr's explorations of embodiment, embeddedness, and situated perspectives, rather than from Indigenous theorizations, to describe Spahr's poetic explorations as a non-Indigenous, settler-colonial epistemological project. What Spahr tries to understand by thinking through her own situated perspective in and through her poetry, I argue, is what it means for a continental American migrant and settler to engage in ecopoetic place-making in relation to Hawai'i.

Spahr's poetry collections *Fuck You—Aloha—I Love You* (2001) and *Well Then There Now* (2011) are highly evocative when it comes to exploring "multiple modes of embedding" and experimenting with a "view from above, from nowhere, from simplicity" versus the "view from [...] a complex, contradictory, structuring and structured body" to recall Haraway's phrasing. As if to signpost a shift in Spahr's publications toward a poetry of dis/location invested in situated perspectives, "localism or t/here," the first poem of *Fuck You—Aloha—I Love You* (2001), traces the progression from a painful sense of placelessness to an exuberant, though in no way stable sense of place. In ways similar to, yet also different from, the blissful immersion in nature evoked in "Gentle Now," the exuberant sense of place in "localism or t/there" is figured as physical intimacy between the poem's plural speakers and the natural world of their new place of residence. Employing a poetic language reminiscent of Gertrude Stein's poetics of repetitions and grammatical variations (Altieri 134), "localism or t/here" begins as follows:

> There is no there there anywhere.
> There is no here here or anywhere either.
> Here and there. He and she. There, there.
>
> Oh yes. We are lost there and here.
> And here and there we err.
> And we are that err.
> And we are that lost.

(Fuck You 3)

The first lines of "localism or t/here" conjure an abstract, almost existential sense of being "lost there and here" that evokes feelings of displacement experienced by Spahr's migrant speakers as much as feelings of disconnection and confusion experienced by "err[ing]" lovers. Rather than reading like an environmentally suggestive poem of place, "localism or t/here" initially reads like a poem of dis/location that expresses—through the repeated insistence on the absence of a "here" and of a "there"—a deep-seated longing for the kind of stable, uncontested sense of place commonly associated with settler emplacement.

While the poem's speakers are trying to reorient themselves in relation to their new place of residence, they realize that they have been "misunderstanding fullness and/ emptiness" (*Fuck You* 3). Where they initially felt dislocated, they begin to see a "here" that becomes increasingly concrete and tangible. By using punctuation that skillfully inverts subject and object relations, Spahr turns the poem's marker of location "here" into the speakers' addressee ("Oh here, you are all that we want"; *Fuck You* 3). Switching from expressions of loss and longing to a song of love and praise—a reversal of the narrative progression in "Gentle Now"—the poem begins to invoke the fullness of "here," which becomes the object of the speakers' adoration. At the same time, appealing to all the senses, "location or t/here" starts to imagine the more-than-human world Spahr's plural speakers encounter in highly sensual terms, stressing its almost excessive materiality: the natural environment is "rich and dark with soil" (3) and made fertile by "soft rain" that "refreshes and stimulates" (3); it is "encouraging of growing" (3) and "full of seeds" (4). Given the sensual language in this passage, one may be tempted to read these lines as evocative of what Catrin Gersdorf, in following Susan Griffith, calls "an *ecology of intimacy*" ("Ecocritical Uses" 179; emphasis original), that is, as an expression of deep appreciation for and attraction to nature that "articulates ideas of interrelatedness and interdependency as well as experiences of pleasure and joy" (Gersdorf 179). Yet, because "localism or t/here" is not concerned with the abstract act of establishing human-nature relations but with the aftermath of the speakers' work-related migration from the continental United States to Hawai'i, the poem's celebration of nature's receptiveness and fertility cannot simply be reduced to an environmentally suggestive erotics of place.

In light of Hawaii's occupied status and history of colonization, it is a risky poetic move to figure the longing of U.S. continental migrants for emplacement as a desire for physical intimacy with a "rich and dark" natural world, risky because the poem's ironic play with the tropes of conventional nature poetry can easily be overlooked or misunderstood. At the same time, there is subtle irony in the poem, I would argue, for example when a personified natural world receives these migrants like it receives the rain, "without complaint" (*Fuck You* 3), as the poem stresses, using an odd metaphor that I read as mockery of the conventional imagery of 747 poetry, in which the trope of the lush (female-coded) island paradise awaiting (sexual) conquest has been as pervasive as in U.S.-American settler-colonial depictions of Hawai'i at large (Wilson x). In this light, Spahr's use of an erotically charged rhetoric in a poem that depicts settler place-making in the aftermath of migration risks perpetuating the racist and sexist discourses of colonization that structure western understandings of human-human and human-nature relations in the Pacific. At the same time, Spahr's ironic use of an eroticized, gendered language may be said to challenge the destructive patriarchal "*economy of power*, in which language functions in concert with and in support of techniques and tactics of domination and subjugation" (Gersdorf, "Ecocritical Uses" 178–79; emphasis original). The fact that Spahr portrays the gradual embedding that follows the migrants' arrival on the archipelago as an effect of place-making, not just as a natural consequence of arriving in a place, is significant as well. What this portrayal of empowered speakers cannot undo, however, or indeed what it foregrounds, are the problematic settler-colonial dimensions of the environmentally suggestive place-making that Spahr's speakers engage in.

Indeed, even though the speakers of Spahr's dis/located poems noticeably struggle with the realization that their position as settlers changes the political and ethical implications of their place-making, what one might view as migrants' understandable longing for an intimate connection with their new place of residence cannot necessarily be seen as culturally sensitive or ethically defensible in the case of settler migration to Hawai'i.

Instead of insisting on the colonial trope of the welcoming island paradise, one can argue, "localism or t/here" dramatizes the migrant speakers' struggle with the politics of place and the politics of place-making in the context of colonization.[10] In the last stanza of the poem, Spahr counters the idea of a blissful union between its migrant speakers and the natural world by undercutting it with the everyday realities of "banal globalization" as they are enacted in "tourist discourse" (see Thurlow and Jaworski). Troubling the trope of the welcoming island paradise, the poem ironically alleges that the island's natural world is "as accepting of the refrigerator" as it is "of the bough loaded with/ fruit" (*Fuck You* 4), criticizing the false colonialist and capitalist logic that the resources of an exoticized "there" ("the bough loaded with/ fruit" 4) are and will always remain plentiful and available for consumption. The poem also draws attention to the fact that seemingly mundane actions—such as one's unquestioning reliance on common amenities of modern life (represented by "the refrigerator" 4) and casual far-distance travel ("And you and you and you are here and/ there and there and here" 4)—may have far-reaching environmental consequences and implicate people in larger systems of exploitation and oppression. Even though Spahr's speakers seek to establish a relation of intimacy with the islands' natural environment, their place-making does not lead to a balanced, let alone mutually enriching exchange. Rather, the final line of "localism or t/here" suggests that the speakers' move to Hawai'i and the mass mobility of other people like them—whether other continental migrants or tourists—produces a "tear[ing]" or disruption. This disruption points to the cultural, social, and political conflicts that have been caused by settler mass mobility between the continent and Hawai'i and the considerable stress this movement imposes on the archipelago's environment. Continental migrants coming to Hawai'i, such a reading suggests, would do well to

---

10   In her memoire *The Transformation*, Spahr too addresses the problems of writing poetry about Hawai'i as a "continental haole" (109), that is to say, as a white American migrant and temporary inhabitant of the archipelago. As a result of becoming aware of her own and her lovers' position as settlers, Spahr notes, she/they devised a very specific set of rules for writing about the place they had moved to: "Whenever they discussed the island, they had the responsibility to address the legacy of colonialism on the island" (*The Transformation* 108), they had "to point out both that they supported the sovereignty movement and that this movement was larger than them" (108), and "they should not claim to understand the culture that was there before the whaling ships arrived" (109). While many of her poems about Hawai'i follow these rules, others, like "location or/there," wrestle with them.

critically examine their longing for emplacement, their impulses toward place-making, and the responsibility that comes with the significant ecological agency they derive from their specific position of privilege.

Like other poems in *Well Then There Now*, "localism or t/here" suggests that continental migrants' longing for emplacement and acts of place-making are understandable but difficult to justify amidst ongoing Indigenous demands for decolonization. It is especially difficult to justify, where settler place-making comes into direct conflict with Native Hawaiian land rights, as the poem "gathering palolo stream" from the collection *Fuck You—Aloha—I Love You* demonstrates. The poem's title points not only to a little stream approximately four miles east of downtown Honolulu, O'ahu, and to the island's name, which means "the gathering place" in Native Hawaiian, it also to different acts of engaging with places and the nonhuman world ("gathering"). From the onset, the poem thus draws attention to the material-discursive dimensions of place, different forms of place-making and conflicts surrounding land rights:

A place allows certain things.

A place allows certain things
and certain of we of a specific
place have certain rights.

(*Fuck You* 19)

In its very first line, "gathering palolo stream" avoids a human speaker and instead establishes "place" as a grammatical subject. The open-ended, ambiguous phrasing implies that places "allow[/] certain things" within their bounds while keeping other things out and permit certain interactions to take place while preventing others. While the second line may initially only seem to repeat the first line, it marks the beginning of a short stanza that introduces a hierarchy between the "things" that constitute a place such as Palolo Stream through their presence and activities. It differentiates between "things" and "we," a pronoun that sometimes refers to a very specific group of people in Spahr's poetry and sometimes to every human and nonhuman being on the planet. In "gathering palolo stream" the pronoun "we" is more narrowly defined insofar as the poem discusses the relationship of "certain of we of a specific / place" to the stream. Rather than being a grammatical object that the stream acts upon, as in the first line, "certain of we of a specific/ place" in the second sentence of the poem is a grammatical subject, which not only tells the reader that the people in question have agency but emphasizes that "certain of we of a specific / place *have certain rights*" (19; emphasis added). The insistence on rights implies that "certain of we" in this particular instance neither refers to all living beings nor to all human beings on the island. Instead, it refers only to "*certain of we* of a specific / place" (19; emphasis added), that is, to certain human beings but not others. This distinction adds an explicitly social and political dimensions to the material relations evoked in the text and draws attention to the contested politics of place in Hawai'i.

By specifying that "certain of we *of a specific / place* have certain rights" (19; emphasis added), the poem indicates that peoples' places of origin matter when it comes to their right of access to and use of the land. In the case of Hawai'i, where Indigenous control of the land has long been limited by haole settlement and codified by settler law, this is not only to say that mobility can affect a person's or group's relationship to place, in the settler state of Hawai'i it is also to say that racial politics determine peoples' rights, access, and, relationship to the land, a fact that Spahr explores, for instance, in her poetic photo-essay "2199 Kalia Road" also included in the collection *Well Then There Now*. Like Waikīkī's beaches and coastal waters, which has been turned into a wasteland "full of silt and/ pesticides and oils and other urban run-off" (*Well Then* 119) by mass tourism and made almost inaccessible for Kanaka Maoli while they remain accessible for continental migrants (103), Palolo Stream, the plural speakers explains in "gathering palolo stream," too is difficult to access, because it is blocked by "a fence," "buildings," and a "parking lot" (*Well Then* 24). Instead of pointing to tourism as the culprit, Spahr here points to the transposition of continental American car culture to the much less spacious geographies of Hawai'i as the cause for disrupted access to public lands on the island chain: "It is because *certain of we* are / always driving," her speakers note, "that the parking lot / matters" (28; emphasis added). Put differently, it is at least in part because the land and mobility rights of some—here the right to private property and automobility rights—matter more than the land and mobility rights of others—here the right to access to certain sections of public land—that locales such as Palolo Stream remain contested spaces in which the ecological agency of some is legally heightened, while it is severely limited for others.

Spahr's poems are highly ambiguous in how they speak about rights of access to and rightful versus ethical use of public land. This ambiguity points to a tension that emerges in her ecopoetry about Hawai'i between her anti-colonial views, which lead her to support Indigenous claims to the land, and what one might describe as her anarchist views, which lead her to promote common uses of the land. More or less explicitly, some of Spahr's poems thus also explore the problems that arise for settlers invested simultaneously in anti-colonial, anti-capitalist, and environmental politics. Over the course of several pages, each of which only consists of a few lines, "gathering palolo stream" explores this tension along with the discrepancies between ecological agency and land rights through word-play and code-switching:

To go to the stream is a right for
certain people.

To go, to gather.

[page break]

The stream is right.

It is a place for gathering.

A place for gathering āholehole

or for gathering guava, mīkana,
maiʻa

or for gathering palapalai.

(*Fuck You* 20–21)

Playing with different connotations of the word *gathering*, the poem alludes to the multiple meanings that places accumulate and to the different functions that places fulfill for different people in different social and cultural contexts. A distinction that matters in Hawaiʻi, as the poem indicates by combining references to legal discourse and Native Hawaiian words, is the one between the meanings and uses of places in Native Hawaiian cultural practices as opposed to the meanings and uses of these places in settler-colonial practices. What matters, too, the poem implies, is which of these meanings and uses are given priority, both legally and in everyday material and discursive practices.

As Spahr explains in a note following "gathering palolo stream," the Supreme Court of Hawaiʻi ruled in a 1995 landmark case—*Public Access Shoreline Hawaii US vs. Hawaiʻi County Planning Commission (PASH)*—that state agencies had the right to protect "indigenous Hawaiians' traditional and customary rights of access to gather plants, harvest trees, and take game" (*Fuck You* 31). Despite this law, the note adds, Indigenous land rights in Hawaiʻi are still "constantly eroded by property owners who restrict physical access by fencing" (*Fuck You* 31). Or as the last stanza of "gathering palolo stream" puts it:

Certain of we have rights and
these rights are written so that
there is a possible keeping, a

keeping away, that denies
gathering.

(Fuck You 30)

Subtly modifying phrases, the text lays out an intricate chain of cause and effect that evokes what I discuss in more detail in my chapter on Craig Santos Perez as the practice of colonial enclosure, that is, a fencing in of land and a "keeping away" of Indigenous (and other non-propertied) people. In line with the logics of colonial enclosure, which depends on the idea of land as legal property, the "written" word (of law) in Spahr's poem stands accused of perpetuating the marginalization and dispossession of Native Hawaiians. Insofar as the poem's speakers exhibit a certain self-consciousness about their own social positioning—after all they are members, one can infer, of the group that has historically claimed land rights in Hawai'i at the expense of Native Hawaiians, namely continental haole—this charge in the poem against the written word is also one that poetry as a practice of place-making en-acted by a continental migrant poet must grapple with.

In the Native Hawaiian tradition, "gathering palolo stream" suggests, the stream is a place "to gather" or come together as well as one "for gathering āholehole" (a type of sweet water fish), guava, "mīkana" (papaya), "mai'a" (banana or plantains), and "palapalai," a fern-like plant used for *lai* and *hula*-making. In such a tradition, places like Palolo Stream would be understood as environments that sustain a community physically, culturally, and spiritually by way of accommodating a range of place-making practices. Yet, places can only sustain communities this way if the larger ecosystem does not change too drastically or too quickly and if the communities in question have rights of access to and use of the land. In the case of Palolo Stream neither is guaranteed. Hinting at the dangers of ecological degradation, Spahr's poem depicts Palolo Stream as a local ecosystem that "gathers" many disparate "things" with potentially dire environmental consequences. Punning on two differ-ent connotations of the word *thing*, which can refer to a concrete material object as well as to an abstract idea or meaning, Spahr asserts: "The stream is many things. / Is busted television and niu [= coconut]" (22). Although they may be fenced off, the poem suggests, places such as Palolo Stream are porous environments, open to intrusions. Apart from being impacted by pollution, the extended ecosystem surrounding Palolo Stream too has changed as a result of introduced species. In-deed, in the list of flora and fauna from the excerpt just quoted, only the first and the last, "āholehole" and "palapalai" (21) refer to native Hawaiian plants. The other three, "guava," "mīkana" (papaya) and "mai'a" (banana) are tropical transplants, although they can easily be mistaken for native species given their ubiquity on the archipelago. By listing these transplants together with native plants, the poem high-lights the extent to which nonhuman mobilities have shaped Hawaii's ecosystem. At the same time, the presence of these plants on the islands points to the (colonial) human migrations that led to the introduction of foreign species to and spread of these species on Hawai'i. The place-making practice of poetry, Spahr's poem shows, can obscure these intertwined histories or make them visible. Drawing attention to her speakers' ecosocial position and imbrications in larger structures of domination as well as to the conflicts that arise from settler migrants' interactions with Hawaii's more-than-human world, Spahr attempts the latter, although her poetry also demands of her readers to be informed. By writing "ecological text[s]" that "highlight[/] the tangle of nature and society" (Ergin 32), she revisions poetry as a situated practice that reveals the potential pitfalls of settler place-making in the specific context of continental American migration to the Hawaiian Islands, even though it can never completely avoid all of them.

Dis/Entangled Poetry, Diffractive Ecopoetics, and Anti-Colonial Place-Making

Spahr's poetry draws attention to the agency of nonhuman beings and the agentive potential of matter, not least by highlighting their mobility, while also emphasizing human agency by examining the ways in which ecological agency, including settler ecological agency, is conditional on the individual's position within larger ecosocial structures. In the remainder of this chapter I elaborate on the tensions produced by these different understandings of ecological agency: first, as an ability to act and have an impact on the world that is more widely dispersed among nonhuman agents than commonly assumed and, second, as a power to act and a tendency to impact that some human agents possess to a much greater degree than others for histori-cal, political, economic, social, and cultural reasons. More specifically, I explore how Spahr uses experimental language and form to investigate place-making by settler subjects moving back and forth between Hawai'i and the continental United States, that is to say, settler ecological agency and responsibility in the context of settler mi-gration more broadly conceived.

Among recent work on matters of representation in materialist ecocriticism and materialist feminism, Karen Barad's notion of "agential realism" is particularly in-structive not only for understanding ecological agency as dispersed among human and nonhuman agents, but also for thinking about how the material reality of such dispersed agency can be made seen or known and understood. Drawing from physi-cist Niels Boer amongst others, Barad recasts human-nature interactions as "intra-actions" and hence proposes the idea of "representation" with the idea of "agential re-alism" as an epistemological and ontological framework that depends on a "posthu-manist notion of performativity" (Barad 808). Rather than being a purely human activity and product of human agency alone, posthumanist performativity, as con-ceptualized by Barad, "incorporates important material and discursive, social and scientific, human and nonhuman, and natural and cultural factors" (808) and thus continues to examine the ever-shifting boundaries between human bodies and non-human natures, instead of (cl)aiming to describe phenomena in the world. As a result, all "intra-actions," among which human efforts at describing phenomena in the world are just one example, are open-ended "*[m]aterial-discursive practices*" as well as "*specific iterative enactments*" (Barad 822; emphasis original) involved in the continuous re-constitution of human bodies in relation to nonhuman entities as well as in the constant reconfiguration of the shifting boundaries and constellations of meaning these processes of materialization produce (815). What happens, Spahr's eco-materialist poetry invites readers to ask, if one reads her poetries about different places not merely as an attempt at representing human-nature relations but as an attempt at foregrounding poetry as a material-discursive practice? Or, for my purposes, what happens when one reads Spahr's poetry as a material-discursive practice that conceives of poetic place-making as an iterative enactment of human-non-human relations in the context of mobility? As I will suggest, it shows the im/possibility of settler attempts at anti-colonial place-making, whether through poetry or otherwise.

Rather than conceiving of representation in terms of "reflection," Barad suggests, much like Donna Haraway, the work accomplished by material-discursive practices should be thought of in terms of "diffraction" (Barad 803). As Filippo Bertoni notes, both Barad and Haraway propose diffraction as a figure for a "method of inquiry, a technique for writing and reading, a genre of storytelling, an ethics, and a politics" that "embraces the situated, modest interventions that it makes possible, and uses them towards bringing about different worlds" (178). Such an understanding of writing as inquiry as well as a political practice and ethical project has much in common with the ideas of ecopoetics as an investigative practice discussed earlier. As Paulina Ambrozy notes in drawing in part on Lynn Keller's reflections on the experimental poetic works of Adam Dickinson and Evelyn Reilly, "a diffractive approach [to reading poetry] helps to uncover fluid entanglements as well as intra-actions between poetry and science, reworking their boundaries and actualizing their new possibilities as well as ecosophical concerns" (381–82; see also Keller, *Recomposing Ecopoetics* 67–97.). As it examines the boundary-making processes resulting from the intra-actions of human and nonhuman agents, writing as inquiry—whether in the form of scientific discourse, critical theory, or in Spahr's case investigative ecopoetry—remains interested in the shifting distribution of agencies as well as in the responsibilities of the situated and embodied human subject, precisely because the anthropocene subject's boundaries with and position in the world is never fixed:

> Agency is about the possibilities and accountability entailed in reconfiguring ma-
> terial-discursive apparatuses of bodily production, including the boundary artic-

ulations and exclusions that are marked by those practices in the enactment of
a causal structure. Particular possibilities for acting exist at every moment, and
these changing possibilities entail a responsibility to intervene in the world's becoming, to contest and rework what matters and what is excluded from mattering.
(Barad 827)

In Spahr's experimentalist poetry, place-making in and through poetry is the kind
of situated, open-ended, material-discursive practice Barad describes here. As such,
it asks questions about different subjects' changing positions and "possibilities for
acting" in the world rather than providing simplistic answers for social or environmental problems. Employing para-lyrical experimentations with poetic voice and
perspective, ungrammatical sentence structures, and language defamiliarized by
translation machines, Spahr's poems constantly prod and reconfigure what could be
perceived as naturally occurring material-discursive entanglements of human and
nonhuman agents in the context of mobility as well as the gradations of ecological
agency that these entanglements produce. At the same time, Spahr's poetry thinks
about what Barad describes as humans' "responsibility to intervene in the world's becoming" (Barad 827), or what Haraway discusses as humans' responsibility "to make
a difference in the world, to cast our lot for some ways of life and not others" (Mod-
est_Witness 36). The ways of life Spahr casts her lot for with her diffractive ecopoetics
are more ecologically viable and socio-politically just ones, which is why she continues to address settler colonialism.

Among Spahr's collections to date, Well Then There Now is most invested in examining the ethical implications of mobile subjects' entanglements with the more-
than-human world. In the poem "Sonnets," as in "location or/here," the initial
response of Spahr's migrant speakers to the overwhelming physical presence of
Hawaii's natural world is a mixture of intense attraction and confusion. The recent
arrivals are unsettled by "[t]his growing and this flowing into all around [them]"
(Well Then 28) and the breaking down of barriers between themselves, "others," and
"the land" (28). In an attempt to maintain (a sense of) control over the transformative
encounter with the more-than-human world in Hawai'i, Spahr's speakers decide to
"uproot," "buil[d]," and "bunker" (Well Then 28). Their acts of place-making, which
at this point aim at separation and mastery, are destructive, although they lead to
a sense of belonging. Or rather, they lead to a sense of entitlement and possession
equated with a sense of belonging, as a later passage implies:

And because we could not figure it out bunkering was a way for us
    to claim what wasn't really ours, what could never really be
    ours and it gave us a power we otherwise would not have had
    and we believed that this made the place ours.

(Well Then 29)

Once the speakers' place-making has been marked as an act of land-taking, it is implicitly contrasted with a different form of place-making that leads to a more critical understanding of human-nature relations in Hawai'i. Rather than relying on notions of intimate entanglements with the non-human world as something that occurs naturally as a result of moving from one place to another, this critical understanding depends on the speakers' acknowledgement of their ecosocial positioning as continental migrants and settlers in a colonized/occupied place and a reckoning in poetry with the realization that the material-discursive entanglements resulting from continental settler migration to Hawai'i are in many ways highly unnatural:

> But because we were bunkered, the place was never ours, could
> 	never really be ours, because we were bunkered from what
> 	mattered, growing and flowing into, and because we could not
> 	begin to understand that this place was not ours until we
> 	grew and flowed into something other than what we were we
> 	continued to make things worse for this place of growing
> 	and flowing into even while some of us came to love it and let
> 	it grow in our own hearts, flow in our own blood.

(Well Then 29)

Rather than continuing "to claim what wasn't really [theirs]" and "what could never really be / [theirs]," some of the speakers "let / [this place] grow in [their] own hearts, flow in [their] own blood," even though doing so "make[s] things worse for the place of growing / and flowing." It is significant, I believe, that the two final lines of the passage of "Sonnets" just quoted are similar to the lines from the poem "Gentle Now, Don't Add to Heartache," discussed earlier. This echoing of a poem about Spahr's place of origin raises the question in how far, for Spahr's speakers and other continental migrants, place-making in the "house where [they] are from" (25) is different from place-making in Hawai'i, "the house where [they] live" (25). At the same time, this passage urges readers to ask whether, and in what contexts, the difference between Hawai'i and Appalachian Ohio matters, given that the United States as a whole is a settler state.

"Sonnets" explores questions of identity and belonging, place-making and place-taking in relation to Hawai'i by addressing discourses of migration as well as discourses of blood. The right side of every page consists of passages like the one quoted earlier, in which the speakers comment on the experience of arriving in Hawai'i and being confronted with the more-than-human world in their new place of residence as well as its history of colonization. The first two stanzas point to flying and walking as two ways of encountering Hawai'i from two vastly different perspectives, one from above, one more planar:

We arrived.
We arrived by air, by 747 and DC10 and L1011.
We arrived over the islands and we saw the green of them
       out the window.
We arrived and then walked into the green.

Things were different.
The air was moist and things were different.

Plants grew into and on top of and around each other and things
       were different.
The arrival of those before us made things different.

                                   (*Well Then* 19)

While the right side of each opposing page of the poem evoke a process of arrival, the left side of each page (with the exception of the last pair of pages) consists of lists of blood components, including different types of white blood-cells (20), different enzymes, fatty acids, and proteins (21, 22), and the levels of essential minerals as well as of certain waste products produced by biochemical processes in the body (24, 26). In some ways similar to the record of "the chemical self" that experimental Canadian poet Adam Dickinson proposes in his latest pataphysical poetic project (Ambrozy 376), where he conceptualizes poetry "as an alternative form of science in its own right capable of expanding what matters in semiotic and material environments by interrogating the distinctions between culture and nature, and between human and nonhuman" (A. Dickinson, "Pataphysics" 147), Spahr uses the test results to explore the measurable and immeasurable-but-sensed consequences of being an American settler poet and continental migrant living in Hawai'i. As she puts it in one of the sections of "Sonnets," she is compiling

A catalogue of the individual and a catalogue of us with all.
A catalogue of full of thought.
A house where we with all our complexities lie.
A catalogue of blood.

                                   (*Well Then* 25)

While Adam Dickinson uses "microbiological and chemical burden tests" to write "the potentialities and intensities of 'the transversal' self" (Ambrozy 376), "opening [it] up to new levels of interiority, intimacy, and relationality" (376), Spahr's "catalogue of blood" is at once an indictment of racist discourses and an acknowledgement of decolonial discourses converging on the metaphor of blood. Without excluding the possibility that Spahr may be "shift[ing] her focus from the search for an originary identity based on lineage and blood to the urgent need to speak collectively against capitalist-military build-up and environmental destruction" (Ergin 177), as Meliz Ergin suggests, I want to highlight that "Sonnets" evokes the opposition between "[t]hose who had a home" and "have a right to a home" (*Well Then* 25) and "[t]hose who took" or at least "stayed with the taking" (25), even if she doesn't ultimately affirm this opposition. One of the "complexities" that arises in a place such as Hawai'i, a reading of her poems focused on issues of mobility indicates, is that continental migrants are at the same time human beings who "had a home" and "have a right to a home" and privileged individuals "who took" and "stayed with the taking." Another complexity is that there may be no form of settler place-making, however critical or consciously anti-colonial, that can resolve this tension. Viewed in this way, any form of settler ecopoetic place-making intent on producing a deeper sense of belonging and a more stable sense of emplacement, just like any form of settler place-making affirming a settler migrant's uncritical sense of place and right to emplacement, for example by depicting continental migrants' arrival in Hawai'i as an unavoidable entangling with the archipelago's natural world, can be said to perpetuate a settler-colonial logic of land-taking.

"Sonnets" suggests that place-making can all too quickly become an act of land-taking in the sense of an appropriation by which settlers come to lay claim to or maintain control over a given place. The poem "Things of Each Possible Relation" too asks this question while it imagines alternative forms of (ecopoetic) place-making from a perspective of migration. As Spahr points out in the short commentary following "Things of Each Possible Relation" mentioned earlier, the poem was in part inspired by the two complementary views that define positioning practices in the Pacific, one from the sea and one from the land (*Well Then* 71; see also Ergin 184).[11] As Rob Wilson explains, the directional distinction that new arrivals in Hawai'i have to

---

11   Spahr refers to *Islands and Beaches: Discourses on a Silent Land: Marquesas 1774–1880* (1988) by Australian historian Greg Dening in her commentary (*Well then* 70), when she mentions this double view. In *Islands and Beaches*, Dening reflects on the beach as a zone of cultural contact and conflict, describing islands as places defined by mobility: "Every living thing on an island has been a traveler. Every species of tree, plant and animal on an island has crossed the beach. In crossing the beach every voyager has brought something old and made something new" (Dening 31–32). As can be seen here, Dening's description conflates different kinds of mobility in ways that is highly problematic because it does not distinguish voyaging from settling and settling from colonizing, a fact that becomes even plainer in the following passage: "Human beings are voyagers to islands, as any plant or any other animal. They might land naked on an empty beach, but in their minds, their languages, their relationships they bring a world with them. The island might be to them something given. They inherit its soils, its climate, its products. But they are also the creators of the world they come to live in. They give names to all its parts and in naming they order and divide. The colours, the winds, the mountains, the valleys, the fruits, the fish, the peoples, all things are theirs because they name them and give them separate being" (32). By differentiating between different kinds of mobility and place-making, my analysis tries to avoid such conflations, as does Spahr's poetry, I would argue.

learn as quickly as possible is the one between "*mauka* ('inland toward the mountain') and *makai* ('toward the sea')" (126), a distinction Spahr refers to in her collection as well (*Well Then* 36, 38). In the version of this double view included in "Sonnets," the Native Hawaiian positioning practice is revised from and for a perspective of migration as "a view from the sea (*the view of those who arrived from elsewhere*) and the view from the land (those who were *already there*)" (*Well Then* 71; emphasis added). Before Spahr's poem arrives at a "view from land" (65) toward the end of the poem, it opens with "the view from the sea" (55):

> the view from the sea
> the constant motion or claiming, collecting, changing, and taking
> the calmness of bays and the greenness of land caused by the
>   freshness of things growing into
> the arrival to someplace else
> the arrival to someplace differently
>
> (*Well Then* 55)

The "arrival to someplace else" is described here as a prolonged and active process that engages all the senses of the unidentified speaker/s ("calmness of bays and the greenness of land caused by the freshness of things"). In conjunction with the shifting perspective, the emphasis in the poem on bodily sensations recalls what Jonathan Skinner in his discussion of "somatics" as a concern of ecopoetics calls "proprioception," that is, "those stimuli perceived within an organism connected with the position and movement of the body, amongst other indicators" (*Jacket 2*, "Somatics" n. p.). Even though "Things of Each Possible Relation" presents proprioception, the embodied speaker(s) remain somewhat elusive in large parts of the poem, which omits pronouns, even where conventional sentence structures would demand their use. Rather than featuring a lyrical "I" or a lyrical "we" like so many of Spahr's other poems about Hawai'i and continental North America, these passages avoid explicit speakers, without eliminating evocations of embodied experiences or allusions to situated, yet mobile perspectives.

Importantly, "Things of each possible relation" evokes many different kinds of human and nonhuman mobility, ranging from peoples' historical and contemporary migrations to Hawai'i to the small-scale biochemical processes that produce the islands' lush vegetation. Viewing Hawai'i while approaching the islands by ship, as the poem's beginning indicates, the speaker/s emphasize/s "the freshness of the things increasing / the greenness of the ground / the calmness of the compartments" (*Well Then* 55). Through repetition and anaphora as well as through the use of gerunds that allows for a collapsing of subject and object positions, the poem depicts the islands' more-than-human world as a strange and wonderful system "of things growing into [each other]," that is, of emergent interconnections and intra-actions:

> the constant movement to claim, to gather, to change, and to
>   consider sea
> constant motion
> the green of the soil which increases the freshness of things
> then calmness and the sail
> the requirement on meeting to modify and to regard
> the inbound of this someplace differently
> the constant movement

(Well Then 55)

The migrant subjects' encounter with Hawaii's more-than-human world is associated here with the emergence of interdependencies that never settle into permanently fixed formations (see Ergin 185). On the one hand, the speaker/s recognize/s the "requirement on meeting to modify," that is, the inevitability of her/their material-discursive impact on the local ecosystem; on the other hand, she/they must "regard / the inbound of this someplace differently," that is, they must consider how the "constant movement" they become part of is changing them in return.

While "Things of Each Possible Relation" insists on a certain degree of reciprocity in migrants' engagements with the islands' more-than-human world, then, it does not pretend that the field is leveled between the different actors when it comes to questions of ecological agency. One of the ways in which the text points to the differences rather than the similarities between the various inhabitants of Hawai'i is by alluding to the harm some migratory species have caused to the archipelago's ecosystem. While "the snipe" and "the plover" (*Well There* 57), two vagrant bird species mentioned in the poem, are seasonal migrants that appear naturally on the archipelago, at least as long as their migrations are not disturbed by changing climatic conditions, the "tree of heaven" and the "cow" (57) mentioned in the same passage were introduced on the islands in order to increase their agricultural profitability and with the least regard to the far-reaching effects on the local ecosystem. Using numerous similes and comparisons that withhold the stable second element of comparison and thus a resolution, "Things of Each Possible Relation" suggests that both human and nonhuman migrations have caused "a series of great and extremely fast changes" (57) in Hawaii's more-than-human world. At the same time, the text warns against "the problems" of drawing this kind of "analogy" (57; see also Ergin 186). As Tana Jean Welch notes in her reading of the poem, "analogy contributes to the violence and justification of colonialism by perpetuating a singular perspective that reduces everything to type" (13). Overly simplistic equivalences such as the one that equates a migratory bird to a human migrant, Spahr's poem warns, risk obscuring how ecological agency, political power, and social responsibility are distributed unevenly within the "diverse formed assemblies" (*Well Then* 57) that different human and nonhuman agents enter into as a result of their respective mobility.

Referring to the intertwined physical and cognitive processes at work in poetic human-place engagements, many of Spahr's poems can be read as meta-poetic commentaries on ecopoetic place-making as a self-conscious and self-reflexive process. Rather than proposing without any reservation that poetry is always an appropriate means of place-making for all types of migrants, Spahr emphasizes the epistemological limits, representational challenges, and ethical quandaries involved in enlisting poetic language for the project of place-making:

while what we are knows the unalike and
while one becomes the various compositions formed by nature
the problems of the analogy
are the sight of the trace
and nature as the way to see the fly-catcher
and the series of large and extremely fast modifications
in the sight of the land
and the introduction of the plants and the animals, others, exotic
when it is we, it is the unalike knowing and
if one were to transform nature's given forms
then the problems of the analogy of it appear

(Well Then 64)

When poetry tries to account for the complexity of natural processes and humans' entanglement by way of analogy, this dense passage suggests, it faces the double-challenge of trying to represent inherently mutable phenomena from a perspective that is equally mutable because "what we are" cannot be kept separate from "the various compositions formed by nature." And yet, even if takes such a perspective on the world and the subject's place in it as one's analytical point of departure, it is still possible to "know" which phenomena are "unalike" others at a given moment in time. At the same time, it would be difficult, if not impossible, to argue for the general likeness of two phenomena, even though this is precisely the idea that poetic techniques of comparison and "analogy" rely on. Indeed, "problems of analogy" not only reveal themselves in "the sight of the trace," which is to say in those constantly changing aspects of complex phenomena that testify to their processual and mutable character, they also lie in conceptualizations of "nature as the way to see the fly-catcher," that is, in an equation of natural phenomena with humans' perception of these phenomena. Last but not least, the "problems of analogy" Spahr's poem addresses also result from "the series of large and extremely fast modifications in the sight of the land," or put differently, from the kinds of anthropogenic environmental changes that threaten to make old analogies meaningless. While analogy may thus be a useful tool to explain unfamiliar phenomena with the help of familiar ones, Spahr's poem questions the logic of analogy because it is wary of the fixed ontologies it presupposes.

Like several other poems in *Well Then There Now*, "Things of Each Possible Relation" foregrounds "the interconnectivity of the various elements of the ecosystem as a means for resisting colonial taxonomies and exposing irregularities of identification as well as the eco-ontological ambiguities at the heart of all existence" (Ergin 8–9). "Things" uses a variety of poetic strategies of diffraction (i.e. of inquiry and investigation rather than representation or reflection) to portray Hawai'i as a place in which the boundaries between some phenomena that may conventionally be presumed to be clearly distinct in western/ settler-colonial thought begin to blur (see also Ergin 191), while other differentiations *stay in place* because they are *kept in place* through material-discursive processes of boundary-making. One such differentiation, and a highly contentious one, is that between settlers and natives, a differentiation that has stabilized in some contexts while it is contested in others, such as when settlers lay claim to land and resources in Hawai'i by claiming non-Indigenous nativeness. The strategies in Spahr's poem uses to explore this kind of boundary-making are repetitions with slight modifications, agrammatical sentence structures that verge on the nonsensical, and analogies that either fail to make clear which phenomena they mean to compare or offer equivalences that remain highly obscure even as they suggest the interrelatedness of thing. Indeed, the "things sewn together" (*Well Then* 59) on the "pages" (62) of Spahr's book range from individual "cells" (62) to entire organisms, from inanimate to animate nature (the "wings of the blow[hole]" 62), from human to more-than-human bodies ("the tongue of humans and the tongue of hummingbird" 62). This poetic stitching questions the boundaries between the paired phenomena, between human subjects and the natural world, and between nature and culture ("analogy/ drives pages together on the branch"; *Well Then* 62). Engagement with place here becomes an open-ended process of diffraction that crucially depends on "things of each possible relation hashing against one another" (67).

Ecopoetic place-making as an activity that should allow subjects to establish meaningful relationship to the natural world in cases where long-term intimate engagement with a place is not an option is re-conceptualized here as an ongoing practice that depends crucially on the place-maker's socioecological positioning and the ecological agency that results from it. Importantly, the "view from land" Spahr's speaker/s eventually arrive/s at via a "sight from the earth" (*Well Then* 64), mentioned right before the shift from one perspective to the other, is a sight that highlights Spahr's environmentally-oriented approach to place-making. Contrary to what the poem's transition from a "view from the sea (*the view of those who arrived from elsewhere)*" to "a view from land" (65; emphasis original) might suggest, however, the more ecologically informed perspective "from land" that Spahr's speaker arrive at in the poem is not one based on notions of stability, mastery, or ownership, nor is it the view of "(*those who were already there)*" (65; emphasis original), i.e. a perspective that claims any kind of native-ness. Instead, it is a perspective that acknowledges different kinds of mobility as both harmful for and constitutive of the islands' more-than-human world and humans' entanglements with it. Conceived of as a situated yet mobile material-discursive practice, the ecopoetic place-making that "Things of Each Possible Relation" is and investigates, challenges humanist notions of bounded subjectivity, while still emphasizing bodily perspectives and the unique position, agency, impact, and responsibility of the continental migrant who is also a settler-colonial subject.

While poems such as "Sonnets" and "Things of Each Possible Relation" reflect on the discontents of settler ecopoetic place-making in Hawai'i, "Some of We and the Land That Was Never Ours" transposes these reflections onto continental North America. Written in response to Robert Frost's "The Gift Outright" (1923; see Ergin 194), a poem about human-place relations in (North) America written from a settler-perspective that famously begins with the claim that "The land was ours before we were the land's" and ends by suggesting that America was "unstoried, artless, un-enhanced" before the arrival of European settlers (Frost 224), "Some of We" weaves together impressions from Spahr's travels from California to France with allusions to her French grandfather's migration to Canada over half a century prior, reflecting on the longer history of European migration to and settlement in North America. "Some of We" constructs interlinked thematic sections based on the repetition and variation of sentences translated, as Spahr notes, back and forth between the colonial languages of English and French with the help of an online translation machine (*Well Then* 15). Arranging the resulting de-familiarized, often ungrammatical and unidiomatic phrases into constantly shifting poetic constellations, the poem explores what it means to live off and—through the everyday material, trans-corporeal exchanges of eating— "to be of" land that "was never/ some of ours" and of "ground [that] was never sure with us. Is never some/ of ours. Be never certain with us. Never will be rightly some of ours" (*Well Then* 12). Unable to deny the appeal of a hard-won intimacy with place that comes from practices such as farming ("the green/ of the ground is the possession of the ground of us" 12), but equally unable to ignore the historical reality of colonial land-taking and the dramatic present-day consequences of treating land only or primarily as property and resource, the speakers of "Some of We" interrogates traditional notions of settling:

> What it means to settle. What means it arrangement. To we are all
> in this world together. We all the small ones are together in this
> world. To eat the grapes and not to plant the seed. To eat the grapes
> and not to plant seed. To hold on too tight. To be too strongly held in
> the function. To change. To change. To make the change. To make
> the change. To change the land. To change the ground.
>
> (*Well Then* 14)

In this excerpt, a way of settling reminiscent of the type of agrarianism also evoked in the U.S. passages of Walcott's poetry is criticized here for its disavowal of Indigenous claims to the land. Settler-capitalist ways of living off the land are put under scrutiny for valuing the land only based on its "function" or usability and for fostering a disconnection between processes of production and consumption. Both historical forms of settler agriculture and the land-use practices of contemporary agribusiness, the poem suggests, can be blamed for having disturbed inter-species relations in a global ecosystem in which "all the small ones"—a phrase that alternately refers to birds and to all human and nonhuman beings—"are together" (*Well Then* 14).

Bringing into relief different forms of being in the world and different modes of exploiting the land, "Some of We" raises urgent questions about ecological agency and the ethics of (ecopoetic) place-making in the context of migration and settler-colonialism. Self-consciously engaging with North America's heritage of territorial expansion, Spahr's poem points to the need for anti-colonial approaches to place-making that consider the complex politics of mobility and settlement in North America:

> [...] How to
> move. How to move from settle on top to inside. How
> to move stabilization on the top inside. To embrace, to not settle. To
> embrace, not to arrange. To speak. To speak. To spoke. With the
> spoke. To poke away at what it is that is wrong in this world we are
> all in together. To push far what is with it is incorrect in this world
> which all the small ones are us in the unit.
>
> (*Well Then* 14)

While the poem does not give any concrete instructions on how to "move from settle on top to inside" and how to "embrace" instead of arranging, it tries out possible ways of thinking, speaking about, and acting differently while living with and off the land. Moreover, it demands a critical interrogation, not least through poetry, of how historical forms of social and environmental injustice continue to shape human-nature relations in the twenty-first century.

When mobile settler subjects hope to find a way of relating to the places they inhabit temporarily without settling/land-taking, Spahr's poetry indicates, they must "speak" about "what is wrong with the world" and "push far what is with it is incorrect in this world which all the small ones are us in the unit" (*Well Then* 14). Ultimately, however, Spahr's diffractive ecopoetics of mobility poses the question how collective settler ecological agency relates to the responsibility of individual privileged settler migrants:

> We tried not to notice but as we arrived we became a part of arriving
>   and making different.
> We grew into it but with complicities and assumptions
>   and languages

and kiawe and koa haole and mongooses.
With these things we kicked out certain other things whether we
    meant to or not.
Asking what this means matters.
And the answer also matters.

(Well Then 19)

Questions about settler ecological agency in the context of mobility and about the ethics and politics of settler place-making matter and so do the answers to these questions. While Spahr's poetry asks these questions, it only provides tentative answers, perhaps because, ultimately, she may not be the person to recommend a certain course of action. Still, insofar as settler ecological agency figures in her poems alternatively as the power and will to take and destroy or as the power and will to engage in/ join in a making and repairing, any attempt at imagining an anti-colonial approach to settler place-making, in poetry or otherwise, Spahr's poems indicate, requires that mobile settler subjects examine their own material-discursive position and their ecosocial impact on the places they inhabit. At the same time, Spahr's poetry implies, reckoning with the concrete ecosocial impact of settler ecological agency also means for settler subjects to make careful choices about when to allow themselves to become entangled with the more-than-human world of a place and when to try to disentangle themselves, when to stay and when to leave, when to engage and when to withdraw.

3. Lyricizing the Planetary Epic:
Genre Mixing and Discrepancies of Scale
in Derek Walcott's *Omeros*

One of the most acclaimed English language poets of the twentieth and early twenty-first century, Derek Walcott received the Nobel Prize in Literature in 1992 and the British T. S. Eliot Prize for Poetry for his last collection *White Egrets* in 2010. After a long and prolific career that reached well beyond the Caribbean, his region of origin, he died in 2017 at the age of 87. Born on the island of St. Lucia in 1930, Walcott lived and worked in Jamaica, Trinidad, the United States, and Europe for extended periods, publishing nine plays, over twenty books of poetry as well as numerous essays and other writings concerned with poetics and politics. Since Walcott's works first began to attract scholarly attention during the early 1970s, his plays and poems have been the object of countless articles and book-length critical studies. In contrast to most of the other poets analyzed in this study, Walcott already garnered scholarly interest during the rise of postcolonial criticism in the late 1970s and early 1980s and during the emergence of ecocriticism in the early 1990s. Even more, due to the ubiquity of representations of the natural world in his work and the increasingly transnational themes in his texts, his work became a touchstone for scholars working in the fields of postcolonial and transnational ecocriticism as well as for scholars interested in poetries of migration and travel. Walcott's poetry thus presents a paradigmatic case to demonstrate some of the larger issues that are at stake when examining poetries of migration as ecopoetries engaged in poetic place-making. Analyzing his 1990 book-length poem *Omeros*, I focus in this chapter on Walcott's reluctant and conflicted ecopoetics of mobility which, as I will show, relies crucially on genre-mixing. Combining the genre of epic with the travel poem, the pastoral, the (pastoral) elegy, and the confessional lyric, *Omeros* can be read as an environmentally resonant lyricization of epic that is ripe with tensions between the universal and the particular, the communal and the individual, the global and the local, the postcolonial and the transnational. Indeed, as I argue, Walcott's book-length poem *Omeros* can be described as a lyricized planetary epic that emphasizes the discrepancies of scale and the poetic as well as ethical problems of representation that come to the fore when an Afro-Caribbean migrant poet engages in poetic place-making in the United States.

Derek Walcott always wrote about the natural world (see Mootry, Ramchand, and Izebaye). While some scholars suggest that the early poems of his "Caribbean phase" (Ismond 1) treat nature primarily as a metaphor for abstract social, cultural, and political phenomena (see Lane), Graham Huggan, in prefiguring later ecocritical and geocritical approaches to Walcott's work, noted already in 1987 that Walcott frequently infuses his Caribbean landscapes with "the dimensions of height and depth which [human geographer Yi Fu] Tuan considers to be disappearing in the Western world's predominant aestheticization of nature" (24). The motif of travel, too, is important in Walcott's poetry (Gray, *Mastery's End* 178–211). During his "American Phase" (Handley, *New World Poetics* 14)—a period starting in the 1980s that was marked by the poet's frequent work-related travels back and forth between Trinidad and the United States—Walcott not only increasingly began to write about places beyond the Caribbean, he also began to engage more directly with questions of mobility in his poetry. Scholars discussing his poetry collections *The Fortunate Traveller* (1981) or *Midsummer* (1984), for instance, have commented on Walcott's preoccupation with the figure of the "poet as permanent traveler" (Breslin 219) suggestive of "our [postmodern] sense of homelessness" (Lane 325) as well as of the postcolonial subject's sense of "imaginative dislocation" (Döring 195). Comments like these raise the question, of particular import for my present discussion, under what circumstances evocations of mobility in poetry matter not only figuratively but also as literally. What is more, if one assumes, as I do here, that mobility invoked in poetry and particularly in poetries of migration matters as geographical movement, the next question would be whether such movement must always lead to an "uneasy sense of dislocation" (Breslin 216) or to a problematic "tendency [...] toward the mythology of placelessness" (Huggan 26), as scholars have claimed in the case of Walcott's poetics. Or, put differently, it raises the question whether the sense of dislocation that mobility can produce must necessarily be debilitating, also in environmental terms. I propose that it does not. Instead, I argue, it can produce an ecologically suggestive sense of place that is deepened by experiences of mobility, rather than being made shallower by them.

Because I am invested in evocations of various types of geographical movement in conjunction with evocations of American geographies, I focus here on Walcott's epic *Omeros* (1990). *Omeros* marks the culmination of Walcott's "American Phase" and the beginning of what could be called his "Transnational Phase," a period in his oeuvre when Walcott increasingly began to evoke concrete, multilayered European geographies in addition to Caribbean and North American ones. I turn to *Omeros*, because it features multilayered geographies in the United States and elsewhere as well as many different kinds of mobilities. I also turn to *Omeros*, because it is a poetic work of remarkable complexity that anticipates many of the themes and literary strategies at work in later eco/poetries of migration, even as it demonstrates how some debates, for example surrounding Indigenous representation and settler-colonialism have progressed considerably in the past thirty years. Much like *The Arkansas Testament* (1989), the collection that directly preceded *Omeros*, Walcott's epic poem is centrally concerned with places in North America and its narrator's movements between them. At the same time, *Omeros* is concerned with human-nature relationships as shaped by past and present movements of people, whether in the form of European immigration and colonial settlement, as a result of the transatlantic and intra-American slave trade, in connection to people's present-day migrations between the Caribbean and the United States, or in connection to modern leisure tourism. Moreover, prefiguring important themes in later collections such as *The Bounty* (1997) and *White Egrets* (2010), *Omeros* marks the beginning of a period in Walcott's career in which his poetry gained more explicitly environmental undertones (see DeLoughrey, Gosson, and Handley 13; Handley "A Postcolonial Sense of Place"). What emerges as all of these concerns converge in Walcott's epic poem, I suggest, is an ecopoetics of mobility that goes beyond postcolonial and transnational sensibilities, gesturing instead toward the planetary.

Derek Walcott and Omeros: A Transnational Poet and his Planetary Epic

The main narrative of *Omeros* follows the transnational movements of the first-person narrator and poet Derek, who has left his native Caribbean to live and work in the United States. During his time in the United States, Derek travels extensively, visiting many different places and reflecting on the violent histories of displacement that mark them. When Walcott's narrator returns home to visit the island of St. Lucia, his perspective is no longer only that of an Afro-Caribbean postcolonial writer. It is also that of a Black transnational poet. According to Jahan Ramazani, the lives and works of "transnational poets" (6)—a term he uses in reference to Derek Walcott, among other poets—are characterized by "various global and ex-colonial criss-crossings" (6), that is, by many different kinds of figurative and physical movements. For Ramazani, as well as other scholars who have used the designation, the term "transnational poet" thus evokes the lived experience of transnational migrants, that is to say, people for whom "international moves are only part of a biography of movement between places, with some moves being more permanent than others, and many being part of a regular circulation between different places" (Boyle, "Migration"). The idea of a "biography of movement between places" is apt both for Walcott and for his poetic alter-ego Derek. It is thus not only because Walcott's long poem evokes many different physical geographies (the U.S. Northeast and the Pacific West Coast, the U.S. South, and the Western Plains) and many different forms of human mobility (the transatlantic slave trade, European immigration to North America, the westward movement, Native American removal, contemporary transnational migration, and various kinds of travel), that *Omeros* is pertinent for this study. Walcott's epic poem is also of interest because one of the key elements of its main narrative is the ongoing—if at times conflicted and reluctant—efforts at (eco)poetic place-making undertaken by Walcott's narrator, a constantly mobile transnational poet.

In contrast to many other scholars who have discussed the environmental undertones of Walcott's poetry, I do not focus in my reading on his Caribbean poetry but on his poetry about the United States. While there are similarities between Walcott's representations of Caribbean and U.S.-American environments, I do not see the same kind of "poetics of conservation" (Handley, "Walcott's Poetics" 212) at work in Walcott's poetry about the United States that scholars such as George B. Handley find in Walcott's poetry about the Caribbean. Still, comparisons between Walcott's poetry about the Caribbean and his poetry about the United States are useful, such as when Roy Kamada suggests in his reading of Walcott's Caribbean poetry that Walcott replaces Romantic notions of nature with a historically conscious "postcolonial romanticism" that casts the more-than-human world as "traumatic as well as sublime" (91). As I show in this chapter, the U.S. passages of *Omeros* too are filled with landscapes haunted by the violent histories of the American (post)colony, including violent histories of displacement and removal. In similar yet also different ways than in the Caribbean passages of *Omeros*, the landscapes that the poet-narrator encounters while living in and traveling through the United States are ripe with tensions between experiences of the sublime and historical trauma. These tensions point to discrepancies between human and nonhuman scales of time and place, which take shape not only in the changing relations of the local and the global to be found in Walcott's work (see Clark 132–134), but also in his engagement with different forms of mobility, ranging from individual short-term travel to large-scale movements and displacements of entire peoples.[1] Conscious of these tensions and discrepancies, Walcott's epic poem examines the limitations of an ecopoetics of mobility that takes form when the individual mobile subject encounters—and tries to account for—the intertwined human and environmental histories that have shaped human-nature relations in the 'New World' more broadly and in the United States more specifically.

---

1   Timothy Clark discusses Walcott in a subsection of a longer chapter on "Questions of Scale: The local, the national, and the global" in his *Cambridge Introduction to Literature and the Environment* (2011). The relevant subsection is entitled "Literary 'reinhabitation'?" and asks, in drawing from Peter Berg and Dasmann, whether literature can be used to as a means of "learning to live-in-place in an area that has been disrupted and injured through past exploitation" (Berg and Dasmann qtd. in Clark 133). Clark's notion of Walcott as a poet interested in literature as a means of reinhabitation is instructive for my reading, especially since Clark notes that Walcott's "own Caribbean is particularly suited as a testing ground of the force and coherence of bioregional ideas" (Clark 133), a challenge that the poet responds to with an "affirmation of the Adamic possibilities of the archipelago" (134).

In his influential study *The Future of Environmental Criticism* (2005), Lawrence Buell discusses Walcott's intensive engagement with Caribbean island landscapes as an example of literary bioregionalism (81). Later, when he emphasizes the need for "a place-responsive ecoliterature of global scope" (Buell, *The Future* 92), Buell again points to Walcott. Indeed, Buell views *Omeros* as an especially "resonant example" (*The Future* 92) for such an ecoliterature of global scope, because Walcott's long poem exhibits, according to Buell, "a global sense of place" (92) and is "centered" (95), yet also "migratory, global, and world-historical in its evocations of place" (95). Buell contends that Walcott's poetry "bears out the possibility of imagining placeness in multi-scalar terms: local, national, regional, transhemispheric; topographically, historically, culturally" (*The Future* 96). Taking Buell's observations as a starting point for my analysis, I begin this chapter by providing a brief discussion of the Caribbean passages of *Omeros*, before I turn to the text's U.S.-American passages to explore the "multi-scalar placeness" as well as the "migratory, global and world-historical evocations of place" of Walcott's epic in a transnational American context that is conscious of postcolonial as well as settler-colonial histories. Focusing primarily on these frequently neglected U.S. American passages of *Omeros*, I illustrate how the narrator's migrations between the Caribbean and the U.S. and his confrontations with histories of displacement during his travels in the United States change his perspective on the more-than-human world in both places. As I propose, the U.S.-American passages in Walcott's poem are not negligible, as many critics have suggested.[2] Rather, they are crucial for the critical transnational and emphatically glocal place-sense that comes to the fore at the end of Walcott's epic. What I emphasize in my reading, too, is how a deliberate mixing of poetic genres allows Walcott to re-examine different Anglo-American poetic traditions of representing nature and mobility together with the clashing scales of the local and the global as well as of human and nonhuman histories. By integrating various genres that are associated with nature and mobility into his epic poem, his text points to some of

---

2   Most critics so far have treated the U.S. passages of *Omeros* alternatively as irrelevant, odd, weak, or outright offensive (see Leithauser, Benfey "Coming Home," or Mason). Even Robert Hamner, one of the few Walcott scholars who has discussed the U.S. passages of *Omeros* in some more detail, refers to the Dakota sections as one of the "least defensible aspects of the poem" (*Epic of the Dispossessed* 95). Arguing that "each of [the text's] protagonists is *a castaway* in one sense or another" (3; emphasis added), Hamner reads the long poem as an "epic of the dispossessed" (3) that focuses on several "*transplanted individuals* whose separate quests all center on the fundamental need to strike *roots* in a place where they belong" (3; emphasis added). Hamner's use of metaphors such as "castaway" and "transplanted individuals" in search of "roots" reveals that many of the instances of dispossession he discusses are in fact the result of physical displacement. At the same time, his use of nature imagery evokes issues of place-attachment and belonging and, at least inadvertently, suggests that the natural world too is a crucial element in *Omeros*.

the profound ways in which the experience of migration changes mobile subjects' perspective on the more-than-human world in all its multi-scalar dimensions as well as their perspective on place-making as a means to establish or maintain meaningful relationships to the places they encounter, leave behind, and return to.

Engagements with literature and evocations of different literary tradition play a central role in Walcott's place-oriented poetry (Buell, *Future* 64–65; DeLoughrey, Gosson, and Handley 13); so do revisions of poetic modes, genres, and forms, as Sarah Philips Casteel points out in her reading of Walcott's *Tiepolo's Hound* (2000). Like Casteel, although I do not use that specific wording, I analyze representations of "rural and wilderness settings" in Walcott's poetry that I find to be "uniquely informed by experiences of cultural and geographical displacement" (Casteel 1), while paying special attention to the "modes of landscape representation" (1) it employs. Also, like Casteel, I hope to make explicit in my reading how Walcott articulates alternative "forms of emplacement" (Casteel 3). More so than Casteel, though, I focus on the means by which Walcott's poetry about the United States produces complex environmental imaginaries suited for our present age of mobility and ecological crisis. In particular, my reading of Walcott asks what happens when a poet—who was born on a colonized island that was "physically transformed in the service of plantation economies" (Casteel 32) and grew up with the idealized images of English landscapes projected in metropolitan literature (Casteel 32)—interrogates U.S.-American landscapes and U.S.-American histories from a migratory perspective. I argue that the result is twofold: by engaging with U.S.-American landscapes in and through poetry, Walcott's poet-narrator recalibrates both his historical and environmental sensibilities and, by consequence, his strategies of and attitude toward practices of poetic place-making in different locations. After engaging with U.S.-American places and U.S. histories of displacement from a perspective of mobility, the traveling poet returns to his native island in the Caribbean with a heightened awareness of how a privileged transnational migrant like himself can become implicated in, and indeed complicit with, neocolonial forms of exploitation and the environmental destruction these exploitative systems produce. It is at least in part through his move to and subsequent travels in the United States, I want to suggest, that the poet's sense of place shifts from a postcolonial to a critical transnational sense of place that foregrounds the many different experiences of mobility that have shaped and continue to shape human-nature relations in North America and carries subtle but important environmental undertones.

Where scholarly discussions of *Omeros* have centered on matters of genre, critics have often debated whether Walcott's book-length poem should be called an epic and, if so, what kind of epic it represents. Four different positions have dominated this debate:[3]

1) *"[t]raditional classicists"* (Jay 545; emphasis added) have celebrated *Omeros* as a modern epic in the European tradition;

2) *critical classicists* have emphasized the ways in which *Omeros* engages with those facets of the ancient epic associated with its oral and folkloristic origins;

3) *traditional postcolonialists* have accepted Walcott's own demonstrative rejection of the genre of epic (see Davis 326–328) and thus avoid the label of epic due to the genre's Eurocentric and imperialist associations;

4) and finally, *critical postcolonialists* have stressed Walcott's creative engagement with the European epic tradition and consider *Omeros* an anti-imperialist revision of the epic as a classic metropolitan genre.

Among these different critical traditions, the work of scholars who explore how Walcott challenges the generic conventions of epic is most pertinent for my purposes. Taking inspiration from Line Henriksen, who describes *Omeros* as a "heteroglossic" text that "incorporates other voices and genres, and parodies of these" (238), and Tobias Döring, who analyzes the ways in which Walcott integrates elements of travel writing, nature poetry, the adventure tale, autobiography, and ekphrastic writing into his epic (169–202), amongst others, I highlight the specifically *ecopoetic* dimension of Walcott's place-making through genre-crossing. Specifically, I argue that it is through a self-conscious interlacing of epic with different genres of lyric, that is to say, through a self-conscious "lyricization of epic" (see Dimock, "Low Epic" 619), that an environmental imaginary of mobility begins to emerge in Walcott's epic *Omeros*.

While the wide range of places and the broad scope of histories of migration and displacement featured in *Omeros* may be said to call for the genre of epic, the text's simultaneous investment in the narrator's personal engagements with those places and histories demand the genre of lyric. In my analysis, I show that Walcott's ecopoetic place-making depends on his interlacing of epic with three lyrical genres or modes: the travel poem, the pastoral, the (pastoral) elegy, and the confessional lyric. By integrating different lyrical modes into his epic, a genre that has often served nationalist, settler-colonialist, and imperialist purpose (see Quint, Graham, or Adair), Walcott's *Omeros* challenges a Western poetic tradition in which representations of nature and mobility have more often than not erased histories of violence, displacement, and exploitation. In doing so, it gestures toward a critical transnational sense

---

3   This four-part categorization follows Paul Jay's summary of early scholarship on *Omeros* in "Fated to Unoriginality: The Politics of Mimicry in Derek Walcott's *Omeros*" (2006), which in turn draws on Joseph Farrell's "Walcott's *Omeros*: The Classical Epic in a Postmodern World" (1997). However, the titles for the categories two to four are mine.

of place with significant environmental resonances that accounts for the challenges ecopoetic place-making confronts when the subject engaging in it—like Walcott's poet-narrator Derek—is not only a Black postcolonial subject, but also a relatively privileged transnational migrant of color. Emphasizing Walcott's engagement with these histories, but also the limits of his engagement, I read *Omeros* as a lyricized *planetary epic* that draws attention to the discrepant scales of human and nonhuman histories as well as to the possibilities and limits of an ecopoetry of migration.

Discussed by such thinkers as Nelson Maldorado-Torres, Gayatri Chakravorty Spivak, and Wai Chee Dimock, whose writings counter "local-, ethno-, anthro-, or other centrisms" in favor of "intercultural networks that negotiate relationships between people and environments" (Thornber 25), notions of the planetary have been used in the past two decades as an ethically charged alternative to notions of the global. In the work of sociologist and cultural critic Paul Gilroy and ecocritic Ursula K. Heise, for example, the concept of *the planetary* for instance draws attention to the importance of rethinking globalization in relation to histories of colonization and imperialism as well as in relation to large-scale environmental change. In *Postcolonial Melancholia* (2005), Gilroy suggests that "[t]he planetary [...] specifies a smaller scale than the global, which transmits all the triumphalism and complacency of ever-expanding imperial universals" (xv). For Gilroy, "the planetary" thus allows for an anti-imperialist critique of discourses around globalization; for Heise, it represents an alternative to those environmental theorizations of the global that rely on an "erasure of political and cultural differences" (*Sense of Place* 24). When Heise proposes an eco-cosmopolitanism in *Sense of Place, Sense of Planet* (2008) that rethinks local, regional, as well as national ecological discourses on the basis of "a thorough cultural and scientific understanding of the global" (59), she envisions a "planetary 'imagined community'" (61) that extends into the non-human world. Drawing from these and similar grounded conceptualizations of "the planetary" that highlight the anti-colonial/anti-imperialist as well as the environmental dimensions of the term, I argue that the U.S. passages of *Omeros* dramatize the process by which the mobile narrator's postcolonial sense of place transforms into a critical transnational and environmental, or in short, a planetary sense of place.

Epic, Travel Poem, and the Critical Planetary Sensibilities of *Omeros*

While *Omeros* can be productively read as an epic, it can also be read as an expansive example of the prolific Anglo-American tradition of the travel poem.[4] Indeed, the

---

4   Although not a genre as well-established as the pastoral or the elegy, the travel poem goes back at least to the tenth century with such Old English poems as "The Wanderer" or "The Seafarer," two Anglo-Saxon laments recorded in the so-called *Exeter Book* (c. 975). Famous Amer-

travel poem is a useful lens with which to analyze Walcott's epic, because *Omeros* presents Derek as a postcolonial poet of mobility who constantly wavers between his positions as transnational migrant and tourist.[5] As Jahan Ramazani notes, "the travel poem [...involves] a macro-level transition, a mimetically plotted border crossing from home to foreign land" (*A Transnational Poetics* 53). Ramazani's emphasis on "border crossing from home to foreign land" is consistent with the most common definitions of travel writing, although in the U.S. in particular the genre also routinely includes texts by writers who are traveling within their home country.[6] As Jeffrey Gray explains, travel poetry has generally been "associated with agency and power, whether as exploration, conquest, adventure, or, more recently, tourism" (*Mastery's End* 3). The agency and power accorded to Derek stems from his relative economic privilege compared to his fellow St. Lucians, economic privilege that is directly linked to his mobility. This privileged position comes with the potential to effect change through representation as well as with a certain risk of abusing the (writerly) authority that comes with this power. At the same time, his conflicting experiences of mobility give him insight into the complex glocal processes that are increasingly affecting the environment on St. Lucia. By having the narrator engage in poetic place-making that self-consciously evokes the divergent perspectives on the more-than-human world of the local, the traveler, the migrant, and the tourist, the ending of *Omeros* consolidates a planetary sense of place that remains conscious of place-specific historical and socio-political circumstances while also pointing to the imminent dangers of, as well as the interconnections between, local environmental degradation and global climate change.

The passages of *Omeros* in which Derek travels back to St. Lucia hinge on a tension between the narrator's self-styling as the prodigal son returning to his native island and his self-presentation as a privileged visitor from the United States. Like

---

ican examples of travel poetry include works by Hart Crane (*White Buildings* 1926, *The Bridge* 1930), Elisabeth Bishop (*North and South/A Cold Spring* 1955, *Questions of Travel* 1965, *Geography III* 1976), Joan Kyger (*Desecho Notebook* 1971, *Mexico Blonde* 1981, *Patzcuaro* 1999), Campbell McGrath (*Road Atlas* 1999), Rafael Campo (*The Enemy* 2007), Kazim Ali (*The Far Mosque* 2005, *Bright Felon* 2009), and Naomi Shihab Nye (*Yellow Glove* 1986, *Red Suitcase* 1994, *Fuel* 1998, *Transfer* 2011).

5   As Jahan Ramazani notes, tourism studies challenge the distinction between the traveler and the tourist, a distinction associated with dichotomies such as "work vs. pleasure, active vs. passive, solitary vs. mass" ("Poetry and Tourism" 460). I uphold this distinction in my argument, at least initially, to highlight Derek's conflicted position rather than to suggest that the line of demarcation between tourist and traveler are clear-cut.

6   Judith Hamera and Alfred Bendixen imply as much when they include essays in the *Cambridge Companion to American Travel Writing* that discuss Margaret Fuller's non-fiction account of her journey to the Midwest (*Summer on the Lakes* 1843), William Cullen Bryant's collection of popular tourist attractions in the United States (*Picturesque America* 1872), or John Steinbeck's travelogue *Travels with Charley: in Search of America* (1962).

Walcott, who admitted that he sometimes felt like "a Tourist [...] from America" (Hirsch, "The Art of Poetry" 78), when visiting the Caribbean after taking up residency in the United States, his alter ego Derek experiences a split perspective. This can be seen in chapter 49, canto III, of *Omeros* where Derek simultaneously distances himself from and aligns himself with the tourists at his hotel:

> [...] too much happiness was shadowed with guilt
> like any Eden, and [the tourists] sighed at the sign:
> Hewannorra (Iounalao), the gold sea
>
> flat as a credit card, extending its line
> to a beach that now looked just like everywhere else,
> Greece or Hawaii. Now the goddamn souvenir
>
> felt absurd, excessive. The painted gourds, the shells.
> Their own faces as brown as gourds. Mine felt as strange
> as those at the counter feeling their bodies change.

(Walcott, Omeros 229)

Struggling with what sociologist John Urry has called the "tourist gaze" (*The Tourist Gaze* 1990), which resembles what E. Ann Kaplan has discussed as the "imperial gaze" (xii), Walcott's narrator here contemplates to what extent his perceptions of his native island have become aligned with those of the tourists around him. He acknowledges that St. Lucia is threatened by a commodification of space (Melas 151), which opens the island's natural environment up to foreign consumption just like the souvenirs mentioned in the canto, but he cannot shake the feeling that he too is implicated in what Walcott elsewhere calls the "benign blight that is tourism" ("The Antilles" 81).

While Derek's fear of unduly romanticizing the St. Lucians' poverty and the island's beauty is certainly justified, his perspective on the island's people and environment is made more complex on account of the postcolonial sensibilities his Afro-Caribbean heritage afford him, his migratory experience, and his extended travels throughout the United States, where he visits places associated with U.S. histories of settler-colonialism and slavery. In the canto just quoted, the sign of Hewannorra International Airport, the main airport of St. Lucia, points to those pre-colonial Caribbean Indigenous cultures that colonization has all but erased as well as to those new forms of mobility that are reshaping human-nature relations on the island in the present. In a different yet related manner, chapter 13, canto II, of *Omeros* evokes the Caribbean's history of slavery, while drawing attention to the harm modern tourism inflicts on the island's people and its natural environment. In this canto, Derek remembers a stroll he took with his father down to the wharves of Castries, St. Lucia's capital. Described as having a "hull bright as paper" (Walcott, *Omeros* 72) and as "preening with privilege" (72), the cruise liner represents to Derek his dependence on white patronage and the distancing his social advancement has produced between him and his fellow St. Lucians. At the same time, the ship comes to represent the exploitation that the Caribbean suffered as a result of colonization and slavery, histories made manifest by the lines of "women" Derek and his father saw climbing the ship like "ants" (73) to load it with "baskets of coal" (73). Reminiscent of Virgil and Dante's journey into hell, the narrator and his father's walk down to the tourist-flooded harbor, is a figurative descent into the hellish parts of the Caribbean island.

Mass tourism as represented by the cruise ship is a threat for St. Lucia, according to the narrator, because it perpetuates the power imbalance between the continental tourists and the inhabitants of the island. It is also a threat because it has highly detrimental effects on the island's natural environment. While the tourist industry does create some revenue for the island, the costs St. Lucia pays for this revenue is far greater, the narrator implies. Observing the tourists who toss small coins into the water to encourage a few young boys to dive after them, Derek notes that the children use "old tires" to rest between dives and swim in a harbor into which the ship's "humming engines spew[...] expensive garbage" (Walcott, *Omeros* 73). Comparing the children to "fishes" and little "porpoises" (73), the narrator points to the fact that the more-than-human world of St. Lucia is in as much danger due to the excesses of the cruise industry as the island's human inhabitants, if not more immediately so. Mass tourism in this canto is thus not only presented as a modern-day version of the institutionalized dehumanizing systems of exploitation that have harmed the Caribbean in the past, it also threatens the St. Lucia's future along with one of the island's greatest assets: its natural environment.

Environmental degradation in the Caribbean is addressed several times in the long poem. In chapter 60, canto I, the narrator alludes both to problems of pollution and to the local effects of global climate change that have begun to manifest on the island. After speaking to Seven Seas, a local wise man, storyteller, former sailor, and world-traveler like, yet also unlike the privileged narrator, the fisherman Achille notices disturbing changes on the island. Interlacing multiple layers of storytelling, Derek relates Achille's musings, which in turn recall the comments of Seven Seas:

He had never seen such strange weather; the surprise
of a tempestuous January that churned
the foreshore brown with remarkable, bursting seas

convinced him that 'somewhere people interfering
with the course of nature'; the feathery mare's tails
were more threateningly frequent, and its sunsets

the roaring ovens of the hurricane seasons,
while the frigate hung close inland and the nets
starved on their bamboo poles. The rain lost its reason

and behaved with no sense at all. What had angered
the rain and made the sea foam? [...]

(Walcott, *Omeros* 299–300)

Having closely observed the local natural world for years as part of his daily work, Achille displays intimate knowledge of the island's ecosystem, which is also why he begins to notice the increase in "feathery mare's tails" (a cloud formation that precedes a depression zone) and other unusual weather patterns that point to the local effects of global warming. As Seven Seas suggested to him, the weather is changing because "somewhere people [are] interfering/ with the course of nature." What begins to manifest in this canto, which is narrated by Derek even if he does not take part in the conversation represented in it, is a planetary perspective on the world that stresses the interconnections between local and the global environments as well as the catastrophic effects of humans' interference with glocal ecologies.

A fisherman by trade, Achille is not only concerned about the "strange weather" and the "bursting seas;" he is also alarmed by the dwindling numbers of sea life around the island. The gradual disappearance of certain species may well be linked to the changing climate in the region and to the pollution caused by the burgeoning tourist industry. However, Achille—whose musings are presented with commentary by the narrator—is more enraged about "the trawlers / who were dredging the banks the way others had mined / the archipelago for silver" (Walcott, *Omeros* 300). The text here identifies industrialized overfishing as a major threat to Achille's livelihood, with the narrator providing the larger political context of this practice and the longer history as well as the environmental impact of foreign resource extraction in the Caribbean. "[T]he steely blue albacore/ no longer leapt to [Achille's] line," the narrator notes, and "the shrimp were finished, their bodies were curled/ like exhausted Caribs in the deep silver mines" (300), he adds, once again linking the present-day economic exploitation of the island to the region's settler-colonial history. Whether it takes the form of the modern cruise industry, industrialized fishing, or mining operations, the text implies, this exploitation has its roots in the racist ideologies of colonialism. The environmental degradation this exploitation causes is not only a matter of concern because it will ultimately affect all human and nonhuman life in the region; it is also a matter of environmental injustice, because it affects the region's most vulnerable inhabitants first.

According to the narrator, Achille interprets the dramatic changes in the local weather and the disappearance of certain species from the ocean around the island as "signs of a hidden devastation under the cones of volcanic gorges" (Walcott,

Omeros 300), that is, as indicators of a worse catastrophe yet to come. Seven Seas too foresees future catastrophe, one that threatens humans and nonhumans alike:

[...] Seven Seas would talk
bewilderingly that man was an endangered

species now, a spectre, just like the Aruac
or the egret, or parrots screaming in terror
when men approached, and that once men were satisfied

with destroying men they would move on to Nature.   (300)

Referring back to an earlier canto in the epic poem, in which the narrator links violent displacement of Indigenous peoples to the destruction of the natural world in the settler United States ("First men, then the forests," 207), this canto repeats Seven Seas' view that "once men were satisfied/ with destroying men they would move on to Nature" (300). Seven Seas' speech confirms Derek's logic, according to which settler-colonial ideologies are responsible for the decimation of Indigenous people as well as for the environmental degradation of the New World, while also echoing those environmental discourses that challenge the idea that humans are separate from the natural world. The passage just quoted thus emphasizes that human beings are one among many species threatened by environmental change, even though they are the only species responsible for the approaching catastrophe. The wordplay on "species" and "spectre" in the above excerpt along with the listing of birds ("the egret, or parrots") alongside "the Aruac" (St. Lucia's disappeared Indigenous peoples), sounds a dire warning of impending mass extinction. At the same time, the poem refrains from blaming all of humanity for global environmental change indiscriminately. Instead, it suggests that the past and present empires of the Global North are primarily responsible for the contemporary environmental crisis, while marginalized peoples, such as the poor Black Caribbean fishermen of St. Lucia are its primary victims. By commenting on Achille's and Seven Sea's speculations on the causes and future consequences of environmental change in the Caribbean, the narrator foregrounds marginalized voices as well as his own ambiguous position within the global political and economic system that the United States and the other great powers of the Global North have established by building on the legacies of colonialism. What is more, the narrator-poet raises questions about his own complicity in existing systems of oppression and about his responsibility to challenge them.

The ending of *Omeros* asks if the responsibility of the privileged toward the more vulnerable can be fulfilled, at least in part, through practices of poetic place-making that draw attention to matters of social and environmental injustice, even if (or perhaps especially when) the poetry in question employs modes of representation that have historically been used these injustices. The epic's last chapter suggests as much by including references to the different lyrical genres employed by Walcott in the course of the text. Canto I of chapter 64 begins by evoking Homer's *Odyssey* and Eliot's *Waste Land* ("I sang of quiet Achille [...] whose end, when it comes, will be a death by water;" Walcott, *Omeros* 320). It thus alludes to two very different kinds of epic, the main genre in whose tradition *Omeros* places itself, albeit reluctantly. In the same canto, which begins by praising the beauty and resilience of Caribbean peoples and their environment, the narrator notes: "now the idyll dies" (321). This brief remark points to the poet's critical engagement throughout his epic with the postcolonial pastoral and the pastoral elegy as a means to highlight the detrimental cultural, social, and environmental effects of centuries of colonization. It also em-phasizes the narrator's struggle to represent in poetry the landscapes and peoples that are affected by different kinds of oppression and displacement. In the chap-ter's second canto, the narrator's own story comes back into focus. Here, the poem evokes the highly ironic confessional passages of Walcott epic that I discuss later in this chapter as well as the narrator's self-critical engagement with the poem of travel:

> [...] For three years
> Phantom hearer, I kept wandering to a voice
> Hoarse as winter's echo in the throat of a vase!
>
> Like Philoctete's wound, this language carries its cure,
> its radiant affliction; [...]   (323)

Directly addressing a ghostly reader ("Phantom hearer"), the "wandering" narrator expresses hope as well as doubt that his "language" will provide a "cure" for what ails the world. The last line of *Omeros* is equally ambiguous: "When [Achille] left the ocean, the sea was still going on" (325). Some scholars have read the end of *Omeros* as implying that the healing of the many personal and communal wounds referenced in the text will one day be possible, also with the help of Walcott's poetic "cure," because "the sea [is] still going on." From an environmental perspective, however, the word "still" here introduces a crucial caveat: healing will only be possible *if* or *as long as* the ocean goes on and someone is there to bear witness. Given the kind of global environmental change that Walcott addresses in some of the Caribbean passages of his epic, including disastrous storms, such permanence is no longer self-evident. Rather, it is something humans must work toward with direct environmental and political action and by engaging with complex planetary imaginaries like the one evoked in *Omeros*. A crucial part of the critical planetary imaginary that emerges in Walcott's text is its exploration of human-nature relations in light of different forms of mobility, an exploration that takes place in the epic's U.S.-American passages.

Epic, Pastoral, and Countering Epic Amnesia in *Omeros*

In the U.S. passages of *Omeros*, Walcott's narrator is frequently traveling between different places in the United States. While on the move, he reflects on the histories of the places he encounters and describes the natural environments he sees around him, engaging in place-making with a certain troubled reluctance. When faced with "nature's opaque and deep history" (Handley, *New World Poetics* 6) in the United States rather than in St. Lucia, Walcott's mobile narrator struggles to conjure those human histories that the natural world tends to obscure as time passes and memories fade. The first canto of chapter 35, a canto set in the U.S. South, dramatizes this pained effort of recovery:

> "Somewhere over there," said my guide, "the Trail of Tears
> started." I leant towards the crystalline creek. Pines
> shaded it. Then I made myself hear the water's
>
> language around the rocks in its clear-running lines
> and its small shelving falls with their eddies, "Choctaws,"
> "Creeks," "Choctaws," [...]
>
> (Walcott, *Omeros* 177)

The guide's uncertainty about how to narrate the Trail of Tears as a history of place/s as much as a one of dis-placement in this passage points not only to the erasure from national consciousness of state-sanctioned acts of violence against Indigenous peoples during U.S. expansion, but also to the ways in which the regenerative powers of nature cover up the traces of human history. Where Derek expected to see a landscape marked by the injustice it has been witness to, an injustice which consisted not least in the violent disruption of land-based practices, an idyllic scene presents itself to the visitor. Despite what a cursory reading of the second stanza quoted above might suggest, nature is not telling the story of the Creek (Mvskoke Creek) and Choctaw (Chahta'), who were forced from their ancestral homelands in south-eastern Mississippi and parts of Alabama to the Indian territory of what is now Oklahoma in the aftermath of the Indian Removal Act of 1830. Instead, it is the narrator who wills himself to perceive in nature traces of the murdered and the displaced. The "clear-running lines" are the narrator's—and by extension—the lines of poetry on the page, not the river's; and what will see "shelving" are not the river's waters, but Walcott's poems, poems that imagine the stories that nature does not, and cannot, tell. Where the regenerative powers of nature (along with human forces) erase human histories of violence, Walcott implies here, poetry can reconnect these histories with the places in which they occurred. In order to achieve this deepening of place-sense through a re-joining of human and nonhuman histories of place, poets need to engage in poetic place-making in locally specific ways that counter national(ist) forms of "epic amnesia" (Breslin 241).

In the canto quoted above, the narrator struggles for a mode of representation that will do justice to the complex settler-colonial history of the places he visits during his travels through the U.S. South. The poetic genre Walcott turns to in these passages is a version of what Rob Nixon has called the "postcolonial pastoral" (*London Calling* 161), that is, a kind of pastoral that "brings into tension idealizing and historicizing visions of landscape" (Casteel 13). When Gregson Davis points to "a few key *loci*" in *Omeros* in which pastoral motifs are "elaborated and complicated" ("Pastoral Sites" 43; emphasis original), all the places he lists are on St. Lucia; none are in the United States. And yet, Davis's characterizations of Walcott's Caribbean pastorals also apply to his American ones: "sophisticated and multilayered" (fn.1, 43), they foreground "metapoetic issues" and employ "the bucolic scaffolding" for a "subtle exploration of important issues—ethical, epistemological, and aesthetic" (43). In the canto about the starting point of the Trail of Tears, the "metapoetic issue" addressed is how to write about the seemingly innocuous natural beauty of U.S.-American sites of injustice and trauma from the perspective of a Black Caribbean migrant and traveler. More bitterly and brutally than the Caribbean sections, the complex pastoralism of the U.S. passages of *Omeros*, I would like to suggest, subverts idealized representations of the natural world to expose hardly visible ideologies of oppression and exploitation that have shaped human-nature relationships in North America and specifically in the U.S. South. In the U.S. passages of *Omeros*, "the real" that troubles "the ideal" of the pastoral idyll (Davis 47) are histories and legacies of Native American displacement and dispossession as well as the histories and legacies of the transatlantic slave trade.

Upon evoking the Trail of Tears, the first canto of chapter 35 addresses the history of chattel slavery in the United States. Using richly metaphorical language and playing with the semantic field associated with the classical pastoral, the passage recalls the historical transmutations of settler-colonial and planter-colonial rhetoric employed in relation to the U.S. South, drawing attention to two different, yet ideologically and materially imbricated racialized regimes of oppression and their lasting effects in the narrator's present:

> [...] I thought of the Greek revival

> carried past the names of towns with columned porches,
> and how Greek it was, the necessary evil
> of slavery, in the catalogue of Georgia's

marble past, the Jeffersonian ideal in
plantations with its Hectors and Achilleses,
its foam in the dogwood's spray, past towns named Helen,

Athens, Sparta, Troy. The slave shacks, the rolling peace
of the wave-rolling meadows, oak, pine, and pecan,
and a creek like this one. From the window I saw

the bundles of women moving in ragged bands
like those on the wharf, headed for Oklahoma;
then I saw Seven Seas, a rattle in his hands.

(Walcott, Omeros 177)

Recalling Greek antiquity as a model for a culture of enslavement that—unlike the removal of Indigenous peoples—has become manifest in the landscapes of the U.S. South, this canto suggests that the success of the United States as a "new empire" (169) depended on the interlinked domination of people of color and the nonhuman world. What is more, it suggests that pastoral (and georgic) ideals have historically helped, first, to justify and, later, to cover up the atrocities perpetrated against Native American and enslaved Africans and their descendants for the sake of turning the so-called New World into a "Garden." The "Jeffersonian ideal in / plantations" referenced in the passage above makes this political dimension of the American pastoral promise plainly explicit, a promise that originated, as Terry Gifford notes in drawing from Leo Marx, "in the georgics and advertisements of Beverley (1705), Crèvecoeur (1782), and Jefferson (1785)" ("Pastoral" 23). Indeed, Thomas Jefferson's glorification of the yeoman farmer not only arguably found its most perverse permutation in the slavery-based plantation culture associated primarily with the U.S. South; it also promoted the westward movement of European and American settlers and thus led to the forced relocation, violent dispossession, and genocide of Indigenous peoples on the territory of what are now the United States.

Using one of the "hybridizing literary strategies" typical of both postcolonial and transnational poetry (Ramazani, *A Transnational Poetics* 101), Walcott's U.S.-based pastorals rely on a complex "super-position" (101) of different places and time frames. As Derek evokes the different rustic scenes he saw while driving "past towns named Helen, / Athens, Sparta, Troy" (Walcott, *Omeros* 177), his references to the natural world continue to allude to the atrocities of Native American removal and chattel slavery. The mention of the "dogwood's spray," that is to say, of the opulent flowering of one of the most common ornamental trees in the U.S. South, is particularly resonant in this context. Known as "Cherokee Chief," "Cherokee Brave," and "Cherokee Princess," the names of individual cultivars of the dogwood invoke racist stereotypes masked as romantic ideas concerning Indigenous life.

What these Anglo-European names recall but also actively obscure, then, is the fact that the Cherokee are a living people whose ancestors were violently driven out of Georgia and other states in the U.S. South. What is more, the image of the "dogwood's spray" (Walcott, *Omeros* 177) is suggestive because the flowers of certain white dogwood variants look as if sprinkled with blood. Commonly associated with the crucifixion of Christ, the tree as well as the echoes of African American spirituals in the passage quoted above ("the rolling peace / of the wave-rolling meadows") hint at how religion, and Christianity in particular, has been used in the United States and elsewhere to justify what Walcott wryly refers to as "the necessary evil of slavery." At the same time, the metaphorical cross-fading of meadows and ocean in the passage, a figurative link struck between landscapes and oceanscapes that is crucial to Walcott's innovation of the pastoral (Davis 44), evokes the horrors of the Middle Passage. With all these resonances in Walcott's descriptions of a seemingly idyllic Southern landscape, this canto presents a version of postcolonial pastoral that has been carefully adapted to its U.S.-American location.

While the first six stanzas of chapter 35, canto I, juxtapose pastoral evocations of idyllic natural beauty with subtle evocations of histories of violence, the second half of Walcott's American postcolonial pastoral gains almost (southern) gothic undertones that allow for the true horrors of the region's slave-holding past to come to the surface. Against the ominous backdrop of an approaching thunderstorm, the narrator imagines "shadows" (Walcott, *Omeros* 178) of enslaved individuals being chased by the "hounds" (178) of unseen masters. The hunt leads through the same "pines/ and [...] pecan groves" (178) that were part of the pastoral scene of "meadows, oak, pine, and pecan" (177) a few lines earlier. Re-inserting histories of slavery back into a seemingly past-less place, the landscapes depicted in the poem transform into a "'resonant' natural environment" (Davis 44) in which "echoes of brutality,/ and terror" (Walcott, *Omeros* 178) reverberate in the narrator-poet's present. In such an environment made resonant through poetic language, trees like the "oaks [growing] along red country roads" (178) can no longer be viewed as mere ornamentation. Instead, they evoke the crime of lynching, while "[h]ooded clouds" (178) recall the threat of the Ku-Klux-Klan. Any faith that the migrant narrator may be expressing in the redemptive power of nature's beauty in the Caribbean passages of *Omeros* is pushed past its breaking-point when Derek is confronted with U.S.-American landscapes and histories. Indeed, in the pastoral U.S. passages, Walcott reaches beyond the "postcolonial romanticism" of the Caribbean passages of *Omeros*, which, as Roy Kamada asserts, continue to insist on "beauty in the midst of [...] devastation" (98). What emerges instead in the passages of *Omeros* that are set in the U.S. South is a decidedly unromantic American pastoral that emphasizes the horrors of American history, a horror that the beauty of nature (and the kind of poetry foregrounding it) could never adequately address, let alone begin to redress.

Repeatedly indicating that the narrator of *Omeros* is not only a Caribbean post-colonial subject but also a Black migrant "from the hem of a frayed empire" (Walcott 170) traveling in the U.S., the pastoral passages of *Omeros* insist that American geographies and histories must be considered in larger transnational contexts. In this insistence, Walcott's American pastorals resemble, but are also different from, what Heather I. Sullivan has described as the "the dark pastoral" (85).[7] According to Sullivan, the dark pastoral is a (post-)pastoral genre "undergirded by postmodernism's rejection of the possibility of unmediated language and things" (87), informed by a "rejection of the artificial delineation of local and global" (85) and marked by "the beauty and the horror of [...] interconnectivity" (85). Replete with world-as-text figures and metapoetic commentary, the U.S. passages of *Omeros* reflect on the possibilities and limits of representing histories of displacements and local-global exchange in poetry. And yet, Walcott's transnational pastorals evoke a different kind of "horror of [...] interconnectivity" than the texts Sullivan discusses, which describe European ecosystems made toxic by war.[8] When Walcott's narrator mentions "a silk-

---

7   Sullivan here draws on Timothy Morton who proposes "dark ecology" as an alternative ecological aesthetics that seeks to replace Romantic notions of nature with the postmodern, ecological concept of the "mesh" and aims to put "hesitation, uncertainty, irony, and thoughtfulness back into ecological thinking" (*Ecology* 16). Unlike Morton, Sullivan argues that twenty-first-century critics should not prematurely reject Romantic ideas and textual strategies as outdated. On the contrary, she insists that "we need full recognition of our own pastoral impulses juxtaposed with current and scientifically informed skepticism" (87). Sullivan's idea of the dark pastoral bears some resemblance to Terry Gifford's notion of the post-pastoral, "a pastoral informed by ecological principles of uneven interconnectedness, as well as an educated understanding of the symbiotic link between environmental and social justice, at both the local level and beyond" (*Pastoral* 156).

8   It is one of my main arguments that analyses of contemporary ecopoetries need to pay attention to the specific contexts and politics of different forms of mobility. Sullivan's essay demonstrates why this kind of attention is important. In her article, Sullivan defines the dark pastoral as a genre that engages with the problem of "dirty traffic," which is to say with the fact that "[p]ollution has no place but rather is everyplace" (83) and the idea that the world we live in is shaped by "all types of material, bodily, ecological, and cultural flows" (84). When Sullivan summarizes her analysis by observing that the texts she analyzes "express concerns regarding the altered flows of resources, people, and bodies that are deterritorialized in the Anthropocene" (96), her listing of mobile "resources" alongside mobile "people" requires unpacking. Of course, Sullivan does not describe refugees as just another kind of "dirty traffic"; indeed, elsewhere in the essay she notes that refugees are "driven to flee amid war's dirty traffic" (89). Econativists do, though, when they compare im/migration to pollution, depicting it as a threat to environmental, racial, and national purity. For a detailed discussion of how a racist and settler-supremacist rhetoric of pollution enters U.S.-American environmental discourses about immigration and Indigenous mobility, see, for example, Sarah Jaquette Ray's chapter on "The Poetics of Trash: The Environmental Impact of Immigration in Organ Pipe Monument" from her 2013 study *The Ecological Other*.

cotton tree / from which Afolabes hung like bats" (*Omeros* 178), he on the one hand points to tropical West Africa, where his narrator meets his ancestor Afolabe during a dream voyage, and on the other to the Caribbean, where "silk-cotton" or Ceiba trees were venerated as spirit trees and used for canoe making by Indigenous people such as the Taíno. What is more, he points to the historical connection that existed between the U.S. South and the Caribbean due to the intracontinental slave trade and the trade in agricultural products such as cotton, a connection that is still visible because the landscapes of both places were radically transformed by the plantation system established there. Driving through the U.S. South, the narrator sees "islands reflected on windscreens" (178) and hence begins to imagine enslaved field-workers "moving through the foam of pods, one arm for an oar, / one for the gunny sack" (178). Here and elsewhere in *Omeros*, Walcott critically examines the ways in which the narrator's own "pastoral impulses" (Sullivan 87) are counteracted both by his postcolonial sensibilities and by the transnational sensibilities stemming from his perspective as a world traveler and migrant in the U.S. Read from a joint ecocritical and critical mobility studies perspective, the U.S. passages of *Omeros* set in the U.S. South demonstrate the violence inherent in an American pastoral tradition imbricated in the long history of obscuring settler-colonialism and romanticizing chattel-slavery. They do so by transforming an American pastoral rhetoric into a critical transnational pastoral informed by postcolonial sensibilities and made complex through evocations of different kinds of transnational and transregional mobilities, migrations, and displacements.

Epic, Elegy, and Ecopoetic Witnessing in *Omeros*

The canto discussed in the previous section features the narrator Derek as a transnational migrant who reluctantly engages in poetic place-making as he traverses the countryside of the U.S. South. Within the larger structure of Walcott's epic, this canto is framed by three cantos (Ch. 34, cantos III; Ch. 35, cantos II and III) in which the narrator alternately tells the story of and ventriloquizes another migrant: Catherine Weldon, a nineteenth-century white woman, artist, and social activist who emigrated to Boston from Switzerland with her mother in 1852, but eventually moved west to act as the secretary to famous Lakota (Teton Sioux) leader Tetanka Yotanka, or Sitting Bull. Walcott also included Weldon in his play *Ghost Dance*, which was first performed in 1989, a year before the publication of *Omeros*. In the Weldon passages of *Omeros*, Walcott's narrator addresses the events leading up to, and the aftermath of, the massacre at Wounded Knee as well as the death of Catherine Weldon's son. Moving back and forth between epic, pastoral, and elegiac modes, Walcott experiments with poetic voice and the poet's position as (non-)witness to personal and collective histories of displacement and loss. Natural environments are central in these passages and play a key role in the narrator's self-conscious struggle for adequate expressions of grief and appropriate modes of commemoration, raising questions about the ethics as well as the aesthetics of (eco)poetic witness. What Walcott dramatizes in the Weldon passages of *Omeros*, is a migrant poet's attempt to come to terms with the burden of representation placed on him: he reluctantly begins to develop more profound relationships to the places he encounters while on the move and in the process feels compelled to account for histories of displacement and loss far removed from, but also relatable to, his own experience. Evocations of nature in the Weldon passages link individuals across time and space as well as across boundaries of gender and race without eliding their specific personal backgrounds and stories. In exploring transnational, transhistorical, and transethnic connections, the elegiac cantos not only draw attention to the fragility of place-based imagined communities, but also to the fragility of the natural world itself.

What little is known about Catherine Weldon's life must be gleaned from a few newspaper-clippings and Weldon's personal letters to Sitting Bull and his antagonist, the government agent James McLaughlin, materials which Walcott is known to have read (Bensen 119).[9] Catherine Weldon was a member of the New England National Indian Defense Association who traveled to Standing Rock Reservation in 1889 after her husband's death to support the Hunkpapa Lakota, a Sioux tribal band of the Great Plains. Weldon went west in order to work for and speak on behalf of Sitting Bull, perhaps the most famous Native American leader during the time of the second Ghost Dance Movement. The Ghost Dance Movement was a cross-tribal religious and political movement founded by the Paiute spiritual leader Tävibo in 1869/70 and revived again in 1889/1890 by another Paiute holy man, Wovoka, who prophesied a return of the spirits of the dead, an end of white settler-colonial rule, and a subsequent age of freedom and peace for Indigenous peoples in North America (Dunbar-Ortiz 153–54). Although Weldon left the Hunkpapa before the desperate hunger winter of 1890 and the Wounded Knee Massacre on December 29 of that same year, a military attack on an unarmed band of Lakota refugees that left 300 of them dead, many of them women and children (Dunbar-Ortiz 155), Weldon witnessed some of the final, but ultimately futile attempts at resistance by the Sioux (Oceti Sakowin) and other Plains peoples against the U.S. government's policies of relocation and dispossession. Inspired by these events and the sketchy historical records of Weldon's time with Sitting Bull, several of the U.S. passages of *Omeros* provide an ac-

---

9   Already during Catherine Weldon's own lifetime, the details of her life among the Lakota were cause for speculation, as rumors circulated in the press and among government agents that she had been married to Sitting Bull and become pregnant with his child, stories Weldon herself continued to refute as slander in her correspondences. For more information on the Weldon documents, see, among others, Dorothy Johnson's *Some Went West* (129–36) and Eileen Pollack's *Woman Walking Ahead: In Search of Catherine Weldon and Sitting Bull* (2002).

count of Catherine Weldon's life on the Midwestern plains infused with reflections on her son's death as well as the mass-murder of the Lakota.

Early reviewers of *Omeros* were either puzzled by the Weldon passages or they completely ignored them (Gidmark and Hunt 13; Bensen 119). Robert Hamner, in his 1991 review of Walcott's book, for example, questioned the poet's motives for including the plight of Native Americans, when he could as well have focused on Caribbean postcolonial histories ("Epic of the Dispossessed" 114). Hamner later revised his position, conceding that the Weldon passages had "a thematic purpose" (*Epic of the Dispossessed* 94), suggesting that Weldon functions as a "representative of white imperialism" (97) in the text, yet one who rejects "the trappings of hegemony in favor of [living with] people who are traditionally victimized as racially inferior" and who, as a result of losing her son during her life on the plains, experienced her very own kind of "dispossession" (97). George B. Handley posits that Walcott must have been "tempted by the notion that indigenous experience throughout the Americas is cut from the same cloth and that all diasporas are perhaps created equal" (*New World Poetics* 394). What Handley does not mention is the fact that "indigenous experience" is always self-consciously mediated and poetically refracted in *Omeros*, like in the Weldon passages, where the migrant narrator channels the voice and perspectives of a nineteenth-century white woman who is an agent, albeit a reluctant one, of European settler-colonialism. This mediation and refraction in Walcott's text suggest that not all experiences of and perspectives on histories of dispossession and displacement are comparable, let alone that all these experiences are "equal."

While some of Walcott's representations of Indigenous people must be considered overly simplistic and stereotypical, the Weldon passages complicate these representations by creating a highly elaborate construct of narrative embedding, carried by a complex constellation of narrators and speakers from vastly different backgrounds. It is through the resulting refraction of perspectives and voices in the Weldon passages, rather than by adopting a seemingly objective perspective or endowing his narrator with an unchallenged, authoritative voice, that Walcott attempts to bear witness in poetry to the history of Native American removal. By interlacing the voices of a Black, late-twentieth-century transnational migrant from the Caribbean and a nineteenth-century white, European, female immigrant to the U.S, who was known for her ultimately failed attempts to speak *in favor of*, and indeed to speak *for*, the Lakota in her function as secretary to Sitting Bull, Walcott indicates that neither Weldon, nor his narrator, nor his lyricized epic as multi-voiced text can claim to speak with definite authority to all the histories of displacement and dispossession that inform the North American past and present. The U.S. passages of *Omeros* foreground the impossibility and even dangers of the outsider's desire to act as witness, even as it continues to attempt precisely such witnessing in and through poetry.

The few scholarly texts that have considered the Weldon passages address the problems and functions of representing history in poetry. Jill B. Gidmark and Anthony Hunt, for example, suggest that Walcott invokes the figure of Catherine Weldon in order to construct "a cameo of her to represent yet another direction in his quest for the truth about fictionalized history" (12). Similarly, Robert Bensen reads Walcott's recourse to the Weldon persona as "a conversation about history registered as personal loss" (119). Jahan Ramazani's brief analysis of *Omeros* in *The Hybrid Muse* (2001) too emphasizes that Walcott "crosses and recrosses lines of race, nation, and gender" along with "the line between narrative and lyric poetry" (68) by intermingling historical events and personal histories in this part of the text. Building on these insights, I suggest that Walcott uses the pastoral elegy to explore the ethics of bearing witness in poetry to losses that go beyond personal experience. The pastoral elegy is well suited to interrogate the challenges and benefits of approaching the histories and experiences of others from a perspective that remains personal without presuming that all histories and experiences are identical. Relying on representations of nature and human-nature relations, these passages tentatively imagine a common ground for people to connect across spatial, temporal, and ethnic boundaries through a shared experience of grief. Rather than producing lasting imagined communities or "imagined individualities" (Müller 250), Walcott's pastoral elegies evoke what one could describe as temporary, place-based, and localized yet open *imagined communalities* that depend on acts of (eco)poetic place-making.[10]

Chapter 34, canto III of *Omeros* places Catherine Weldon in an ostensibly idyllic rural setting. From the onset, it uses pastoral and elegiac elements to create a sense of foreboding:

The elegies of summer sighed in the marram,
to bending Virgilian reeds. Languid meadows
raised their natural fly-screens around the Parkin farm.

Larks arrowed from the goldenrod into soft doors
of enclosing thunderheads, and the rattled maize
threshed like breaking surf to Catherine Weldon's ears

(Walcott, *Omeros* 176)

The reader encounters Weldon on the farm of Mr. and Mrs. V. Solen Parkin, where, according to some historical accounts, her son Christie stepped on a rusted nail that would eventually cause his death from tetanus (Vestal 103). While the poem makes

---

10   Reading several contemporary Black poets alongside Walcott, Timo Müller contends that "transnational poetry is about imagined individualities" (250). This is particularly so, Müller contends, because "transnational poets tend to be more interested in redefining their individuality through the various cultures, languages, and identities their diasporic experience holds in store for them" (250) than in the "old or new promises of communal homogeneity" (250).

obvious its thematic and formal debt to the tradition of the complex "Virgilian" pastoral, the reference to "elegies" in the first line of the poem introduces the theme of death. From the very beginning, then, chapter 34, canto III of *Omeros* presents itself as a pastoral elegy, a genre that, as Graham Huggan and Helen Tiffin note, has "particular resonances in the context of postcolonial settler societies which are marked by the death and/or dispossession of their original inhabitants" (89).

The description of the Plains in Walcott's poem blends images of sprawling midwestern farmland with those of the seaside, evoking the Caribbean passages of *Omeros* and the narrator's life on the East Coast near Boston, on the one hand, and Catherine Weldon's personal history of migration from Switzerland to the East Coast and further to the Midwest, on the other. It is due to the shared experiences of im/migration that both Catherine Weldon and the narrator, who imagines Weldon's thoughts in the poem, would have reason to compare the storm over the Plains rattling the "maize" and "[l]anguid meadows" of the Parkin farm to the sound of an ocean's "breaking surf" (Walcott, *Omeros* 176). The places the migrant characters have inhabited and left behind—Switzerland/St. Lucia and then New England—inform the descriptions of the natural world presented to the reader in this scene. The canto revises the pastoral elegy, a genre which traditionally emphasizes locality and immobility, by considering various migratory movements within and across national borders. It infuses the narrator's poetic account of Weldon's life with recollections of personal experiences of displacement, while also conjuring the dispossession, displacement, and strategic annihilation of Indigenous peoples of the Plains at the hand of the U.S. government.

As the poem progresses, the pastoral idyll initially evoked by Derek through the eyes of Catherine Weldon begins to include more and more allusions to U.S. colonialism and various ominous signs of future violence and death. At the same time, the poem begins to reveal Weldon's personal losses, highlighting how this section of Walcott's epic fuses the postcolonial pastoral and the pastoral elegy:

> Ripe grain alchemized the pheasant, the pelt of mice
> nibbling the stalks was unctuous as the beaver's,
> But the sky was scribbled with the prophetic cries
>
> of multiplying hawks. The grass by the rivers
> shone silvery green whenever its nub of felt
> was chafed between the thumb and finger of the wind;
>
> rainbow trout leapt arching into canoes and filled
> their bark bodies while a clear wake chuckled behind
> the gliding hunter. An immensity of peace

across which the thunderheads rumbled like wagons,
to which the hawk held the rights, a rolling excess
from knoll and pasture concealed the wound of her son's

death from a rusty nail. [...]

(Omeros 176)

In the above passage, Weldon's and Derek's minds mingle, as is implied through intertextual references which draw attention to the themes of displacement, loss, and
grief, but also to the different historical and socio-cultural positions held by Weldon and the narrator. It makes sense that a passage from Exodus describing the
Promised Land of Canaan (Genesis 45:17-18) would resonate with a nineteenth-century Christian woman like Weldon determined to make a life for herself in the American West, while the evocation of Steinbeck's tragic novella of migrancy and longing for place-attachment, *Of Mice and Men* (1937), would resonate with the migratory
narrator who, like Steinbeck, calls into doubt myths of America as a Land of Opportunity. By contrast, the reference to the proto-environmentalist poem "To a Mouse"
(1785) by Robert Burns, from which Steinbeck borrowed his title, may come from
both Walcott's Weldon and Derek, pointing to the construction in Walcott's text of a
shared Anglo-American literary canon that is invested in representations of human-
nature relations resonant with grief and thwarted hopes. Taken together, these references evoke the disastrous consequences of those "fiction[s] of entitlement" (Huggan and Tiffin 86) that infuse the colonial pastoral imagination and, in the case of the
United States, arguably contributed to settler-colonial expansion into the West; the
references thus not only inject Walcott's poem with a general sense of sorrow and
dread, they also fill them with subtle anticolonial and environmental resonances.

In Derek's account of events, the dying of the Lakota Sioux constituted a deeply
personal tragedy for Catherine Weldon, who witnessed, albeit only briefly, the disastrous effects of the government's strategies of attrition on Indigenous peoples such
as the Sioux. Walcott's evocation of genocidal violence against Indigenous people
together with the death of Weldon's son in the elegiac passages of *Omeros* juxtaposes
events of very different kind and scale. While I would not call this comparison a complete success in terms of the emotional responses it tries to invoke, I see it as an attempt on Walcott's part to make sense of incomprehensible and inexpressible loss,
while also acknowledging the impossibility of such a project via his alter ego Derek
who tries to imagine Weldon's perspective on the topic:

[...] An immensity of peace

across which the thunderheads rumbled like wagons,
to which the hawk held the rights, a rolling excess
from knoll and pasture concealed the wound of her son's

death from a rusty nail. [...] That summer did not last,
but time wasn't treacherous. What would not remain
was not only the season but the tribes themselves,

as Indian summer raced the cloud-galloping plain,
when their dust would blow like maize from the furrowed shelves,
which the hawks prophesied to mice cowering in grain.

(Walcott, *Omeros* 176–77)

Revising seasonal imagery, which has a long tradition in pastoral poetry as well as in elegy, the canto's "elegies of summer" mourn the death of Catherine Weldon's son as well as the arrival of "Indian summer," a phrase repeatedly associated in the long poem with settler-colonial displacement of Indigenous peoples. At the same time, the narrator's elegies of summer foreshadow the "ghost dance of winter" (*Omeros* 213), that is, the hunger winter of 1889/90 and the Wounded Knee Massacre in December 1890.

As a non-Indigenous white woman, Catherine Weldon was able to leave the Dakotas to travel southward with her son when conditions on the Standing Rock Reservation became increasingly dramatic (Gidmark and Hunt 14). Making use of the freedom of mobility afforded to her as a white European-born settler in the expanding United States, she survived the winter of 1890/91, while many Sioux, confined to the reservation, did not. Like the migrant narrator of *Omeros*, who relates Weldon's story and the plight of the Lakota one hundred years later, Weldon observed the suffering of the Sioux and other Plains peoples as an emotionally involved, yet unaffected outsider. By juxtaposing a personal tragedy with acts of settler-colonial violence, Walcott's pastoral elegies explore the limits of poetic representations of grief as well as the paradox of trying to give an account in poetry of atrocities committed against a marginalized group from a distanced position of relative privilege. Parallel to this, evocations of nature become a powerful, albeit conflicted, vehicle for emotions in the explorations of the discrepant scales of loss and grief in the U.S. passages of *Omeros*. In drawing from a long tradition of politically-minded poetry of mourning centered on nature, Walcott's pastoral elegies counter stationary notions of emplacement and exclusive notions of community by inter-connecting displaced people from diverse backgrounds and across time. What must be acknowledged too in the specific context of the Weldon passages, though, is the fact that a settler's desire for place-based community, however temporary and seemingly innocuous, must be considered a form of colonialism that assumes "access to Indigenous Land and its ability to produce value for settler and colonial desires and futures" (Liboiron 11). One question the Weldon passages raise through their narrative layering is how the desire for place-based community of an arrivant like Derek or Walcott should be judged in this context.

The Weldon passages exploit the conventions of the pastoral elegy to full effect at the same time that they wrestle with the potentially problematic dimensions of the genre. As Walcott himself once noted in an interview, modes such as the elegy "are sometimes suspicious because they so often focus on the person writing them [rather] than on the subject" (Baer 196). The narrator's struggle with this suspicious self-centeredness of the elegy comes to the fore in chapter 35, canto III. In this canto, Catherine Weldon reflects on her life on the Plains by contemplating the natural world, which she finds replete with omens of death. The text evokes traditional elements of the pastoral elegy, such as the dead bird as a symbol of mortality and the limits of poetry, but it also subverts such common tropes by figuring a dead crow—a harbinger of death in Western culture, but a symbol of wisdom in the cultures of many Plains peoples, drawing attention to the vast landscapes of the western and northern Plains as a historical site of intertribal as well as Native-settler conflict:

> I have found, in bleached grass, the miniature horror
> of a crow's skull. When dry corn rattles its bonnet,
> does it mean the Blackfoot is preparing for war?
>
> When the Crow sets his visage on Death, and round it
> circles his eyes with moons, each one is a mirror
> foretold by his palm. So, the bird's skull in the grass
>
> transfixed me, parting the spears of dry corn, just as
> it would your blond soldiers. As for the herds that graze
> through lance-high grasses, drifting with the Dakotas,
>
> are not the Sioux as uncertain of paradise,
> when the grass darkens, as your corn-headed soldiers?
> Doubt isn't the privilege of one complexion.

(Walcott, *Omeros* 181–82)

Catherine Weldon does not primarily view the bird's skull as a reminder of her own mortality or of mortality as a universal human condition here. Instead, Walcott's narrator suggests (or alleges in his presentation of Weldon), she sees it as an emblem of the tragically doomed resistance of the Sioux and the Crow (Apsáalooke)—historically neighbors and then enemies, when the Sioux began to be pushed westward, which briefly led the Crow to form an alliance with the U.S. government in its war against the Sioux—against the U.S. government's violent project of resettlement and dispossession. The juxtaposition of the "crow's skull" with the war/death mask of the "Crow" turns the Midwestern grasslands through which Weldon moves, but which she and the narrator also re-imagine, into one unfathomable Native American mass grave.

The image of the (singular) grave in nature is a stable of the Anglo-European pastoral elegy, as represented by Milton's *Lycidas* (1638), Thomas Gray's "Elegy on a Country Churchyard" (1759), Percy Bysshe Shelley's *Adonais* (1821), or Alfred Lord Tennyson's "In Memoriam A. H. H." (1849), amongst others. In American literature, there is a similar tradition represented by such poets as Henry David Thoreau and Walt Whitman, in which nature itself is the grave.[11] Indeed, both in content and imagery, the lines above are reminiscent of the passage "A child said *What is the Grass*" from Whitman's "Song of Myself," in which the speaker views the "dark grass" as "the beautiful uncut hair of graves" and as a "uniform hieroglyphic" that is "sprouting in broad zones and in narrow zones" and "among black folks as among white" (*Leaves of Grass* 31–32). These lines have been read as evidence for Whitman's belief in "the continuity of individual lives and regional or racial types" (Killingsworth 34) and as "an originating moment" for all other moments of "noticing small nature" in *Leaves of Grass* (Gerhardt, *A Place for Humility* 60). Like Whitman's "Song of Myself," Walcott's poem points to different functions and scales of N/nature and reflects on the racial politics of human relations in light of the shared human experience of death. In his version of death as the great equalizer, Whitman presents the natural world as a regenerative force that is able to erase racial difference. Although Catherine Weldon's elegiac meditations on the landscape of the Midwestern prairies suggest that doubt about life after death may be an experience she shares as a grieving mother with the Sioux and the "corn-headed soldiers" (Walcott, *Omeros* 182)—perhaps due to colonialist ideas of her own missionary duties and failures—Walcott's poem troubles over-simplistic equations. Instead, it emphasizes the fact that the genocidal wars waged by the U.S. government against Indigenous peoples were motivated by white supremacist ideas and used religion to justify racist notions of Indigenous inferiority and moral deficiency.

When Catherine Weldon tries to distance herself from the U.S. government by referring to its troupes as "*your* blond soldiers" (Walcott, *Omeros* 181; emphasis added), one must ask whether there is any possibility that Weldon can position

---

11   Henry David Thoreau, for instance, rejects the Romantic motif of the lonesome tomb in *A Week on the Concord and Merrimack Rivers* (1849), his pastoral elegy for his brother John, when he writes: "It may be that I am not competent to write the poetry of the grave. The farmer who has skimmed his farm might perchance leave his body to Nature to be ploughed in, and in some measure restore its fertility" (171). In related yet different ways, Walt Whitman famously imagined the land as a mass grave for the fallen soldiers of the Civil War, pointing to the possibilities of national renewal in and through nature. In other English-language traditions, the motif remained common. As Ivor Indyk notes in his article "Pastoral and Priority: The Aboriginal in Australian Pastoral," for example, one of the most common motifs of the Australian (settler-)colonial pastoral is the Aboriginal grave (842).

herself outside the racist settler-colonial system and discourses of her time, even if she has made it her mission to support the Lakota. Walcott's poem does not answer in the affirmative. Without completely invalidating the gestures of personal and collective mourning inherent in Catherine's (and the narrator's) elegy for the Lakota, the poem raises questions about the limits of transethnic identification (in poetry) and the problem of bearing witness in poetry to histories of colonial and racial violence from an outsider perspective, even when this outsider perspective is occupied by the Black migrant and (reluctant) arrivant Derek, but especially when it is occupied by the white immigrant and considerably less reluctant settler Weldon.

The romanticized portrayal of both Native warrior and American soldier in the passage above showcases the extent to which Catherine Weldon's elegiac musings remain indebted to settler-colonial discourses. Weldon's reference to the *"miniature horror/ of a crow's skull"* (Walcott, *Omeros* 181; emphasis added) in chapter 35, canto III, speaks both to the marginalization of the horrors of Indigenous extermination in U.S.-American narratives of nation-building and to a marginalization of these same discourses in nineteenth-century American memorial culture more broadly. Highly popular during the nineteenth-century, the art of miniature painting was brought to the U.S. by the earliest European settlers and commonly consisted of small portable portraits painted on ivory lockets on the occasion of births, marriages, or deaths. If these portable portraits frequently functioned, as Robin Jaffee Frank suggests, as "substitutes for an absent loved one" (*Love and Loss* 1), Catherine's description of the skull as "miniature horror" links the murder and displacement of American Indigenous peoples to a highly sentimental and private form of nineteenth-century mourning. Walcott's poem draws attention to the problematic nature of such a sentimental rhetoric by reminding readers that what they read are not in fact Weldon's words but those of the narrator of *Omeros*, whose voice supplants Catherine's in Walcott's pastoral elegies for the Indigenous peoples of the Plains.

Another questions the Weldon passages of *Omeros* raise, then, is what Walcott's tendency to speak not only *for* but also *as* others means for his epic's gestures of poetic witness. I would argue that it calls them into question without condemning the poet to silence and that this tension is what Walcott seeks to express. The poem quoted above does not hide its deliberate supplementation of historical and autobiographical details with imaginary histories and experiences; hence it frequently disrupts its own pastoral-elegiac mode through meta-commentary. By the end of the canto, Weldon's musings about the omnipresence of death on the Plains become legible not only as an interrogation of nineteenth-century colonialist ideologies and sentimentalist rhetoric, but also as a critical engagement with the poetic tradition of the pastoral elegy and its conventions. At the heart of this critical engagement lies a cautious affirmation of what Robert Bensen describes as a "merging [of] human identity in an imaginative act, across time and space" (122), but also an interrogation of the limits of such poetic identification along with poetic witnessing.

A later section from *Omeros* highlights how such a temporary merging of identity depends in crucial ways on the natural world as a conduit. In Chapter 41, canto II, a canto replete with references to Indian Summer as a figure for Native American removal and genocide, Walcott's narrator declares: "This was the groan of the autumn wind in the tamaracks/ which I shared through Catherine's body, coming in waves/ through the leaves of the Shawmut, the ochre hands of the Aruacs" (*Omeros* 208). As in several other places in the epic, human grief in *Omeros* is echoed by the natural world. As Timothy Morton argues, "the reverberation of nature is the way in which elegy imagines how grief is brought into language" ("The Dark Ecology of Elegy" 253). Indeed, it is a physical experience of the natural environment during the Indian summer in Boston—"Shawmut" (Walcott, *Omeros* 208) being a name for the area derived from Algonquian—that allows the narrator to do more than merely speak *for* or *as* Catherine Weldon in her moment of grief. He experiences her grief for the displaced and murdered tribes and her son in an explicitly and inevitably visceral manner. The reverberation of nature, we might say by misappropriating Morton's phrasing, is the way in which Walcott's elegy imagines how grief is shared across time and space.

Because both the grief and the natural world in the canto are experienced by people who live centuries apart in separate bodies and socio-cultural positions, Walcott's layered acts of ecopoetic witnessing—in the voice of Weldon or as the narrator-poet Derek (and on a meta-level as the author-poet Walcott)—retain their respective historical specificity and uniquely (if in part imaginary) personal quality. Catherine Weldon's story and perspective is refracted by the narrator's perspective on Native American histories of displacement and colonial oppression, a perspective influenced and further complicated by his experiences as a Black Caribbean poet and recent migrant to the United States. Where Catherine Weldon mourns the Lakota and the death of her son, Walcott uses his migratory narrator to evoke the fate of racial minorities and Native peoples throughout the Americas, in particular the Sioux and the Aruac of his native Island of St. Lucia. In important ways, the act of mourning presented in the U.S. American passages of *Omeros* is both personal and more than personal. If Walcott's poet-narrator is able to bear witness to the suffering of the Sioux, he can only do so from a position twice removed. Walcott's choice of the pastoral elegy in this context is significant exactly because it speaks to the poet's desire to do more than merely report on historical events. Instead, the pastoral elegies in the U.S. passages—which are also critical transnational elegies informed by postcolonial sensibilities—enable a trans-historic, trans-ethnic, highly self-aware, and explicitly situated act of mourning.

The natural world plays a key role in this act of poetic mourning, which is also an act of place-making that—if one takes seriously Indigenous rights to land and sovereignty, including their right to make decisions about who to allow on their land and in their communities—verges on place-taking. Walcott's use of the pastoral elegy as a means of poetic place-making/place-taking has environmental relevance because it depends crucially on a natural world that can serve as a mediator between mourners, while also drawing attention to nature as a (potential) object of mourning itself. For as the narrator begins to notice upon observing seasonal changes upon his return to the East Coast and then understands during his return visits to the Caribbean, the relative permanence amidst gradual change that allows natural environments to become places of depth and resonance for those who encounter them while on the move and across time is no longer a given in a world affected by spreading environmental degradation and accelerated global climate change.

Epic, Confessional Lyric, and the Posthuman Comedy of Scale

Most of the U.S. passages of *Omeros* not concerned with Catherine Weldon's story are dedicated to the narrator's account of his life in the United States after the separation from his wife. Like the Weldon passages, these sections deal with loss. It is a loss, however, that pales in comparison with Weldon's loss of her child and, even more significantly even though in a less individuated manner, the losses of the Lakota. Traveling westward over the Great Plains on an airplane and musing about "a land that was lost" and "a woman who was gone" (Walcott, *Omeros* 175), Walcott's narrator combines a personal, at times blatantly self-centered perspective with the kind of impersonal, distanced perspective that has historically served U.S. settler-colonial projects and their imperialist successors by erasing the humanity of those Native peoples targeted for dispossession and displacement. The text makes this connection between a rhetoric of distance and a politics of violence explicit when Derek points to the countless broken treaties between the Sioux and the U.S. government as evidence for how "Empires [such as the U.S.] practiced their abstract universals of deceit" (Walcott, *Omeros* 181). The fact that the narrator sees his own "expression" (175), that is, both his face and his poetry, reflected in the plane's window and thus superposed onto the landscape at a far distance below him implies that he, too, is practicing such "abstract universals of deceit" (175) with his poetry. Rather than being unaware of the risk involved in choosing to speak to issues that one might consider of no concern to him, as some scholars seem to suggest, Walcott employs intentionally lopsided comparisons in the Dakota passages to expose "abstract universals" (*Omeros* 181) as dangerous distortions. Instead of seriously implying that Derek's personal losses could and should be compared to the loss of Indigenous peoples and cultures, the Dakota passages dramatize the poet's failure to find an appropriate poetic language for representing the places he encounters and the settler-colonial histories that have shaped them. This failure, Walcott's text suggests, is not just a personal or moral one. It is also a failure of the poetic language of universalization commonly associated with the traditional epic and of the language of individualization commonly associated with the confessional lyric, a failure that becomes even more obvious when the two genres are combined.

Derek's struggle and ultimate inability to find a poetic language suited to the immensity of North American landscapes, the weight of North American history, and his own relationship to both is especially pronounced in chapter 34, canto I, a canto which conjures the striking landscapes of the American West. Contemplating the awe-inspiring sight of "Colorado" and the "Dakotas" (Walcott, *Omeros* 174) during a westward flight, the transnational migrant Derek envisions a statuesque Crow horseman, a romanticized heroic figure representative of a long-gone past, who points his "lance" to the "contrail" (174) that the narrator's plane leaves in the sky in a tragically futile gesture of defiance and/ or recognition.[12] Like the "interstate" (Walcott, *Omeros* 175) mentioned a few lines later and the "contrails" visible on the window's "Plexiglas" (174), the plane's condensation trail is symbolic of an America constantly on the move and constantly claiming new territory. The word component *trail*, together with the "white wagons" (Walcott, *Omeros* 175) mentioned in the third stanza, points to the Westward Expansion and the resulting Native American removal which not only affected Indigenous peoples of the U.S. South displaced by the Trail of Tears and similar forced acts of relocation, but also Plains Peoples such as the Dakota who the passage alludes to as well. The way in which these different Indigenous peoples are evoked is problematic: the warrior's "whitening" by the "[c]louds" (Walcott, *Omeros* 175) highlights the ambiguity of the poetic gesture that brings Indigenous people into passages centered on Derek. The horseman's gradual erasure by the passing time and by a natural world that does not provide a reliable historical record unless the poet intervenes is paralleled with the Crow warrior's eventual disappearance "into the page" (Walcott, *Omeros* 175) of the narrator's account of his travels westward—and by extension of Walcott's poem. The long and diverse histories of Indigenous peoples of North America are therefore quite literally "narrowed from epic to epigram" (175) in Walcott's epic poem in which Native American histories remain on the margin. Put differently, in the very moment in which Walcott's "poetry of subjectivity or confession" (Gray, *Mastery's End* 193–94) tries to challenge the restraints often imposed on poetry of migration by weaving together personal experiences and larger settler-colonial histories, the poet is confronted with the impossibility of such an endeavor.

---

12   This mention of a statuesque Crow horseman may be an allusion to James Earle Fraser's well-known bronze sculpture *The End of the Trail* (1918) which depicts a Native warrior on horseback, collapsed back upon himself, letting his lance trail on the ground in defeat. It might as well point toward an abyss right in front of him, into which he and his horse, which has come to an abrupt halt but is barely able to stand, are about to fall.

The narrator's description of the Colorado and Dakota plains is rich in metaphors that are oddly mismatched and strangely out of scale. Natural phenomena as clearly visible yet still incomprehensible in their temporal and geographical scale as the geological formations left behind by "the crumbling floes/ of a gliding Arctic" (Walcott, *Omeros* 174) are figured as marks left by "angelic skis" (174) and then compared to scratches on the airplane's windows, which are in turn compared to the trails of "comets" (175). These lopsided comparisons do more than deconstruct what might otherwise appear as a sublime vision of the Dakota Plains and "Colorado's/ palomino mountains" (Walcott *Omeros* 174) from the mobile perspective of the air traveler. The intentional awkwardness of Walcott's language here highlights the incomprehensible horrors of human history as well as the unthinkable timespans that have led to the formation of the landscapes he surveys. Poetic gestures like this one characterize the Dakota passages and by consequence Walcott's epic at large as a "posthuman comedy" (McGurl 537) of scale. Responding to Wai Chee Dimock's call for scholars to study American literature in a historical context that goes beyond the conventional timeframes of historiography governed by colonial, nationalist, and imperialist interests, Mark McGurl proposed the project of the posthuman comedy that is, of critical fiction "in which scientific knowledge of the spatiotemporal vastness and numerousness of the nonhuman world becomes visible as a formal, representational, and finally existential problem" (McGurl 537). Although Walcott's epic is neither fiction, nor oriented toward scientific knowledge, the Dakota passages nonetheless strikingly render the "vastness and numerousness of the nonhuman world" through densely figurative evocations of histories and places that highlight the clash of human time with deep time, of human perspectives with the scales of (continental American) nature. The canto just discussed shows how the poet struggles with the realization that even the "most epic productions" of human existence are "cosmicomically small" (McGurl 538) when compared with the vast scales of the more-than-human world. It is precisely because of the mind-boggling nature of these posthuman scales—"posthuman, not in the affirmative sense suggested by Hayles and Haraway, but in the devastating sense that, on any order of magnitude other than our own, human individuation is statistically insignificant" (Dimock, "Low Epic" 616)—that Wai Chee Dimock in a response to McGurl emphasized the particular ability of poetry to "represent something like a lyricization of epic—our brain's way of telescoping in reverse, turning unthinkable orders of magnitude into thinkable ones" (619). Walcott's Dakota passages capitalize on the ability of poetry to make the unthinkable thinkable with a single image, even as his text draws attention to that which is lost in the resulting processes of re-scaling. His posthuman comedy is one of ultimately incommensurable scales, histories, and voices that nonetheless produce relevant insights when combined in a text such as *Omeros*.

While the transnationally mobile narrator displays some confidence in his ability to adequately represent nature and its history in the Caribbean passages of *Omeros* (see Handley, *New World Poetics* 290–92), he is more doubtful in the cantos about the United States. In the Dakota passages, he sardonically admits to having "mis[taken] mountains for lakes" (Walcott, *Omeros* 175) while attempting to describe the northwestern plains. What this may be highlighting is that poetic place-making from too great a distance, without immersing into the places in question, is exceedingly difficult, if at all possible. What it also implies is that such poetic place-making, whatever insights it may yield with regard to the grandness of the nonhuman world (or because it yields such insight), entails the risk of becoming implicated in forms of place-based violence that stem from universalization and distancing. Indeed, I would argue, the narrator's self-conscious display of his failure to account fully for the complex, multi-layered and multi-scalar placeness and historicity of the American landscapes he only passes over by plane in the Dakota passages, implies an awareness that arrivants such as Derek are easily roped into the discursive project of obscuring, romanticizing, and thus perpetuating settler-colonialism in the United States. While they are not settlers, they too can become implicated in practices of writing that lead to a flattening of N/nature and a thinning out of places of depth into abstract political geographies void of meaning. They too can become complicit in the erasure or trivialization of the culturally, socially, politically, and ecologically significant human-land relations that other marginalized and displaced peoples have established, whether through place-making or other place-based practices. When this happens, a reading of the U.S.-passages of *Omeros* attuned to matters of place and displacement suggests, arrivant acts of place-making—whether undertaken out of a deeply felt desire for place-attachment and belonging, as in the case of Agha Shahid Ali discussed in the following chapter, or, undertaken with a certain reluctance and ironic distance, as in the case of Derek Walcott—become ethically fraught.

Throughout the Dakota passages, Walcott explores the problems that arise when a migrant poet like himself engages in poetic place-making in a U.S.-American context where such place-making has historically been tied, and continues to be tied, to a poetic self-fashioning that relies on a rhetoric of justified conquest and heroic individualism. Phrases like "Manifest Destiny" and "American dream" (Walcott, *Omeros* 175), and attributes like "paradise" (175) in the last stanza of Chapter 34, canto I, suggest that the narrator struggles with his role as a poet of place and displacement in the United States. In a certain sense, the Dakota passages renegotiate a dominant poetic instantiation of the myth of the "American Adam," namely that of "the poet-prophet, the artistic self who shapes the world" (Patea 23).[13] As Viorica Patea

---

13   In "The Muse of History" (1973), Walcott famously wrote: "In the New World servitude to the muse of history has produced a literature of recrimination and despair, a literature of revenge

notes, the myth of the American Adam has provided the foundational framework for "the drama of the American self" as well as for "interpreting space and time" (17) in the 'New World.' Following Myra Jehlen, Patea emphasizes that the Adamic project of self-definition crucially depends on "the existence of a 'garden'" (29), which in the U.S. American context also came to be mapped onto the open spaces of the American West, despite the obvious resistance of the landscapes and residents of the Midwest to such a figuration. George B. Handley reads Walcott's (Caribbean) New World Adam as a "postlapsarian Adam, a 'second Adam'" (2), who does not deny violent histories but expresses "'awe' before the wonders of a New World whose beauty has survived or has even, paradoxically, been nurtured by the wreckage of colonialism" (2). Walcott's U.S. passages too acknowledge histories of colonial violence and the (sublime) beauty of U.S. nature. Yet, if they express any "awe" for the "wonders" of the more-than-human world in the United States, the resulting elation is short-lived, tempered by grief or irony and undermined by the narrator's use of jarring metaphors and maladroit comparisons. The American Adam of the bitterly ironic Dakota passages is a reluctant one: the natural world Walcott's narrator encounters during his travels through the United States are ancient and saturated with human and nonhuman histories, not new, let alone made anew by his words. Rather than confidently presenting himself as a poet-prophet who (re-)creates the world, Walcott's narrator is a failing American Adam as much as a reluctant (eco)poetic place-maker. However, given the violent implications of such adamic place-making, for which erasure and misrepresentations are crucial, Walcott's self-conscious display of the poet's failures in *Omeros* may be read as an at times heavy-handed but necessary troubling of settler-colonial ideologies through a posthuman comedy of scale and thus as an achievement in its own right, especially for an Afro-Caribbean transnational migrant like Walcott's narrator.

Walcott's critique of the myth of the adamic poet-prophet not only challenges settler-colonial violence, it also has remarkable environmental implications. "The Adamic hero," Viorica Patea notes in drawing from Richard Slotkin, frequently "translates his self-assertions into acts of violence against the garden" (34), which is why "in his wake, the earthly Eden is transformed into a wasteland marked by ruin and debris" (34). Following Derek's return to the East Coast after his trip to the U.S. South and his voyage across the Great Plains, he recognizes New England as precisely such a wasteland. In chapter 41, canto II, he muses:

---

written by the descendants of slaves or a literature of remorse written by the descendants of masters. [...] The great poets of the New World, from Whitman to Neruda, reject this sense of history. Their vision of man in the New World is Adamic" (37).

[...] The widening mind can acquire
the hues of a foliage different from where it begins
in the low hills of Gloucester running with smokeless fire.

There Iroquois flashed in the Indian red, in the sepias
and ochres of leaf-mulch, the mind dyed from the stain
on their sacred ground, the smoke-prayer of the tepees

pushed back by the Pilgrim's pitchfork. All over again,
diaspora, exodus, when the hills in their piebald ranges
move like their ponies, the tribes moving like trees

downhill to the lowland, a flag-fading smoke-wisp estranges
them. First men, then the forests. Until the earth
lies barren as the dusty Dakotas. [...]

(Walcott, *Omeros* 207)

Figuring Native peoples as trees or leaves, as he also does in other passages in the epic poem, but also suggesting that migratory movements profoundly affect individuals and their perspective on the world, the traveling poet confronts the legacy of American settler-colonialism "in the low hills of Gloucester." The name Gloucester recalls Charles Olson's *The Maximus Poems* (1960, 1968, 1975), another twentieth-century American epic of place with environmental undertones that chronicles the European settlement of North America. The narrator's references to the "Iroquois" in this canto, like his references to the Choctaw, Sioux or Crow in other parts of *Omeros*, is marked by a blurring of the line between historical facts and (settler-colonial) fantasies and thus by a problematic erasure of cultural differences between the many different Indigenous tribes that were "pushed back by the Pilgrim's pitchfork" (Walcott, *Omeros* 207), as the narrator puts it. The Six Native nations of the Northeast commonly referred to as Iroquois, that is to say, the Seneca, Cayuga, Oneida, Onondaga, Mohawk, and Tuscarora, did not live in "tepees" as suggested in the passage above, but in longhouses.[14] This kind of oversight, or as one might say, this kind of universal abstraction, is a problematic feature of *Omeros*, even if the text strongly implies that some of the stereotypical repertoire of images the narrator draws on

---

14   Historically, the confederacy of five Northeastern tribes known as Iroquois called themselves *Kanonsionni*, "people of the longhouses" before receiving the more commonly known, European name Walcott uses in his text. Today, the confederacy comprises six Northeastern Native nations—the Seneca, Cayuga, Onondaga, Oneida, Mohawk and Tuscarora (Ortiz 24)—and calls itself "Haudenosaunee," meaning "They made the house." For more information on the Haudenosaunee Confederacy, see the Confederacy's official website (Haudenosaunee Confederacy).

for his description of landscapes and their histories—a repertoire evoked for instance through the allusion to "sepia" (Walcott, *Omeros* 207) colored films and photographs—in fact be a critical commentary on hegemonic U.S.-American representations of Indigenous peoples, rather than a mere repetition of stereotypes. When
Walcott's narrator represents the historical victims of European colonization in the
Americas with recourse to the same settler-colonial stereotypes that were used to le-
gitimize Native American genocide and dispossession, the Gloucester canto seems
to imply, it is at least partly because the migrant narrator's "mind" has "acquire[d]/
the hues of a foliage different from where it beg[an]" (Walcott, *Omeros* 207) during
his stay in the United States, where the cultural and popular imagination continues
to erase Indigenous diversity along with Indigenous histories, cultures, and experiences.

Importantly, the devastation resulting from conquest and expansion mentioned in the Gloucester canto does not only concern humans but also the nonhuman world. After Indigenous peoples have been driven off the land in the East
and replaced by settlers and arrivants like himself, the narrator suggests, "the earth"
will soon lie "barren as the dusty Dakotas" (Walcott, *Omeros* 207), an ominous proph-
esy not only given the historical westward progression of the U.S.-American colonial
project, but also in reference to the (late) twentieth-century U.S. neocolonial expan-
sions into the Caribbean, depicted in the Caribbean sections of *Omeros*. When the
narrator temporarily returns to the Caribbean to visit St. Lucia during his sojourn
in the United States, he cannot help but draw comparisons between both regions'
histories of slavery and Indigenous genocide. As I have outlined in the beginning of
this chapter, he also becomes painfully aware of the devastating manner in which
mass tourism—depicted as a modern-day form of colonialism—affects his native
island. What the Caribbean passages suggest is that the narrator's migratory experiences and his travels in the United States have not only changed his sociopolitical
and socioeconomic status in ways that affect his perspective on human-nature
relations, they have also made him acutely aware of his own complicity in systems
of oppression and exploitation, including those that have caused and continue to
exacerbate our current ecological crisis.

It is at least in part due to the increasingly complex perspectives of nature and
mobility that the narrator develops during his travels through the United States,
I argue, that a critical transnational and environmental sense of place emerges in
Omeros. As Richard Kerridge notes, our current moment of escalating environmental crisis calls for "forms of epic realism that combine long perspectives with zooms
into intensely realized local settings" (372) as well as for genres such as "confessional
lyric poetry" that are "equipped to explore people' current reactions and evasions
(such as 'splitting') and the emotional and behavioral shifts that would occur if we
began to change" (373). Derek Walcott's text can be said to have responded to these
conflicting demands on literature in the Anthropocene a decade before the term was

introduced to the public and at a moment in time when ecocriticism was only beginning to emerge as a field of inquiry. *Omeros* explores "long perspectives" and "local settings" as well as a transnational migrant's "reactions [to] and evasions" of his own implications in or at least complicity with systems of oppression and exploitation through a mixing and revision of genres. Walcott's frequently uncomfortable, but in many ways prescient, lyricized planetary epic does not erase the tensions and personal conflicts arising from the clash of the universal and the particular, the communal and the individual, the global and the local. Instead, it confronts them, allowing readers to explore with Walcott's mobile narrator and the other characters of *Omeros*, but also at a distance from them, what the discrepancies of scale inherent in the Anthropocene mean for human beings driven by their desire to engage more deeply with the world around them but also troubled by what their acts of place-making reveal.

4. Reimagining Ecological Citizenship: Environmental Nostalgia and Diasporic Intimacy in the Poetry of Agha Shahid Ali

Like Derek Walcott, Agha Shahid Ali is a poet of migration born in a former British colony whose poetry reaches toward the transnational and the environmental. Or rather, as I propose, Ali's poetry reaches toward the *translocal* and the environmental as it engages with a crowded cartogram of U.S.-American places, histories, literatures, and art. In this light and unlike much of what has been written about Ali to this date, my analysis of his work does not focus on his poetry about Kashmir, his place of origin, nor does it focus on his *ghazals*, the poetic form Ali promoted in the United States and used in most of his later poetry, as can be seen for example in the posthumous collection *Call Me Ishmael Tonight: A Book of Ghazals* (2003). Rather, I turn to one of Ali's mid-career collections, *A Nostalgist's Map of America* (1991), to explore the form (eco)poetic place-making takes in his poems about the United States. Many of Ali's poems are what Jahan Ramazani calls "gloco-descriptive" (*Poetry in a Global Age* 66), that is to say, filled with references to one specific place as well as with references to places elsewhere. In *A Nostalgist's Map of America*, his poems revolve around desert landscapes in the U.S. Southwest, while also suggesting that the speaker of the poems, a Kashmiri migrant and poet who calls himself Shahid, has already moved on to the East Coast. In his texts about the American Southwest as well as in poems featured in the collection that are set elsewhere in the United States, such as the Northeast and New England, Ali does not just express longing for Kashmir. Contrary to what might be expected from a migrant poet living in self-imposed exile from his war-torn homeland, Ali's speaker also expresses a desire to develop meaningful relationships to his new place(s) of residence, including those parts of the United States he only passes through. It is this backward but also forward-oriented nostalgic longing for place-attachment without an insistence on permanent emplacement, I show in the following, that characterizes the project of (eco)poetic place-making in *A Nostalgist's Map of America*.

Ali often employs highly figurative language and figures of memory to evoke complex human-nature encounters in his place-based poems. As I posit, however, many of his poems about the United States do not rely with the same authority on personal and collective memories of place as his poems about Kashmir. As a migrant who lived in the U.S. Southwest only for a short time before moving on to the Northeast, that is to say, as an arrivant who remained mobile after migrating to the United States, such personal and collective memories about his different places of residence in the U.S., his poems suggest, were not always available to him. Neither were large parts of the Indigenous history and culture in the Southwest, not only due to historical erasures by European colonial powers and the U.S. settler-state that succeeded them, but also due to the complex position that non-white immigrants occupy in relation to both settlers and Native peoples in a settler-colonial nation such as the United States. In response to these limitations of knowledge and lived experience, Ali combines in his poetry about the Southwest the personal experiences and memories of the places he has encountered with the place-experiences and place-memories of other residents. What is more, he supplements the available human and environmental histories of the Sonoran Desert with imagined ones.

Pervaded by an intense sense of loss as well as longing, Ali's poetic engagements with nonhuman environments in the United States acknowledge the profound and varied ways in which human-place relations in the United States are shaped by human mobilities, both voluntary and forced. His poems about nature and mobility, or rather, about place and displacement, are both nostalgic and environmentally suggestive, two qualities that have sometimes been considered incompatible by scholars who promote realist modes of environmental writing (see Ramazani, *Poetry in a Global Age* 172). Relying heavily on a place-based yet mobile poetic imagination, highly figurative language, and suggestive intertextual references for his project of place-making, Ali embraces an ecopoetics of mobility informed by environmental nostalgia that depicts places as lived-and-imagined and as complexly layered and translocal formations. By evoking physical human-nature encounters as well as encounters with places in memory and through literature, I show in the following, *A Nostalgist's Map of America* points not only toward mobile forms of place-attachment, it also points to what I understand in expanding on Svetlana Boym's notion of "diasporic intimacy" as a migrant's *diasporic intimacy with the world*. This diasporic intimacy with the world, I argue, challenges exclusive notions of ecological citizenship, instead affirming the mobile subjects' desire and ability to forge meaningful connections to the places they only pass through as well as their capacity to care deeply for places they only inhabit temporarily.

Agha Shahid Ali: A Kashmiri-American Poet in the Sonoran Desert

Born in Delhi and raised in Kashmir, a conflict-torn region in the northernmost part of South Asia that is divided between India, Pakistan, and China, Agha Shahid Ali spent three years in the U.S. as a teenager. Later, he began his university education in India before moving once more to the United States, where he earned a Ph.D. in English from Pennsylvania State University and an MFA in creative writing from the University of Arizona. After finishing his studies, Ali remained in the United States, teaching at the University of Massachusetts-Amherst, Princeton College, in the MFA program at Warren Wilson College, and at the University of Utah until his premature death from brain cancer in 2001, shortly after he became naturalized as an American citizen. Due to Agha Shahid Ali's migration history, his divided cultural allegiances, and the multi-locality of his poetry, scholars have alternatively identified him as an Indian postcolonial poet, a diasporic Kashmiri poet in exile, an immigrant or Asian American poet, or as a diasporic, transcultural, or transnational poet. Ali himself sometimes used the phrase "Kashmiri-American-Kashmiri" to indicate his non-uni-directional migratory identity as well as the mobile cultural location and geographic locale from which he wrote his poetry (Shankar and Srikanth 378). In using the double hyphen, Lavina Dhingra Shankar and Rajini Srikanth suggest, Ali followed Arjun Appadurai who, in his essay "The Heart of Whiteness" (1993), pointed to the increasing tensions between traditional, nation-based conceptions of Americanness and the "large variety of trans-nations" (804) constituting the United States in the late twentieth century. In light of these changes, Appadurai observes, "the hyphenated American might have to be twice hyphenated [...] as diasporic identities stay mobile and grow more protean" (804). Mindful of the importance of place-attachments for the migratory subject, Ali's poetry about the United States carefully examines how such a new kind of diasporic identity that remains mobile and withholds permanent arrival shapes human-place relations in the U.S. trans-nation of the Southwest.

Reflecting on questions of the *postnational* and *transnational*, Appadurai advocates for a "widening of the sphere of the postcolony [...] beyond the geographical spaces of the ex-colonial world" ("The Heart" 796). More specifically, he claims,

> the study of postcolonial discourse should include the United States, where debates about race, urban violence and affirmative action index more general anxieties about multiculturalism, about diasporic diversity and thus about *new forms of transnationality*. (807; emphasis added)

Agha Shahid Ali's poetry evokes such "new forms of transnationality," or more precisely, as I read it, of *translocality*, a point I will come back to later. For where Appadurai's "*transnation[s]*" as well as the diasporic identities and collectivities that emerge from them are profoundly "delocalized" (804), as Appadurai insists, Ali's poetry imagines diasporic identities and collectivities that retain attachments to place and affinities for the local and the regional. Moreover, rather than associating these identities and collectivities primarily with urban spaces, as Appadurai does in the excerpt above, Ali's tentatively environmental imaginaries of belonging emerge from a distinctly mobile perspective as well as from a sustained engagement with nonurban landscapes and environments.

Pervaded by postcolonial and transnational, modernist and postmodernist sensibilities (see Needham, Ramazani *A Transnational Poetics*), Agha Shahid Ali's poetry is critical of objective truths and fixed origins. Although his poems show acute awareness toward the complexities of personal and cultural identity formation, the precariousness of memory, and the instability of language, Ali does not engage in complacent language games or universalizing abstraction in his poetic works, nor does he use irony or biting wit to draw attention to the violence of history and the everyday injustices of life as a migrant of color in the United States, as Walcott does. Reflecting on the tenuous relationship of displaced subjects to the world, including the more-than-human world, his texts use highly figurative poetic language and a gentle lyric voice enriched with narrative elements to create meaning and coherence where meaning and coherence seem to be lacking (King 258). Much like Walcott's *Omeros*, Ali's poems about the United States feature nonurban environments as sites of encounter with other cultures and times as well as with the nonhuman world, casting places both as cultural and natural spaces, metaphorical and literal landscapes. Indeed, many of his poems refer to the natural world as a touchstone for poetic and philosophical reflection on experiences of displacement and matters of belonging.

In the poem "No," Ali for instance employs ostensibly figurative language to evoke the materiality as well as the cultural texture of places:

[No,]
not in the clear stream,
I went fishing in the desert sky.
With rain-hooks at the sun's end,
I caught a rainbow, its colors
slippery in my hands.
I gently separated,
like the bones of a trout,
the blue from the red,
the green from the yellow,
my knife sharp, silver-exact,
each color lean,
impeccably carved.

(Ali 85)

Ali uses synesthesia in the quoted passage to make tangible what can only be seen and thus creates a concrete, albeit in no sense realist representation of a "desert" landscape in his poem. "No," points to a world outside the text, but more importantly, it draws attention to itself as poetic text by evoking literary forbearers, whose works raise questions about human-world-text relations. Indeed, this passage echoes not only Emily Dickinson's poem "Split the Lark – and you'll find the Music" (Fr905), an ironic, metapoetic text that foregrounds problems of representation and artistic production; the poem also echoes the famous dialogue between Hermit and Poet from the ecocritical ur-text *Walden: or, Life in the Woods* (1854) by Henry David Thoreau, in which fishing is described as "the true industry for poets" (Thoreau 296).[1] As different critics have remarked, fishing in *Walden* stands for "truth seeking," whereby the truth sought is that of man's position in relation to nature and civilization (Lee 134, Dolis 131). While I would not describe Ali as a truth-seeker in the Thoreauvian sense, he carefully examines the poet's position in relation to the natural environments and cultures of different places, a process made literal in lines quoted above.

Ali's poetic engagement with human-place relations shows a particular sensitivity to those historical processes that make places contested territories, whether politically or culturally. The natural environments he depicts frequently function as repositories of histories, memories, and imaginaries for voluntarily mobile or violently displaced subjects. His poem "Desert Landscape" can help to illustrate this approach:

> Stringing red serrano peppers, crushing
> cilantro seeds—just a few yards from where,
> in 1693, a Jesuit priest
> began to build a boat, bringing rumors
> of water to an earth still forgetting
>
> the sea it had lost over two hundred
> million years ago—three white-haired women,
> their faces young, are guarding the desert
> as it gives up its memories of water
> (the fossils of vanished species) [...]

(Ali 94)

Employing a startling line-break between "hundred" and "million years" and mentioning both the year "1693" and "fossils of vanished species," the above passage draws attention to the clash of human and nonhuman time-scales, human memories and nonhuman histories, as well as the different kinds of loss and longing that result from this clash. Alluding to the history of European mission, colonization, and settlement of the Southwest, "Desert Landscape" references the Tyrolean Jesuit Eusebio

---

1   I want to thank Christoph Irmscher for pointing out this particular intertextual connection to me in a discussion about a conference paper, in which I developed an earlier version of this reading.

Kino, who had just "beg[u]n to build a boat" (Ali 94) in order to expand the Jesuit mission from what is now Arizona across the Gulf of California, when a gift of blue shells from local Indigenous peoples caused him to change his plans, because the shells indicated to him that what is now Baja California was not in fact an island but could be reached and had been reach by the Native peoples of the Southwest via land.[2] When Ali includes this story in his poem, he suggests that the Indigenous peoples of the Southwest have always been highly mobile. He also portrays the Southwest as a place that has been marked by many different kinds of human (and nonhuman) mobilities. Among these, European colonization and settlement stand out not only because they dramatically changed Indigenous social and political life in the region, but also because they had lasting effects on human-nature relations in the Sonoran Desert.

Indeed, the reasons why Kino is still known today is not only because he helped to establish the first mission in the region, but because he introduced European practices of agriculture. This second intervention had drastic effects on Indigenous ways of living in and with the desert, a fact I will come back to later in this chapter. Viewed in this context, the "three white-haired women" (94) mentioned in the second stanza of "Desert Landscape" can be seen as Indigenous survivors of a long history of European colonization and settlement in the Southwest. The disastrous consequences of this history are powerfully, if obliquely, evoked in the second part of Ali's poem, which fuses nature and religious imagery to turn the description of a heavy rain shower during sunset into an apocalyptic vision of death and destruction. While the three women are "guarding the desert" (Ali 94)

> [...] the sky opens its hands above
> a city being brought to memory by rain:
> as silver veins erupt over the peaks
> and the mountains catch fire, the three women
> can see across the veiled miles the streets turn
>
> to streams, then rivers, the poor running from
> one another into each other's arms;
> can see the moon drown, its dimmed heart gone out
> like a hungry child's; can see its corpse rising—

(Ali 94–95)

---

2   For Father Eusebio Kino's own account of his missionary work and travels in those parts of the Sonoran Desert that are now part of Northern Mexico, Arizona, and Southern California, see *Kino's Historical Memoir of Pimería Alta: Contemporary Account of the Beginnings of California, Sonora, and Arizona, by Father Eusebio Francisco Kino, S. J., Pioneer Missionary Explorer, Cartographer, and Ranchman (1687–1711)*, a transcription and translation of Kino's original manuscripts published by Herbert E. Bolton in 1919.

Highly figurative and full of allusions, the above passage describes a desert land-scape completely transformed before the Native women's eyes by a great flood, a scene reminiscent of Indigenous stories about floods as much as of the Bible story of the great deluge. Apart from pointing back to the long history of colonial violence, the poem's ending can also be said to conjure a future destruction of those settle-ments established in the desert by missionaries, colonizers, and settlers. Indeed, the second half of the poem refers back to the poem's epigraph, which quotes Isaiah 40:12, a bible verse that suggests that, next to God's creation, even the most powerful "nations are like a drop in a bucket" and "dust on the scale" (Isaiah 40:15). Referencing the Bible to emphasize the grandeur of Southwestern desert landscape, but also, I would argue, the vulnerability of human cultures to destruction, the poem imagines the devastating losses experienced by the Indigenous nations of the Southwest and possible future devastations of the two settler nations that claim territorial control over the desert landscapes north and south of the U.S.-Mexico border. The image of the spring flood in Ali's poem is particularly resonant in this context, given that the increasingly extreme weather conditions in the American Southwest caused by an-thropogenic climate change have not only led to ever more severe draughts in the three decades that have passed since the publication of Ali's poem, they have also led to ever more severe floods in the region.

Saturated with accounts of troubled colonial past and present by a migrant poet whose sense of place is shaped by deep emotional connections to places and cultures elsewhere, the desert environments figured in Ali's collection come to hold multiple, at times divergent meanings. While most of the topographical poems in Ali's larger oeuvre focus on Kashmir, Ali's topographical poems about the United States present readers with just as much attention to the arresting beauty as well as the embattled nature of some of those places that hold particular meaning for the (myths of the) nation. Ali's collection *A Nostalgist's Map of America* (1991) was written in large parts, if not entirely, before the political conflict between Indian, Pakistani, and separatist Kashmiri forces escalated in 1989/1990. It is this escalation, Raza Ali Hasan suggests, that caused Ali to concentrate more intensively on his place of origin in his later po-etry (Hasan 118–119), collected for example in *The Country Without a Post Office* (1997) and the posthumous *Rooms Are Never Finished* (2002). In contrast to these collections from the mid-1990s to the early 2000s, *A Nostalgist's Map of America* prominently fea-tures the Sonoran Desert and U.S. Southwest, a region that resembles Kashmir in that it is characterized by great natural beauty and dazzling cultural diversity, while also having a long history of colonization and territorial conflict.

The Sonoran Desert is a subtropical North American desert that not only cov-ers parts of Arizona and California but also reaches into the Mexican states of Baja California, Baja California Sur and Sonora. Divided by the U.S.-Mexican border, the Sonoran Desert forms an extraordinarily diverse bioregion that supports many dif-ferent kinds of vegetation zones and a great variety of species. Home to cities such as Hermosillo and Guaymas on the Mexican side and to Tucson and Phoenix on the American side as well as to several Indigenous communities inhabiting land on both sides of the U.S.-Mexican border, the region covered by the Sonoran Desert is culturally diverse and marked by a complicated history of settlement, displacement, and migration. This history continues to this day in the form of uncontrolled urban sprawl and the resulting encroachment of non-Indigenous settlement on Indigenous lands. Despite this urban expansion, the region still comprises vast areas of scarcely populated land. This fact has made the Sonoran Desert a popular but also deadly route for illegal border crossings, ever since border control near the region's urban centers was intensified during the late 1990s and early 2000s. *A Nostalgist's Map of America* was published before the fortification of the U.S.-Mexican border under Bill Clinton and George W. Bush. It was also published before the effects of climate change became increasingly visible in the Southwest in the form of the devastating droughts that present an acute threat to the ecosystem of the Sonoran Desert today. And yet, although Ali's collection does not explicitly address environmental degradation and climate change, whether in relation to the Sonoran Desert or beyond, *A Nostalgist's Map of America* can be read as ecopoetry of migration that registers the complex ways in which human-nature relations in the U.S. Southwest have been affected and continue to be affected by human mobility, whether socially, culturally, or ecologically.

A Nostalgist's Map of America intertwines lyrical evocations of personal loss with historical and mythical evocations of collective loss. While only some of the poems in the volume mention their speaker by name, the speaker of the topographical poems set in the Sonoran Desert can be identified as the migrant poet Shahid. Together with selected other poems featuring Shahid on the road, these desert poems speak to the sustained struggle of their continuously mobile speaker for a meaningful sense of place. Frequent intertextual and intermedial references serve a double function in the poems: on the one hand, they help to deepen the emotional connection between the migratory poet and the places he encounters, while on the other, they challenge those theories of place-attachment that consider long-term inhabitation and personal experience as the most important factors for an individual's sense of place and belonging. Resisting such a logic, Ali not only describes personal encounters with the nonhuman world; he also draws on the accounts of others, infusing his poems about U.S. landscapes with a multiplicity of histories of mobility and place-based imaginaries. It is this multiplicity of histories and imaginaries that shapes Ali's ecopoetics of mobility and allows *A Nostalgist's Map of America* to resist exclusionary notions of belonging and place-attachment. When examined with a double-focus on nature and mobility, Ali's U.S.-centered poetry thus provides valuable insights into how the changing realities of an increasingly globalized world come to matter in relation to the changing demands of an increasingly burdened ecosphere.

Moving Beyond Memory in the Poetry of Agha Shahid Ali

Even as scholars increasingly address the transnational and transcultural orientation of Ali's poetry (see Islam, Ramazani *A Transnational Poetics*, Sajid) much of the
existing scholarship on his work remains within the recognizable bounds of postcolonial critique, discussing questions of identity, loss, exile, as well as issues of
cultural translation (see Needham, Tageldin, Kabir, Woodland). Influenced by the
spatial turn in literary studies, some scholars have drawn attention to the importance of issues of space and place in Ali's poems (see Newman, Islam, Katrak, Ramazani *Poetry in a Global Age*). Ketu Katrak, for example, suggests that Ali provides
what she calls an "imagistic recreation of actual spaces" (130) and then goes on to argue that Ali's poetry portrays "acutely observed geographical locations" (130), while
also comingling times and places in ways that create "imaginative ways of returning
home through the imagination" (136).[3] Jahan Ramazani, on his part, argues that Ali's
poetry illustrates "the translocational nature of loco-descriptive poetry, particularly
in a global age" (*Poetry in a Global Age* 73) and thus "poetry's peculiar ways of articu-
lating the translocalization of locality and [...] its reinvigoration of the topographical
imagination for our time" (75). Pointing beyond a spatial toward the possibility of an
ecocritical reading, Robert T. Hayashi notes that "[t]he American landscape" in Ali's
poetry "becomes a multifaceted and multilayered place, one more faithful to historical reality and the range of traditions that have shaped the environment" than to the
"literature and scholarship that has [traditionally] defined what the land has meant
to us" (62). Advocating for a widening of the range of texts considered in ecocritical analysis in general, Hayashi urges critics to reconsider their definition of texts
deemed fit for ecocritical analysis and lists Ali's works as an example of the kind of
poetry that may "offer new perspectives on the relationship of the self to the environment" (63). As I will suggest by reading *A Nostalgist's Map of America* from an ecocritical perspective enriched by considerations of mobility, Ali's translocational and
multilayered poetry of place about the United States offers such new perspectives
on human-environment relationships by rethinking conceptualizations of place and
traditional notions of place-attachment in the context of displacement.

One of the issues frequently addressed in relation to Ali's poetry is his treatment
of memory and nostalgia (see Freitag, Katrak, King, Tageldin, Woodland). More or

---

3   By calling Ali's use of language "imagistic," Ketu Katrak establishes a link between the Kash-
     miri-American poet and American modernist poetry, in particular the writings of T. S. Eliot.
     The link between Eliot and Ali is undeniable, not least because Ali published *T. S. Eliot as Edi-
     tor*, a critical study based on his graduate work on the modernist poet, in which he examines
     Eliot's work for *The Criterion*, while also repeatedly commenting on Eliot as poet. Indeed, sev-
     eral scholars analyzing Ali's poetry have suggested that it was influenced by Eliot (see Ra-
     mazani, *A Transnational Poetics*; Ghosh; King).

less explicitly, all of these readings participate in a larger theoretical debate on the role of nostalgia in postcolonial, ethnic, and world literatures.[4] They either reject nostalgia as "ersatz, vulgar, demeaning, misguided, inauthentic, sacrilegious, retrograde, reactionary, criminal, fraudulent, sinister, and morbid" (Lowenthal 27) or argue for its rightful place in the postcolonial or transnational poetic repertoire. Of the scholars writing about memory and nostalgia in Ali's works, many favor memory over nostalgia. Lawrence Needham, for instance, posits that Ali's poetry "safeguards against nostalgia by refusing to sentimentalize the past" (Needham 69). In a similar vein, Kornelia Freitag argues that Ali performs a "careful balancing act between [...] nostalgia and reality check" (211) in his self-conscious engagement with personal and cultural memory, and ultimately uses "ironic deflation" to counter moments in which "memory [threatens] to become arresting nostalgia" (221). While most critics thus acknowledge the importance of nostalgia in Ali's work, they tend to see its presence in the text critically. We can observe this, for example, in Malcom Woodland's reading of Ali's poetry, which suggests that Ali's ghazals leave "a real but *problematical* place for nostalgia in the hybrid text" (267; emphasis added). Where nostalgia is not considered ideologically or ethically questionable, it often figures as an emotional affliction expressed through poetic means. In his reading of a poem from Ali's collection *The Half-Inch Himalayas* (1987), Shaden M. Tageldin, for example, describes the "impossible nostalgia" experienced by the postcolonial migrant living in (self-imposed) exile as a torturous, unescapable condition to which poets like Ali react by "violently disrupt[ing] the syntax of language, identity, geography, and temporality" (Tageldin 234). Rather than viewing nostalgia as a problem, I will explore nostalgia's critical potential as "expansive memory" (Hashmi 183) and as a means of evoking place-attachments despite geographical and temporal disruptions that are suggestive in environmental terms because they challenge the idea that meaningful emplacement can only result from long-term inhabitation.

While scholarly examinations of the role of nostalgia for people's place-sense are a comparatively recent phenomenon, the role of places for individual and collective memory as well as the role of memory in the production of places have long been

---

4   For a brief summary of different arguments about the place of nostalgia in postcolonial literature and literatures of migration, see, for example, Malcom Woodland's discussion of Homi Bhabha's and Jahan Ramazani's takes on the subject (Woodland 253–54). As Woodland suggests, nostalgia is surpassed by the hybrid text according to Bhabha (see *The Location of Culture*), whereas Ramazani explores the role nostalgia continues to play in postcolonial literatures (see *The Hybrid Muse* 83–84). For a more in-depth study of nostalgia in the context of (im)migration, see Andreea Deciu Ritivoi's study, *Yesterday's Self: Nostalgia and the Immigrant Identity* (2002), which examines the function of nostalgia as "an interpretive stance in which a person is aware of the element of discordance in her life" (165). Nostalgia in this account allows immigrants to construe coherent life-narratives, which in turn help them come to terms with the ruptures and discrepancies following from displacement.

a concern of scholars interested in questions of memory and spatiality.[5] Ecocritics, too, examine memory as a constitutive element of the process by which people forge a sense of place over time (see Buell *The Future* 71–76; Goodbody; and Gerhardt "Nothing Stays Put"). Some of these scholars use the term "environmental memory" to indicate the need for a more systematic discussion of issues of memory and environmental politics. According to Lawrence Buell, environmental memory can be defined as

> the sense (whether or not conscious, whether or not accurate, whether or not shared) of environments as lived experience in the fourth dimension – i.e., the intimation of human life and history as unfolding within the context of human embeddedness in webs of shifting environmental circumstance of some duration, whether these be finite time spans (a lifetime, a generation, an epoch, a dynasty), or stretching back indefinitely into remotest pre-history. ("Uses and Abuses" 96)

In his definition, Buell describes environmental memory as the awareness of the temporal dimensions of environments and people's sense of place. He implies that this awareness is only on one level the product of personal memory; on another, he suggests, it is in conversation with cultural memory, an observation that Axel Goodbody makes as well. Reconfiguring Aleida and Jan Assmann's "figurations of memory" for an ecocritical context, Goodbody defines the concept as "a constantly evolving archive of narratives and images deriving from the Bible, Greek myth, fairy tales, history, world literature, etc." (59) and then argues that "figurations of memory focusing on places serve as particularly important vehicles for the communication and redefinition of understandings of our relationship with the natural environment" (59). Both Buell's insistence on the importance of individual and collective "environmental memory narrative[s]" ("Uses and Abuses" 107) as a means to counter "environmental generational amnesia" (Kahn, qtd. in Buell "Uses and Abuses" 96) and Goodbody's emphasis on the crucial role that cultural "narratives and images" play for the constitution of environmental figurations of memory are pertinent here, especially because Ali relies so heavily on the repository of American as well as non-

---

5   In *The Poetics of Space* (1969, Fr. 1958), philosopher Gaston Bachelard undertakes a phenomenological investigation of space that makes repeated use of poetry to think about how humans come to understand the "specific reality" (xv) of poetic images and is very much interested in the imagination as well as the memory of places. French historian Pierre Nora, author of the multi-volume *Les lieux de mémoire* (1984–92), on his part discusses "realms" and "sites" where "memory crystallizes and secretes itself" ("Between Memory and History" 7). Aleida Assmannn, a key figure in the field of memory studies, in turn, has extensively written about the role of (sacred) places as media for collective or cultural memory (see, for example, part V "Orte" of her study *Erinnerungsräume*). For a discussion of the many ways memory and place can be thought together, see Dylan Trigg's *The Memory of Place: A Phenomenology of the Uncanny* (2012).

American myths, literature, and art in his depiction of the Southwest. Rather than only evoking "figurations of memory," however, Ali's project of place-making also self-consciously evokes complex "figurations of nostalgia." Indeed, at the end of his article "Sense of Place and Lieu De Mémoire: A Cultural Memory Approach to Environmental Texts" (2011), Goodbody concludes in part in drawing on Ursula K. Heise, that despite the obvious importance of memory for a person's environmentally-oriented place-sense, "[i]t may be unwise to dismiss place-identity, and even the nostalgic idealization of places, as factors contributing to a caring attitude toward the environment" (66). Building on these and similar insights, I am interested for my discussion of Ali's poetry in the environmental affordances of an environmental nostalgia informed by what Kate Soper and Jennifer K. Ladino refer to as "avant-garde nostalgia" (Soper) and "counter-nostalgia" (Ladino) respectively.

Environmental philosopher Kate Soper defines "avant-garde nostalgia" as "a movement of thought that remembers, and mourns, that which is irretrievable, but also attains to a more complex political wisdom and energy in the memorializing process itself" ("Passing Glories" 23). Nostalgia, in her reformulation, allows for critical reflection on the past and is thus able to "stimulate desire for a future that will be at once less environmentally destructive and more sensually gratifying" (24). In her book *Reclaiming Nostalgia: Longing for Nature in American Literature* (2012), Jennifer K. Ladino, too, suggests that what she calls "counter-nostalgia" can be "a mechanism for social change, a model for ethical relationships, and a motivating force for social and environmental justice" (8). "Nostalgia," she notes in her concluding remarks, which touches on questions on migration, "can highlight the material and political dimensions of dislocations" and in the process "inspire empathy and, potentially, alert more people to a future we should take steps to avoid" (230). Ladino here alludes to what Svetlana Boym, in her influential monograph of the same title, famously refers to as "the future of nostalgia." Indeed, revisiting *The Future of Nostalgia* (2001) with a focus on questions of place and displacement allows me to sketch how an overtly nostalgic ecopoetry of migration like Ali's might go beyond merely commemorating an invented past in order to imagine more eco-ethical futures in the context of mobility.[6]

In *The Future of Nostalgia*, Boym defines nostalgia as "a longing for a home that no longer exists or has never existed," which expresses itself in "a sentiment of loss and displacement" but also represents "a romance with one's own fantasy" (xiii). Nostalgia, she notes, "can be retrospective but also prospective" (xvi) and is a political

---

6   The term "environmental nostalgia" also appears in the works of film studies scholars Robin Murray and Joseph Heumann. Both in a 2007 essay on Al Gore's *An Inconvenient Truth* and in their monograph *Ecology and Popular Film* (2009), which includes a revised version of the essay, they define the term as "a nostalgia we share for a better, cleaner world" (n. p.; 196), a definition my analysis of Ali's poetry seeks to complicate.

force insomuch as "[f]antasies of the past determined by needs of the present have a direct impact on realities of the future" (xi). Whether it takes the form of an emotional attachment to a (partially) invented past or whether the longed-for conditions are projected into the future, nostalgia comes in one of two shapes, Boym explains: while "[r]estorative nostalgia protects absolute truth" (xviii) and tends toward simplification for the sake of false coherence, "reflective nostalgia" (xviii) is complex and contradictory. This is why it can produce critical awareness as well as a drive to action. As Boym puts it:

> Reflective nostalgia dwells on the *ambivalences of human longing and belonging* and does not shy away from the contradictions of modernity. [...] Reflective nostalgia does not follow a single plot but *explores ways of inhabiting many places at once* and imagining different time zones; it loves details, not symbols. At best, reflective nostalgia can present an ethical and creative challenge. (xviii; emphasis added)

Boym here emphasizes nostalgia as an at-once spatial and temporal phenomenon with an explicitly political, ethical, and creative set of dimensions, and proposes reflective nostalgia as a generative combination of "longing and critical thinking" (49). Such a complex understanding of nostalgia is crucial for my analysis of environmental nostalgia in Ali's poetry. Indeed, one can say that his nostalgic ecopoetics of mobility "explores ways of inhabiting many places at once." At the same time, it is invested in balancing migrants' "longing" for meaningful relationships to their temporary places of residence with the "critical thinking" necessary to challenge exclusionary notions of "belonging" and place-attachment in the context of mobility, U.S. settler-colonialism, and environmental change.

Ali does not reject nostalgia in favor of memory as a seemingly more reliable and ethical basis for poetic creation. Instead, he embraces reflective nostalgia in *A Nostalgist's Map of America* as a place-, history-, and ultimately environmentally conscious affect that is especially well suited for migrants who cannot depend on memories and experiences alone in order to build meaningful relationships to the places they only encounter in passing. Ali's nostalgic ecopoetics of mobility manifests in two main ways: first, in a translocal sense of place that relies in crucial ways on migratory perspectives and literary imaginaries of displacement to evoke mobile forms of place-attachment and, second, in a nostalgic longing for a diasporic intimacy with the world that abandons the desire for an original or ultimate home without relinquishing the desire for meaningful human-place relations. Overall, Ali's nostalgic ecopoetics of mobility challenges theories of belonging that privilege long-term residency, personal experience, and/or first-hand knowledge as the basis of meaningful place-attachment. Instead, it points toward non-localist, anti-nativist models of ecological citizenship that take seriously displaced people's desire for place-attachment and mobile perspectives on human-nature relations. For the theorization of such alternative models of diasporic belonging and ecological citizenship as well as of the mobile environmental imaginaries on which they might be based, literature and art more generally are of crucial importance, Ali's poetry insists. This is one of the reasons, I propose, why Ali relies on intertextual references, including in particular the works of desert poet Richard Shelton, the nature poems of Emily Dickinson, the desert paintings of Georgia O'Keeffe, and the ethnobotanist writings of Gary Paul Nabhan.

Mobile Forms of Place-Attachment

Subjects in motion and evocations of various kinds of mobility abound in *A Nostalgist's Map of America*. The motif of travel not only appears in poems such as "I Dream I Return to Tucson in the Monsoons," "Leaving Sonora," "A Nostalgist's Map of America," "In Search of Evanescence," "I See Chile in My Rearview Mirror," and "Snow on the Desert," poems I address in some detail in this chapter, it is ubiquitous throughout Ali's collection. In "Beyond the Ash Rains," the speaker first leaves his home to join his lover in "the northern canyons" and then leads said lover away for both to "walk through the streets/ of an emptied world" together (Ali 23); in "A Rehearsal of Loss," the speaker is driving through the desert and away from his lover's house at night (25), while the poem "Crucifixion" depicts someone who is driving through New Mexico, noticing many different kinds of landmarks and contemplating many different kinds of mobilities (26–28). Given this ubiquity of different forms of mobility, one might even go so far as to call the title of Agha Shahid Ali's collection a misnomer in that it hardly constitutes a "Map of America." Rather, *A Nostalgist's Map of America* stages ongoing processes of mapping that Ali's mobile subjects engage in while traversing the Sonoran Desert and other regions across the United States.

While the many journeys in the collection conjure the "*topoi* of the travelling American" (King, *Modern Indian Poetry* 271), the poems in which Shahid travels by car recall the classic American road narrative (see also Kazim Ali, "Introduction" 1). Like the topoi of the traveling American, this literary genre evokes American ideals of individuality and freedom, qualities also associated with mobility more generally (Tölölyan 67; Cresswell 3; Leyda 25). When the traveler is a transnational migrant, like Shahid or Walcott's narrator Derek, the conventional interpretation of the American road narrative has to be rethought, however. After all, displacement rather than emplacement, routedness rather than rootedness, are the norm for many migrants. In consequence, rather than a desire to assert his individuality and independence, it is a want of community, belonging, and place-attachment that preoccupies the migratory subject in *A Nostalgist's Map of America*. For Ali's speaker, establishing and maintaining meaningful connections to the places and communities he encounters, and not breaking free from them, seem to be the primary goal. By depicting Shahid as both highly place-conscious and highly mobile,

A Nostalgist's Map of America suggests that place-attachment is anything but a given, especially for migratory subjects. At the same time, Ali's poetry indicates, mobility is not necessarily the obverse of place-attachment. Rather, as I will show, in Ali's poems, place-attachment is portrayed as the accumulative effect of place-making that the migrant subject engages in while constantly being on the move. Because this ongoing process of place-making continues to integrate different perspectives of mobility, ranging from travel and voluntary migration to forced displacement, it does not lead to traditional emplacement or a purely local sense of place. Instead, it produces a *trans*local sense of place and mobile forms of place-attachment.

When I use the term "translocal" to describe the environmentally suggestive sense of place evoked in *A Nostalgist's Map of America*, I do so in reference to Jahan Ramazani's influential work on transnational and translocal poetics. In his study, *A Transnational Poetics* (2009), and in his later publications, Ramazani invokes the translocal as "an alternative to understandings of the relation of poetry to place as either rooted or rootless, local or universal" (*A Transnational Poetics* xiii; emphasis original). Borrowed from the Prologue of James Clifford's *Routes: Travel and Translation in the Late Twentieth Century* (1997) and employed by Ramazani in distinction to "the transnational," the translocal indicates a move away from purely abstract cultural spaces to concrete places, and from too exclusive an emphasis on mobility to an acknowledgement of those forces of emplacement at work in imaginaries of place. In suggesting that the sense of place Ali's poetry evokes is translocal rather than transnational, I thus mean to highlight the ways in which his poems sidestep the nation as a privileged site of territorial attachment and identity construction, despite what the title of his collection suggests. When I speak of mobile forms of place-attachment, I am building on Christine Gerhardt's notion of a "mobile sense of place." According to Gerhardt, a mobile sense of place "becomes tangible" ("Imagining a Mobile Sense of Place" 425) in the contemporary poems she analyzes

> through three interrelated poetic tactics: the construction of places that are significantly shaped by nonhuman mobilities, of speakers whose environmental insights are critically informed by their geographical movement, and of broader cultural frameworks characterized by overlapping movements of people, materials, goods and ideas. (425–26)

Many of Ali's poems represent the kinds of mobilities Gerhardt mentions here. What is more, a nostalgic place-based literature and art sensible to past and present mobilities constitute a broader cultural framework of mobility that shapes the poems' depiction of places as translocal and of place-attachments as "mobile."

In *A Nostalgist's Map of America*, histories of human displacement are often discussed in association with specific landscapes that the speaker encounters during his travels. Places that might initially seem bounded and neatly circumscribed are revealed to be translocal spaces: they are open to and constituted by different forms of human and nonhuman mobility and connected to places elsewhere through these mobilities. In "Crucifixion," for instance, the speaker follows an unnamed traveler who is "driving clear of memory,/ north from Las Cruces" (Ali 26). On his journey, the traveler passes different geographical landmarks, including "dunes of whitest gypsum" (26), that is, geological formations moved by the wind, "the timbered forests of the Penitentes" where "the blue pines / are like men, descending from the summits" (26) and "the rock that once sprouted wings and bore/ the besieged Navajos to safety" (26). Referred to as *Tsé Bit'a'í* or "winged rock" by the Navajo (Diné), Shiprock is situated in San Juan County, New Mexico, and plays a crucial role in a number of ancient Diné myths that explain how the Navajo Nation came to be located in the Southwest. According to these myths, "the rock that once sprouted wings" carried the Navajo from the lower worlds of the Holy People to their traditional homeland of Dinétah.[7] When the Navajo came to the Southwest, the area that is now northeastern Arizona, northwestern New Mexico, parts of southeastern Utah, and parts of southwestern Colorado was already inhabited by the Pueblo people commonly known as the Anasazi. Navajo and Anasazi population movements, together with the consequences of colonization, led to an extremely complex history of mobility and displacements in the region.[8] Ali's reference to Shiprock points to these precolonial migrations of Indigenous peoples as well as to colonial histories of displacement. Indeed, the English name of this natural site, Shiprock, alludes both to the colonization of the Southwest by European missionaries and seafaring nations, such as the Spanish, and to the region's mid-nineteenth-century incorporation into the United States, which led, amongst other things, to the so-called "Long Walk," a term used to describe the forced removal of thousands of Navajos from Dinétah and onto a reservation in southwestern New Mexico.

---

7   For accounts of the Navajo myth referred to here, see, for example, Marta Weigle and Peter White's book *The Lore of New Mexico* (1988, p. 27) and the entry on "Shiprock Pinnacle" in Laurance D. Linford's *Navajo Places: History, Legend, Landscape* (2000). Archeological finds and studies of the Athabaskan language family from the early twentieth century have led anthropologists and linguists to argue that the ancestors of the people today known as the Navajos and the Apache may have migrated to the Southwest from what is now West Canada. Given the possible political implications of such arguments, they have not been without controversy. In his guide to Navajo places, myths, and histories, Linford—who collaborated for his book with members of the Navajo Nation—, for example, notes that the name of Shiprock "gave rise to a White man's myth in the first half of [the twentieth] century: that the Navajos once lived on the Pacific Coast" (265).

8   For a reconstruction of the history of Anasazi and Navajo settlement of the Southwest including New Mexico, see for example *Anasazi America: Seventeen Centuries on the Road from Center Place* (2000) by David E. Stuart, where he suggests that the challenge of building sustainable communities, both in environmental and non-environmental terms, can help to explain precolonial migrations in the Southwest, including those of the Navajo and the Anasazi.

By alluding to Indigenous and settler-colonial histories of mobility in poems that chronicle a migrant's travels and acts of poetic place-making, Ali's collection highlights the fact that powerful place-attachments can arise from story-telling and figurative language-use—crystalized in his poems in such names as *Tsé Bit'a'í*, "winged rock," or Shiprock. It also alludes to the fact that stories/metaphors can be used to naturalize some forms of movement (such as settler migration) and certain kinds of human-place-relations (such as settler-colonial notions of individualized landownership), while delegitimizing others (such as Indigenous notions of place-belonging or Indigenous semi-nomadic lifestyles). Human mobilities and their representations, *A Nostalgist's Map of America* indicates, can have far-reaching consequences for an individual's or a community's sense of place and place-attachment; so can narratives of rootedness, whether they come in the form of stories or metaphors. Ali's poetry shows awareness of the power of story-telling and poetic language in the context of place-making, as can be seen in his mentions of storied places such as Shiprock. It also shows awareness toward the complex position that migrants such as Ali's speaker, Shahid, occupy as arrivants in a nation marked by a centuries-old conflict between natives and settlers. Rather than abandoning place-making in the context of settler histories of place-taking, Ali gives expression to the migrant's desire for place-attachment and responds to the challenges place-making poses in the American (post-)colony/settler-colonial America by enriching the representations of places in his poems with a variety of Indigenous and non-Indigenous stories and histories of mobility. In doing so, he evokes a form of mobile place-attachment that tries to avoid settler logics of place-taking without conflating the position of migrants with that of Indigenous peoples, whether they have been displaced or remain on their ancestral homelands and whether they live more mobile or more sedentary lives.

A Nostalgist's Map of America highlights the fact that, despite their migrations and the ravages of settler-colonialism, Indigenous peoples of the Southwest, whom Ali's speaker in one poem explicitly refers to as "survivors of Dispersal" (Ali 44), have been able to forge and retain meaningful connections to the places they (used to) inhabit, also in environmental terms. At the same time, Ali's poems draw attention to the fact that Indigenous survivors of displacement, like other displaced peoples, experience the fragility of human-place relations in particularly acute ways. Ali's poetry refuses to romanticize sedentarism and in doing so offers material for a critique of the "place-essentialism" (Ray 26) and environmental nativism that discourses of belonging and sustainable living sometimes fall into.[9] Ali's poetry suggests that migratory subjects like his speaker do not have to become sedentary (let alone settlers) in

---

9   In her book, *The Ecological Other: Environmental Exclusion in American Culture* (2013), Sarah Jaquette Ray speaks of "blood-and-soil nativism," a form of environmentalism that operates by "denying other places and processes that constitute any given place" (26) and thus can be

order to develop meaningful place-attachments. Instead, the mobile forms of place-attachment his poetry evokes are built on the notion that a shared experience of displacement and longing for a meaningful sense of place can be the basis for viable alliances between (im)migrants and Indigenous peoples, even if their respective experiences of displacement are vastly dissimilar.

Many poems in *A Nostalgist's Map of America* feature multilayered places as well as mobile subjects who engage with these places on different levels and through different means. They explore how migratory, displaced, or traveling subjects interact with the spaces they cross by experiencing their environs with all senses. They also explore the ways in which mobile subjects revalidate existing place-attachments or form new ones by imbuing places with personal and cultural memories and thus with historical depth and emotional investment. Poems, such as "I Dream I Return to Tucson in the Monsoons" or "Leaving Sonora," highlight the importance of experiences as well as of memory when it comes to establishing meaningful human-place relationships in the context of migration. They also represent moments in Ali's work when experience and memory give way to a poetic imagination informed by complex feelings of loss and longing.

As other poems in the collection confirm, the title of "I Dream I Return to Tucson in the Monsoons" alludes to Ali's speaker's return to the Southwest after his move away to the Northeast of the United States. The fact that Shahid returns to Tucson "in the Monsoons" (Ali 30) hints at his migratory background, linking the U.S. Southwest to Kashmir by way of a weather phenomenon that occurs in both regions. As the poem's speaker dreams about driving toward the Tucson Mountains in "the afternoon sun" (30), sensory perceptions begin to trigger memories of a walk the poet took in the desert at nightfall. The sight of sunlit streets wet with rain as well as "pieces of blue glass" (30) scattered in the desert bring to mind an earlier time in the speaker's life "when [he] was alone" (30) and "there was nothing but the rain/ [...] nothing but silence" (30). Gradually, the speaker's experiences, memories, and dream images begin to blur, as do timeframes and locations in the poem. "I Dream" disorients its readers spatially and temporally by omitting all punctuation and using irregular capitalization at the beginning of lines. Adding narrative layer upon layer—the speaker relates a dream of a visit to Tucson, which conjures memories of a night walk in the desert, which in turn causes the speaker to reflect on a "vanished love" (30)—the poem draws the reader into the speaker's past as well as into his imagination. Shahid's dream and his memories of a walk among the "rocks" near "Gates Pass" (30), a scenic road along the crest of the Tucson Mountains, are suffused with feelings of loss and intense longing. The emphatically imaginary nature of the poet's return to the desert does not lessen its emotional effect on the speaker, however. Rather, both the remembered

---

linked to what historian Peter Coates calls "the eco-racism of American nativism" (187) in his study *American Perspectives of Immigrant and Invasive Species: Strangers on the Land* (2006).

and the imagined encounters with the landscape affirm Shahid's attachment to the Sonoran Desert, even as he has already moved elsewhere.

The intense feelings of loss and longing that pervade the speaker's dream of the Southwest are neither strictly personal nor strictly anthropocentric, insomuch as the mourned "vanished love" does not necessarily refer only to an individual human being. Heavily indebted to the poets Mirza Ghalib and Faiz Ahmed Faiz in its use of imagery, language, and tone, "I Dream" recalls a tradition of Urdu poetry in which the longed-for beloved can stand in for anything from a lost political cause to the loss of one's cultural heritage, sense of identity, or homeland.[10] The "vanished love" Shahid thinks of during his walk in the desert can thus represent many different things. Among them are lost Indigenous cultures of the Southwest, as the poem preceding "I Dream" indicates, which mourns the "perished tribes" (Ali 29) and the "vanished village[s]" (29) of Sonora ("Leaving Sonora"). The migrant poet also mourns the loss of his former home of Kashmir and the loss of his temporary home in the Southwest. Indeed, by revisiting past encounters with the landscapes of the Sonoran Desert, Ali's multilayered, polylocal, and polytemporal poem, to return to Ramazani's description of translocal poems in global age, produces a deepening of these attachments as well as a deepening sense of loss of, and longing for, the different places he has left behind. "I Dream" thus engages in a form of poetic place-making that emphasizes an emphatically retrospective yet persisting desire for meaningful place-attachment.

As the references to ancient Indigenous cultures in poems such as "Desert Landscape" and "I Dream" indicate, the layering of places in Ali's desert poems does not merely rely on personal experiences and memories. It also relies on the poet's imaginative engagement with the region's long human and nonhuman history, or what Lawrence Buell calls "'biogeological' time" ("Uses and Abuses" 97):

The moon touched my shoulder
and I longed for a vanished love

The moon turned the desert to water

For a moment I saw islands
as they began to sink

---

10   Several scholars have remarked on the influence of Urdu poetry on Ali's work (see Caplan, Islam, Tageldin, Woodland). In his introduction to *The Rebel's Silhouette: Selected Poems*, a translation of the ghazals of Faiz Ahmed Faiz that appeared in the same year as *A Nostalgist's Map of America*, Ali himself not only talks about the "highly sensuous language" and key motifs of Urdu poetry, such as the moon, he also discusses how Faiz's ghazals extended the meaning of the figure of the longed-for Beloved, which Ali calls "an archetype of Urdu poetry," so that it could refer to the revolution.

The ocean was a dried floor

Below me is a world without footprints
I am alone I'm still alone
and there's no trace anywhere of the drowned

The sun is setting over
what was once an ocean

(Ali 30–31)

While walking through the Tucson Mountains, Shahid imagines the desert landscape before him as the "dried floor" of an "ocean" that swallows entire "islands."
Apart from conjuring the myth of Atlantis, and thus the sudden loss of an entire
society and culture, the reference can also be read as a nod to the geological history
of the Tucson area and the Sonoran Desert more generally. Rather than suggesting,
however, that "fossils of vanished species" (Ali 94) can be unearthed as physical manifestations of the past, as in the poem "Desert Landscape," the speaker of "I Dream"
emphasizes the limits of the natural world when it comes to preserving records of
the displaced and the disappeared. Where the poem's migrant speaker hopes to find
traces of those who used to walk the Sonoran Desert before him, he only sees "a
world without footprints" that bears "no trace anywhere of the drowned" (31). Like
those passages in Walcott's *Omeros* that contemplate the impossibility of pinpoint-
ing a precise location for the Trail of Tears, "I Dream" suggests that it is the poet's task
to imagine those histories that colonial violence and natural processes have erased.

The traveling poet's responsibility toward former inhabitants of the Southwest
and, by consequence, his determination to testify to the powerful human-place relations of others, is most explicitly addressed in the poem "Leaving Sonora." Placed
right before "I Dream," the text stresses the complex layering of places and the importance of imagination in the migrant's poetic quest for a meaningful sense of
place, while also emphasizing how the speaker's feelings of loss and nostalgic longing blur the lines between personal and extra-personal place-imaginaries. "Leaving
Sonora" begins with a quotation attributed to Richard Shelton, whom the speaker
identifies as "a poet of this desert" (Ali 29). Shelton is an environmentalist writer and
poet who published several collections of poetry and nonfiction about the Sonoran
Desert during the 1970s, '80s, and '90s after moving to Arizona for his studies.[11] "Liv-

---

11   Richard Shelton is the author of eleven books of poetry, including *The Tattooed Desert* (1971),
      Among the Stones (1973), *Chosen Place* (1975), *The Bus to Veracruz* (1978) and *Hohokam* (1986), all
      of which seem to have had a great influence on Ali's desert poems. He has also written several
      nonfiction books such as the memoir *Going Back to Bisbee* (1992). In an interview published
      together with his poem "Local Knowledge," as part of W. T. Pfefferle's *Poets of Place: Interviews
      & Tales From the Road* (2005), Shelton summarizes his place-bound environmental poetics as

ing in the desert," Ali quotes Shelton in the epigraph of "Leaving Sonora," *"has taught me to go inside myself / for shade"* (Ali 29; emphasis original), a lesson Ali's speaker seems to have learned as well. Instead of suggesting that the poet withdraws from the external world into an internal one in which he himself becomes the center of poetic inquiry, however, Ali's speaker advocates for critical introspection enriched by a place-based imagination as a means to commemorate those at risk of being forgotten or written out of dominant histories of such places as the U.S. Southwest. Concrete natural environments and specific geographic locations play an important role in this process of commemoration, itself also an act of (re-)imagination. "Certain landscapes insist on fidelity," Shahid notes and, in doing so, establishes himself as "a poet of this desert" (Ali 29) in Shelton's footsteps. Like Shelton, Ali's migrant speaker takes his cues from the iconic landscapes of the Southwest, testifying to the history of the place and to the intense human-place relationships engendered by the extreme environmental conditions of the desert, while also forging a connection between himself and the desert's (former) inhabitants across time and across cultures.

"Leaving Sonora" suggests that people who are aware of the histories of the Southwest and those have engaged with the region's literatures experience a more intense appreciation when they encounter the landscapes of the Sonoran Desert. They also experience a more acute sense of loss and, consequently, of responsibility. This sense of loss and responsibility is based on a shared experience of place and displacement rather than on a shared cultural, ethnic, or racial background. "The desert insists, always: Be faithful, / even to those who no longer exist" (Ali 29), Shahid reminds himself and the reader, revealing the maxim of his place-based, yet mobility-conscious poetics of witness. In "Leaving Sonora" and several other desert poems in *A Nostalgist's Map of America*, those who no longer exist are "[t]he Hohokam [who] lived here for 1500 years" (29).[12] Contemplating the disappearance

---

follows: "I think what I have done in my poetry is [that I have] interpreted the desert, the Sonoran desert, through the lens of my own despair at its destruction" (130).

12   As Shepard Krech notes in his chapter on the Hohokam in *The Ecological Indian: History and Myth* (1999), the history of the Hohokam is difficult to reconstruct. There are no written records by the Hohokam and the oral histories of the Akimel O'odham, who live in the same parts of Arizona where relics of the Hohokam have been found, are divided on whether the local Native peoples descend from the Hohokam or whether they had left the region before the O'odham arrived. The accounts also provide different reasons for why the Hohokam disappeared. In the language of the Akimel O'odham, the word *Hohokam* is not only used for this ancient people, but also as an adjective, in which case it refers to people and things that have "vanished" or "perished" or that are "gone" or "finished" (Krech 45). From an ecological perspective, the Hohokam practices is noteworthy because they relied on elaborate dry and floodwater farming techniques to build a civilization under difficult environmental conditions. This fact, Krech explains, led many archeologists to celebrate the Hohokam's agricultural ingenuity and adaptability to the desert. At the same time, other scholars have argued that, as a result of waterlogging and salinization, the very methods of irrigation that allowed

of these precolonial Indigenous desert people, about whose culture and ultimate fate relatively little is known, Ali's speaker goes "deep inside himself for shade" (29), the only place where "the perished tribes live" (29). Imagining a scene from the everyday life of the Hohokam, Shahid envisions "one of their women, / beautiful, her voice low as summer thunder" (29), tending to "the culinary ashes" (29). What her "fire" achieves "in minutes" (29), the poet suggests, "earth" achieves "only through a terrible pressure": transforming "coal into diamonds" (29). Read as meta-poetic commentary, this image highlights the underlying premise of Ali's ecopoetics: writing place-based poetry that is conscious of histories of displacement is a laborious and emotionally taxing process. Yet, it is the poet's responsibility to translate the many layers of places—as well as the various experiences, memories, histories, and literary imaginaries that shape them—into multilayered poetic formations of heightened beauty and expressivity.

The third and last stanza of "Leaving Sonora" reiterates this portrayal of poetry writing (and the place-making it both represents and constitutes) as a place-based and simultaneously mobile practice that depends on textual strategies of layering descriptions, allusions, and thus meanings. At the same time, it illustrates how Ali's poetics of place is shaped by a perspective of migration similar to, but not entirely identical to Shelton's, who, as Scott Sanders observes, "made the major theme of his poetry his desire to join spiritually with a land not of his birth, but of his choosing" (n. p.). At the beginning of the final stanza of "Leaving Sonora," Shahid recalls watching the desert from a plane right after takeoff from Tucson international airport. Halfway through the poem, the text thus reframes the speaker's earlier musings about human-place relations by highlighting the speaker's perspective of mobility and pointing to his identity as a transnational migrant. Shahid remarks that he "left the desert at night – to return/ to the East" (Ali 29), that is, presumably to the East Coast of the United States, where Ali spent the last years of his life, even while occasionally traveling even further "East" to Kashmir. Looking back at the day when he left the Southwest, the speaker of "Leaving Sonora" remembers how he "saw Tucson's lights/ shatter into blue diamonds" (29), when his airplane rose above the clouds—an image that refers back to the poem's second stanza, creating a link between the migrant Shahid and the Hohokam woman of his earlier vision. Traveling by airplane, Shahid remembers looking down at "Tucson's lights" through "a thin cloud" and suddenly seeing, or rather imagining "blue lights fade/ into the outlines of a vanished village" (29). It is thus in a situation that has perhaps come to symbolize the life of

---

the Hohokam to survive in the Arizona desert for centuries may have eventually turned the land infertile and thus caused their culture's demise. Other explanations, usually inspired by the environmental issue of most concern at the time, point to earthquakes, droughts, and catastrophic floods as events that drove the Hohokam away from their settlements by the Salt and Gila rivers (Krech 57–64).

transnational migrants at the end of the twentieth century like no other—that of aeromobility, also briefly discussed in the previous chapter—that Ali's speaker conjures up traces of "the perished tribes" (29), mentioned throughout the collection. For a short instant captured in the poem, the speaker imaginatively superimposes the region's precolonial past onto a present that is characterized by urban sprawl as well as increasing (trans)national mobility. This momentary convergence of vastly different time-periods is represented in explicitly spatial terms. Such a textual layering of places is environmentally resonant because it takes the migrant's desire for a sense of place seriously and suggests that mobile forms of place-attachment and meaningful relationships of mobile peoples with the natural environment may be achieved through sustained engagement with the many dimensions of places, ranging from physical to symbolic spaces and from material environments to their representations in (literary) texts.

Longing for Diasporic Intimacy with the World

The collection's title poem "A Nostalgist's Map of America" is a particularly interesting example for how Ali's uses intertextual references to produce a complex layering of places suffused with environmental undertones as well as a sense of loss and longing. Like several other poems in the collection, including the poem "No," discussed earlier, Ali's title poem engages in poetic place-making from a perspective of mobility by referencing the poetry of Emily Dickinson. In "A Nostalgist's Map of America," most of these references allude to Dickinson's famous poem "A Route of Evanescence." Quoted in full and placed before "A Nostalgist's Map of America," Dickinson's short nature poem engages with themes of loss as well as the sense of environmental nostalgia that pervades Ali's title poem and *A Nostalgist's Map of America* at large.

Dickinson wrote extensively about both nature and loss. In effect, her poetry stands out among her contemporaries for her scientifically accurate and detailed depictions of the natural world (Gerhardt, *A Place for Humility* 27–29). Like in Ali's poetry, Emily Dickinson's descriptions of places, such as her garden, are both detailed and richly textured, creating the effect of a tangible, though not necessarily easily graspable natural world through highly metaphorical language (Knickerbocker 9–13). "A Route of Evanescence," one of Dickinson's most well-known poems about "small nature" (Gerhardt, *A Place for Humility* 31, 35), exemplifies the way in which Dickinson combined concreteness and elusiveness, materiality and mobility in her poetry. The version of "A Route of Evanescence" reprinted in *A Nostalgist's Map of America* reads as follows:

A Route of Evanescence
With a revolving Wheel –
A Resonance of Emerald –
A Rush of Cochineal –
And every Blossom on the Bush
Adjusts its tumbled Head –
The mail from Tunis, probably,
An easy Morning's Ride –
         – *Emily Dickinson*

(Dickinson qtd. in Ali 33)

Despite its brevity, "A Route of Evanescence" renders the minutiae of natural phenomena in vivid detail, producing an arresting double effect of tangibility and
ephemerality. Like many of Dickinson's poems, "A Route of Evanescence" is a poem
"of aftermath" (Benfey, "A Route of Evanescence" 90) that reflects on and seeks to
capture the traces of a vanishing object (Kang 57–58.). The focus on the "loss" of
a hummingbird and the effects of this loss on the consciousness of the speaker,
however, do not necessarily imply a transcendence of the physical world, or a mere
"bracketing of reality" (Hagenbüchle 34). On the contrary, in Dickinson's poetry as
in Ali's, the "minute revelatory elements" of the more-than-human world in and
of themselves are "worthy of careful attention and veneration" (Martin 364). Aside
from alluding to the fact that Ali worked for many years as a director of the writing
program at the University of Massachusetts in Dickinson's hometown, Amherst,
where he would also die and be buried (Merrill 88), Ali's integration of Dickinson's
poems into his collection speaks to the fact that his poetry too relies on the careful
direction, via rhythm and sentence structure, toward the minute revelatory elements drawn together by a certain locale and woven together into intricate poetic
patterns in his texts.

Dickinson's poems frequently and skillfully draw attention to material processes
and matters of perception—here, the immediate effects that the hummingbird's
movements have on its surroundings, including the speaker. By linking sounds and
sights through synesthesia, the poem explores the manifold sensory impressions
that the bird produces, focusing especially on the gradually intensifying feelings of
loss and longing that its disappearance engenders in the onlooker. When re-contex-
tualized and integrated into poems such as "A Nostalgist's Map of America" or "In
Search of Evanescence," the act of producing a feeling of (imminent) loss and (anticipatory) longing, oriented also, though certainly not exclusively, toward the physical
world, becomes part of what I describe as Ali's nostalgic ecopoetics of mobility. Indeed, a "Nostalgist," one might say, is not just be a person who feels nostalgic, but
potentially also someone whose aim or even vocation it is to evoke nostalgia in oth-

ers.[13] As Ali integrates quotations and poetic features of "A Route of Evanescence" into his own text, the tangible yet ephemeral, and subtly nostalgic quality of Dickinson's natural world carries over into Ali's poem (see Newman).

The first lines of "A Nostalgist's Map of America" take up the excess of sense impressions evoked in Emily Dickinson's hummingbird poem and projects them onto the landscapes his speaker encountered while driving through "the dead center of Pennsylvania" to "Philadelphia" (Ali 35). As the reader learns later in the poem, Shahid remembered the car ride, which took place some years earlier, when he received a call from his friend Phil, the poem's addressee and driver of the car, who revealed to him that he was dying. In the speaker's poetic recollection of the drive, which is colored in retrospect with a painful sense of the anticipated loss of his friend, the trees alongside Route 322 appear ominously "hushed in the resonance/ of darkest emerald" (35), as the whispering of their leaves is drowned out by the car and transmuted into color effects. The trees fly by and disappear in the distance. Just like Dickinson's hummingbird, they become symbols of transience, while retaining their material presence. Neither a mere backdrop, nor a conventional symbol of life and renewal, the trees in the poem rouse a sense of longing in Ali's speaker. Rather than trapping the poet in the past, his nostalgic longing for a time (and place) before he learned of Phil's sickness also points the speaker toward the future. At the end of a "Nostalgist's Map of America," Shahid sets out for a poetic quest: he begins to seek a place of refuge, a search that acquires subtle environmental undertones.

Shahid recited "A Route of Evanescence," the reader eventually learns, on a road trip through Philadelphia, a scene that part of the poem describes. Inspired by Dickinson's poem and the landscape flashing by outside the car window, Ali's speaker, he tells us, began to muse about the possibility of making a home in Pennsylvania or elsewhere in America, a thought that still preoccupies him many years later when he remembers the trip:

[...] The signs
on Schuylkill Expressway fell neat behind us.
I went further: "Let's pretend your city

is Evanescence – There has to be one –
in Pennsylvania – . . .

(Ali 35)

---

13   Thanks to Mahshid Mayar for alerting me to the potential relevance of the common connotations in English of the suffix -ist (as in nostalgist) compared to the suffix -ic (nostalgic), a fact I had never considered in connection to the title of Ali's poem and my thinking about his project of poetic place-making.

Looking back at numerous exit signs, a line of vision that emphasizes the speaker's nostalgic perspective, Shahid fails to find the kind of place he is longing for. He thus continues driving and eventually proceeds to invent a home for Phil, the imaginary "boyhood town" of "Evanescence" (36). Referencing the central word in Dickinson's poem, the town's name evokes both a "gradual removal" and a "fleeting moment" (Kang 58). Yet, even while the speaker imagines that he and Phil are driving on a "route that takes [them] back, back to Evanescence" (Ali 36), it becomes obvious that the return to such a place of origin is impossible. When the imaginary city of Evanescence reappears at the end of the poem, it is no longer only Phil's boyhood town but also the imaginary home that the migrant poet Shahid is in search of in America. As we read on, Shahid conjures different versions of Evanescence, all of which he offers to Phil (and himself): first, a safe haven, he built himself, "for America/ was without one" (37); then a mysterious, shadowy place he "found – though/ not in Pennsylvania" (37); and, finally, his poem, which is filled with imaginary "souvenirs of Evanescence" (37). This last despairing gesture speaks not only to the speaker's struggle to cope with the impending loss of his friend, it also speaks to Shahid's own unfulfilled desire for a sense of belonging that emplacement promises and the role that a nostalgic longing for real and imagined places plays in his project of (eco)poetic place-making.

Despite the public image of Dickinson as an almost excessively local, immobile, and firmly rooted poet, a closer examination of "A Nostalgist's Map of America" reveals that Ali responds not only to Dickinson's nature poetry of loss and nostalgic longing. He also responds to what Jane Eberwein calls the "global impetus" (34) of Dickinson's poetic imagination and to what Christine Gerhardt describes as Dickinson's poetic "Vision of Global Dwelling" (A Place for Humility 197, emphasis and capitalization original). While the importance of the small nature of Amherst and its immediate surroundings for much of her poetry cannot be denied, Dickinson showed significant interest in foreign countries and geographies (see Hallen, Hamada, Giles). Indeed, much like Ali, Dickinson frequently references places beyond the U.S. in her poetry, specifically ones in South America, North Africa, and Southeast Asia (see Hamada). Importantly, then, "A Route of Evanescence" ends with the lines "[t]he mail from Tunis, probably,/ An easy Morning's Ride" (Dickinson qtd. in Ali 33), lines which Ali takes up in "A Nostalgist's Map of America," along with Dickinson's imagery and her idiosyncratic punctuation. Thinking back to his car ride with Phil, Shahid addresses his absent friend, musing:

Let's pretend [...] that some day –
the Bird will carry – my letters – to you –
from Tunis – or Casablanca – the mail

an easy night's ride – from North Africa."

(Ali 35)

In comparison to Dickinson's poem, in which the speaker receives "mail from Tunis" (Dickinson qtd. in Ali 33), while she is at home in New England observing a hummingbird in her garden, Ali's speaker is a migrant and traveler who imagines sending "letters" back to the U.S. "from North Africa." More so than Dickinson's text, Ali's poem emphasizes the concrete geographical location of Tunis by associating it with a city from the same region, Casablanca, and by naming the exact part of the world in which both are situated. Shahid's reformulation of Dickinson's "easy Morning's Ride" into an "an easy night's ride" can be read as a comment on what has been described as the "time-space compression" (Harvey 260–307) brought on by globalization and commercial air travel. While Dickinson's "easy Morning's Ride" can refer either to the act of imaginary travel by reading (letters) or perhaps to telegraphy, in Ali's late 20th-century poem a plane (a steel "Bird") carries people around the world at least as swiftly as it does letters. By drawing from and transforming Dickinson's poem, then, the title poem goes beyond reiterating the tension between the local and the global, the familiar and the exotic in Dickinson's nineteenth-century lyric. It rearticulates such an impetus from the perspective of mobility of a late-twentieth-century migrant, who continues to look back at the places he has left behind—Kashmir, Pennsylvania, the Sonoran Desert—and in doing so expresses a longing for belonging and a longing for a meaningful relationship to places, including the natural world that makes these places both alike and distinct.

Just like Ali, Emily Dickinson not only paid minute attention to natural phenomena, she also frequently translated these natural phenomena into movement in her poetry. Her poems rarely describe specific isolated objects. Instead, she tends to put these objects in relation to their environments and dissolves them "in pure movement" (Hagenbüchle 34), a poetic technique for which "A Route of Evanescence" serves as a case in point. Indeed, the key characteristic ascribed to the hummingbird in Dickinson's poem is its startling mobility. Rather than representing a static tableau of the natural world, "A Route of Evanescence" presents a micro-environment marked by movement. Ali capitalizes on this dimension of the poem, using the idea of a place/home of Evanescence as the central theme of the sequence "In Search of Evanescence." In addition to emulating Dickinson's idiosyncratic poetic diction, his poem translates Dickinson's images of a markedly mobile nature into a reflection on human mobilities and human-place relations at a much grander scale. It is this transposition of Dickinson's nature-oriented, mournful, and subtly mobile poetic sensibilities onto the place-based, nostalgic, and diasporic sensibilities of Ali's poetry that allows for a distinctly mobile perspective on the natural world and on the process of poetic place-making to emerge in his poetry.

Many poems in *A Nostalgist's Map of America* express a sense of loss of home as well as nostalgic longing for a sense of place that is meaningful because it is intimate. The speaker's longing for place-attachment relies heavily on an engagement with places he has left behind, yet the feelings of nostalgia he expresses are not purely retrospective. They are also "prospective," to borrow again from Svetlana Boym, that is, they are also directed at the speaker's present and future. The sequence "In Search of Evanescence" indicates how such a nostalgic longing for place-attachment without permanent emplacement may transform into a more mobile and environmentally suggestive longing for belonging that one may describe, with Boym, as a longing for a diasporic "sense of intimacy with the world" (251). Rather than glorifying rootedness or giving priority to places of origin, such a "diasporic intimacy" (Boym 254) with the world describes a being in the world (and, as I submit, in place and with nature) that "is not opposed to uprootedness and defamiliarization but is constituted by it" (252). According to Boym, a nostalgic longing for diasporic intimacy with the world does not depend on "utopian images of intimacy as transparency, authenticity, and ultimate belonging" (252). Instead, it is characterized by "a suspicion of a single home" and by "shared longing without belonging" (252). This emphasis on "shared longing without belonging" resonates with my reading of Ali's poems because it revises traditional notions of emplacement and gestures toward alternative forms of place-attachment in light of mobility. It is also suggestive for my analysis of *A Nostalgist's Map of America* because it allows for a reconceptualization of community and community building in an age of global environmental change and mass mobility in which notions of national borders and nation states are frequently called into question, even as they are being reasserted through violence, oppression, and practices of exclusion.

Intertextual references help to establish a diasporic intimacy between Ali's mobile speaker and the places he encounters throughout "In Search of Evanescence." According to Roland Hagenbüchle, the final lines of Emily Dickinson's "A Route of Evanescence" ("The mail from Tunis, probably,/ An easy Morning's Ride –," Ali 33) correlate that which is "infinitely far away [...] to what is nearest" (48). Hagenbüchle's choice of words resonates especially with section 5 of "In Search of Evanescence," which not only borrows Dickinson's characteristic staccato phrases and idiosyncratic capitalization (Islam 266), but also alludes to Georgia O'Keeffe's famous desert painting *From the Faraway, Nearby* (1937). Modeling his speaker's ruminations about the relationship between the faraway and the nearby after Dickinson's formally innovative yet also famously constrained poetry, Ali's poem alternates between stanzas composed almost entirely of titles or descriptions of paintings by O'Keeffe (stanzas one and three) and stanzas consisting of quotes from a letter O'Keeffe wrote to Alfred Stieglitz in September 1916 (O'Keeffe, Stieglitz, and Greenough 26). In my rendering of the poem below, I have italicized direct references to titles of paintings by Georgia O'Keeffe (capitalized by Ali in an allusion to Dickinson's own idiosyncratic capitalization); I have also italicized indirect references to O'Keeffe's paintings (un-capitalized in Ali's poem). Section 5 of "In Search" reads:

> *From the Faraway Nearby* —
> Of Georgia O'Keeffe – these words –
> *Black Iris* – *Dark Iris* – *Abstraction, Blue* –
> her hands – around – a *skull* –
>
> "The plains – the wonderful –
> great big sky – makes me –
> want to breathe – so deep –
> that I'll break –"
>
> From her *Train* – *at Night* – *in the Desert* –
> I its only – passenger –
> I see – as they pass by – her *red hills* –
> *black petals* – *landscapes with skulls* –
>
> "There is – so much – of it –
> I want to get outside – of it all –
> I would – if I could –
> Even if it killed me –
>
> (Ali 46; emphasis added)

O'Keeffe's painting *From the Faraway, Nearby* (1937) depicts a giant deer scull floating above a desert landscape. According to the painting's description on the website of the Metropolitan Museum of Art, O'Keeffe's *From the Faraway Nearby* uses a "realistic painting technique" without regard to scenic "verisimilitude," while the painting's "poetic title" conveys "longing and loneliness," depicting "an emotional state of mind as well as a physical location" (n. p.). Ali's poem invokes similar themes by using textual instead of visual means to express a sense of loss, longing, and loneliness as well as his speaker's desire to develop a close connection with a natural environment that is so grandiose and undeniably physical that it threatens to overwhelm the onlooker.

By referring to Georgia O'Keeffe's paintings and letters, section 5 of "In Search of Evanescence" approaches the desert through the eyes and art of another temporary inhabitant of the Southwest who maintained strong connections to the East Coast.[14]

---

14   O'Keeffe had fallen in love with the desert landscapes of the Southwest during several visits and shorter stays in the region during the 1920s. In 1929, she established herself more perma-

Like many poems in Ali's collection, Georgia O'Keeffe's abstract-realist paintings can be seen as a mobile subject's artistic engagement with her temporary place of residence that link the "faraway" to the "nearby" and vice versa. Also like many poems in *A Nostalgist's Map of America*, O'Keeffe's letters comment on the artist's struggle to capture the overwhelming grandeur of the southwestern desert landscapes in her art. Even while acknowledging the impossibility of such an endeavor, both of these representations—the paintings as well as the poetry—fulfill an important function. As section 5 of "In Search" implies, approaching the natural world through someone else's art can intensify a person's affective connection to the place represented. Ali's itinerant speaker completely immerses himself in O'Keeffe's desert paintings by imagining himself as the "only – passenger" of her "*Train – At Night – In the Desert*." It is from this imagined perspective of mobility that Ali's speaker observes O'Keeffe's "red hills –" and her "*landscapes with skulls –*," landscapes that resonate with the loss and nostalgic longing discussed in so many of Ali's poems. In the complex textual configuration of the poem, place-based art that accounts for perspectives of mobility is reaffirmed as a crucial means of place-making in the context of displacement. By imitating the characteristic form of an Emily Dickinson poem and referencing O'Keeffe's abstract representations of the desert, the text interrogates the potential and the limits of poetry as a means of expressing the migrant's longing for a diasporic intimacy—in the sense of a strong affinity coupled with the desire for (mutual) understanding, appreciation, and proximity—with the nonhuman world, especially when confronted with landscapes that resist such intimacy even more so perhaps than other environments. "In Search of Evanescence" recounts Shahid's poetic quest for a home in displacement. This home remains forever fleeting, forever eluding. What Shahid finds during his journey instead, is a precarious intimacy with "the near – faraways – of the heart" (53), that is to say, a diasporic intimacy with the places he encounters and then leaves behind. Ultimately, it is by withholding the comfort of arrival while still emphasizing the importance of place-making for the mobile subject that Ali's poems imagine a way of being in the world that balances diasporic and environmental sensibilities.

---

nently in New Mexico, even as she continued to move back and forth between the Southwest and New York City. For more information on Georgia O'Keeffe's life, works, and aesthetics, see, for example, Jan Garden Castro's *The Art & Life of Georgia O'Keeffe* (1985), Barbara Haskell's *Georgia O'Keeffe: Abstraction* (2010), and Debra Bricker Balken's book on O'Keeffe and her fellow modernist Arthur Dove, *Dove/O'Keeffe: Circles of Influence* (2009).

Environmental Nostalgia and Ecological Citizenship

A Nostalgist's Map of America traces the geographical and imaginary journeys of a migrant speaker, whose nostalgic longing for a home is gradually supplemented by a diasporic sense of intimacy with the world. And yet, if Boym notes in the conclusion to *The Future of Nostalgia* that such a "[d]iasporic intimacy could be seen as the mutual attraction of two immigrants from different parts of the world or the sense of a precarious coziness of a foreign home" (254), my reading of Ali's poems seeks to demonstrate how such affinities can acquire environmental significance. In this vein, I attempt here to highlight moments in *A Nostalgist's Map of America* where a place- and nature-oriented diasporic intimacy with the world allows for the emergence of a sense of community—or at least a sense of imagined communalities, to harken back to my proposal of this alternative term in my chapter on Derek Walcott—between mobile subjects with vastly different histories of displacement (even if the affinity must remain one-sided in Ali's lyrical poetry). More broadly, then, I wish to point to moments in contemporary poetries of migration where evocations of the "precarious coziness" (Boym 254) of a temporary home entail an awareness of the precariousness of human-nature relations and perhaps even a sense of responsibility for the nonhuman environment. Toward the end of *A Nostalgist's Map of America*, Ali's poems begin to express exactly such an awareness of precariousness and sense of responsibility, suggesting how traditional notions of belonging may be revised in ways that help us to mobilize notions of ecological citizenship.

In *Citizenship and the Environment* (2004), Andrew Dobson uses the term "ecological citizenship" to refer to a "specifically ecological form of post-cosmopolitan citizenship" (89) that is concerned with "non-contractual responsibility [...and] the private as well as the public sphere" (89). I opt for the term "ecological citizenship" rather than for the alternative "environmental citizenship" here both because I am interested in human-world relations that reach beyond the legal, political, and geographical frameworks that the nation-state has historically established in its definitions of citizenship and because it points to a sense of responsibility for the more-than-human world that is important for discussions of belonging and place-attachment without emplacement. Such an expansive notion of ecological citizenship is similar to the one Joni Adamson and Kimberly N. Ruffin discuss in their introduction to *American Studies, Ecocriticism, and Citizenship* (2013). For Adamson and Ruffin, the term "ecological citizenship" brings to the fore questions surrounding "the 'politics of life,' 'nature,' 'environment,' 'justice,' 'citizenship,' and 'belonging'" (2) that matter most in the context of discussions of "cosmopolitanism, nationalism, localism, and environmentalism" (2). Ali's poetry addresses many of the issues just mentioned and in doing so offers glimpses at an expansive, radical kind of ecological citizenship that acknowledges histories of displacement, experiences of migration, and other perspectives of mobility, without erasing the harm that can be caused for human and nonhuman others by people's desire for emplacement.

Maybe more clearly than any other poem in *A Nostalgist's Map of America*, "I See Chile in My Rearview Mirror," the second to last poem in the collection, exposes the extent to which Ali's "mapping of America," his physical, mnemonic, and poetic place-making, depends on a similar sense of critical environmental nostalgia that is informed by perspectives of mobility. The poem depicts the speaker as he is "driving in the desert" in Arizona, where "the rocks/ are under fog, the cedars a temple" (Ali 96, 97). Later in the text, he arrives "in Utah," where he continues "driving, still north" (98), even while continuously looking back south, "keeping the entire hemisphere in view" (96). At the break of the third and fourth stanzas, the speaker notes: "There's Sedona, Nogales// far behind" (96). With the startling economy of an elliptical sentence, Ali here evokes three locations at once: "Sedona" Arizona, as well as the two towns of "Nogales," abutting cities located in the Sonoran Desert on opposite sides of the U.S-Mexican border. The poem alludes to the cities' special geographical position through the line and stanza break "Nogales // far behind" (96), which signals both proximity and distance and calls attention to the arbitrary drawing of borders in service of the modern settler-colonial nation-state. Although the poem does not explicitly address questions of immigration, the speaker's ruminations about the political situation of countries such as Chile, Paraguay, Colombia, and Peru during his own unimpeded northward journey through the United States gestures toward other, more perilous northward journeys undertaken by individuals living southward of the U.S. border with Mexico. At least implicitly, then, the speaker's own mobile perspective—as a recent migrant to the U.S. and temporary inhabitant of the Southwest—raises questions about U.S. immigration policies in the context of the Americas' complex colonial history and the political conflicts that have both fed into and resulted from that history. What is more, it points toward alternative forms of (ecological) citizenship and belonging that do not rely on an anti-immigrant rhetoric of fortified borders.

The beginning of "I See Chile in My Rearview Mirror" evokes the colonial history of the Americas through metaphors of map-making and painting and as such "grimly elaborates the playfully fantastical evocations of Elizabeth Bishop's 'The Map' [1946]" (Ramazani, *Poetry in a Global Age* 73). The allusions to different forms of spatial visualization in the poem draw attention to (geopolitical) processes of territorialization as well as to the (artistic) processes of representation involved in such a project:

The dream of water – what does it harbor?
I see Argentina and Paraguay
under a curfew of glass, their colors
breaking, like oil. The night in Uruguay

is black salt. I'm driving toward Utah,
keeping the entire hemisphere in view –
Colombia vermilion, Brazil blue tar,
some countries wiped clean of color: Peru

is titanium white. [...]

(Ali 96)

By comparing the night in Uruguay to "black salt" and by associating Colombia with "vermillion," Brazil with "blue tar" and Peru with "titanium white," while the "colors" of Argentina and Paraguay are described as "breaking, like oil" (Ali 96), Ali produces a rich tableau of Central and South America in several senses of the word: on one level, his description sketches a portrait of Latin America that seems to emphasize geo- and biodiversity; on another level, it hints at centuries-long economic and environmental exploitation of the region by way of resource extraction. On yet another level, the above lines conjure up a brightly colored schematic map that links the geopolitical (re-)organization of the Americas to the violence of colonization as well as to its legacies. This violence becomes manifest on the continent's map in the form of "countries [that have been] wiped clean of color" (Ali 96), a metaphor alluding to the erasure of Indigenous cultures and the extermination of Indigenous peoples in the Americas by European, and later U.S.-American, colonial powers and their twentieth-century authoritarian successors.

Shahid is in the Southwest driving toward Utah when he commemorates "the disappeared" (Ali 98) of General Pinochet's rule in Chile, people who are all too easily forgotten in the global North. The traveling poet's act of poetic commemoration, his act of poetic witnessing, relies on a critical look back in time and beyond the southern border of the United States, which keeps U.S. settler-colonial and imperial histories in view. What is more, it evokes environmental degradation as a current and future threat to the Americas at large:

... And what else will
this mirror now reason, filled with water?
I see Peru without rain, Brazil
without forests – and here in Utah a dagger

of sunlight: it's splitting – it's the summer
solstice – the quartz center of a spiral.
Did the Anasazi know the darker
answer also – given now in crystal
by the mirrored continent? [...]

(Ali 98)

The above lines play with the notion of turning points and reversals, as marked by the allusion to "the summer/ solstice" and the spiraled stone constructions the Anasazi used to record significant solar events such as the solstice.[15] Apart from acknowledging the scientific achievements of one of the foremost pre-modern high cultures of the Americas, this passage once more centers on the mirror as the poem's pivotal image: it is a symbol of poetic language as a means of representation and a symbol of the speaker's perspective of mobility and retrospection.

According to Jahan Ramazani, the mirror in "I See Chile" constitutes "both a spatial and a temporal metaphor for reflecting on the global South, even as [the poem's speaker] journey's northward" (*Poetry in a Global Age* 72). Ali's poem, he adds, also brings to mind Jean Baudrillard's philosophical travel diary *America* (1989), which begins with an account of a drive through U.S. American deserts that comes to stand metaphorically for "endless futurity and the obliteration of the past in an instantaneous time" (Ramazani, *Poetry in a Global Age* 72). By choosing the image of the mirror, a metaphor that also features in the poem "Amsterdam" by James Merrill quoted in the epigraph to "I See Chile," Ali's poem suggests that it is art's purpose to make visible what could otherwise not be seen, even if artistic representations are necessarily selective and distorting. What is more, Shahid's poem acknowledges and writes against these distortions, as it projects faraway geographies and histories of violence back onto the U.S. If the Americas are figured as a "mirrored continent" in Ali's text, this is also to imply that the (post-)colonial violence and environmental destruction that Shahid observes in Latin America have their counterpart in the U.S. The last poem of the collection, "Snow on the Desert" suggests as much, while also tentatively evoking place-based affiliations between different migratory and displaced peoples that are tentatively decolonial and environmental and thus point to the particular kind of ecological citizenship I believe emerges in Ali's text.

"Snow on the Desert" begins by situating the speaker precisely in time and space. Shahid is driving through the Sonoran Desert in order to take his sister Sameetah to Tucson International Airport "on January 19, 1987" (Ali 100). Together with the speaker's memories of a concert by Begum Akthar, the "Queen of Ghazals," in New Delhi also mentioned in the text, the poem's narrative once more alludes to Shahid's migratory background and his identity as a world traveler among other world travelers. On the way to the airport, Shahid contemplates the frozen cacti on the roadside and then muses:

---

15   See, among others, the archeological site described by Anna Sofaer, Volker Zinser, and Rolf M. Sinclair in their article "A Unique Solar Marking Construct" from the October 19, 1979, issue of *Science*.

The Desert Smells Like Rain: in it I read:
The syrup from which sacred wine is made

is extracted from the saguaros each
summer. The Papagos place it in jars,

where the last of it softens, then darkens
into a color of blood [...]

(Ali 100–101; emphasis original)

The Desert Smells Like Rain is the title of a 1982 book by the renowned agricultural ecologist, conservation biologist, sustainability activist, and poet Gary Paul Nabhan. Nabhan's book about the Sonoran Desert carries the subtitle *A Naturalist in O'odham Country*, a phrasing that resonates with the title of *A Nostalgist's Map of America*. An ethnobotanical study, *The Desert Smells Like Rain* not only provides detailed descriptions of the flora of the Sonoran Desert, it also records stories and cultural practices of the Tohono O'odham, who are referred to by their Anglo-American name, Papago, in Ali's poem.[16] In particular, Nabhan's book describes the *O'odham Himdag*, or the "Papago Way" of cultivating the desert, a sustainable form of agriculture that has been practiced by the Tohono for centuries (Nabhan xi). Having survived in competition with other agricultural techniques introduced to the Tohono by early Spanish missionaries, the *O'odham Himdag* is nowadays threatened due to urban expansion and the increasingly severe droughts plaguing the Southwest. Together with Tohono-led projects, the work of non-Indigenous ethnobotanists such as Nabhan has been part of an effort to keep Tohono environmental knowledges about the deserts of the Southwest alive and, where possible, learn from the century-old practices in order to respond more effectively to the current climate crisis.

Ali's reference to Nabhan's book in "Snow on the Desert" suggests that the speaker's perception of the natural world around him is, at least in part, influenced by the Tohono view of the desert. Or, more accurately, it is influenced by the poet's

---

16   The Indigenous people today referred to by their own name as the "O'odham" were once considered three separate tribes by anthropologists who used settlement patterns to differentiate between the sedentary Pima (also known as the Akimel O'odham or "River People"), the nomadic Hia C'ed O'odams or "Sand People," and the seasonally migratory Papago (also Tohono O'odham or "Desert People"). As Peter M. Booth observes, the Tohono O'odham abandoned their seasonal migrations at the beginning of the twentieth century, when U.S. government-sponsored wells allowed for new methods of year-round irrigation and farming ("Tohono O'odham"). For a short history of the Tohono O'odham, see Booth's entry on the Tohono O'odham in the *Encyclopedia of North American Indians*. For a more detailed account of the O'odham of Santa Cruz Valley, located between Tucson and the Mexican border town of Nogales, see Thomas E. Sheridan's *Landscapes of Fraud: Mission Tumacácori, the Baca Float, and the Betrayal of the O'odham* (2007).

reading of *The Desert Smells Like Rain*, that is, of a book by a non-Tohono natural-ist and environmental activist of Lebanese-American descent, who is known for his interdisciplinary and community-focused writing and his Thoreau-inspired "practice of sauntering in the Sonoran borderlands" (Fiskio 141). Nabhan's own ethnic background, family history of migration, and habit of walking and driving in the desert to connect with different people, cultures, and knowledges mean-ingfully link the author to the migrant poet Shahid and to the mobile as well as environmental sensibilities Ali expresses in "Snow on the Desert." The Lebanese-American ethnobotanist's commitment to recording and transmitting the cultural and environmental knowledges and practices of the Tohono O'odham to a broader audience, where such knowledges furthermore echoes Ali's interest in the human and geological histories of the Sonoran Desert.

Much like *The Desert Smells Like Rain*, "Snow on the Desert" reflects on the strange beauty of the desert environments of the Southwest, the conditions of human exis-tence in view of the unfathomable geological age of the desert, the land-based wis-dom of Tohono ritualistic practices, and the region's complex history of settlement and displacement. Like the references to Richard Shelton and Georgia O'Keeffe dis-cussed earlier, the juxtaposition of quotes from Nabhan's book with Shahid's per-sonal impressions and memories of the desert emphasize the speaker's desire to en-gage deeply, and through a range of different source materials, with his temporary place of residence. The fact that Ali does not engage with Indigenous sources here, but instead turns to Nabhan's book about the Tohono, just as he turns to Shelton and O'Keefe's representations of the desert, must be acknowledged. What I would argue, though, is that Ali's choice of source materials, whether intentional or not, is what makes his approach to ecopoetic place-making so intriguing: it is an approach to place-making that highlights the perspective of migrants and arrivants like him-self, without disavowing the vastly different place-sense that comes from long-term inhabitation and the place-specific and community-centered cultural and environ-mental practices that can emerge from this kind of emplacement.

By entwining descriptions of Sonoran Desert landscapes with quotations from literary and non-literary texts about them, "Snow on the Desert" depicts places as material and cultural, real and imagined. At the same time, the representations of human-nature relations in the poem acquire a distinctly social and ethical dimen-sion, especially because they link people of different origins through their shared experience of particular geographies as well as through their collaborative produc-tion (in the case of Nabhan and the Tohono as well as in the case of Nabhan and Ali) of environmentally resonant texts about them. After situating Ali on the road toward Tucson International Airport, "Snow on the Desert" continues:

the saguaros have opened themselves, stretched
out their arms to rays millions of years old,

in each ray a secret of the planet's
origin, the rays hurting each cactus

into memory, a human memory –
for they are human, the Papagos say:

not only because they have arms and veins
and secrets. But because they too are a tribe,

vulnerable to massacre. [...]

(Ali 101–02)

Probably the most iconic mega-flora of the Southwest, Saguaros are endemic to the Sonoran Desert and threatened in particularly dramatic ways by urbanization, pollution, and the effects of climate change on the region. By calling these giant cacti a "tribe," Ali evokes a community of victims of violence, oppression, and displacement that includes both his speaker Shahid and the Tohono, whose culture barely survived Spanish colonization and settlement, Mexican rule, and, later, the U.S.-American take-over of the region since the second half of the nineteenth century (Nabhan 68). Ali's acknowledgment of O'odham oral traditions and mythology as the source for his representation of Saguaros as a tribe ("for they are human, the Papago say," Ali 102) constitute an attempt to establish trans-ethnic affiliations with the Tohono. Or at least it imagines that (temporary) peaceful cohabitation is possible and that the sense of place of mobile subjects, but especially of arrivants like Ali's speaker can be enriched by an encounter with the place-based culture and history of displacement of natives like the Tohono, as long as the encounter is based on a shared appreciation for the local natural world and respectful engagement with the cultural practices it has inspired—be they dry-gardening or story-telling.

By including in his poem aspects of the traditional Tohono worldview that challenge anthropocentrism, "Snow on the Desert" draws attention to the limits of settler-European perspectives on nature and nature poetry. What if one were to read the reference to the personhood of the Saguaros not only as a metaphor? The arising implications would certainly be of an eco-ethical nature, raising urgent questions of the kind addressed by Joni Adamson and Kimberly N. Ruffin in their introduction to *American Studies, Ecocriticism, and Citizenship* (2013), which discusses radical notions of ecological citizenship in order to explore "ancient and new trans-species understandings of who and *what* can be granted the right to exist, maintain, and regenerate life cycles and evolutionary processes" (11–12). By figuring the endangered nonhuman species of the Saguaros as a tribe "vulnerable to massacre," Ali's poem establishes an ethical framework in which the cacti may be granted a "right to exist, maintain, and regenerate life cycles and evolutionary processes" (Adamson and Ruffin 4). What is more, the poem opens a space of social-ecological inquiry in which such a right must be negotiated with an eye to the region's colonial history while also attention to the different forms of marginalization that are relevant to debates surrounding (ecological) citizenship in the U.S., debates which include the ongoing marginalization of Indigenous people and (im)migrants when it comes to environmental concerns.

Aside from reinforcing the poem's environmental implications, the references to Nabhan's book in the poem pay respect to the traditional Tohono O'odham way of thinking about and inhabiting the desert, which, if we believe Nabhan and researchers like him, can provide valuable lessons for more sustainable ways of living in the deserts of the Southwest and, perhaps, in the expanding deserts of the world at large. One of these lessons is the importance of taking seriously precarious Indigenous environmental knowledges, a point I also address in my chapter on CHamoru poet Craig Santos Perez. Since the late 1980s and early 1990s when Ali wrote and published *A Nostalgist's Map of America*, lessons of "ecosystem people" (Gadgil and Guha qtd. in Buell, "Uses and Abuses" 108) such as the Tohono O'odham have perhaps become even more valuable, not least because the ecosystems they inhabit have become more precarious. After all, water shortage and irresponsible urban planning are not only increasingly infringing on already limited Indigenous land rights but also increasingly putting bioregions such as the Sonoran Desert at risk. The works of contemporary ecopoets writing about the deserts of the Southwest such as poet and geographer Eric Magrane, co-editor with poet and nonfiction writer Christopher Cokinos of *The Sonoran Desert: A Literary Field Guide* (2016) and with Linda Russo, Sarah de Leeuw, and Craig Santos Perez of *Geopoetics in Practice* (2019), testify to the environmental challenges the region faces. Written several decades earlier, Ali's collection is less explicit about these changes and challenges, while highlighting all the more forcefully why emerging environmental imaginaries for the Southwest must acknowledge histories of displacement and perspectives of mobility.

While comparisons of humans and trees are common in ecopoetry, such as in Eric Magrane's Sonoran Desert poem "Mesquite," probably because such a comparison is expedient from an environmental perspective, images of rootedness cannot do full justice to the mobile environmental imaginaries that emerge in Ali's poems about transitory desert dwellers. As noted earlier, Ali does not compare Saguaros to human beings on accounts of their roots (Saguaros commonly only have one deep root, the tap root, and otherwise rely on a rhizomatic network of shallow roots near the surface), but on accounts of their shared vulnerability to violence. *A Nostalgist's Map of America* is environmentally resonant, then, not because every poem in the collection is explicitly environmentalist, but because it employs figurations of environmental nostalgia together with other poetic strategies of place-making to imagine alternative forms of place-attachments that are attuned to perspectives of mobility. Toward the end of Ali's collection, his nostalgic ecopoetics of mobility begins to gesture not only toward the migrant's longing for a diasporic intimacy with the world but also toward alternative kinds of ecological citizenship, suggesting that histories of oppression and displacement do not preclude an individual's ability to establish meaningful relationships to the land, while also acknowledging that these kinds of histories and experiences affect people's relationship with the nonhuman world in crucial ways.

A critical and open notion of ecological citizenship, I want to suggest in closing, must be based on environmental imaginaries that acknowledge perspectives of mobility and engage in one way or another with the ongoing impact of settler-colonialism, environmental racism, and eco-nativism. Acknowledging the place-making practices of migrants and victims of displacement, Ali's poems affirm, is crucial for the development of more mobile environmental imaginaries and more inclusive forms of ecological citizenship, as is creating opportunities for migrants to engage with a variety of literary and non-literary texts as well as with works of art about the places they inhabit, whether only temporarily or more permanently. Although *A Nostalgist's Map of America* is pervaded by the poet's intense longing for community, belonging, and a home, this longing is never fulfilled. While the collection thus offers clues about what a diasporic intimacy with the world and more inclusive forms of ecological citizenships might look like, it can do so mainly because it continues to place its migrant speaker into a world devoid of people except an occasional close friend or relative. Put differently, the reasons why migrants such as Ali might look for a sense of belonging and meaningful place-connection in nature rather than in the company of people may not only or even primarily stem from an environmental interest in and care for the nonhuman world of a certain place, but also from the experience of not being welcomed into the *human* community of a certain place, region, or nation. In order for alternative forms of ecological citizenship to effectively counter econativist arguments for why some people, and specifically people of color and migrants from the former colonies of the Global South, should not be or live in certain places, they need to be attentive to environmental racism and xenophobia, even as they have to acknowledge the right of some marginalized communities, including Indigenous communities, to make decisions about who is welcome on their land and for how long.

5. Queering Ecological Desire: Post-Mobility and Apocalyptic Environmental Ethics in the Poetry of Etel Adnan

As I have suggested in the previous chapter, Agha Shahid Ali's collection *A Nostalgist's Map of America* (1991) uses intertextual references to place-based works of literature and art to express a deep longing for a diasporic intimacy with the world that challenges econativist ideas about belonging and emplacement and, in doing so, points toward more mobile and more inclusive forms of ecological citizenship that acknowledge the experiences and perspectives of the displaced. A similar nature-oriented longing can be found in Etel Adnan's poetry, which expresses a queer ecological desire for an intimate connection with the more-than-human world from a different perspective toward mobility. Where Ali's migrant speaker Shahid is looking back at past migrations but also at those still constantly on the move, the perspective evoked in Adnan's poetry is one informed by two different kinds of post-mobility: a re-orientation toward nature in the aftermath of the disorientation caused by migration and in light of an acute awareness of the increasing immobility that comes with old age.[1]

In a short poetic essay, entitled "The Cost for Love We Are Not Willing to Pay," published on the occasion of the exhibition of her paintings at the thirteenth docu-

---

1   The term "post-mobility" occasionally appears in publications in the social sciences, usually in the context of work-related mobility or migration, such as in the introduction to the edited collection *Spatial Mobility, Migration, and Living Arrangements* (2014), edited by Can M. Aybek, Johannes Huinink, and Raya Muttarak. As the editors argue, the "Post-mobility Phase" (9) is one of three stages in the life course of mobile individuals, or in *Spatial Mobility of Migrant Workers in Beijing, China* (2015) by Ran Liu. Most of these economic, sociological, and political science publications use the term in a fairly commonsensical manner, denoting a time period of indeterminate and flexible length after an especially significant act of mobility, in which the aftereffects of that previous act of mobility remain felt. This is one way in which I use the term. Additionally, I use the term to denote a time after mobility in a related yet slightly different sense that is connected to the use of the term mobility in the context of disability studies, namely as a time in which the subject is no longer mobile, i.e., able to move in the same ways as it was before.

menta 2012 in Kassel, Germany, the Lebanese-American artist and poet Etel Adnan contemplates the different kinds of love she has been exploring in her art throughout her long and prolific career. Before discussing her anti-war activism and her lesbianism, she uses this essay to reflect on a world in crisis and on the reasons why it may already be too late to avoid environmental catastrophe:

> Planet Earth is [...] the house we are discarding. We definitely don't love her [... b]ecause the price for the love that will save her would reach an almost impossible level. It would require that we change radically our ways of life, that we give up many of our comforts, our toys, our gadgets, and above all our political and religious mythologies. We would have to create a new world [...]. We're not ready to do all that. So we are, very simply, doomed. (Adnan, "The Cost" 6)

Adnan's assessment of the current state of "Planet Earth" palliates nothing. It is because, she argues, those of us living in relatively more affluent countries do not appreciate nature enough and instead cling to our luxuries and outdated ways of thinking, even if they are destructive of the world, that "we are, very simply, doomed." In light of the apocalyptic scenario Adnan conjures here, one might expect her to give herself over to quiet despair. Yet, Adnan continues to speak. Despite the apparent hopelessness of the situation, her poetry expresses a radical love for nature that hopes to seduce readers into loving it enough to consider paying the price necessary to save the world. Indeed, Adnan understands her poetry not only as a means to capture what we are about to lose but also as a means "to create [the] new world" we so urgently need.

Adnan's poetry about the more-than-human world addresses matters of politics, ethics, and poetics by reflecting on human-nature relations from a perspective of migration. While there are no ecocritical publications on Adnan's poetry yet, at least to my knowledge, a few scholars have addressed issues of import to my own analysis. Mahwash Shoaib, for instance, examines the complexity of spatial configurations in Adnan's collection *There*. Shoaib's ideas about questions of location in this extended poem sequence are relevant to my discussion of place-making in Adnan's work. Teresa Villa-Ignacio's argument about the ways in which *There* "envisions and discursively practices ethical encounter as the making-present of a virtual, postapocalyptic, planetarily-conscious community of the future" (305), in turn, resonates with my analysis of the temporal dimensions of Adnan's environmental imaginary. So does Eric Keenaghan's assessment of Adnan's poem "Sea" as a text that "point[s] to the future" by engaging with past and present traumas as well as "global crises" (601) and as a text that draws readers "into continuous movement, buoyed by sensuous thought and feeling" (601). Taking inspiration from these and selected other publications, I focus on the mobile environmental imaginary put forward by Adnan's collections *There* (1997), *Seasons* (2008), *Sea and Fog* (2012), and *Night* (2016), collections that evoke a migrant's desire for meaningful encounters with the more-than-human world as well as an apocalyptic environmental ethics informed by experiences of mobility that grapples with the certainty of death, but does not abandon hope for a better future.

In order to show how mobility troubles and makes strange human-nature relations in Adnan's poetry, I draw from concepts and theories of queer ecocriticism and queer phenomenology. Specifically, my analysis is indebted to a number of "'queer ecocritical' trajectories" (Sandilands, "Queer Life" 305) that Catriona Mortimer-Sandilands has outlined in her writings over the past two decades: first, her suggestions that a queer phenomenology might help us to challenge the kind of ethics of proximity that is often promoted by ecocriticism ("Whose There is There" 66); second, her observations concerning a radical rethinking of human-nature relations of the kind Adnan demands in her documenta essay that require a queering of our desire for nature ("Desiring Nature, Queering Ethics"); and finally, her argument that a "genuinely queer ecology" entails an interrogation not only of the narratives that structure humans' relations to place but also to time, that is, not only of humans' relations to nature but also of humans' relations to "future nature" ("Queer Life?" 309). Drawing on these and related queer ecocritical trajectories, I show by building on Sara Ahmed's work that Adnan's ecopoetry of migration engages in a *queering of dwelling* by transforming her speaker's *migrant orientation* into a perpetual process of reorientation toward nature. Approaching the natural world from a perspective of post-mobility, I argue in drawing on Catriona Sandilands, that Adnan's poetry is invested in a queering of *ecological desire* that points to the value as well as to the limits of an *erotogenic ethics* based on touch in the context of migration. Examining human-nature relations in light of post-mobility in yet another sense, namely the kind that recognizes the limits imposed on physical mobility by old age, I conclude the chapter by demonstrating how Adnan's poetry employs poetic strategies of disorientation to reach toward what can be described with Nicole Seymour as *queer ecological empathy* and an imagination of a *queer ecological futurity* in the face of apocalypse.

Etel Adnan: A Lebanese-American Poet of the World

Born in Lebanon in 1925, Etel Adnan attended the École Supérieure des Lettres in Beirut, before moving to Paris in 1950 to study philosophy at the Sorbonne. Having completed her studies in Paris in 1955, Adnan moved to the United States to pursue postgraduate work in philosophy at U.C. Berkeley. After a short stay at Harvard during the academic year of 1957/58, she moved back to California and took up a lecturer position at the Dominican University of California in San Rafael, where she taught philosophy of art for fourteen years. During her time in the Bay Area, Adnan met many poets associated with emerging countercultural movements such as the San

Francisco Renaissance, whose poetic practices changed her perspective on poetry in profound ways, as did the French-Algerian War (1954–1962), eventually leading her publish her first poems in English in protest of the Vietnam War (1954–1975). In 1972, Adnan moved back to Beirut to work as a journalist, which is where she met her life partner, the Syrian painter and sculptor Simone Fattal, and experienced the outbreak of the Lebanese Civil War. In 1977, Adnan and Fattal returned to Paris, where Adnan wrote her acclaimed anti-war novel *Sitt Marie Rose* (Orig. Fr. 1978; Transl. Arab. 1977), a fictional account of life in Beirut before and during the civil war. In 1979, the couple once again moved to California, where Adnan continued to work as a writer and painter, while Fattal founded Post-Apollo Press, a small pressed focused on poetry and experimental writing. After having lived in Sausalito, a small town to the north of San Francisco, for several decades, the pair again moved to Paris, where Adnan died in 2021 at the age of 96. During the final decades of her life, Etel Adnan wrote politically engaged and emotionally engaging nature poetry full of details of the physical world, while also examining life in a time of many wars. Adnan was thus not only a "poet of the world" in a cosmopolitan sense insomuch as she continued to cultivate affiliations and connections to multiple places and cultural traditions in her poems. As I propose in this chapter, she was also a "poet of the world" in an environmental sense, particularly because she wrote poetry that addresses human beings' relationship to and responsibility toward the natural world in the context of mobility.

Etel Adnan is the author of several works of non-fiction and more than a dozen books of poetry, the last of which was published in 2020, a year before her death in November 2021. Despite her incredible productivity during the last two decades of her life, Etel Adnan's literary oeuvre at large remains woefully understudied (see Majaj and Amireh 1–2). To this day, her best known and most widely discussed publication beside her novel is *L'Apocalypse Arabe* (Fr. 1980, Engl. 1989), a graphically innovative collection of poetry that deals with the 1976 Tel al-Zaatar massacre, during which Christian Syrian militia forces killed several thousand Palestinian civilians in a refugee camp northeast of Beirut (see Mejcher-Atassi, Seymour-Jorn, Donovan). In contrast to *The Arab Apocalypse*, Etel Adnan's poetry collections *There: In the Light and the Darkness of the Self and of the Other* (1997), *Seasons* (2008), *Sea and Fog* (2012), *Night* (2016), *Surge* (2018), *Time* (2019), and *Shifting the Silence* (2020) have so-far only received very little critical attention, which seems to be, at least in part, due to the fact that the more-than-human world features prominently in many of these volumes. Indeed, when scholars analyze Adnan's literary works, they often do so by reading them as Arab American literature and/or war literature.[2] Her treatment of nature

---

2   Yasir Suleiman and Michelle Hartman, for example, identify Adnan as one of those Arab American poets who use jazz to negotiate their own ethnic/racial identity in an U.S. American context. Philip Metres mentions Adnan in an essay on the poetry of Abu Ghraib, classi-

seems to pose a challenge to such classifications. And yet, as Gregory Orfalea and Šarīf al-Mūsā note in their introduction to the anthology *Grape Leaves: A Century of Arab American Poetry* (2000), the natural world in Adnan's oeuvre "is to be [...] negotiated with" (xxvii), even if one wants to maintain that her "apocalyptic poetry [...] in beat fractures" (xix) offers "very little of what is an American (Emersonian) genre: nature, or pastoral, poetry" (xxvii). In this chapter, I attempt precisely such a negotiation, demonstrating how the human-nature relations Adnan evokes in some of her more recent and indeed increasingly apocalyptic collections are shaped by experiences of (im)mobility.

In recent years, including the years following her death, Etel Adnan has received more attention as a painter than a poet. Adnan turned to painting while living in the U.S. during the late 1950s, a time when the ongoing anti-colonial struggles in the Middle East and North Africa caused her to look beyond the French she had grown up with and for "a language without a language problem" (Adnan qtd. in Khal 102). A detailed investigation of the many ways in which her visual art is in conversation with her poetry is outside the scope of this chapter. Suffice it to say that there are interesting parallels in how Adnan approaches depictions of landscapes in her paintings and how she approaches evocations of natural phenomena in her poetry. Indeed, what Cole Swensen notes in relation to Adnan's paintings is also to a large extent true for her poetry: "[Adnan] has made the act of painting into the bridge between self and world that lets consciousness disperse, lets the I overflow the body and spread out across that world as a field of bright attention traversing an earth that will not stop" (145). As this description of Adnan's artistic process as an act of translation of perception and experience suggests, thinking about the environmental imaginary of mobility that emerges in her poetry does not only entail thinking about place and time, it also entails thinking about the traveling body as well as the traveling mind.

---

fying her as one of many Arab American poets who, after 9/11 "dramatized the complexities not only of the Arab world but also of Arab American life, of living in the hyphen" ("Remaking/Unmaking" 1599). Susan S. Friedman reflects on the "Poetics of Home and Diaspora" in the works of several ethnic American women writers, noting that "[l]ong before 9/11, Etel Adnan wrote about living, speaking, and writing in the body of an Arab woman traveling away from 'home' where no one feels 'at home'" (207). Scholars focusing on Adnan's war writing too have often emphasized her position as an Arab woman writer, who "has used women's traditional role as witnesses and keepers of memories to write a different story about motherhood and suffering" (Afshar 186) in times of conflict, or who, as a result of that conflict has "interrogated the hierarchic power structures of Arabic society—the lingering national, political, communal, sexual, and aesthetic issues that only emerged more clearly during the war—in a more radical way than had previously been attempted" (Alcalay 88). More recently, Christiane Schlote has discussed Adnan's choice of the genre of literary non-fiction in texts such as *In the Heart of the Heart of Another Country* as a choice that foregrounds the special pressures surrounding "civil rights, the ethics of engagement, committed writing, and their experience of living abroad" (284) for Arab American women writers in the context of the Iraq War.

Etel Adnan's nature poetry is often arranged in long sequences of solid blocks that one might mistake for poetic prose, if it weren't for the very deliberate placement of line breaks. Despite her poetry's emphasis on natural phenomena typical of Northern California and San Francisco Bay, the Middle Eastern landscapes of her youth continue to shape Adnan's migratory poetic imagination, as the following two stanzas from the beginning of *Seasons* demonstrate:

> O the Syrian desert mounted by its young emperors in the steel
> days of Rome! Its salt has melted in the Euphrates. Further north
> the spring has planted miles of orchards. Frantic flowers whisper
> to the wind. Birds use corridors of air within the air for their flight.
> Their shadows come from the soul. It is necessary not to stay still;
> the voyage is family.
>
> I want to walk in mountainous countries. Some nations are
> sitting and crying in front of screens larger than their borders.
> Their brains are starting to fall apart. I listen. Of course, all this
> is perceived as silence, in the midst of storms, under heaven's
> explosion.

(Adnan, Seasons 3–4)

Concerned with history, politics, the ethics of speaking/writing in a time of crisis, as well as with questions of nature and mobility, Adnan's poetic language is sparse yet colorful, producing effects of concreteness without relinquishing the possibility of a complex, at times idiosyncratic symbolism. In the quote above, for example, references to the Syrian desert and fallen empires as well as to "storms" and "heaven's explosion" allude to military conflict. At the same time, the arrival of "spring" points to the reawakening of the natural world, urging both birds and human beings to move in a defiant affirmation of life. Like this excerpt, Adnan's poems frequently bring together seemingly contingent aphoristic statements into highly evocative scenes with multiple layers of meaning. Pervaded by a stubborn hope for renewal and change, her political nature poetry alternates between seemingly disengaged, descriptive passages, in which the speaker recedes to the background, and more traditionally lyrical, contemplative passages, in which an emotionally involved speaker voices her perspectives on the natural world. These perspectives are often perspectives of mobility.

Even those collections in which nature features most prominently make it clear that the non-human world can never be separate from the human world. The following stanza from *Seasons*, for instance, suggests that experiences of migration shape not only people's perceptions about the world but also their preferences for certain types of cultural and artistic production, in this case for the fast-paced, more immediately accessible art of film as opposed to literature. At the same time, it conjures up the threat humanity's insatiable hunger for space and careless acts of pollution pose to the environment:

> In a season of migration movies are preferred to books. Luminosity is a different language, the result of a confluence of methods used by Nature. A reel played backwards, that's the future. Wherever one looks one finds that space is filled with the past along with steep cliffs, big fires. Although the moon escaped the disaster, the future will not. Poisons connect with their destination in beautiful plants. A lawyer loses his argument. The voyage is delayed.
>
> (Adnan, *Seasons* 2)

In this quote, like at various other moments in her collections, Adnan's poetry weaves together evocations of nature, history, and culture into a series of thought-provoking tableaus that often allow for multiple, sometimes contradictory readings. By drawing attention to processes of perception and representation, Adnan's poems hint at the special role that allusive poetic language might play for a project of ecopoetic place-making that views writing about the non-human environment in a world in crisis as a necessary labor of love. Importantly, then, Adnan is not only a poet of the world for whom the (aftermath of) mobility is key for understanding her own place in a world moving toward different kinds of endings, she is also a poet of the word who assigns poetic language and expression an important role in producing alternative environmental imaginaries in the face of impending apocalypse.

Queering Dwelling: Migrant Orientations and the Politics of Reorientation

In her documenta essay, Adnan discusses migration as a profoundly unsettling and disorienting experience that lastingly affected her relationship to the natural world. Reflecting on her indebtedness to ideas of a "fundamental unity of love" (Adnan, "The Cost" 5) expressed in both Western and Sufi mysticism, Adnan recalls "two passions that did not concern human beings, but that at turns took center stage" (5) in her life. As she reveals, the first of these passions was directed at the Mediterranean Sea of her childhood. The second one, she explains, only manifested once she arrived at the West Coast of the United States:

> A few decades later, I settled in California. During the first years there, I carried within me the feeling of a deep uprootedness. Living north of San Francisco, near the other side of the Golden Gate Bridge, I developed a familiarity with Mount Tamalpaïs, a mountain that dominates the scene. Gradually, the mountain be-

came a reference point. I began to orient myself by its presence, or a view of it in the distance. It became a companion. ("The Cost" 5)

Adnan here emphasizes the "feeling of a deep uprootedness" that plagued her after relocating to Sausalito, a feeling that only began to abate, when she started to develop a "familiarity" with the place she had moved to. Specifically, her sense of displacement lessened once she started "to orient" herself by the "presence" of Mount Tamalpais, a mountain that not only quite literally "dominates the scene" in Marin County, but that would also dominate her artistic imagination, at least as far as her paintings are concerned. According to Adnan, Mount Tamalpais became more than just an important "reference point" in her new place of residence; it became a cherished "companion," implying an intimate, emotional connection to this landmark. In Adnan's poetry, the mountain as a primary means of orientation is frequently replaced by other natural phenomena such as the seasons, the sea, or fog, as her collections' titles indicate. This shift in focus, I suggest, is indicative of the *mobile* as well as the complex *temporal* environmental imaginary in Adnan's poetic works. To expand on this, in the following, I begin to explore how this environmental imaginary is shaped by experiences of mobility by asking what it means for Adnan's migrant speaker to be oriented by and toward the natural world. Specifically, I suggest that Adnan's poetry depicts place-making in the aftermath of migration as a never-ending process of reorientation toward nature that produces a queering of traditional notions of dwelling.

In her book *Queer Phenomenology: Orientations, Objects, Others* (2006), Sara Ahmed re-conceptualizes the politics of being in the world as a matter of being oriented in space and toward certain objects rather than other ones. All orientations, she argues, either fall in line with dominant social, cultural, and moral codes, or run counter to them. Orientations thus "shape not only how we inhabit space, but how we apprehend this world of shared inhabitance as well as 'who' or 'what' we direct our energy and attention toward" (Ahmed 3). "Queer orientations," she suggests, are "those that don't line up, which by seeing the world 'slantwise' allow other objects to come into view" (Ahmed 107). Hinting at the difference between the conventional objects of phenomenology and these queer "other objects," Ahmed notes that phenomenology traditionally offers a way of thinking about "the importance of lived experience" as well as about "the significance of nearness or what is ready-to-hand" (2). By contrast, "queer phenomenology," she suggests, "might start by redirecting our attention toward different objects, those that are 'less proximate' or even those that deviate or are deviant" (Ahmed 3). Similarly, Adnan's nature poetry foregrounds questions of inhabitance and processes of apprehension from a deviating perspective of migration. In the course of her poetic career, Adnan has increasingly turned toward the more-than-human world as the primary subject of her poetry, even though the human tragedies of a world in turmoil, which are so central to her earlier works, have never disappeared entirely from her poems. Furthermore, although Adnan's poetry values lived experience and that which is "ready-to-hand," nature remains a deviant object of orientation in her poems not only because of the persistence with which she engages with it in a world that does not have enough love for it, but also because she continues to approach it from the perspective of post-mobility, which makes it a "less proximate" object of attention.

While Ahmed does not actually discuss the natural world as a queer object of orientation in *Queer Phenomenology*, she addresses how experiences of migration effect a queering of people's orientations toward the world. Suggesting that orientations do not only matter for what objects we turn our attention to but also for "how we 'find our way'" and "how we come to 'feel at home'" (Ahmed 7), she writes:

> Migration could be described as a process of disorientation and reorientation: as bodies 'move away' as well as 'arrive,' as they reinhabit spaces. [...] The disorientation of the sense of home, as the 'out of place' or 'out of line' effect of unsettling arrivals, involves what we could call a *migrant orientation*. This orientation might be described as the lived experience of facing at least two directions: toward a home that has been lost, and to a place that is not yet home. (9–10; emphasis added)

Adnan's poetry dramatizes the disorienting effects of migration and displacement as well as processes of reorientation in and through nature, and in doing so engages in what Ahmed calls the "work of inhabiting space" (7), or as I would call it, an (eco)poetic project of place-making. If Adnan's poems thus act as "homing devices" (Ahmed 9), they do not do so under the premise that a migrant's sense of place can simply be restored to its pre-mobile state, or that such a restoration would necessarily be desirable.

Instead of figuring a "migrant orientation" as a transitional state that can be overcome by successful reorientation and emplacement, Adnan's poetry draws attention to the fact that human-place relations may permanently acquire a different quality as a consequence of migration and forced displacement, even if migrants or displaced individuals eventually return to a life of relative immobility. As Adnan writes in her collection *Seasons*: "We live in many places, experience different telluric spirits. At / the end, we'll live in all these various places simultaneously" (43), and later in *Sea and Fog*: "What does it mean to belong to land? For those of us who live / away from our private history, the question never heals" (73). If, as Ahmed suggests, "the starting point for orientation is the point from which the world unfolds: the 'here' of the body and the 'where' of its dwelling" (8), and if orientations thus are about "the intimacy of bodies and their dwelling places" (Ahmed 8), then the queer orientations toward nature evoked in Adnan's poetry are exactly the ones that deviate from those conventions in that they neither present mobility as a necessary obstacle to nor bodily proximity as a necessary condition for such intimacy. In doing so, they challenge the eco-nativist logic that the idea of dwelling is sometimes associated with, particularly in its Heideggerian, "geophilosophical" tradition (Garrard, "Heidegger, Heaney" 167).[3] Paying attention to orientations in Adnan, I read her collections *There*, *Seasons*, and *Sea and Fog* as works of ecopoetry that explore the lasting aftereffects of migration on human-nature relations by enacting a queer reorientation toward nature. I argue that Adnan's poetry moves from evocations of the disorientations caused by (forced) displacement in *There* to evocations of continuous reorientation toward the natural world in *Seasons* and *Sea and Fog*. Through extended poetic and philosophical musings on the profound materiality and locatedness of Being, Adnan's poetry questions ideas of permanent emplacement as a prerequisite for authentic dwelling and instead points to an ecopoetics of post-mobility.

Many of Adnan's poems allude to migration, displacement, and mobility more generally as events with a potentially disorienting effect. As the poet puts it in "The Manifestation of the Voyage" from *The Spring Flowers Own & The Manifestation of the Voyage* (1990): "Between one airplane and / another / space is disoriented" (44). The book of poems in which this disorienting effect of mobility is explored most prominently is *There: In the Light and the Darkness of the Self and of the Other* (1997), a collection in which, as Mahwash Shoaib points out, "the material political world [...] is coordinated with the inner landscape of thought and memory" (21). *There* consists of thirty-nine sections that combine descriptions of concrete sensory impressions and reflections on human life in a world of conflict, pointing at once to the limits of individual lived experience and the expansiveness of a compassionate imagination. Thirty-eight of the sections that constitute the collection are entitled "There," while the section at the collection's center is entitled "Here," a structure that speaks—to use

---

3   It would go beyond the scope of this study to include a discussion of Heidegger's notion of dwelling, in particular how it relates to poetry; indeed, much has been written on the topic, including about how Heidegger developed his idea of dwelling by thinking about the poetry of the German Romantic poet Friedrich Hölderlin (see Malpas, *Heidegger's Topology* 2006; or Young, *Heidegger's Philosophy of Art* 2000). Suffice it to say that for Heidegger *dwelling* (*wohnen/ Wohnen*) meant a "being-in-the-world" as opposed to *Dasein* (as a "being-here" or "being-there") or the Cartesian "being-in-thought." For Heidegger, dwelling thus not only gestures beyond Being (*Dasein*) because it points to the ways in which human existence is profoundly emplaced and temporal and can only be experienced as such, it also gestures beyond notions of "physical inhabitation" or literal, architectural "home-making" insofar as Heidegger, especially in his later writings, frequently insisted that poetry may be the best way for human beings to approach dwelling, that is, to approximate what "being-in-the-world" means or to engage in "home-making" (or indeed place-making). As Heidegger wrote in an essay that used a phrase from one of Hölderlin's poems as its title: "Poetic creation, which lets us dwell, is a kind of building. Thus, we confront a double demand: for one thing, we are to think of what is called man's existence by way of the nature of dwelling; for another, we are to think of the nature of poetry as a letting-dwell, as a—perhaps even the—distinctive kind of building. If we search out the nature of poetry according to this viewpoint, then we arrive at the nature of dwelling" ("...Poetically Man Dwells..." 213).

Ahmed's phenomenological terminology—to the vertiginous multiplicity of the "less proximate" in comparison to that small part of the world that is "ready-to-hand." At the beginning of the book-length poem, philosophical questions, asyndetic sentence structures, and metaphorical references to human existence as uncontrollable movement through time and space evoke a profound sense of confusion. The speaker asks:

Where are we? where? There is a *where*, because we are,
stubbornly, and have been, and who are we, if not you and
me?

Where are we? Out of History, of his or her story, and back
into it, out in Space and back to Earth, out of the womb, and
then into dust, who are we?

Where is where, where the terror, the love, the pain? Where
the hatred? Where your life, and mine?

(Adnan, *There* 1)

Conjuring a world in which the "terror," "pain," and "hatred" that define both "History" with a capital "H" and "his or her story" appear to outweigh the "love" between "you and / me," the speaker seems to have lost all sense of place or location and, in consequence, also a sense of self, which can only ever exist in relation to others and to the world. The speaker emphasizes that being always means "stubbornly" existing in a specific time and place; yet at the moment evoked in the poem she can find no stable point of reference by which to orient herself, neither in relation to others nor in relation to a world that has descended into chaos. In her reading of *There*, Mahwash Shoaib argues that for Adnan "subjectivity is simply not tied to a single place or time" (25) because an appreciation of "the irony of dwelling as permanent ownership, and the complications of constant mobility [...] leads the poet to a space beyond the dogma of nationalism and other codified aspects of subjectivity as gender and race" (25). While I would agree that *There* frequently troubles the boundaries between the self and the other rhetorically and calls into question notions of permanent or authentic dwelling from a perspective of mobility, I find that the speaker's position in the world, her socio-cultural as well as geographical location in the moment of speaking/writing, continues to reasserts itself in the text. In the end, *There* does not suggest that a life in exile and a life on the move transcend place or identity and defy all borders, whether of nation, gender, ethnicity, or race. Rather, the text explores how subjects react to the disorientation produced by experiences of displacement through reorienting themselves with the help of, and toward, the natural world.

While the beginning of *There* evokes an existential sense of dislocation, the collection later suggests that the speaker's disorientation is, at least in part, the result of physical displacement:

> Am I always going by boat, and where from? Am I crying, and
> why? Are the roads blocked by angels or by soldiers?
>
> I'm asking you to run ahead of yourself and tell me why my
> bones are cold, or am I wanting you to leave my trees alone and
> search for water where the rivers overflow?
>
> Going, into a train and stopping nowhere, because *it is*
> nowhere, with people pouring in, like ripped bags of wheat,
> birds helplessly flying overhead.
>
> (Adnan, *There* 3; emphasis original)

Moving about in a world in turmoil, always "[g]oing," the speaker ends up "nowhere," a place which, as the poem puns, seems to represent both a "NowHere" and a "NoWhere" (see Friedman), as indicated when the speaker projects her feelings of disorientation and vulnerability onto the migratory birds described as "helplessly flying overhead" (Adnan, *There* 3).[4] Being thus disoriented in place, the speaker identifies with many different groups of people. Indeed, in the excerpt, the speaker considers many possible geographical locations and socio-cultural positions for herself: of someone travelling on a "boat" lost on the ocean, maybe a migrant or refugee; of people trying to move through a war zone where roads may be "blocked by angels or by soldiers" at any time; and finally, of people trying to protect their "trees" against encroaching enemy forces. Whether the speaker on the "train" is herself a displaced person or whether she is merely a traveler or commuter contemplating these tragedies from a safe distance, this passage speaks to the profound disorientation produced by physical dislocation. Juxtaposing different kinds of travel, migration, and forced displacement, the poem emphasizes that mobilities must be considered in larger political contexts in order to allow for an examination of how they affect people's relations to place in general and people's perception

---

4   I borrow the orthography of NowHere and NoWhere from Susan S. Friedman's essay "Bodies on the Move: A Poetics of Home and Diaspora," which mentions Adnan's book of travel meditations *Of Cities and Women* (1993) together with several other texts in connection to what Friedman calls "an exploration of the poetics of dislocation" (189). Friedman develops this orthography by drawing from the sociologists Roger Friedland and Deirdre Boden (*NowHere: Space, Time, and Modernity*, 1994) to argue for the home as a "utopia – a no place, a nowhere, an imaginary space longed for, always already lost in the very formation of the idea of home" (192). My reading of Adnan's poetry puts a different stress by emphasizing the importance that place in general and the natural world of different places retains for the poet.

of the natural world in particular. Or to expand on the examples Adnan gives in the text: migrating birds acquire a very different meaning for migrants like the speaker—who interprets their erratic flight as a sign of disorientation—than they do for the common traveler, who might be more likely to enjoy the spectacle of the birds' aerobatics. The same is true for trees, which for Palestinians or the people of Lebanon have become powerful symbols of national identity, contested territorial claims, and displacement of populations, while they may have more economic, romantic, or indeed environmental significance for people in comparable situations elsewhere.[5]

While the locations referred to as "There" and "Here" in the collection initially remain relatively elusive, *There* gradually begins to reveal more information about the particular place in time Adnan's poems speak from and the distant places that occupy the speaker's mind due to personal connections and due to the tragic histories that have been unfolding there. One of the sections of *There*, for example, emphasizes that the speaker belongs to a long line of people who were born elsewhere and then moved "to the Americas" where "Columbus landed [...] bringing stench, / disease and mortal wounds, logs to crucify Indians on" (Adnan 5). Pointing to American colonial history and U.S. involvements in different oversea conflicts as well as her own position in relation to these histories and current events, the speaker reveals that she now lives "somewhere on the West Coast, away from / the front line" (7).[6] Yet, as the speaker emphasizes when contemplating a "conversation" (Adnan 7) she hopes to have with an unidentified addressee, her "twin enemy-brother" (5), possibly an American or Israeli friend or solider, "war is around us, visible at different / degrees of sharpness" (7). For Adnan, who moved to the United States from the same region in which the U.S. was engaged in military action throughout most of the 1990s and 2000s, as for her speaker, what is "There" cannot neatly be kept separate from what is "Here."

---

5   In the poetry of Palestinian-American poets like Naomi Shihab Nye, the olive tree frequently features as a symbol of land loss and for the willful destruction of Palestinian property, family structures, and community by Israeli forces (see, for example, her collection *Transfer*, 2011). For Lebanon, too, trees symbolize the sovereignty of the nation and its territorial integrity. Indeed, not only does the so-called Lebanon cedar crown the country's flag, in the conflict between Lebanon's Hezbollah groups and Israeli forces trees have sometimes been represented as victims of war in their own right, as in a piece written about the environmental consequences of the 2006 Lebanon War by Hassan M. Fattah for the *New York Times* entitled "Casualties of War: Lebanon's Trees, Air and Sea."

6   The reference to a single "front line" in this stanza is deceptive insofar as Adnan refers to many different military conflicts in the poem. As Shoaib notes, *There* not only invokes conflicts in Lebanon and Palestine, but also the Vietnam War (see Adnan, *There* 69) and war in Bosnia. Indeed, as the acknowledgement section of *There* indicates, parts of the poem previously appeared in a special issue of the American literary magazine *Lusitania* on the war in Sarajevo edited by the Jewish Serbian American poet Ammiel Alcalay.

Gradually in *There*, the initial disorientation gives way to what Ahmed calls a "migrant orientation," that is, the "lived experience of facing at least two directions: toward a home that has been lost, and to a place that is not yet home" (10). It is precisely at such a moment, in which both the world "there" and the world "here" come into view simultaneously, that the speaker directs her attention to the natural world:

> Floods, as persistent as the sun could be. It is in the early mornings of the Bay that a peace I would share with you invades my awareness. The light steams out from the ground and carries the soul into a sensation of beginnings. Things seem possible, which have something to do with the thrust of living.

> You may claim the privilege to such an experience. How to assess your mind's clarity, its innocence? It's clear there, over there, as I see it from my window, my brain getting sharper than a radio satellite. I don't need to travel if I wanted to visit the disappeared streets of my hometown, and you are doing the same, I'm sure, even if your birthplace stands gloriously under its flag, but you lost forever the particular light which accompanied you to school between ages four to six.

(Adnan, *There* 8)

The "disappeared streets of [the speaker's] hometown" stand in sharp contrast to her addressee's "birthplace [which] stands gloriously / under its flag," marking the speaker as someone who has been exiled from a region of conflict. The speaker's loss of home, which is representative of the devastating losses of millions of peoples displaced by war and affected by foreign occupation, by far outweighs the more common losses her addressee has suffered as a result of the passage of time. Yet, for the speaker who compassionately compares different losses, these disparate experiences can still be the grounds for empathy and a genuine human connection. In light of the conflicts and wars waged in the Middle East, the constancy of the natural world in the Bay Area, the incoming "[f]lood as persistent as the sun could be," offers the speaker a momentary sense of constancy and orientation. It offers her "a peace" she "would share" with those she addresses, particularly, one can assume, her American readers whose lives were—at the point of the collection's publication in 1997—only rarely, if at all impacted by the wars fought overseas with U.S. involvement. Watching the movements of the Pacific Ocean from the "distance of her window" and falling back on memories and her imagination in order to also look "over there," to the sea of her youth, the natural world becomes a navigational and indeed orientational tool, albeit not an entirely stable one, as the choice of the sea rather than a mountain as a reference point in this scene suggests.

When Adnan evokes mountains in her writing, they usually represent fixity and stability, often in explicit or implicit comparison to the sea. As the speaker notes in Adnan's most recent collection, *Premonition* (2014): "Beyond, there's solidity, a mountain. My fluidity is measured by what seems not to move" (2). In contrast to mountains, the sea and the ocean in Adnan's poetry are characterized by mutability and (the potential to produce) mobility: "Universe and sea made an agreement: the one provides substance / and the other, movement" (*Sea and Fog* 17). More ambiguous than it may initially seem due to the unusual use of punctuation, this quotation implies that the sea provides "substance" as well as "movement." This idea is suggestive of Adnan's treatment of the sea as a queer object of orientation that is permanent yet inconstant, forever close but never ready to hand. Precisely because of this quality, the sea functions as a useful metaphor as well as an important constitutive element for how the speaker experiences her being-in-the-world, or dwelling, in the aftermath of migration. As the only section from *There* entitled "Here" puts it:

> If we were not tied to a place what of us? I will introduce the
> sea into the frame and that would be tentative. Not an answer.
> Not a question.   (47)

If the natural world provides orientation for Adnan's migrant speaker, and if the ocean and the sea come to represent the primary objects of orientation and means of reorientation in her late poetry, this orientation is never complete. Rather, due to its mutability and constant movement, the sea only ever offers momentary orientation and thus forces the speaker to keep engaging with it, be it physically or mentally. It is through this ongoing engagement with nature that Adnan rethinks ideas of *Being* and *dwelling* as open-ended processes at once driven by and sustaining the speaker's orientation toward nature in the context of post-mobility.

As Mahwash Shoaib perceptively notes in her reading of *There*, the initial impression that "Adnan's poetry has no local base in its investigation of existential subjectivity" (21) is deceptive. However, rather than identifying what the essay's title describes as "Etel Adnan's Location in *There*" primarily by way of the poet's "socio-political references" (Shoaib 21), I want to stress that the "statements and questions [...] she poses of the specific reality of existence in regions of war and conflict" (Shoaib 21–22) are frequently and importantly ones about human-nature relations in the aftermath of dislocation. In my reading, *There* represents the tentative beginnings of a queer reorientation toward the natural world in Adnan's poetry, introducing an increasingly contemplative, philosophical poetic voice that would become more pronounced in collections such as *Seasons* and *Sea and Fog*. When Adnan's speaker notes in the excerpt from *There*, discussed earlier, that "[t]he light steams out from the ground / and carries the soul into a sensation of beginnings" in "the early / mornings of the Bay" (8), Adnan invokes a question that dominates all her poetry collections published after *There* and one she explicitly asks in the only stanza of *Seasons* that consists of a single line: "What's meant by 'Being'?" (62). For Adnan, the answer to this question not only involves the relationship of mind and matter, self and world, it also suggests that the question must take into account an interrogation of human-nature relations. As Adnan reflects on the important role that both thinking about nature and physical encounters with nature play for the question of Being, she recasts it as a question of "being-in-the-world," that is, of dwelling.

Throughout *Seasons*, the speaker's orientation toward the natural world manifests in an almost obsessive preoccupation with the ways in which Being—the question of what it is like to be in the world in terms of a felt sense of one's existence—depends on an exchange between the mind and the world. "Being is mind and outside / the mind" (*Seasons* 34), Adnan notes, adding a few pages later: "At the confluence of spirit and matter, or mind and environ- / ment, there's a continuous spark" (37). For Adnan, a person's felt sense of existence is experienced especially acutely when the individual is in close contact with the natural world. In this encounter, the natural world represents a co-constituting force, as the following excerpt from *Seasons* suggests, which recalls the writings of phenomenologist Maurice Merleau-Ponty who, especially in the unfinished and posthumously published manuscript of *Le visible et l'invisible* (1964), used the image of light to explore the role of vision and touch in the process of the making-conscious of Being:[7]

> Master of velocity, light bores into the tree trunks of these woods.
> Blue moon over green waters. The beach's impenetrable beauty
> lends its transparency to the soul in order to institute Being, in a
> joint creation.
>
> (Adnan, *Seasons* 11)

Because human-nature encounters "institute Being, in a / joint creation," Being cannot be reduced to mere thinking; it is not immaterial or transcendent, because it depends on both thinking and on perceiving the world with all senses, including vision, touch, and taste:

> In Yosemite Valley the body felt weightless. All the way to the
> Merced River's beginning. No past or future there. Only to eat
> drink and touch granite. There, awareness detaches itself from
> thinking. The mind becomes a sense added to the other senses. No
> concepts; just a total, uncluttered way of being.
>
> (*Seasons* 37)

---

7   For an account of Merleau-Ponty's challenge to purely consciousness-based conceptualizations of the interactions between bodies and the world and of his argument about the materiality and corporeality of vision, perception, and consciousness, see Cathryn Vasseleu's *Textures of Light: Vision and Touch in Irigaray, Levinas and Merleau-Pont* (1998), especially pp. 21–72.

By evoking immediate sensory impressions, Adnan here suggests that in order to think/feel Being one must become aware that "being" is corporeal and acknowledge one's place in the world and relationship to the natural world. What is more, she also implies that the encounter with nature, especially with sublime landscapes such as those of "Yosemite Valley," can overwhelm the rational mind.

When Adnan reflects on questions of Being in her poetry, she frequently evokes ecomystical experiences in which—as David Tagnani suggests for the ecomysticism he identifies in the nature writing of Edward Abbey—"the object with which union is achieved is translated from a supernatural entity or force into the material world" (318).[8] For Adnan, these ecomystical experiences also depend on physical mobility, as in the following stanza from the poem "Sea":

> Soon, disoriented but keeping full speed, a body intact throws
> itself against demented waters: the two masses, the single spear-
> like and the oceanic other meet, clash, then fuse their weight in
> an ultimate reckoning with Being.
>
> (*Sea and Fog* 9)

In this excerpt, Adnan imagines the act of swimming or diving as a physical encounter between the swimmer and his/her "oceanic other." Adnan evokes a "meet[ing]" with the more-than-human world that provides momentary orientation and elation to a "disoriented [...] body" in the form of a fleeting yet all the more powerful "ultimate reckoning with Being." Rather than just depicting an ecstatic unification of a "single" self with an ineffable transcendent entity, the emphasis in this scene lies on materiality, physicality, and movement as indicated by the "two masses" that "meet," "clash," and "then fuse their weight." Altogether, the scene can be said to conjure an ecomystical experience of nature that depends on "a state of consciousness brought about via the five senses interacting with the rest of the material world" (Tagnani 319). What is more, it also draws attention to the fact that physical mobility is an inherent part of being and indeed of dwelling the way Adnan understands it. When read metaphorically, the scene furthermore suggests that the mobility of the swimmer, the "disoriented [...] body," which can be said to stand for the subject disoriented by the experience of migration, does not impede meaningful human-nature relationships but provides the motivation for the kind

---

8   Tagnani uses the term *ecomysticism* to distinguish his conceptualization of a "synthesis be-
     tween materialism and mysticism" from theistic notions of mysticism, whether ecological in
     orientation or not, that view mystical ecstasy as a means to experience union with the god-
     head or another kind of immaterial being, concept, or force (318–20). He also uses the term
     to indicate that older ideas of nature mysticism (see, for example, the one proposed by J. Ed-
     ward Mercer in *Nature Mysticism* 1913) need to be revised in order to allow for an ecomysticism
     to emerge that is capable of addressing the wider implications of "the ecological crises of the
     twenty-first century" (319).

of intensive engagement with the nature that may eventually lead to a more viable environmental ethics. The fact that the non-human in this passage is the sea is particularly significant, because it foregrounds a mutable and mobile/ mobilizing natural phenomenon. Rather than acting as a relatively stable point of reference that will fade into the background as soon as the speaker has permanently oriented herself by its constant, immutable presence, the sea encourages a sort of place-making that requires continuous reorientation toward an always changing non-human world, effectively challenging essentialist notions of authentic dwelling as the effect of arrival and successful emplacement.

Queering Ecological Desire: Re-thinking Erotogenic Environmental Ethics

In her dOCUMENTA essay "The Cost for Love We Are Not Willing to Pay," Etel Adnan not only discusses how her migration affected her view of nature, but also recalls how she learned to swim as a young child in the Mediterranean Sea, off the coast of Beirut. Her anecdote speaks to the poet's life-long attachment to the landscapes of her childhood, despite having led a migratory life. What is more, it invokes her love for the Sea as a queer desire for nature:

> The sea beat directly against the edges of the town, and there were rocks with little pools just half a mile from my house. My mother would sit on one of these rocks and let me paddle in the water. As a measure of security, she passed under my arm a string or a cord, something like a leash that she held carefully. Thus, I developed from my early years a sensuous response to the sea, a fascination, a need that I lived like a secret. It enchanted me, and it isolated me. It has lasted all my life. (Adnan, "The Cost" 5)

Remembering how she used to live in the immediate vicinity of the sea and frequently came into direct contact with nature already at a young age, Adnan evokes the beginnings of a life-long desire for a close physical, intellectual, as well as emotional relationship with the natural world characterized by "a sensuous response to the sea, a fascination, a need." When she suggests in this passage that her longing for an intimate connection with the sea made her feel "isolated" and when she implies that she felt like she had to conceal this longing that "enchanted" her so much, she frames her desire for nature using traditional elements of the queer coming-of-age narrative. Specifically, she recounts a scene of initiation and awakening followed by a period of secrecy, a life in the closet marked by confusion as well as elation. The poet's lifelong desire for nature as she depicts it in her essay is queer in the two senses Sara Ahmed spells out in *Queer Phenomenology*, first as "'oblique' or 'offline' (i.e. askew, aslant)" and, second, as a reference to "those who practice nonnormative sexualities" (161) as well as their practices and desires. On the one hand, Adnan expresses concern that her desire for nature might be considered odd, if not outright deviant, by society at large, and on the other she makes sense of this desire by using a language of queer awakening. If Adnan indeed "lived" her desire for nature "like a secret" during some parts of her life, as she suggests in the excerpt, the poetry of her later life brings her queer/ecological desires out into the open. In collections such as *Seasons* or *Sea and Fog*, the poet's longing for an intimate connection to nature takes center stage. Acknowledging the disorienting experience of migration, Adnan's nature poems explore the speaker's intensely sensual, emotional, and intellectual relationship to the landscapes of Lebanon and California by overlaying them with evocations of profound longing for a lover who appears at once overwhelmingly close and increasingly out of reach.

In effect, Adnan's nature poetry gives expression to what Catriona Sandilands refers to as a queer "ecological desire" ("Desiring Nature" 170). Sandilands, in turn, draws from feminist social ecologist Chaia Heller, who, in *Ecology of Everyday Life* (1999), rethinks notions of desire "in the hope of radicalizing our approach to ecological questions" (7). Criticizing the idealization of nature and the narrow understanding of the function of desire in traditional "romantic ecology" (13), Heller argues for a "new kind of *social* desire for a just and ecological society" (69; emphasis added).[9] This social and ecological desire, she suggests, manifests in an "eco-erotic" (Heller 125) that is based on principles of "mutualism, differentiation, and development" (Heller 137) and attends to "the qualitative dimensions of our relationship to the natural world that are sensual, cooperative, creative, and elaborative" (Heller 141). Language and literature are crucial for imagining a political eco-erotic, according to Heller. Indeed, liberatory ecological desire, as she defines it, must be more than a personal, "associative desire for nature" (141). In other words, it must exceed the individual's desire to be close to nature. Rather, it must be transformed into or combined with a "[c]reative differentiative desire for nature" (142), which is to say a "yearning to sensitize ourselves to our relationship to the natural world" (143) as "unity in diversity" (142). According to Heller, the necessary critical sensibility can be fostered through "such mediums as philosophy, poetry, song, dance, or painting" (142). Instead of being merely aesthetic, then, poetic and non-poetic creative expressions of an eco-erotic must be informed by a critical social and historical consciousness,

---

9   In developing her argument on ecological desire as social desire, Chaia Heller builds not only on the radical socialist ecology of Murray Bookchin, she also discusses Audre Lorde's essay "The Uses of the Erotic: The Erotic as Power" and James Baldwin's "The Creative Process." Drawing from these queer, feminist, socialist, Black authors, who were interested in the poet's role as the one who re-imagines and ultimately transforms social and political relations, Heller speaks of the "socio-erotic" as "a continuum of social and sensual desires endowed with ethical, personal, and political meaning" (79) and as "a metaphor for a relational orientation that may counter capitalist rationalization" and in doing so "places social and cultural criticism on much firmer ground" (95).

Heller insists, and they have to interrogate cultural practices and conventions of representation:

> [A] radical love of nature entails that we become aware of the history of ideas of nature in addition to politically resisting social hierarchies that nurture distorted understandings and practices of nature as well. In particular, we must extend this critical self-consciousness to our poetic and visual expressions of our desire for nature. We must be critical of our use of metaphors and images of natural processes, making sure that they do not reproduce racist or sexist cultural stereotypes. (36)

Heller's language and argument here bear a striking resemblance to the language and argument Adnan uses in her documenta essay. Indeed, much like in Heller's feminist socialist ecological critique, Adnan asserts that the radical new "love" necessary to save the planet asks us "to give up many of our comforts, our toys, our gadgets, and above all our political and religious mythologies" ("The Cost" 6).

Etel Adnan's poetry promotes a radical love of nature similar to the one Heller conjures in her discussion of ecological desire. I say 'similar,' because Adnan's writing, unlike Heller's or that of Juliana Spahr discussed earlier in *Ecopoetic Place-Making*, focuses less on a structural critique of global capitalism and U.S. imperialism and more on an evocation of a utopian space in which the individual's capacity to love nature makes such a critique redundant. Still, Adnan's poems evoke a queer eco-erotic that enriches her representations of human desire for the natural world with references to the human tragedies of loss and displacement that result from global conflict. In doing so, Adnan's poetry gives voice to a politically-conscious queer/ecological desire that, to quote Catriona Sandilands, "does not suggest the 'liberation' of sensory pleasure in/for nature from its social context, but rather that the enculturation of desire includes and shapes different bodily relations to nature" ("Desiring Nature" 171). The specific "enculturation of desire" highlighted in Adnan's poems—one that takes experiences of migration and dislocation into account—indicates how the kind of "bodily relations to nature" that Sandilands describes become more complex as a result of mobility. Indeed, what Adnan's poetry suggests is that for the displaced persons living far from some of those places they are most deeply attached to, a queer/ecological "erotogenic ethics" (Sandilands, "Desiring Nature" 169) based on touch has to be revised in order for it to consider the sensuality of thought as an alternative, equally powerful source for a radical love for nature in the context of post-mobility.

Desire for nature in Adnan's poetry frequently takes the form of an erotically charged longing for a female sea, as in the following excerpt from "Sea," one of the two poems collected in *Sea and Fog* (2012):

> Even when I'm swimming she seems to be at a distance. Her
> waters feel like an intimate encounter of differences. There's no

transgression. We're mesmerized by immensity touching our
body, and instead of a prison, being a liberation.   (39)

Insisting on the sensual, emotional, and intellectual foundation of human-nature relations, this excerpt conjures an "intimate encounter of differences" that suggests a desire to be in close bodily contact with the sea and to fathom its "immensity," while also recognizing the natural world's essential otherness. Rather than merely viewing the feeling of "distance" that results from this "unity in diversity" (Heller 142) as proof of humans' limited capacity to comprehend the non-human environment, the speaker is "mesmerized" (Adnan, *Sea and Fog* 39) by the intimate physical encounter with the sea's "immensity" and experiences it as "a liberation." Preceded by a transition from the lyrical, embodied "I" of the first two lines to a collective, experiencing "we" in the second half of the stanza, the emphatic use of the word "liberation" at the end of the stanza's last line seems to signal both a liberation of the speaker from the confines of the individualized, rational self—again conjuring an ecomystical union with the more-than-human world as an explicitly material other—and a liberation from those societal conventions that position the queer/ecological desire for nature depicted here as a "transgression."

By acknowledging nature's strangeness, Etel Adnan's depiction of her speaker's desire for the sea gestures toward an eco-erotic that does not reduce queer desire to a desire for sameness. Instead, Adnan's work raises questions about the conventional symbolic organization of human-nature relationships in the Euro-American tradition, which, as Heller suggests, both exacerbates humans' exploitation of the environment and ignores social injustices (13). Adnan's poem "Sea" exposes these representational conventions and the structures of thought that form their basis by repeatedly employing poetic imagery that tries to make the otherness of non-human nature graspable through cultural metaphors—particularly erotic ones—while also trying to make a world in turmoil graspable through natural metaphors. In doing so, "Sea," like many of Adnan's poems, suggests that poetry invested in an eco-erotics that seeks to surpass the trappings of (heteronormative) romantic ecology must exhibit critical consciousness toward its specific and expanded historical context and engage in a sustained critique of dominant cultural, political, and religious mythologies as well as of the metaphors for human-nature interaction these mythologies provide:

The sea. Nothing else. Walls ruptured. Sea. Water tumbling.
Oil. Transparency. The sea. Field of stirring liquid. Gathering
of pouncing waves going to battle. Into one's mythology, trees
intrude, expand, shed shadows.

A wave, a mouth; a horse arrives, submits, drowns. Streaked and
bleeding sky. What is sky? To climb mountain peaks to overlook
clouds. Water on water reverberates memory's mechanism.

(Sea and Fog 3)

Combining descriptions of the more-than-human world with images of war reminiscent of H.D.'s meditation on WWII in *The Walls do not Fall* (1944), this passage
depicts a tumultuous, dangerous sea and simultaneously conjures scenes of violent conflict. While references to "Walls ruptured" or a "bleeding sky" might apply
to many different disasters and conflicts Adnan witnessed during her lifetime, the
collection's publication in 2012 and the mention of "Oil" in the above passage seem
to point at once to the Deepwater Horizon oil spill of 2010 and to the U.S.-led invasion of Iraq, about which the poet asks at the end of *Seasons*: "Are the pipelines of
blood running in the bodies of the Arabs less / worthy than the oil running under
their grounds?" (73).[10] Descriptions such as "pouncing waves going to battle" emphasize the extent to which the migrant speaker's perceptions of the natural world
are shaped not only by "memory's / mechanism," that is, by personal recollections,
but also by a more elusive yet all the same powerful cultural "mythology." In the case
of Adnan's speaker, this mythology is a composite of many different cultural imaginaries and has been shaped by experiences of migration as well as by her changed
relationship to the natural world ("Into one's mythology, trees / intrude, expand,
shed shadows"). Refuting the stanza's initial assertion, this passage reveals that the
speaker sees a lot when she sees "[t]he sea. Nothing else." Indeed, the sea "reverberates" with multiple meanings, meanings that challenge traditional representations
without erasing the dramatic consequences caused by U.S. military interventions
abroad.

As Greta Gaard argues, Western alienation from and exploitation of nature has
gone hand in hand with a fear and repression of the erotic more generally and the
queer erotic in particular (129). If we entertain the argument, as Catriona Sandilands
does, that "the ecological crisis is, even in small part, a problem of desire—specifically, of its narrowing, regulation, erasure, ordering, atomization and homogenization" ("Desiring Nature" 186), then a queer revision of the eco-erotic needs to counter
not only conventional representations of nature and human-nature relations, but
also to counter the erotophobia and queerphobia inherent in these representations

---

10   Fueled in part by Western powers' desire to gain control over the Middle East's rich oil de-
posits, the 2003–2011 Iraq War, also known as the Second Gulf War, arguably left the region
destabilized, "tumbling" and "stirring," and profoundly affected even those countries not directly involved in the conflict, including Lebanon, Adnan's country of origin. Beside *Sea and
Fog*, Adnan's collection *Seasons* most explicitly references the 2003–2011 Iraq War, frequently
by emphasizing the suffering of both civilians and soldiers on the "sacrificial ground" and on
the "killing fields" of Iraq (67).

(see Lee and Dow 8). In this context, it is significant that the sea, the principal object of desire in Adnan's late poetry, is not only consistently imagined as female but also associated with nonhuman movement, human mobility, and a queer sexuality that holds both generative and destructive potential:

> Oh fire's explosion from a woman's gut! Organized fearful
> battalions on the march. Soldiers cover their eyes with flowers,
> given the season. Continents of drifting clouds on the move.
>
> Sea insomniac with jealousy, sky moving eastward. White foam
> covers the water. Disquieting silence. Matter's feminine essence
> surging as sea's quiddity.
>
> (*Sea and Fog* 3)

Notably different in tone from the two stanzas quoted in the last paragraph, this excerpt mixes the language of nature poetry, love poetry, and (anti-)war poetry. The speaker's preoccupation with the "sea's quiddity" (the sea's "Being") as a manifestation of "[m]atter's feminine essence" points not only to Adnan's preoccupation with questions of Being and dwelling discussed before, it also points to her speaker's queer desire for nature as a central theme of Adnan's poetry. The conflation of ecological and sexual-erotic desire in this passage is worth examining from a queer-ecocritical perspective, because, as Sandilands notes,

> the social organization of sexuality and eroticism in the late twentieth century
> constrains and organizes the experience of sensual desires in and for (nonhuman)
> nature [...]. These restrictions and constructions not only impoverish our experi-
> ences of nature, foreclosing the apprehension and appreciation of an 'erotic tinge'
> in our relations to other organisms, but they also play into the maintenance and
> proliferation of significant social oppressions." ("Desiring Nature" 172)

By cautiously infusing human-nature relations in her poems with an "erotic tinge," Adnan does not only contest the constraints imposed on depictions of queer desire, she also contests the conceptual limitations imposed on representations of encounters with a more-than-human world on the move.

While the queer eco-erotic in Adnan's poetry most frequently finds expression in the female speaker's desire for an explicitly female sea—a choice that is interesting, given that the word for sea in Arabic (البحر) is masculine, while it is feminine in French (*la mer*)—the speaker's history of migration is what keeps the sea at a distance.[11] Although it may initially look as if Adnan uses the words "sea" and "ocean"

---

11   I want to thank Mahshid Mayar for pointing out to me the fact that the Arabic word for "sea" is masculine and for providing me with the word in the original Arabic script as well as with a transliteration into Latin alphabet.

interchangeably in her poems, many instances in Adnan's poetry suggests that she actually differentiates between the two. In *There*, Adnan's speaker for example mentions "leaving far behind the sea's / whiteness" as she is "carried by the voyage" to a place where "waters / submit themselves to the ocean's attraction" (49), and at the beginning of "Sea," she remarks: "The ocean is / near, the sea, far" (*Sea and Fog* 9). Because the Mediterranean Sea of her childhood and youth is far away, the speaker's longing for the sea's presence is all the more acute, even when she is near the Pacific Ocean. Indeed, even though the ocean is frequently "near" in her texts, it is often curiously out of reach. Several times in *Seasons* a woman is depicted in the process of walking toward the ocean or the cliff overlooking it without actually reaching the water (7, 15, 23, 25). When the speaker mentions the ocean, it is frequently close by but still at a remove, either "[b]y the dusty alley's end" (*Seasons* 15), "[i]n the background" (*Seasons* 28), or "behind the trees" (*Seasons* 30). In the poem "Fog," from *Sea and Fog*, the ocean also remains elusive, even as it exacts a strong pull on the speaker:

> [...] We're driving
> with no visibility down a winding and steep hill, toward army
> barracks, then to the ocean. It's not sure we will make it. But the
> fascination is fatal. It's fused with the world.   (88)

In this moment, like in others in the same poem, the ocean is not only at a distance, it is also concealed from view by the notorious Bay Area fog (*Sea and Fog* 90). The fact that the ocean so frequently appears unreachable for the speaker or out of sight is of import here because in the world of war and conflict that Adnan depicts in her poetry, an immersion into the ocean would promise a deeply sought-after sense of relief in the experience of a becoming-one-with-nature in which one's worries recede into the background, at least temporarily. "Fog" suggests as much only one page later:

> We fear violence, but more feared is its absence. So heavy is the
> world becoming. Heavy in the soul. A few laps in the ocean will
> bring rest.
>
> *(Sea and Fog* 91)

It is no coincidence then, I would argue, that there are several instances in Adnan's poetry describing such a swim. While one of the two swimming scenes—the scene discussed earlier—begins with the remark "[e]ven when I'm swimming she seems to be at a distance" (*Sea and Fog* 39), the other describes the dive of "a body" while the speaker remains at a certain distance to the events that are enfolding (*Sea and Fog* 9).

The third intimate encounter with the sea, this time described from the perspective of the speaker, is framed as a memory rather than an experience in the present. More explicitly than in the other scenes, the speaker here directly addresses the sea as a distant lover and describes their reunion in explicitly sexual terms:

If from so much afar you remember me, send a sign. I used
to walk through flowered gardens down in streets with barely
discernable figures; in full sun I was moving fast, accompanied
by orange trees. Carried by this feast, I was reaching your shores,
and, removing my clothes, I was softly going in, sliding toward
your waters and swimming.

(Sea and Fog 30)

Thinking back to a time when she "used / to walk through flowered gardens" toward
the coast, the speaker calls for the sea to remember her "from so much afar." Apart
from implying that some time has passed, since the speaker "was moving fast" in
this way to reach the "shores" and may no longer be able to do so in the present, a
point I return to later, this section also suggests that the speaker's migrations have
separated her from the object of her longing. More obviously than the two other
scenes, this scene could be read as a sequel to the childhood memory described in
Adnan's documenta essay, in which Adnan recalls how she learned to swim in the
Mediterranean Sea. While that anecdote evokes Adnan's queer/ecological initiation,
the above scene depicts a temporary fulfillment of the speaker's longing for an intimately sensual, emotional, and intellectual connection with nature as an act of
lesbian love-making ("I was softly going in, sliding toward/ your waters and swimming"). By emphasizing the physicality of the encounter as well as the fact that what
she depicts is a distant memory, Adnan suggests that for a migrant and exile like
her speaker, some of the most precious landscapes are anything but readily at hand.
Place-making in such a context, especially place-making invested in evoking a queer
eco-erotic may have to rely on a poetry that takes seriously both an erotics of touch
and an erotics of thought that draws on memory as well as the imagination.

However evocative such scenes of the speaker's complete bodily immersion into
the sea may be for a queer eco-erotic, then, they are also rather unusual for Adnan's
poetry and especially her late poetry. While her collections do in fact depict moments
in which the sensory impressions of intimate physical contact with the natural world
overpower the speaker's faculties of reason, much of Adnan's poetry is concerned
less with pleasures of the body and more with the pleasures of the mind. The erotic
that emerges in Adnan's poetry from the migrant speaker's intimate entanglements
with the natural world is thus not primarily the result of what Catriona Sandilands
describes as a "blurring of bodily boundaries through eroticized tactile apprehension" ("Desiring Nature" 169), of matter touching the body. Rather, it is also importantly the result of thinking and reveling in "the miracle of matter itself" (Adnan,
"Journey" 339). In her poetry, this emphasis on thinking frequently shows itself in
explorations of those moments in which matter and mind encounter each other. As
Adnan puts it in "Sea":

> Sea: mirrored mirror that distracts the soul from ecstasy. The
> uncontrollable desire to think the fleeting elements of the world,
> to fuse them into images, into words, is probably the most
> hypnotic of all of Eros' manifestations.

(Sea and Fog 15)

In this stanza, which emphasizes the speaker's "uncontrollable desire to *think* the fleeting elements of the world" (emphasis added) and describes this act of thinking as "probably the most / hypnotic of all of Eros's manifestations," the touching of matter and mind resolves in a moment of unhurried contemplation and astonished appreciation for the natural world. Or as Adnan's speaker specifies on the same page, it resolves in an act of witness:

> To think is not to contemplate, it's to witness. We have to deal
> with the events that happen in the Palace's danger zone ... By the
> dusty alley's end, the ocean unfolds its unlimited space. That cliff
> is poetry's jumping board. Words are cracked open, reused in bits
> and pieces. There's much agitation. Spring unattached itself from
> its elements. It has become Being.

(Seasons 15)

If Adnan thus suggests in "The Cost for Love We Are Not Willing to Pay" that "[m]ore than another field of expression, mystical texts witness the experience of the fundamental unity of love" (5), she certainly assigns herself and her poetry a similar task, while also noting under what circumstances physical closeness can and cannot be the basis for the kind of ecomystical experience her poetry repeatedly evokes. At the same time, her differentiation between contemplation and what seems to be the worldlier and more outward-turned activity of thinking/witnessing stresses that for Adnan loving nature and loving the world are political acts. Writing "poetry" and using poetic language in which "[w]ords are cracked open" are not a frivolous pastime in this scenario, they are a necessity.

Even though Adnan's poetry returns again and again to the same places and natural phenomena—whether trees, the weather, the seasons, the sea or fog—the intimate encounters of matter and mind her poetry evokes as frequently produce moments of profound confusion as they produce moments of clarity or illumination. This confusion, however, does not lessen the urgency of the speaker's passionate longing for a "fundamental unity of love" with nature, on the contrary. In the following stanza from "Sea," for example, the speaker's desire for the sea is powerfully expressed through negations and the repetition of sounds, which create the effect of an exhilarated mind struggling to comprehend what it will never grasp fully:

> And what is this surge of the stupendous and quasi un-nameable
> entity, where un-numbered amounts of bubbles unbreakably

bound to each other make a eulogy for smallness while creating
the most maddening form of an elusive infinity?

(Sea and Fog 10)

Faced with the sea's and indeed also the ocean's "elusive infinity," Adnan's speaker is fully aware that her desire for nature and the passionate love it engenders is a fantasy: "The sea is momentous duration. / A passion for her is love for an illusion. But what else is there to / be had?" (Sea and Fog 18) she writes. Still, throughout her collections, the speaker affirms her passion for the sea, and by consequence her queer/ecological desire for nature, even if the confrontation with this "quasi un-nameable entity" pushes her rational faculties as well as her capacity for poetic expression to the limit. "Can I comprehend you in ignoring intelligence, and contain your immensity? (Sea and Fog 22), the poet asks and then comments in addressing the sea directly: "When the cold freezes you, it slows down my blood. Under the moon's attraction you rise and fall as my mind vacillates and fails" (22). It is this struggle of the poet, despite the limits increasingly imposed on her by her own body, to continue thinking and writing poetry as a way of bearing witness to nature's incomprehensible "immensity" (Sea and Fog 39), not only for herself but also for generations to come, that I discuss in the following as a queering of ecological futurity.

Queering Ecological Futurity: Ecological Empathy and the Poetics of Disorientation

Etel Adnan's nature poetry can be read as a poetry of place-making that suggests that the disorientation produced by experiences of migration and the reorientation process it sets in motion affect human-nature relations long after the migrant has reached a state of relative immobility. But Adnan's nature poetry is a poetry of post-mobility in yet another sense: Seasons, Sea and Fog, and Night explore not only a queer orientation toward and a queer desire for nature in the aftermath of migration, they also exhibit an awareness of how the speaker's engagements with nature change as a result of aging, also, though not exclusively, with regard to the limitations old age imposes on the speaker's physical mobility and access to nature. The awareness of these limitations in Adnan's poetry is accompanied by an apocalyptic imagination that is both personal and political, spiritual, and ecological. It wavers between despair and hope, resignation, and the determination to affect some kind of social change as it grapples with the certainty of death and what this certainty means for humans' shared responsibility for present and future natures.

In her book Strange Natures: Futurity, Empathy, and the Queer Ecological Imagination (2013), Nicole Seymour discusses contemporary queer novels and films that imagine "empathetic, ethical interrelationships between the queer and the non-human" (23).

Drawing from the "queer optimism" of Michael Snediker and José Esteban Muñoz's take on "queer futurity," which finds utopian potential in cultural expressions of queer desire and sociality that may or may not reflect on the future explicitly, Seymour suggests that works of art may produce both queerer and more ecological futures.[12] Art can do so, she argues, by drawing its audiences' attention to, and inspiring care for, nature without perpetuating "the value set of normative, reproductive heterosexuality [that] establishes strict, moralized limits to futurity" (Seymour 12). Indeed, she proposes, that "any kind of environmentalism that does not operate within those limits—that is, that does not operate out of *immediate or extended self-interest*—is 'queer'" (Seymour 12; emphasis added). Immediate and extended self-interest are conflated in the heteronormative logics of a future-oriented mainstream environmentalism, she explains, because it demands that we protect the environment in order to protect our own future and the future of our children (Seymour 7). According to Seymour, this logic should be countered, or at least complemented, by a "queer ecological empathy" based on the ability to "imagine someone or something to whom environmental destruction *would*, and does, matter" (Seymour 18; emphasis original), but who is not an immediate or close relation (27). I want to posit that Adnan's late nature poetry is queer and ecological in Seymour's sense, for two reasons: first, because it draws attention to an aging speaker for whom the most awe-inspiring natural phenomena and experiences in nature are increasingly out of reach; and, second, because it seeks to inspire care for a future nature that this speaker (nor her descendants) will not live to see. At first glance, Adnan's poems, like many works by writers with a migratory background, seem primarily focused on the past and the present rather than the future. When they evoke the future, especially her late poems seem to do so much more by centering on the inevitability of death rather than on the dangers of future environmental catastrophe. Despite these tendencies, however, Adnan's poetry of post-mobility invites readers to contemplate the very question Seymour asks when commenting on the role of literature for the production of queerer and more ecological futures: "What if we could imagine that environmental catastrophe does matter, even, or perhaps especially, if we are not going to witness its effects?" (18)

---

12   In different ways, both Snediker and Muñoz resist the queer pessimism of Lee Edelman, who in *No Future: Queer Theory and the Death Drive* (2004) proposed a radical new queer ethics based on an uncompromising critique of "reproductive futurism," urging queers to resist rather than to comply with societal demands, symbolically organized around the figure of the child, to sacrifice the present for the sake of an allegedly better future. On the contrary, in *Queer Optimism: Lyric Personhood and Other Felicitous Persuasions* (2008), Snediker rereads lyrical poetry by Emily Dickinson, Hart Crane and Elizabeth Bishop focusing on forms of positive affect rather than on more common critical categories in queer studies such as melancholia or shame, suggesting that queer desires have always also been imagined with an eye to and in the hopes of better futures.

While many of Adnan's collections are infused with references to migration, travel, and other kinds of mobility, her later collections also convey the poet's desire to arrive and make a permanent home for herself, even as her poems acknowledge that such an arrival does not cancel out the changed perspectives on nature produced by previous experiences of mobility. The following passage from *Seasons*, for example, indicates that the speaker is tired and worn out from years of moving: "Pulled down by the afternoon's / implacable passing, there's no way to see the beach. I carry years of / wandering on my back. Would like to shed them" (Adnan 37). The last two sentences explicitly express the speaker's desire to arrive or at least to pause. I am quoting the preceding sentence as well, because the longer excerpt illustrates that instances of mobility, such as the voyage in Adnan's poem "Manifestations of the Voyage" or the "wandering" in the above quotation, also need to be read with close attention to their temporal dimension rather than only their spatial one. Indeed, in the lines just quoted, questions of mobility and temporality are bound together. The excerpt indicates that what has left the speaker feeling "[p]ulled down," that is, what has made her weary and exhausted, are not only her "years of / wandering" but also the "afternoon's implacable passing." This double emphasis on the inexorable passing of time (in both the short and the long run) is suggestive of the fact that the speaker is not only a migrant and world traveler but someone who has reached a moment in her life when time has become a matter of more immediate concern. Significantly, this moment is also one in which her exhaustion, which seems mental as well as physical, keeps the formerly wandering speaker from visiting the beach and thus from encountering the sea she so dearly loves. While there are certainly other ways of reading these lines, I read them as a commentary on human-nature relations in the context of mobility that open up questions about precisely the two senses of the term *post-mobility* addressed in Adnan's nature poetry: post-mobility as the aftermath of migration and post-mobility as the increasing physical immobility associated with old age.

Adnan's most recent works contain countless references to death, aging, as well as to physical and mental decline. "Some people witness / their soul's death before dying. That's an apocalyptic event, a private eclipse" (Adnan, *Sea and Fog* 67), she writes in "Fog." In "Sea," she comments with a combination of puzzlement and resignation: "But the universe is alive, so how can its parts die? Still, we die" (*Sea and Fog* 25). And yet elsewhere in the same poem she muses:

The body produces that superstructure we call mind. When
they work together there's elation. But they can go – too often
– their own ways, the body, damaged beyond repair, the mind
destroyed beyond recourse. All the while the world manifests its
overwhelming power.

(*Sea and Fog* 47)

For a poet who figures place-making not only as a "clash" of the "body" with its "oceanic other" (*Sea and Fog* 9) but also as a "confluence" of "mind and environment" that produces "a continuous spark" (*Seasons* 37), these statements are not only about physiological decline, whether as a consequence of aging or due to the mutilations inflicted on the minds and bodies of people by war. They are also about a diminished capacity to be in and with nature and to enjoy this experience physically as well as intellectually:

> [...] Winds sweep
> the imagination while the spirit dries up. Small memories drift
> away. The brain – soft bag – collapses on itself. Stripped speech
> patterns float in the soul's canyons where things are perennial.
>
> (*Sea and Fog* 4)

As if it wasn't enough that people's physical capacity to encounter the natural world intimately diminishes with old age due to a decrease in mobility that keeps nature at a distance, Adnan suggests here, so does the intellectual ability to remember past encounters and to communicate one's experiences to others. Or, as Adnan puts it quite succinctly in "Sea": "Without a body there's no soul and without the latter there's no / way to speak about the sea" (*Sea and Fog* 22). The prospect of no longer being able to speak about the sea and, accordingly, the prospect of no longer being able to bear witness to her desire and love for nature fills the speaker with deep regret: "There's so much life around me, and I will have to leave" (*Night* 27).

Several more passages in *Seasons*, *Sea and Fog*, and *Night* point to the ways in which old age limits physical mobility and, by consequence, the speaker's immediate access to nature. This is the case, for example, in the passage discussed earlier, in which a dive into the ocean, that is, the merging of body and sea evokes an ecomystical experience and which I quote here again for the sake of readability:

> Soon, disoriented but keeping full speed, a body *intact* throws
> itself against *demented* waters: the two masses, the single spear-
> like and the oceanic other meet, clash, then fuse their weight in
> an ultimate reckoning with Being.
>
> (*Sea and Fog* 9; emphasis added)

Adnan's insistence in this particular scenario on the fact that the body mentioned here is not just any kind of body, but a "body *intact*" and the fact that this body "throws / itself against *demented* waters" rather than "softly going in" (*Sea and Fog* 30), as in the bathing passage quoted earlier, points to bodies and potentially also minds that are not or no longer intact, including bodies and minds harmed by war or affected by illness and old age. To repeat a passage in *Sea and Fog* discussed earlier that strongly resonates with the one above:

The body produces that superstructure we call mind. When
they work together there's elation. But they can go – too often
– their own ways, the body, damaged beyond repair, the mind
destroyed beyond recourse. All the while the world manifests its
overwhelming power.

(Sea and Fog 47)

Whatever intact "body" (Adnan, *Sea and Fog* 9), is referred to in the first passage—the
use of the indefinite article "a" ("a body") indicates that the speaker is either only
an observer to the scene or that she imagines it without her own involvement—the
excerpt implies that an ecstatic union with nature of the kind described above for
the person entering the water has become an experience of the past for the aging
speaker.

Other passages from Adnan's more recent nature poetry corroborate such a
reading. Indeed, while both *Sea and Fog* and *Night* contain verses in which the
speaker remembers climbing mountains (*Sea and Fog* 3, 53; *Night* 12), "Night" also
features in the following passage, which once more alludes to the fact that the
speaker may no longer be as mobile as she used to be:

Not to be able to climb up a mountain, run from this place to
the next, see things improving for friends or nations or even
a clear day, not to stop the torture…

(Night 10)

More explicitly than in the passages already quoted, this excerpt links the speaker's
inability to move about freely in the world and in nature with an inability to witness, let alone effect positive change in a world in which "nations" such as the United
States remain involved in military conflicts in which "torture" is an all too frequent
occurrence. Like in this instance, personal and global scenarios of decline ("Not to be
able to […] see things improving for friends or nations") as well as environmental
and non-environmental scenarios of doom are frequently juxtaposed in Adnan's poetry. While this juxtaposition speaks to Adnan's complex apocalyptic imagination,
it also gestures toward the kind of empathy for strangers and for nature as even
stranger kin that Seymour considers to be crucial for any viable imagination of a
queer ecological futurity. Put differently, Adnan's late poetry gestures toward a queer
and an apocalyptic environmental ethics.

Unlike Craig Santos Perez and Juliana Spahr, who I discuss in previous chapters,
Adnan rarely addresses environmental degradation directly.[13] Indeed, she mentions

---

13   Adnan mentions "global warming" (*Seasons* 49) and its effects on the natural phenomena she
closely observes on several occasions. Keenly interested in weather patterns, Adnan for instances refers to the increasing occurrences of "mega-storms" (*Sea and Fog* 94) and "September
fires" (*Sea and Fog* 72) which have begun to "engulf big chunks / of California" (*Sea and Fog* 74)

environmental degradation more frequently in her earlier publications than in her more recent ones. And when she does, she frequently combines references to global environmental catastrophe with personal musings about death. In the following passage from "Spreading Clouds...," a poem published as part of *The Indian Never Had a Horse & Other Poems* (1985) that she dedicated to June Jordan, for example, Adnan not only warns of the possible future consequences of present-day environmental destruction, she also addresses her parents' death. Employing a language of protest reminiscent of her own beginnings as a poet during the Vietnam War as well as of Jordan's uncompromisingly political and rousing rhetoric, the poem demands that everyone "look what we did to our common / mother Earth!" (Adnan, *The Indian* 69). A little later, in a passage in which the speaker remembers "the Greek eyes of [her] / mother looking over the / agony of [her] Arab father" (71), the tone drastically changes, prefiguring the more introspective and much less combative tone of Adnan's later writings:

> I don't want to watch our
> planet go the way they
>   did:
> reluctantly having learned
> the great secret at the moment
> of the Great Journey.
>
> (*The Indian Had a Horse* 71)

The "great secret" Adnan refers to here, the secret her parents only learn at the moment of the father's approaching death, I would suggest, is the secret of a love that by far surpasses the boundaries of heteronormative romantic love also alluded to in the exchange between the speaker's father and mother. For their daughter, the nature poet who gives voice to a queer ecological desire in her writing, this love is one that turns to the natural world with appreciative attention as well as empathic care. When Adnan insists in this poem that she does not want to "watch our / planet go the way they / did," she implies not only that environmental catastrophe is looming, she also expresses the hope that others will learn the "great secret" sooner than her parents did. For Adnan, this means that they embrace the radical love for the world she

---

more and more frequently in "these times of global over-heat" (*Sea and Fog* 45). Environmental degradation too figures in poems such as "Spreading Clouds..." from *The Indian Never Had a Horse & Other Poems* (1985) and in "The Manifestation of the Voyage" from *The Spring Flowers Own* (1990), both of which contain passionate pleas against environmental destruction. As discussed in more detail above, *Sea and Fog* points to uranium mining as a highly exploitative and destructive activity (85) while both *There* and *Seasons* lament the pervasiveness of chemical pollution (*There* 23, *Seasons* 2).

advocates before it is too late, allowing for even queerer and more ecological futures than her parents' generation or her own may be able to imagine.

A section of the poem "The Manifestation of the Voyage" (1990) is yet another place where she juxtaposes a discussion of impending global environmental catastrophe with very personal reflections about death. In this text a "brutalized" and "devastated" (89) Earth lies dying, just like and yet also unlike the speaker's mother:

> And Earth?
> I found her wounded
> - is she in agony?-
> [...]
> It is not my mother who's dying
> over the silk of her bed
> it's Enormous Death herself [...]
>
> (*The Spring Flowers Own* 89)

Suggesting an incomparability as well as a comparability of two very different deaths, this excerpt raises the question whether and (if so, then) how human beings can make sense of these kinds of imminent catastrophes that push the mind toward its limits of comprehension, whether intellectually, emotionally, or spiritually. While the death of a loved one, and especially that of one's mother, may indeed mean the end of the world as one knows it, "Enormous Death herself," as I understand Adnan here, actually means the end of the world as we know it, if not the end of the world as such. The paradox Adnan seems to express here is that, for those who love nature as passionately and deeply as she does, observing these two kinds of apocalypses, the private and the global one, may in fact feel very similar, while for many others the mere idea of comparing the two might seem absurd. Yet, precisely because of this discrepancy, the event more widely acknowledged to be a tragedy of "Enormous" proportion, that is, the personal experience of having to face the approaching death of a loved one, helps to convey the enormous tragedy of a looming environmental catastrophe. In turn, conveying not only the information that such a catastrophe is ahead or already under way but placing it within a more familiar emotional framework may help to produce what I have described as a radical, queer ecological empathy for nature.

Of course, such a queer ecological empathy has very little political import if it overwhelms those who grieve for nature in ways most only grieve for their closest of kin. As Lynn Keller notes in relation to the political limitations of apocalyptic discourse, anticipating environmental catastrophe, especially when there are clear signs that it may already be well under way as in Adnan's poems, may cause paralyzed inaction rather than a change of thinking and behavior (Keller, *Recomposing Ecopoetics* 101, 104). "The Spring Flowers Own," the companion piece to "The Manifestation of the Voyage" in the collection of the same name, warns about precisely this danger. It suggests that the prospect of one's own death, and indeed in this particular case the growing awareness of its inevitability that comes with aging or other imminent threats to one's life, can dull people's senses toward environmental dangers such as the effects of global warming, especially when the effects in question seem like problems that may never affect them directly in their lifetime:

> temperatures on earth are
> rising
> but we wear upon us some
> immovable frost
> everyone carries his dying as
> a growing shadow.
>
> (Adnan, *The Spring Flowers Own* 35)

Rather than chastising "everyone" for what the poem seems to consider a very human tendency (that is, to hold most dear what is closest to us, including our own lives), Adnan's poetry responds with compassion to the understandable limits of human empathy for nature in the face of mortality. Still, her poems also point to the very real problems arising from this failure of the imagination in the present and the consequences this failure may cause for the world's future. Adnan's poetry insists that our actions in the present—which in Adnan's case means how we interact with, how deeply we think about, and how radically we love nature—are of essence, because they either allow for or preclude the possibility of queerer and more ecological futures.

While much of Adnan's later nature poetry extends compassion and understanding to those who fail to love nature deeply enough, it also occasionally provides clues about how one might develop a radical queer/ecological empathy for the world especially in the face of death and approaching environmental catastrophe. As one stanza from the poem "Night" implies, such a more defiant perspective may be the effect of aging and coming face to face with one's own mortality: "The wedding of history with the coffee we drink in our ever / shrinking days awakes our need to reinvent love" (Adnan, *Night* 9). In these powerful yet unpretentious lines, Adnan conjures passages from the same collection and her earlier writings in which the juxtaposition of everyday occurrences and events of global import create a feeling of desperation and powerlessness in the face of violence and destruction (an example is "To be in a Time of War" from *In the Heart of the Heart of Another Country*). In the passage from *Night* I just quoted, by contrast, this sense of helplessness is transformed into an confirmation of what I take to be Adnan's key concern in her poetry on nature, mobility, aging, and death: a desire to affirm the value of an all-encompassing love for the world in general and the natural world in particular, and—upon being confronted with the fact of "our ever / shrinking days"—to bear witness to this love in her poetry. As I would like to suggest, her poetry stands as a powerful example of the commitment this kind of love requires, introducing those who may yet live to see the future that needs saving to the kind of queer ecological empathy on which a radical love for nature must be based. Put differently, Adnan's nature poetry of post-mobility is "illustrative" (Heller 159) in Chaia Heller's broadly defined critical-pedagogical sense of that term, in that it expresses faith in reading nature poetry as a way of enacting a queer ecological futurity in the present and, in doing so, of making more likely those queerer and more ecological futures that can avoid perpetual conflict and environmental catastrophe. In Adnan's poetry of post-mobility, this enactment of a queer ecological futurity relies on an apocalyptic environmental imagination and ethics.

When Heller speaks of the importance of the "illustrative moment" (159) of ecological desire in *Ecology of Everyday Life*, she speaks of the need to teach and communicate resistance against those practices and ideologies that encourage the exploitation and destruction of nature. According to Heller, "illustrative opposition must be sensual: it should constitute the ultimate body politic in which we literally throw our bodies into social contestation, taking illustrative and expressive direct action" (159). The insistence that those who protest the intersecting oppressions of sexism, racism, capitalism, and environmental exploitation put their actual physical bodies on the line is certainly anything but misguided. Still, Adnan's poetry of post-mobility suggests that there must be options of "expressive direct action" other than the ones insisting on immediate experience. Indeed, her poetry may be considered a form of expressive direct action, insomuch as it highly values thinking as a "sensual" engagement with nature. Following Seymour's line of argument, then, I would stress the value of Adnan's poetry as a "remarkable *achievement* [/] of imagination" (Seymour 10; emphasis original). Seymour's statement harks back to José Esteban Muñoz who, in reading Ernst Bloch, stresses the "anticipatory illumination of art" (3), that is, art's ability to gesture toward politically productive "utopian feelings" (3) that may be put to work in order to imagine and enact better and queerer futures. Like Seymour I want to take this argument one step further in order to explore how art like Adnan's poetry may imagine and enact futures that are not only queerer but also more ecological. As I want to suggest in closing, the "anticipatory illumination" of Adnan's poetry works by way of a poetics of disorientation that attempts to make the experience of disorientation caused by displacement and by a sense of approaching personal and environmental apocalypse graspable in the act of reading.

Aphoristic and impressionistic, contemplative and at times highly philosophical, Adnan's nature poetry requires several re-readings, before larger themes emerge and the meaning of certain passages becomes clear through accumulation. In the same vein, her texts demand patience and make readers work for pleasurable moments of startling insight and new perspectives on seemingly familiar topics. Reading page after page of Adnan's loosely jointed reflections, some readers would certainly come to enjoy the meditational effect of her long poems, which depends on the continual return to similar subject matters from a variety of perspectives. Many readers, however, even those willing to engage in the interpretative labor Adnan's nature poems require, might experience a strong sense of confusion due to abrupt changes of topic between and even within stanzas, the oblique references to mythology, history, philosophy, and art, and the idiosyncratic system of symbols underlying her poetry. And so, if her poetry about nature is in part motivated by the disorientation caused by experiences of migration and records a reorientation process that remains forever incomplete, Adnan's poems about natural phenomena also enact this disorientation on the page. Swept away by "the maddening effect of a /constant present" and allowed only brief moments of "rest" in "memory" (*Night* 13), Adnan's speaker takes her readers on a dizzying journey through time and space, reminiscent of what Gertrude Stein in reference to her own poetry described in her essay on war and poetics, "Composition as Explanation" (1926), as a "continuous present" (499):

> There's space, for sure, we're of it, but where's time? Where
> from? There's change, and it is movement. No doubt. So time,
> abstracted from change, is movement represented by a watch's
> needles. The measure of change we call time. As we fear death, a
> fatal change, we fear its progression in everything. Although we
> love change and marvel at movement.
>
> (Adnan, *Sea and Fog* 43)

In my understanding, the lesson to learn on this journey undertaken "by a watch's / needles," which inevitably takes readers closer to the uncertain futures looming in Adnan's poetry, is to keep searching for the all-encompassing love that drives the speaker, despite the fact that or, maybe exactly because, "death, a / fatal change" manifests "in everything." In other words, the lesson to learn from Adnan's poetry in the midst of a world that is all about "change" and "movement" is to keep looking at nature.

Searching for a radical love that will save the world, Adnan's poems suggest, means to arrive at the realization that the great secret one has been looking *for* is to be found in what one has been looking *at* while on that journey and while reveling in the pleasures this act of looking produces:

> The only absolute this mind can apprehend is the pleasure of
> being only a temporary visitor to this transient garden. That hap-
> pened ten minutes ago. A summer breeze is worth a night of love.
>
> (*Seasons* 67)

Because each and every one of us is "only a temporary visitor in this transient garden," Adnan's poems encourage her readers to look patiently and closely at nature while we still can. The following passage from *Sea and Fog* expresses the urgency behind the prompt that we take the time to look:

The sea is to be seen. See the sea. Wait. Do not hurry. Do not
run to her. Wait, she says. Or I say. See the sea. Look at her using
your eyes. Open them, those eyes that will close one day when
you won't be standing. You will be flat, like her, but she will be
alive. Therefore look at her while you can. Let your eyes tire and
burn. Let them suffer. Keep them open like one does at midday.
Don't worry. Other eyes within will take over and go on seeing
her. They will not search for forms nor seek divine presence.
They will rather continue to see water which stirs and shouts,
becomes ice in the North, vapor in the tropics.

(Sea and Fog 31)

Using staccato phrases, direct reader address, word play, and a repetition of sibilants, this exceptionally long stanza gives the impression of a speaker who stops herself along with the reader, leaving both of them out of breath. Having thus stopped, the speaker once more reorients her readers toward her much beloved sea, pleading with us to "look at her while [we] can" because one day soon "[we] won't be standing" and instead be "flat, like her." Playing with line endings and unsuspected enjambments, this passage suggests that both "[o]ther eyes" and "[o]ther eyes within will take over and go on seeing / her," especially once the speaker and her current companions will have been forced to move on, both literally and figuratively. If we learn to "[s]ee the sea" and to love her radically enough, this poem suggests, those coming after us may "continue to see water which stirs and shouts,/ becomes ice in the North, vapor in the tropics" rather than witnessing the kinds of climatic changes Adnan occasionally alludes to in her poems. Here as in many places in her hauntingly beautiful poetry, Adnan reminds us what we could lose sooner than we might expect, if we fail in the almost impossible task she has set for us: to love nature more than "our comforts, our toys, our gadgets, and above all our political and religious mythologies" and, in doing so, to save nature as the very basis of our existence. As Adnan puts it in *Sea and Fog*:

The forest is shaking terribly. Waves howl and break in jets of
water. What beauty, this fury! Sea: it's because she is that we are,
and when she disappears we'll cease to be. It's only in relation to
her that we find some worth to our existence.   (45)

Conclusion: Environmental Cultures of Im/Mobility

The main argument of *Ecopoetic Place-Making* has been that it is productive to read contemporary ecopoetries of migration from the joint perspective of ecocriticism and mobility studies because the environmental imaginaries of mobility these poetries produce can shed light on some of the many complex ways in which environmental issues and human mobility are connected. In my study, I have examined how contemporary ecopoetries of migration engage in *ecopoetic place-making*, that is, in a (re-)fashioning through poetry of place-sense and place-attachment from perspectives of mobility that has socio-political and environmental significance because it calls into question the idea that long-term residence is the only way by which human beings develop meaningful relationships to the nonhuman world. Contemporary American poetry written by authors of various migratory backgrounds invested in both nature and mobility challenges reductive ecolocalist understandings of emplacement and counters exclusionary notions of belonging, including racist, nationalist, and econativist arguments about whose presence in a given place is to be considered beneficial and whose presence is considered harmful to a particular community or environment. What is more, ecopoetries of migration suggest that experiences of mobility, whether voluntary or forced, do not prevent mobile subjects from establishing emotionally intense, caring relationships to the natural world, even when bodily immersion in the natural world is not, or nor longer a viable possibility. In a world of converging ecological and mobility crises, crises that lead to a simultaneous dissolution of some borders and the strengthening of others, *Ecopoetic Place-Making* claims, we need more inclusive notions of environmental literature, more critical environmental pedagogies, and a better understanding of how we might arrive at conceptualizing and enacting more ecoethical ways of being in the world that take into consideration the perspectives of migrants and other people on the move. Reading ecopoetries of migration, I posit, can help us along the way.

Ecopoetic Place-Making in Contemporary American Ecopoetries of Migration

Examining ecopoetries of migration is important, because the mobile environmental imaginaries these poetries evoke can form the basis of more inclusive models of ecological agency, ecological citizenship, and ecological desire. It requires engaging with intersecting systems of oppression and exploitation in the United States, demonstrating how (racial) capitalism, settler colonialism, and U.S. imperialism shape human-nature relations in ways that are destructive to marginalized communities as well as to the environment, not only by allowing the devastation of some places while investing in the preservation of others, but also by preventing the movement of some people, goods, and ideas, while promoting the movement of others. If it accounts for the uneven regimes of environmental and mobility injustice produced by these systems of oppression and exploitation, reading ecopoetries of migration by Native authors as well as non-Indigenous authors, by white poets as well as by non-white poets of migration, I hope to have shown, can point to more critical forms of environmental thinking and environmental pedagogy as well as to alternative, less destructive approaches to arrivant and settler place-making.

The American landscapes featured in the works of the poets I have discussed range from the occupied territories of the U.S. Pacific over the polluted environments of Appalachia, the deeply historical landscapes of the U.S. South and the Western Plains, to the multilayered places of the Southwestern deserts and the mystifying, yet in no way less historical natural world of the Pacific coast, demonstrating the great variety of environments that migrant poets and the mobile subjects they write about engage with. When contemporary American poets of migration evoke natural environments, they do so by conceiving of places as porous formations open to various translocal, transregional, and transnational connections. The rolling grasslands of Walcott's Western Plains remind the narrator of the tropical seascapes of his native Caribbean; Etel Adnan's musings about the Pacific Ocean always also point to the Mediterranean Sea of her childhood in the Middle East; and when Agha Shahid Ali's speaker contemplates the landscapes of the Sonoran Desert during rainfall, he thinks about the Monsoons of his native Kashmir, to name just a few examples. Portrayed as complex and multilayered, the environments mentioned in the texts are characterized by their many material, social, political, cultural, and historical dimensions, whether one considers Craig Santos Perez's tidelands, which represent an endangered ecological zone as well as contested legal and cultural territory, or Juliana Spahr's rivers, whose ecosocial function as gathering places for human and nonhuman beings is disrupted or at least endangered by toxification and privatization. Where Perez's tidelands challenge dominant legalist conceptualizations of place that only account for dry land, Spahr's rivers dismantle the clear separation between human beings and the physical world around them implicit in dominant settler notions of place and bodily self. In a different manner, the sea in Adnan's poetry and the desert in Ali's poetry appear so immense and strange, yet familiar, that they encourage more capacious notions of desire and longing as well as more radical notions of hope and belonging. At the same time, as all of the works discussed in *Ecopoetic Place-Making* show, the more-than-human environments depicted in contemporary American ecopoetries of migration often appear as complex discursive-material formations imbued with conflicting meanings, highlighting some of the ways in which N/natures and their representations "dodge our expectations and theoretical models" (Snyder v), as do im/mobilites and their representations.

Representations of N/nature in contemporary ecopoetries of migration are diverse and so are representations of mobility. While this study centers on speakers who have migrated to or within the contiguous United States, the texts also feature many other kinds of mobility in conjunction with these migrations. Some of the poems' speakers, such as Perez's seafarers, Walcott's and Spahr's air travelers, Ali's car drivers and walkers, and Adnan's swimmers and mountain climbers re-evaluate their own relationship to nature and position in the world in the moments in which they are moving, or kept from moving. Perez assembles many materials, voices, and stories about mobility and immobilization in order to write *from* the unincorporated territory of Guam about the environmental devastation of Guåhan, while his collections also indicate that he is speaking *from* California and consequently from a perspective of Indigenous diaspora. Juliana Spahr's migrant speakers become acutely aware of their own position of privilege as academic migrants after they have moved away from Appalachian Ohio and of their privileged position as settler migrants after they have moved to Hawai'i. Derek Walcott's narrator starts to perceive himself and the environments of his native island in larger global contexts when he returns to St. Lucia for a visit after having traveled the continental United States. Agha Shahid Ali's descriptions of the Sonoran Desert are tinged with nostalgic longing because his speaker Shahid has left the Southwest for the Northeast, while the desire for N/nature of Adnan's speaker becomes increasingly directed at places she can no longer reach as well as at future natures she will not live to see. Apart from addressing how experiences of mobility affect people's relationship to places and the more-than-human world, then, some of the texts also attest to ways in which limited access to land can impede mobility and how limited mobility can impede access to nature. Adnan's poems reflect on the increased immobility of old age, while Perez's collections denounce Chamoru immobilization in Guåhan as a result of centuries of colonization and decades of U.S. military buildup; Spahr's poems, in turn, think about the legal and physical barriers constructed to keep some people away from or confined to certain places due to their racial or class status. At the same time, both Spahr and Perez also think about the ways in which limited mobility frequently comes to coincide with a heightened exposure to the harmful effects of local forms of environmental degradation. Such differentiations suggest that even while increased human and non-human mobilities—such as the invasion of Guåhan by tree snakes and the U.S. Military in Perez's collections, mass tourism in Walcott's epic poem *Omeros*, and the trans-corporeal mobility of toxins as well as the continental migration of settlers to Hawai'i in Spahr's texts—can mean increased environmental risk, so can a lack of mobility.

Contemporary American poetry invested in nature and mobility not only evokes *experiences* of migration and perspectives on N/nature informed by everyday mobilities, it also evokes *histories* of displacement. In general, the conflicted histories of those U.S.-American places the mobile speakers encounter play a crucial role in the poets' desire for (and in some cases for their attempts at establishing) meaningful relationships to their respective places of residence, however temporary they may be. Rather than conjuring wild or Edenic 'New World' environments as places of refuge from the human world, the five poets I have analyzed here depict places saturated with history, including histories of catastrophic as well as near-invisible environmental change and much -discussed as well as nearly-forgotten histories of violence and oppression. Because of the focus that poetries about nature and mobility direct at human-place, human-nature, and human-land relations, the histories of Native peoples appear as a central motif in contemporary ecopoetries of migration, often accompanied by other histories. Craig Santos Perez, for instance, evokes the variegated Chamoru histories of displacement and dispossession alongside nonhuman histories of displacement. Juliana Spahr's poetry examines the long history of U.S. imperialist occupation of, U.S. settler-migration to, and U.S. mass tourisms in Hawai'i as well as working-class displacements in place as well as between places in her poetry about Appalachia. Derek Walcott incorporates evocations of the forced relocation of enslaved people from Africa to the Caribbean and the United Sates and of Indigenous peoples from the U.S. South to reservations in the American West. Agha Shahid Ali reflects both on the migratory histories of ancient peoples of the Southwest and on the ways in which contemporary Indigenous peoples of the desert such as the Tohono O'odham continue to forge intimate connections to the land by means of land-cultivation and storytelling, despite centuries of encroachment upon their land by settlers and arrivants alike. At the same time, Ali references the colonization of the Southwest by Europeans and alludes, albeit only obliquely, to contemporary migratory movements across the Sonoran Desert and the U.S.-Mexican border that divides it.

One of the problems that contemporary American poetry about nature and mobility foregrounds is the frequent lack of material, or at least visible evidence in nature for settler-colonial and racist histories of violence and displacement, even as it points to the fact and indeed seeks to remind readers of the fact that some environments have been entirely transformed by settler culture. Although industrialization has made Appalachia one of the most polluted regions of the United States, this pollution is rarely made visible, Spahr's poetry notes, and although settler-migration to and tourism on Hawai'i has completely transformed flora, fauna, and many landscapes on the archipelago, ideas of an Edenic island paradise in the Pacific create the illusion of a lush and welcoming natural world reading for the taking by anyone who visits the island chain. While place-names recall some histories of the desert, Ali's poetry asserts, time has erased all but the most minute traces of some of the previous Indigenous inhabitants of the places his speaker travels through. Similarly, in Walcott's poems, the highly regenerative natural world of the Caribbean and the U.S. South makes it seem as if the devastations inflicted on the local communities and environments by violent removal, chattel slavery, and the installation of plantation culture have healed, or were never inflicted in the first place. As the poets I read foreground those histories that nature will not tell, they also draw attention to those representational traditions that have historically contributed to the erasure of settler-colonial histories, be it the imperialist and capitalist fantasies of landscapes figured as always available for consumption (Spahr, Perez), or the pastoral myths of America as a Garden (Walcott) or sublime wilderness (Ali). On the other hand, many of the poets discussed in the present study emphasize, sometimes reluctantly, the importance of critical (Walcott) or nostalgic re-imaginings of history and memory for the creation of meaningful place-sense (Ali), future-projections for a valuable apocalyptic ethics (Adnan), of experimental poetic language as a means to make visible processes that are too small or vast (Spahr, Perez), and the creative poetic imagination more generally, where personal memories or historical records are incomplete (Walcott, Perez).

The poets analyzed in this study not only point to histories that are often forgotten, they actively counter the erasure of histories in traditional nature poetry and beyond by various poetic means: Derek Walcott modifies genre conventions in the Weldon passages as well as the passages set in the U.S. South to draw attention to the violence inherent in traditional Anglo-American (settler) modes of representation. Etel Adnan engages in an ecopoetics of disorientation to orient her readers toward the natural world, while at the same time repeatedly referencing wars that the United States are involved in. Craig Santos Perez tries to retrieve those histories that occupying forces such as the Japanese or the U.S. Military have tried to suppress by using documentary (or as I argue, participatory) modes of combining records and testimonies from various sources. Juliana Spahr too sometimes draws from external sources or works with translation machines to compose her texts. Simultaneously she engages in para-lyrical experimentations to examine the injustices perpetrated against working-class people in Appalachia and Native people in Hawai'i at the hand of (global) corporations, the tourist industry, the U.S. government, pointing to her own implication in and complicity with the harmful practices of these extra-human agents. At the same time, all the poets analyzed here rely in one way or another on highly figurative language to evoke those dimensions of human-nonhuman relations that official histories and hegemonic discourses tend to omit, even as some of them (Walcott, Spahr) remain cautious about the discourses of abstraction and universalization inherent in processes of figuration.

Contemporary American ecopoetries of migration raise questions about identity, subjectivity, community, belonging, and agency together with questions about the potential and the limits of lyrical poetry as a means of expressing the changing human-nature relations in the Anthropocene. The poems in Agha Shahid Ali's collection *A Nostalgist's Map of America* most closely resemble the traditional lyric in form and voice. When confronted with the richly layered and storied landscapes of the Sonoran Desert, Ali's migrant "poet of the desert" humbly adds his own poetic perspective on the places and cultures he encounters, forging translocal, transethnic, and transhistorical affiliations, and expressing a diasporic longing for intimacy with the world. The Weldon passages of *Omeros* revise the pastoral elegy and in doing so explore the limits of (eco)poetic witnessing, while the Dakota passages of Walcott's lyricized epic use jarring images to dramatize the narrator's (and the author's) inability to find the appropriate poetic language and form to express the vast temporal and geographical scales of the American West. In Adnan's meditations, the perceiving and thinking self remains crucial, even though the focus of attention shifts to the changing aspects of such natural phenomena as the seasons, the sea or fog. The more-than-human community evoked in her poems is one determined by a queer ecological empathy for a world of strangers, including the natural world as the strangest kin. Perez's collections, by contrast, evoke the fragile connections formed by individuals across generations and the rerouted ancestral knowledges transmitted by different cultural practices, combining lyrical with experimental sections and weaving multiple fragmented voices together to form suggestive constellations and relations. In her dis/located poems about Appalachia and Hawai'i, finally, Spahr frequently replaced individualized lyrical speakers with evocations of chemical processes or shifting collectivities of speakers, without however completely renouncing the embodied and situated perspectives and the responsibilities that come with the specific ecosocial positioning of an academic migrant and settler and the considerable ecological agency such a positioning affords the privileged anthropocene subject.

When I describe ecopoetic place-making both as a literary and a *poetic* fashioning of place-sense, I do so for three main reasons: first, because I argue that the works of poetry themselves can be read as acts of ecopoetic place-making in the context of mobility; second, because in many of the works of poetry discussed in this study, the use of meta-poetic commentary and other meta-poetic strategies draw attention to the works as text and thus to the acts of ecopoetic place-making that the poems' speakers and narrators engage in; and third, because one of the key poetic strategies the poems employ for the purpose of ecopoetic place-making is the use of intertextual references to other texts about natures and mobilities of varying scales.

These intertextual references perform different functions: in some cases, they gesture toward a similarity in poetics, such as when Perez quotes Olson, when Spahr
revises Whitman, or when Adnan evokes H.D. In other cases, the intertextual references amplify the themes of migration, displacement, and longing for meaningful relationships to place, such as when Walcott references John Steinbeck or when
Ali references Georgia O'Keeffe. Sometimes, they express a shared environmental
sensibility, such as when Ali quotes ethno-botanist Gary Paul Nabhan, or speak to a
comparable place-based, yet mobile poetic imagination, as for instance in Ali's references to Emily Dickinson's poems or the writings of Henry David Thoreau. While
the intertextual references are thus at times employed to deepen the migrant poet's
sense of place (Perez, Ali, Adnan), where s/he cannot fall back on long-term inhabitation of a given place, they are used in other cases to question people's desire for emplacement, whether that of settlers (Spahr) or arrivants Walcott. In all these cases,
contemporary ecopoetries of migration suggest that poetry and other forms of art
and literature can serve as a crucial alternative means of place-making in the context
of mobility and environmental degradation.

From Ecopoetries of Migration to Environmental Cultures of Im/Mobility

In my study, I have read five poets from the joint perspective of American studies, ecocriticism, and mobility studies. Alternatively, I could have chosen contemporary American poets such as Amy Clampitt, Meena Alexander, Ed Roberson, Qwo-
Li Driskill, Haryette Mullen, Myung Mi Kim, Eavan Boland, Tamiko Beyer, Aracelis
Girmay, Arthur Sze, Emmy Pérez, Bill Holm, or Canadian poets of migration such as
Dionne Brand or Fred Wah. Discussing poets like Joy Harjo or Ed Roberson, for example, as I have done elsewhere (Rauscher "From Planar Perspectives"), would have
allowed me to explore in more detail the role of technology in mobile environmental
imaginaries. Adding Harryette Mullen's poetry would have suggested a closer look at
how ecopoetic place-making plays out in urban environments. An analysis of Emmy
Pérez collection *With the River on Our Face* (2016), by contrast, would have thrown into
relief issues concerning U.S-Mexican border ecologies, while focusing on Aracelis
Girmay's book of poems *The Black Maria* (2016) would have brought to attention representations of the more-than-human world in American poetry about the Mediterranean refugee crisis. All of these poets would have provided fascinating material
for analysis. Due to the form that mobilities take in some of the works of these poets
and poets like them, including them would have meant expanding this study from
ecopoetries of migration to ecopoetries of mobility.

Suggesting that many of the larger questions raised by contemporary American
ecopoetries of migration can be asked about ecopoetries of mobility more broadly
and that such an undertaking might be of interest to several different fields in the

environmental and mobility humanities is also to say that literary genres other than poetry and cultural products other than literary texts can be productively analyzed with regard to the practices of place-making they address and the environmental imaginaries of mobility they produce. In the poetic photo essay "Dole Street," included in her collection *Well Then There Now* (2011), Juliana Spahr for example wonders, like in many of her poems, how a continental migrant and settler like herself can develop a meaningful relationship to a place such as Hawai'i. She asks: "how to respect the water that is there, how not to suck it all up with my root system, how to make a syncretism that matters, how to allow fresh water to flow through it, how to acknowledge and how to change in various unpredictable ways" (49). Using imagery that describes herself as a continental transplant and indicating that poetry is not the only kind of art able to explore possible answers to these questions, Juliana Spahr ends her photo essay with a description of a performance piece by "Mudman" Kim Jones that speaks to the potential of art to envision mobile environmental imaginaries for our current times of crisis:

> The artist Kim Jones walked across Wilshire Boulevard in
> Los Angeles one day with a huge apparatus on his back. In the
> photographs of the event it is hard to tell exactly what he used
> to construct the apparatus but it looks like sticks and mud tied
> together in a loose, boxy sort of nest. It looks like the land. The
> apparatus appears heavy and unwieldy on him. It extends above his
> head and off his back by several feet. He wears some sort of mask
> that makes his face featureless as he walks. He is generic as
> he carries his apparatus. In some photographs, Jones draws a
> version of this apparatus over images of himself. One shows
> him crouching in Dong Ha Vietnam in full camouflage with the
> apparatus drawn on his head.
>   Kim Jones, in carrying a heavy and unwieldy nest, on his back
> out in public, might have an answer.
>   Nests draw things together and have many points of contact.
> They swirl into a new thing. All sorts of items end up in them. I found
> one the other day on Dole Street that was full of twigs and leaves
> and feathers and gum and plastic string.
>
> (Spahr, *Well Then* 49–50)

Kim Jones's 1976 performance is commonly interpreted as an engagement on the part of the artist with his experiences as a soldier and life as a veteran of the Vietnam War, a war that led an estimated 125 000 Vietnamese to seek refuge in the United States. As it is presented in Spahr's text, the "Mudman" performance can also be read as a commentary on the ethical responsibility of the artists to make visible to their audiences the messy materiality and mixture of natural and artificial elements used by birds to make their nests and, one can infer, by humans to make homes for themselves in places heavy with history. Read from a joint ecocritical and mobility studies perspective, the performance further points to artistic place-making as a form of human nest-building in the context of mobility and displacement. The idea of artistic place-making as human nest-building, an idea that Craig Santos Perez also evokes in his kingfisher sequence, is intriguing because it raises questions about the function of art in the face of violence and oppression. If art builds imaginary nests or homes, who is invited in and what are people willing to do to protect these homes and against whom do they think these homes require protecting?

Rather than being tied to one location or representing a permanent place of refuge, Jones's "nest" (Spahr, *Well Then* 49) is mobile, Spahr's description of the performance notes. It is carried "in public" (50) by the artist who demonstrates his intention to shoulder his portion of the unwieldy burden of U.S. war-making by putting his own body on display. At the same time, the artist alternatively hides his identity by wearing a "mask/ that makes his face featureless as he walks" (50) and reveals his past as a soldier by integrating photographs of himself "in full camouflage" (50) into his performance. Jones's "apparatus [. . .] looks like the land" (Spahr, *Well Then* 49) but it is constructed from a mix of natural and artificial materials. Art about acts of nest-building (or as I would say, art about place-making), Spahr seems to suggest here, must address the artist's self-positioning and implication in larger structures of violence and oppression and in showing the artist's complicity shoulder at least some of the individual's responsibility of working toward a dismantling of these structures. At the same time, Spahr's reading of Jones's performance point toward what one might describe as a very human but not always ethically defensible desire to make oneself a(t) home, even when such place-/home-making entails both the beautiful and the dreadful dimensions of human beings' enmeshment with the human and the more-than-human world. Engaging with works of art that present more critical perspectives on place-making may help those of us in positions of privilege and power to find ways of stepping a little lighter and living a little less destructively on this planet and in the company of an ever-increasing number of people whose displacements, whether they are caused by conflict or environmental disasters, are at least in part our responsibility.

Being an Indigenous poet from the occupied and highly militarized territory of Guåhan, Perez's approach to evoking what I describe as environmental imaginaries of mobility in the context of converging systems of exploitation and oppression is markedly different from Spahr's and Jones's. His series *from unincorporated territory* portrays the disastrous social, political, cultural, and environmental effects of U.S. imperialism on CHamoru cultures of mobility past and present, cultures of mobility that Perez evokes by referring to ancestral forms of Pacific Islander seafaring as well as to contemporary migratory movements. Because Perez is so invested in educating the public about the ecosocial conditions and political situation on Guåhan, his

254   Ecopoetic Place-Making. Nature and Mobility in Contemporary American Poetry

decolonial ecopoetry continuously reaches toward larger publics and toward popular forms of environmental cultural production. Indeed, Perez himself has long been active in spoken word poetry, one of the most popular forms of political poetry today, especially among younger audiences. Just like fellow Indigenous poets Kathy Jetñil-Kijiner (Marshallese) and Aka Niviâna (Inuk), whose video for the chant-like poem "Rise: From One Island to Another" has been shared widely on social media, Perez not only reads from his collections during public performances, he also engages with readers via social media and shares videos of readings online. Apart from his printed books of poetry and these videos, he has released two CDs, one entitled *Undercurrent: An Album of Amplified Poetry* (2011, with Native Hawaiian poet Brandy Nalani McDougall), and a solo album entitled *Crosscurrent* (2017). In all these activities and projects, Perez makes his poetry accessible to audiences that his printed collections may not reach. If Perez's use of modern media aims to promote his written works and spoken words, it also tries to reach a wider audience willing to inform themselves about the social, political, cultural, and environmental justice issues his poems address. Apart from bridging generations and cultural divides, Perez's work in different media also gestures to a larger repertoire of environmental cultures of mobility.

American studies as a field has long been interested in how popular culture allows for a critical discussion of social and cultural phenomena. Similarly, ecocriticism is increasingly turning toward popular cultural forms such as genre fiction, popular music, blockbuster film, TV series, and comics to think through the multidimensional challenges that life in the Anthropocene poses and to make sense of the role cultural products consumed by wider audiences can play in addressing these challenges. As I have suggested in the introduction to *Ecopoetic Place-Making*, environmental issues and mass mobility are such challenges. At the same time, the refugee camps along the Southern border of the United States and the various U.S. travel bans of the last ten years indicate, each in different ways how immobility and processes of immobilization too are part of environmental and mobility history of the early twenty-first century, the century in which we will either manage to get the global climate crisis and the biodiversity loss it causes under control or witness collectively, albeit in starkly uneven ways, the end of the world as we know it. Whatever the world will look like in fifty years, the people living in it, like the ones today, will engage in different forms of place-making, including we must hope by producing art and literature, and just as many as today, if not more will do so while being on the move or after having migrated in one form or another. If we find it useful to think deeply about cultural representations of environmental crisis in an effort to understand the world we are currently living in, we should also consider questions of mobility and immobility and examine mobile environmental imaginaries across different media as well as the environmental cultures of im/mobility these imaginaries evoke.

Works Cited

Adair, W. Gilbert. *The American Epic Novel in the Late Twentieth Century: The Super-Genre of the Imperial State*. Edwin Mellen, 2008.

Adamson, Joni, and Kimberly N. Ruffin. "Introduction." *American Studies, Ecocriticism, and Citizenship: Thinking and Acting in the Local and Global Commons*, edited by Joni Adamson and Kimberly N. Ruffin. Routledge, 2013, pp. 1–17. Routledge Interdisciplinary Perspectives on Literature.

Adey, Peter. *Mobility: Key Ideas in Geography*. Routledge, 2012.

Adnan, Etel. "The Cost for Love We Are Not Willing to Pay." *The Cost for Love We Are Not Willing to Pay/Der Preis der Liebe, den wir nicht zahlen wollen*. Hatje Cantz Verlag, 2011.

—. *L'Apocalypse Arabe* [1980]. Galerie Lelong, 2021.

—. *In the Heart of the Heart of Another Country*. City Lights, 2005.

—. *The Indian Never Had a Horse & Other Poems*. Post-Apollo Press, 1985.

—. "Journey to Mount Tamalpais." *To Look at the Sea Is to Become What One Is*, vol. 1, edited by Thom Donovan and Brandon Shimoda, Nightboat Books, 2014, pp. 291–339.

—. *Night*. Nightboat Books, 2016.

—. *Premonition*. Kelsey Street Press, 2014.

—. *Sea and Fog*. Nightboat Books, 2012.

—. *Seasons*. Post-Apollo Press, 2008.

—. *Shifting the Silence*. [2020] Nightboat Books, 2021.

—. *Sitt Marie Rose*. [1978] Tamyras, 2010.

—. *The Spring Flowers Own & The Manifestations of the Voyage*. Post-Apollo Press, 1990.

—. *Surge*. [2020] Nightboat Books, 2021.

—. *Time*. [2019] Nightboat Books, 2022.

—. *There: In the Light and the Darkness of the Self and of the Other*. Post-Apollo Press, 1997.

Ahmed, Sara. *Queer Phenomenology: Orientations, Objects, Others*. Duke UP, 2006.

Alaimo, Stacy. *Bodily Natures: Science, Environment, and the Material Self*. Indiana UP, 2010.

—. *Exposed: Environmental Politics and Pleasures in Posthuman Times*. U of Minnesota P, 2016.

Alcalay, Ammiel. *After Jews and Arabs: Remaking Levantine Culture*. U of Minnesota P, 1993.

Ali, Agha Shahid. *Call Me Ishmael Tonight: A Book of Ghazals*. W.W. Norton, 2003.

—. *The Country Without a Post Office*. W.W. Norton, 1997.

—. *The Half-Inch Himalayas*. Wesleyan UP, 1987.

—. *A Nostalgist's Map of America: Poems*. W. W. Norton, 1991.

—. *Rooms Are Never Finished: Poems*. W.W. Norton, 2002.

—. *T.S. Eliot as Editor*. UMI Research P, 1986.

Ali, Kazim. *Bright Felon: Autobiography and Cities*. Wesleyan-UP of New England, 2009.

—. *The Far Mosque*. Alice James Books, 2005.

—. "Introduction." *Mad Heart Be Brave: Essays on the Poetry of Agha Shahid Ali*, edited by Kazim Ali, U of Michigan P, 2017, pp. 1–11. doi:10.3998/mpub.9493485.

Altieri, Charles. "The Place of Rhetoric in Contemporary American Poetics: Jennifer Moxley and Juliana Spahr." *Chicago Review*, vol. 56, no. 2/3, 2011, pp. 128–45.

Ambrozy, Paulina. "The Post-Human Lyric: Diffractive Vision and the Ethics of Mattering in Adam Dickinson's *Anatomic*." *Studia Anglica Posnaniensia*, vol. 55, no. 2, 2020, pp. 375–401. doi: 10.2478/stap-2020-0019.

Appadurai, Arjun. "The Heart of Whiteness." *On "Post-Colonial Discourse,"* special issue of *Callaloo*, vol. 16, no. 4, 1993, pp. 796–807.doi: 10.2307/2932210.

Arigo, Christopher. "Notes Toward an Ecopoetics: Revising the Postmodern Sublime and Juliana Spahr's *This Connection of Everyone with Lungs*." *HOW2*, vol. 3, no. 2, 2008. <www.asu.edu/pipercenter/how2journal/vol_3_no_2/ecopoetics/essays/arigo.html>. Accessed 23 Aug. 2017. (link no longer functional)

Afshar, Haleh. "Women and Wars: Some Trajectories towards a Feminist Peace." *Development & Practice*, vol. 13, no. 2–3, 2003, pp. 178–88. doi: 10.1080/09614520302 949.

Assmann, Aleida. *Erinnerungsräume: Formen und Wandel des kulturellen Gedächtnisses*. C.H. Beck Verlag, 1999.

Aybek, Can M., et al. "Spatial Mobility, Migration, and Living Arrangements: An Introduction." *Spatial Mobility, Migration, and Living Arrangements*, edited by Can M. Aybek, Johannes Huinink and Raya Muttarak. Springer, 2015. 1–21. doi: 10.1007 /978-3-319-10021-0_1.

Bachelard, Gaston. *The Poetics of Space: The Classic Look at How We Experience Intimate Places*. [Fr. 1958; Engl.1964].: Beacon P, 2000.

Bacigalupi, Paolo. *The Water Knife*. Vintage Books, 2015.

Banita, Georgiana. *Plotting Justice: Narrative Ethics and Literary Culture after 9/11*. U of Nebraska P, 2012.

Barad, Karen. "Posthumanist Performativity: Toward an Understanding of How Matter Comes to Matter." *Signs*, vol. 28, no. 3, 2003, pp. 801–31. doi: 10.1086/3 45321.

Bate, Jonathan. *The Song of the Earth*. Harvard UP, 2000.

Bauman, Zygmunt. *Liquid Modernity*. 2000. Polity P, 2001.

Benfey, Christopher. "Coming Home: A Review of *Omeros* by Derek Walcott." *New Republic*, 29 October 1990: 38. <www.newrepublic.com/article/141413/coming-home>.

—. "A Route of Evanescence: Emily Dickinson and Japan." *The Emily Dickinson Journal*, vol.16, no. 2, 2007, pp. 81–93. doi: 10.1353/edj.2007.0007.

Bennett, Jane. "Of Material Sympathies, Paracelcus, and Whitman." *Material Ecocriticism*, edited by Serenella Ioviono and Serpil Oppermann, Indiana UP, 2014, pp. 239–52.

—. *Vibrant Matter: A Political Ecology of Things*. Duke University Press, 2010.

Bensen, Robert. "Catherine Weldon in *Omeros* and *The Ghost Dance*: Notes on Derek Walcott's Poetry and Drama." *Verse*, vol. 11, no. 2, 1994, pp. 119–25.

Berman, Marshall. *All that is Solid Melts into Air: The Experience of Modernity*. Penguin, 1988.

Berry, Wendell. *A Continuous Harmony: Essays Cultural and Agricultural*. Harcourt, 1972.

Bertoni, Filippo. "Resources (Un)Ltd: Of Planets, Mining, and Biogeochemical Togetherness." *Environmental Humanities: Voices from the Anthropocene*, edited by Serpil Opperman and Serenella Iovino, Rowman & Littlefield, 2016, pp. 175–92.

Bevacqua, Michael Lujan. "The Exceptional Life and Death of a Chamorro Soldier: Tracing the Militarization of Desire in Guam, USA." *Militarized Currents: Toward a Decolonized Future in Asia and the Pacific*, edited by Setsu Shigematsu and Keith L. Camacho, U of Minneapolis P, 2010, pp. 33–61. doi: 10.5749/minnesota/9780816665051.003.0003.

Bevacqua, Michael Lujan, and Isa Kelley Bowman. "Histories of Wonder, Futures of Wonder: Chamorro Activist Identity, Community, and Leadership in 'The Legend of Gadao' and 'The Women Who Saved Guåhan from a Giant Fish'." *Rooted in Wonder*, special issue of *Marvels & Tales*, vol. 30, no. 1, 2016, pp. 70–89. doi: 10.13110/marvelstales.30.1.0070.

Bhabha, Homi. *The Location of Culture*. Routledge, 2003.

Bishop, Elizabeth. *Geography III*. Farrar, Straus, Giroux, 1976.

—. *North and South/A Cold Spring*. Houghton Mifflin, 1955.

—. *Questions of Travel*. Farrar, Straus, Giroux, 1965.

Bodansky, Daniel. "The History of the Global Climate Change Regime." *International Relations and Global Climate Change*, edited by Urs Luterbacher and Detlef F. Sprinz, MIT P, 2001, pp. 23–40.

Bolton, Herbert E. *Kino's Historical Memoir of Pimería Alta: A Contemporary Account of the Beginnings of California, Sonora, and Arizona*. 2 vols. Clark, 1919.

Booth, Peter M. "Tohono O'odham Papago." *Encyclopedia of North American Indians*, edited by Frederick E. Hoxie, Houghton Mifflin, 1996.

Boschman, Robert. *In the Way of Nature: Ecology and Westward Expansion in the Poetry of Anne Bradstreet, Elizabeth Bishop and Amy Clampitt*. McFarland, 2009.

Boyle, Paul. "Migration." *International Encyclopedia of Human Geography*, vol. 7, edited by Rob Kitchin and Nigel Thrift, Elsevier, 2009, pp. 96–107.

Boym, Svetlana. *The Future of Nostalgia*. Basic Books, 2001.

Braidotti, Rosi. *Nomadic Subjects: Embodiment and Sexual Difference in Contemporary Feminist Theory*. Columbia UP, 1994.

Brathwaite, Kamau. *The Arrivants: A New World Trilogy*. Oxford UP, 1973.

Breslin, Paul. *Nobody's Nation: Reading Derek Walcott*. U of Chicago P, 2001.

Bricker Balken, Debra. *Dove/O'Keeffe: Circles of Influence*. Yale UP, 2009.

Brigham, Ann. *American Road Narratives: Reimagining Mobility in Literature and Film*. U of Virginia P, 2015.

Bryant, William Cullen. *Picturesque America*. D. Appleton, 1872.

Buell, Lawrence. *The Environmental Imagination: Thoreau, Nature Writing, and the Formation of American Culture*. Harvard UP, 1995.

—. *The Future of Environmental Criticism: Environmental Crisis and Literary Imagination*. Blackwell, 2005.

—. "Toxic Discourse." *Critical Inquiry*, vol. 24, no. 3, 1998, pp. 639–65. doi: 10.1086/44 8889.

—. "Uses and Abuses of Environmental Memory." *Contesting Environmental Imaginaries: Nature and Counternature in a Time of Global Change*, edited by Steven Hartman. Rodopi, 2017. 95–116. doi: 10.1163/9789004335080_007.

Byrd, Jodi A. *The Transit of Empire: Indigenous Critiques of Colonialism*. U of Minnesota P, 2011.

Campo, Rafael. *The Enemy*. Duke UP, 2007.

Caplan, David. *Questions of Possibility: Contemporary Poetry and Poetic Form*. Oxford UP, 2005.

Carr, Emily. "Our Public Tug-of-War with the Private 'We': Proposal for an Eco-Ethical Lyric." *Women's Studies: An Interdisciplinary Journal*, vol. 41, no. 1, 2012, pp. 64–88. doi: 10.1080/00497878.2012.628617.

Casteel, Sarah Philips. *Second Arrivals: Landscape and Belonging in Contemporary Writing of the Americas*. U of Virginia P, 2007.

Castro, Jan G. *The Art and Life of Georgia O'Keeffe*. Crown Publishers, 1985.

Chisholm, Dianne. "Juliana Spahr's Ecopoetics: Ecologies and Politics of the Refrain." *Contemporary Literature*, vol. 55, no. 1, 2014, pp. 118–47. doi: 10.1353/cli.2 014.0002.

Clark, Timothy. *The Cambridge Introduction to Literature and the Environment*. Cambridge UP, 2011. doi: 10.1017/CBO9780511976261.

Clifford, James. *Routes: Travel and Translation in the Late Twentieth Century*. Harvard UP, 1997.

Coates, Peter. *American Perspectives of Immigrant and Invasive Species: Strangers on the Land*. U of California P, 2006.

Cocola, Jim. *Places in the Making: A Cultural Geography of American Poetry*. U of Iowa P, 2016.

Cokinos, Christopher, and Eric Magrane, editors. *The Sonoran Desert: A Literary Field Guide*. U of Arizona P, 2016.

Colvin, Bruce A., et al. "Review of Brown Treesnake Problems and Control Programs." *USDA National Wildlife Research Center*. Staff Publications 631. Washington D.C.: U.S. Department of Interior, 2005. <www.digitalcommons.unl.edu/ic wdm_usdanwrc/631/>. Accessed 12 Dec. 2016. (link no longer functional)

Comer, Krista. "Exceptionalism, Other Wests, Critical Regionalism." *American Literary History*, vol. 23, no .1, 2011, pp. 159–73. doi: 10.1093/alh/ajq043.

Crane, Hart. *The Bridge: A Poem*. 1930. Liveright, 1992.

—. *White Buildings: Poems*. 1926. Liveright, 2001.

Cresswell, Timothy. *On the Move: Mobility in the Modern Western World*. Routledge, 2006. doi: 10.4324/9780203446713.

Crutzen, Paul J., and Eugene F. Stoermer. "The 'Anthropocene.'" *International Geosphere-Biosphere Programme Global Change Newsletter 41*, 2000, pp. 17–18.

Cunningham, Hilary, and Josiah McC. Heyman. "Introduction: Mobilities and Enclosures at Borders." *Identities: Global Studies in Culture and Power*, vol. 11, no. 3, 2004, pp. 289–302. doi: 10.1080/10702890490493509.

Davis, Gregson. "'Pastoral Sites': Aspects of Bucolic Transformation in Derek Walcott's *Omeros*." *From Homer to Omeros: Derek Walcott's Omeros and the Odyssey*, special issue of *Classical World*, no. 93, vol .1, 1999, pp. 43–50. doi: 10.2307/4352370.

The Day After Tomorrow. Directed by Roland Emmerich, 20th Century Fox, 2004.

DeLoughrey, Elizabeth M. "Ecocriticism: The Politics of Place." *The Routledge Companion to Anglophone Caribbean Literature*, edited by Michael A. Bucknor and Alison Donnell. Routledge, 2011, pp. 265–75. doi: 10.4324/9780203830352.

—. "Island Ecologies and Caribbean Literatures." *Tijdschrift voor Economische en Sociale Geografie*, vol. 95, no. 3, 2003, pp. 298–310. doi: 10.1111/j.1467-9663.2004.00309.

—. *Routes and Roots. Navigating Caribbean and Pacific Island Literatures*. Honolulu: U of Hawaiʻi P, 2007.

—. "Toward a Critical Ocean Studies for the Anthropocene." *English Language Notes*, vol. 57, no. 1, 2019, pp. 21–36. doi: 10.1215/00138282-7309655.

DeLoughrey, Elizabeth M., and George B. Handley. "Introduction: Towards an Aesthetics of the Earth." *Postcolonial Ecologies: Literatures of the Environment*, edited by Elizabeth M. DeLoughrey and George B. Handley, Oxford UP, 2011, pp. 3–39.

DeLoughrey, Elizabeth M., Renée Gosson, and George Handley. "Introduction." *Caribbean Literature and the Environment: Between Nature and Culture*, edited by Elizabeth M. DeLoughrey, et al., U of Virginia P, 2005, pp. 1–30.

Denoon, Donald. "New Economic Orders: Land, Labour and Dependency." *Cambridge History of the Pacific Islanders*, edited by Donald Denoon et al., Cambridge UP 1997, pp. 218–52. doi: 10.1017/CHOL9780521441957.008.

Department of the Navy. *Environmental Impact Statement: Guam and the Commonwealth of the Northern Mariana Islands Military Relocation*. Washington D.C.: GPO, July 2010. <www.guambuildupeis.us/documents> Accessed 12 Dec. 2016. (link no longer functional)

Diaz, Vicente M. "No Island Is an Island." *Native Studies Keywords*, edited by Stephanie Nohelani Teves, Andrea Smith, and Michelle Raheja, Arizona State UP, 2015, pp. 90–108.

Dickinson, Adam. "Pataphysics and Postmodern Eco-criticism: A Prospectus." *The Oxford Handbook of eco-criticism*, edited by Greg Garrard, Oxford UP, 2014, pp. 132–153. doi.org/10.1093/oxfordhb/9780199742929.013.011.

Dickinson, Emily. *The Poems of Emily Dickinson: Reading Edition*, edited by R. W. Franklin, Belknap Press, 1999.

Dimock, Wai Chee. "Low Epic." *Critical Inquiry*, vol. 39, no.3, 2013, pp. 614–31. doi: 10.1086/670048.

Dobson, Andrew. *Citizenship and the Environment*. Oxford UP, 2004. doi: 10.1093/0199258449.001.0001.

Dolis, John. *Tracking Thoreau: Double-Crossing Nature and Technology*. Vancouver: Fairleigh Dickinson UP, 2005.

Donovan, Thom. "Teaching Etel Adnan's The Arab Apocalypse." *Harriet: A Poetry Blog*. 10 Feb. 2010. <www.poetryfoundation.org/harriet-books/2010/02/teaching-etel-adnans-the-arab-apocalypse>. Accessed 12 Dec. 2022.

Döring, Tobias. *Caribbean English Passages: Intertextuality in a Postcolonial Tradition*. Routledge, 2001. doi: 10.4324/9780203166901.

Dunbar-Ortiz, Roxanne. *An Indigenous Peoples' History of the United States*. Beacon Press, 2014. ReVisioning American History.

Duncan, Robert. "Uprising: Passages 25." [1968]. *The Norton Anthology of Modern and Contemporary Poetry*, vol. 2, 3rd. ed., edited by Jahan Ramazani, Richard Ellmann, and Robert O'Clair, Norton, 2003, pp. 154–55.

Dürbeck, Gabriele, Caroline Schaumann, and Heather I. Sullivan. "Human and Non-Human Agencies in the Anthropocene." *Ecozon@*, vol. 6, no. 1, 2015, pp. 118–138. doi: 10.37536/ECOZONA.2015.6.1.642.

Dowling, Sarah. *Translingual Poetics: Writing Personhood Under Settler Colonialism*. U of Iowa P, 2018.

Eberwein, Jane Donahue. "Dickinson's Local, Global, and Cosmic Perspectives." *The Emily Dickinson Handbook*, edited by Gudrun Grabher, et al., U of Massachusetts P, 1998, pp. 27–43.

Edelman, Lee. *No Future: Queer Theory and the Death Drive*. Duke UP, 2004.

Eliot, T. S. *The Waste Land*, edited by Michael North. W.W. Norton, 2001. Norton Critical Editions.

Ergin, Meliz. *The Ecopoetics of Entanglement in Contemporary Turkish and American Literatures*. Palgrave, 2017.

Faiz, Faiz Ahmed. *The Rebel's Silhouette: Selected Poems*. With an Introduction by Agha Shahid Ali, U of Massachusetts P, 1991.

Farrell, Joseph. "Walcott's *Omeros*: The Classical Epic in a Postmodern World." *South Atlantic Quarterly*, vol. 96, no. 2, 1997, pp. 247–73.

Farrier, Daniel. *Anthropocene Poetics: Deep Time, Sacrifice Zones, and Extinction*. U of Minnesota P, 2019. Posthumanities.

Fattah, Hassan M. "Casualties of War: Lebanon's Trees, Air and Sea." *The New York Times*. 29 July 2006. <www.nytimes.com/2006/07/29/world/middleeast/29environment.html>. Accessed 18 Jan. 2018.

Fisher-Wirth, Ann, and Laura-Gray Street. "Editors' Preface." *The Ecopoetry Anthology*, edited by Ann Fisher-Wirth and Laura-Gray Street, Trinity UP, 2013, pp. xxvii-xxxi.

Fiskio, Janet. "Sauntering Across the Border: Thoreau, Nabhan, and Food Politics." *The Cambridge Companion to Literature and the Environment*, edited by Louise Westling, Cambridge UP, 2013, pp. 136–51. doi:10.1017/CCO9781139342728.013.

Fletcher, Angus. *A New Theory for American Poetry: Democracy, the Environment and the Future of Imagination*. Harvard UP, 2004.

Fojas, Camilla. *Island of Empire: Pop Culture and U.S. Power*. U of Texas P, 2014.

Folsom, Ed, and Kenneth M. Price. "Walt Whitman." *The Walt Whitman Archive*. <whitmanarchive.org/biography/walt_whitman/index.html>. Accessed 14 Oct. 2016. (link no longer functional)

Frank, Robin J. *Love and Loss: American Portrait and Mourning Miniatures*. Exhibition Catalogue. Yale UP, 2000.

Freitag, Kornelia. "'Eurydice': Agha Shahid Ali's Poetry of Memory." *Recovery and Transgression: Memory in American Poetry*, edited by Kornelia Freitag, Cambridge Scholars, 2015, pp. 209–21.

Friedland, Roger and Deirdre Boden, editors. *NowHere: Space, Time, and Modernity*. U of Chicago P, 1994.

Friedman, Susan S. "Bodies on the Move: A Poetics of Home and Diaspora." *Tulsa Studies in Women's Literature*, vol. 23, no. 2, 2004, pp. 189–212. doi:10.2307/20455 187.

Frost, Robert. "The Gift Outright." *The Norton Anthology of Modern and Contemporary Poetry*, vol. 1, 3rd. ed., edited by Jahan Ramazani, Richard Ellmann, and Robert O'Clair, Norton, 2003, p. 224.

Fukuyama, Francis. "The End of History?" *The National Interest*, vol. 16., 1989, pp. 3–18.

—. *Identity: The Demand for Dignity and the Politics of Resentment*. Farrar, Straus and Giroux. 2018.

Fuller, Margaret. *Summer on the Lakes*. Boston: Charles C. Little and James Brown; New York: Charles S. Francis, 1843.

Gaard, Greta. "Toward a Queer Ecofeminism." *Hypatia*, vol. 12, no. 1, 1997, pp. 114–37.

Ganser, Alexandra. *Roads of Her Own: Gendered Space and Mobility in American Women's Road Narratives*, 1970–2000. Rodopi, 2009.

Garrard, Greg. *Ecocriticism*. 2nd ed., Routledge, 2011. doi: 10.4324/9780203806838.

—. "Heidegger, Heaney and the Problem of Dwelling." *Writing the Environment: Ecocriticism and Literature*, edited by Richard Kerridge and Neil Sammells, Zed Books, 1998, pp. 167–81.

GEPA [Guam Environmental Protection Agency]. *Management of Contaminated Harbor Sediments in Guam*. Coastal Zone Management Act, Section 309, Guam Harbors Sediment Project, Phase III, Final Report, September 2000. <http://www.epa.guam.gov/>, Accessed 13 Nov. 2017.

Gerhardt, Christine. *A Place for Humility: Whitman, Dickinson, and the Natural World*. U of Iowa P, 2014.

—. "Imagining a Mobile Sense of Place: Towards an Ecopoetics of Mobility." *American Studies/Amerikastudien*, vol. 61, no.4, 2016, pp. 421–43.

—. "'Nothing Stays Put': Displacement and Environmental Memory in American Poetry." *Recovery and Transgression: Memory in American Poetry*, edited by Kornelia Freitag, Cambridge Scholars, 2015, pp. 297–312.

Gersdorf, Catrin. "Ecocritical Uses of the Erotic." *Bucknell Review*, vol. 44, no.1, 2000, pp. 175–91.

Ghosh, Amitav. "'The Ghat of the Only World': Agha Shahid Ali in Brooklyn." *Postcolonial Studies*, vol. 5, no. 3, 2002, pp. 311–23. doi: 10.1080/1368879022000032810.

Gidmark, Jill B., and Anthony Hunt. "Catherin Weldon: Derek Walcott's Visionary Telling of History." *Multicultural Versus International*, special issue of *The CEA Critic: An Official Journal of The College English Association*, vol. 59, no. 1, 1996, pp. 8–20.

Gifford, Terry. *Pastoral*. Routledge, 1999. doi: 10.4324/9780203003961.

—. "Pastoral, Anti-Pastoral, and Post-Pastoral." *The Cambridge Companion to Literature and the Environment*, edited by Louise Westling, Cambridge UP, 2013, pp. 913–36. doi: 10.1017/CCO9781139342728.003.

Gilbert, Roger. *Walks in the World: Representation and Experience in Modern American Poetry*. Princeton UP, 1991.

Giles, Paul. "'The Earth Reversed her Hemispheres': Dickinson's Global Antipodality." *The Emily Dickinson Journal*, vol. 20, no. 1, 2011, pp. 2–21. doi: 10.1353/edj.2011.0006.

Gilroy, Paul. *Postcolonial Melancholia*. Columbia UP, 2005.

Girmay, Aracelis. *Kingdom Animalia*. BOA Editions Limited, 2011.

Goodbody, Axel. "Sense of Place and Lieu De Mémoire: A Cultural Memory Approach to Environmental Texts." *Ecocritical Theory: New European Approaches*, edited by Axel Goodbody and Kate Rigby, U of Virginia P, 2011, pp. 55–68.

Graham, Colin. *Ideologies of Epic: Nation, Empire and Victorian Epic Poetry*. Manchester UP, 1998.

Gray, Jeffrey. *Mastery's End: Travel and Postwar American Poetry*. U of Georgia P, 2005.

Greenblatt, Stephen. "Cultural Mobility: An Introduction." *Cultural Mobility: A Manifesto*, edited by Stephen Greenblatt, et al., Cambridge UP, 2009, pp. 1–23. doi: 10.1017/CBO9780511804663.001.

—. "A Mobility Studies Manifesto." *Cultural Mobility: A Manifesto*, edited by Stephen Greenblatt, et al., Cambridge UP, 2009, pp. 250–53. doi: 10.1017/CBO9780511804663.008.

Greer, Allan. "Commons and Enclosure in the Colonization of North America." *American Historical Review*, vol. 117, no. 2, 2012, pp. 365–86. doi: 10.1086/ahr.117.2.365.

Griffiths, Matthew. *The New Poetics of Climate Change: Modernist Aesthetics for a Warming World*. Bloomsbury, 2017.

Guam Legislature. *Committee on Rules, Natural Resources, Federal, Foreign, and Micronesian Affairs*. Bill No. B331-30. An Act Relative to Changing the Official Name of Guam to its Name in the Chamorro Language, Namely 'Guahan'. 2nd Regular Session. 15 Feb. 2010. 1–2. <www.guamlegislature.com/Bills_introduced_30th/Bill%20No.%20B331-30%20(COR).pdf> Accessed 03 Mar. 2018.

Guam Organic Act of 1950. Territories and Insular Possessions. Pub. L. 90–497 .64 Stat. 384. Jan. 8 2008. <www.gpo.gov/fdsys/pkg/USCODE-2011-title48/content-deta il.html>. Accessed 03 Mar. 2018.

Hagenbüchle, Roland. "Precision and Indeterminacy in the Poetry of Emily Dickinson." *ESQ: A Journal of the American Renaissance*, vol. 20, no. 1, 1974, pp. 33–56.

Hallen, Cynthia L. "Brave Columbus, Brave Columba: Emily Dickinson's Search for Land." *The Emily Dickinson Journal*, vol. 5, no. 2, 1996, pp. 169–75. doi: 10.1353/edj.0.0037.

Halttunen, Karen. "Groundwork: American Studies in Place: Presidential Address to the American Studies Association, November 4, 2005." *American Quarterly*, vol. 58, no. 1, 2006, pp. 1–15.

Hamada, Sahoko. "Geography Images." *An Emily Dickinson Encyclopedia*, edited by Jane D. Eberwein, Greenwood, 1998.

Hamera, Judith, and Alfred Bendixen. "Introduction: New Worlds and Old Lands – The Travel Book and the Construction of American Identity." *Cambridge Companion to American Travel Writing*, edited by Judith Hamera and Alfred Bendixen, Cambridge UP, 2009, pp. 1–9. doi: 10.1017/CCOL9780521861090.001.

Hamilton, Amy T. *Peregrinations: Walking in American Literature*. U of Nevada P, 2018.

Hamner, Robert D. *Epic of the Dispossessed: Derek Walcott's* Omeros. U of Missouri P, 1997.

—. "Epic of the Dispossessed." Review of *Omeros* by Derek Walcott. *World Literature Written in English*, vol. 31, no. 1, 1991, pp. 113–14. doi: 10.1080/17449859108589153.

Handley, George B. "Derek Walcott's Poetics of the Environment in *The Bounty*." *Callaloo*, vol. 28, no. 1, 2005, pp. 201–15. doi: 10.1353/cal.2005.0016.

—. *New World Poetics: Nature and the Adamic Imagination in Whitman, Neruda, and Walcott*. U of Georgia P, 2007.

—. "A Postcolonial Sense of Place and the Work of Derek Walcott." *ISLE: Interdisciplinary Studies in Literature and the Environment*, vol. 7, no. 2, 2000, pp. 1–23. doi: 1 0.1093/isle/7.2.1.

Handlin, Oscar. *The Uprooted: The Epic Story of the Great Migrations that Made the American People*. Grosset and Dunlap, 1951.

Hansen, James. "The Greenhouse Effect: Impacts on Current Global Temperature and Regional Heat Waves." *Statement of Dr. James Hansen, Director, NASA Goddard Institute for Space Studies*. Presented to the United States Senate Committee on Energy and Natural Resources. 23 June 1988. <climate-change.procon.org/sourcefiles/1988_Hansen_Senate_Testimony.pdf>. Accessed 28 Jan. 2018. (link no longer functional)

Hao'ofa, Epeli. "Our Place Within: Foundations for a Creative Oceania." *We Are the Ocean: Selected Works*. Honolulu: U of Hawai'i P, 2008, pp. 80–91. doi: 10.1515/978 0824865542-008.

—. "Our Sea of Islands." *The Contemporary Pacific*, vol. 6, no. 1, 1994, pp. 147–161.

Haraway, Donna J. *The Companion Species Manifesto: Dogs, People, and Significant Otherness*. Prickly Paradigm P, 2003.

—. *How Like a Leaf: An Interview with Thyrza Nichols Goodeve*. Routledge, 2000.

—. *Modest_Witness@Second_Millenium.FemaleMan©_Meets_OncoMouseTM: Feminism and Technoscience*. 1st. ed. Routledge, 1997.

—. "Situated Knowledges: The Science Question in Feminism and the Privilege of Partial Perspective." *Simians, Cyborgs and Women: The Reinvention of Nature*. Routledge, 1991, pp. 183–201. doi: 10.4324/9780203873106.

Harding, Wendy. *The Myth of Emptiness and the New American Literature of Place*. U of Iowa P, 2014.

Hartman, Michelle. "'This Sweet/Sweet Music': Jazz, Sam Cooke, and Reading Arab American Literary Identities." *Arab American Literature*, special issue of *MELUS*, vol. 31, no. 4. 2006, pp. 145–65.

Harvey, David. *The Condition of Postmodernity: An Enquiry into the Origins of Cultural Change*. [1989]. Blackwell, 2003.

Harvey, Graham, and Charles D. Johnson, Jr. "Introduction." *Indigenous Diasporas and Dislocations*, edited by Graham Harvey and Charles Johnson, Ashgate, 2005, 1–14. doi: 10.4324/9781315252421.

Hasan, Raza Ali. "The Shifting Nationalisms of Agha Shahid Ali's Poetry." *Mad Heart Be Brave: Essays on the Poetry of Agha Shahid Ali*, edited by Kazim Ali, U of Michigan P, 2017, pp. 118–28.

Hashmi, Shadab Zeest. "Who Will Inherit the Last Night of the Past?': Agha Shahid Ali's Architecture of Nostalgia as Translation." *Mad Heart Be Brave: Essays on the Poetry of Agha Shahid Ali*, edited by Kazim Ali, U of Michigan P, 2017, pp. 183–189.

Haskell, Barbara, editor. *Georgia O'Keeffe: Abstraction*. Yale UP, 2009.

Haudenosaunee Confederacy. Haudenosaunee Confederacy: Oswe:ge Grand River. <www.haudenosauneeconfederacy.com/index.html>. Accessed 27 Apr. 2018.

Hayashi, Robert T. "Beyond Walden Pond: Asian American Literature and the Limits of Ecocriticism." *Coming into Contact: Explorations in Ecocritical Theory and Practice*, edited by Annie Merrill Ingram et al., U of Georgia P, 2007, pp. 58–75.

Heidegger, Martin. "...Poetically Man Dwells..." *Poetry, Language, Thought*, translated and with an Introduction by Albert Hofstadter, Harper Collins, 1971, pp. 209–27.

Heim, Otto. "How (not) to Globalize Oceania: Ecology and Politics in Contemporary Pacific Island Performance Arts." *Unsettling Oceania*, special issue of *Commonwealth Essays and Studies*, vol. 41, no. 1, 2018, pp. 131–45. doi: 10.4000/ces.402.

—. "Locating Guam: The Cartography of the Pacific and Craig Santos Perez's Remapping of Unincorporated Territory." *New Directions in Travel Studies*, Palgrave Macmillan, 2015, pp. 180–98. doi.org/10.1057/9781137457257_12.

Heise, Ursula K. *Imagining Extinction: The Cultural Meanings of Endangered Species*. U of Chicago P, 2016.

—. "Introduction: Planet, Species, Justice – and the Stories We Tell about Them." *The Routledge Companion to the Environmental Humanities*, edited by Ursula K. Heise, et al., Routledge, 2017, pp. 1–10. doi: 10.4324/9781315766355.

—. *Sense of Place and Sense of Planet: The Environmental Imagination of the Global*. Oxford UP, 2008.

Heller, Chaia. *Ecology of Everyday Life: Rethinking the Desire for Nature*. Black Rose Books, 1999.

Hena, Omaar. *Global Anglophone Poetry: Literary Form and Social Critique in Walcott, Muldoon, de Kok, and Nagra*. Palgrave Macmillan, 2015. DOI 10.1007/978-1-137-49661-5.

Henriksen, Line. *Ambition and Anxiety: Ezra Pound's Cantos and Derek Walcott's Omeros as Twentieth-Century Epics*. Rodopi, 2006.

Hirsch, Edward. "The Art of Poetry." Interview with Derek Walcott. *Critical Perspectives on Derek Walcott*, edited by Robert D. Hamner, Three Continents, 1993, pp. 65–84.

Huggan, Graham. "Blue Myth Brooding in Orchid: A Third-World Reappraisal of Island." *Journal of West Indian Literature*, vol. 1, no. 2, 1987, pp. 20–28.

Huggan, Graham, and Helen Tiffin. *Postcolonial Ecocriticism: Literature, Animals, Environment*. Routledge, 2010. doi: 10.4324/9781315768342.

Hungerford, Amy. "On the Period Formerly Known as Contemporary." *American Literary History*, vol. 20, no. 1–2, 2008, pp. 410–19. doi: 10.1093/alh/ajm044.

Hsu, Hsuan L. "Guahan (Guam), Literary Emergence, and the American Pacific in Homebase and from Unincorporated Territory." *American Literary History*, vol 24, no. 2, 2012, pp. 281–307. doi: 10.1093/alh/ajs021.

An Inconvenient Truth. Directed by Davis Guggenheim, written by Al Gore, Paramount Classics, 2006.

Indyk, Ivor. "Pastoral and Priority: The Aboriginal in Australian Pastoral." *New Literary History*, vol. 24, 1993, pp. 837–55. doi: 10.2307/469397.

Iovino, Serenella, and Serpil Oppermann. "Material Ecocriticism: Materiality, Agency, and Models of Narrativity." *Ecozon@*, vol. 3, no. 1, 2012, pp. 75–91. doi: 10.37536/ECOZONA.2012.3.1.452.

Islam, Maimuna Dali. "A Way in the World of an Asian American Existence: Agha Shahid Ali's Transimmigrant Spacing of North American and Indian/Kashmir." *Transnational Asian American Literature: Sites and Transits*, edited by Shirley Gloek-Lin Lim et al., Temple UP, 2006. 257–71.

Ismond, Patricia. *Abandoning Dead Metaphors: The Caribbean Phase of Derek Walcott's Poetry*. U of the West Indies P, 2001.

Izebaye, D. S. "The Exile and the Prodigal Walcott: Derek Walcott as West Indian Poet." *Caribbean Quarterly*, vol. 26, no. 1–2, 1980, pp. 70–82.

Jansen, Anne Mai Yee. "Writing toward Action: Mapping an Affinity Poetics in Craig Santos Perez's *from unincorporated territory*." *Native American and Indigenous Studies*, vol. 6, no. 2, 2019, pp. 3–29. doi: 10.5749/natiindistudj.6.2.0003.

Jay, Paul. "Fated to Unoriginality: The Politics of Mimicry in Derek Walcott´s Omeros." *Callaloo*, vol. 29, no. 2, 2006, pp. 545–59.

Jetñil-Kijiner, Kathy. "Dear Matafale Peinem." *Iep Jāltok: Poems from a Marshallese Daughter*. U of Arizona P, 2017, pp. 70–73.

Johnson, Dorothy. *Some Went West*. U of Nebraska P, 1997.

Kabir, Ananya Johanara. "Language and Conflict in the Poetry of Agha Shahid Ali." *Perspectives on Endangerment*, edited by Graham Huggan and Stephan Klasen, Georg Olms Verlag, 2005, pp. 199–208.

Kamada, Roy O. *Postcolonial Romanticism: Landscapes and the Possibilities of Inheritance*. Peter Lang, 2010. doi: 10.3726/978-1-4539-0480-0.

Kandiyoti, Dalia. *Migrant Sites: America, Place, and Diaspora Literatures*. UP of New England, 2009.

Kang, Yanbin. "Dickinson's Hummingbirds, Circumference, and Chinese Poetics." *The Emily Dickinson Journal*, vol. 20, no. 2, 2011, pp. 57–82. doi: 10.1353/edj.2011.0015.

Kaplan, E. Ann. *Looking for the Other: Feminism, Film, and the Imperial Other*. Routledge, 1996. doi: 10.4324/9780203699614.

Katrak, Ketu H. "South Asian American Writers: Geography and Memory." *Amerasia Journal*, vol. 22, no. 3, 1996, pp. 121–38. doi: 10.17953/amer.22.3.053p640g4491221 7.

Keck, Michaela. *Walking in the Wilderness: The Peripatetic Tradition in Nineteenth-Century American Literature and Painting*. Winter Verlag, 2006.

Keenaghan, Eric. "Queer Poetry in the Long Twentieth Century." *The Cambridge History of Gay and Lesbian Literature*, edited by E. L. McCallum and Mikko Tuhkanen, Cambridge UP, 2014, pp. 589–606. doi: 10.1017/CHO9781139547376.039.

Keller, Lynn. "'Post-Language Lyric': The Example of Juliana Spahr." *Chicago Review*, vol. 55, no. 3–4, 2010, pp. 74–83.

—. *Recomposing Ecopoetics: North American Poetry of the Self-Conscious Anthropocene*. U of Virginia P, 2017.

—. *Thinking Poetry: Readings in Contemporary Women's Exploratory Poetics*. U of Iowa P, 2010. doi: 10.1080/00497878.2011.581557.

Kerridge, Richard. "Ecocritical Approaches to Literary Form and Genre: Urgency, Depth, Provisionality, Temporality." *The Oxford Handbook of Ecocriticism*, edited by Greg Garrard, Oxford UP, 2013, pp. 361–76. doi: 10.1093/oxfordhb/978019974292 9.013.020.

Khal, Helen. *The Woman Artist in Lebanon*. Institute for Women's Studies in the Arab World, 1988.

Killingsworth, M. Jimmie. *Walt Whitman and the Earth: A Study in Ecopoetics*. U of Iowa P, 2009.

King, Bruce. *Modern Indian Poetry in English*. Revised Edition, Oxford UP, 2001.

Knickerbocker, Scott. *Ecopoetics: The Language of Nature, the Nature of Language*. U of Massachusetts P, 2012.

Knighton, Mary A. "Guam, Un-Inc.; Or Craig Santos Perez's Transterritorial Challenge to American Studies as Usual." *The Routledge Companion to Transnational American Studies*, edited by Nina Morgan, et al., Routledge, 2019, pp. 338–46. doi: 10.4324/9781315163932.

Kolodny, Annette. *The Lay of the Land: Metaphor as Experience and History in American Life and Letters*. U of North Carolina P, 1975.

Krech III, Shepard. *The Ecological Indian: Myth and History*. Norton, 1999.

Kyger, Joan. *Desecho Notebook*. Asif Press, 1971.

—. *Mexico Blonde*. Evergreen, 1981.

—. *Patzcuaro: December 17, 1997–January 26, 1998*. Blue Millennium Press, 1999.

Ladino, Jennifer K. *Reclaiming Nostalgia: Longing for Nature in American Literature*. U of Virginia P, 2012.

Lai, Paul. "Discontiguous States of America: The Paradox of Unincorporation in Craig Santos Perez's Politics of Chamorro Guam." *The Journal of Transnational American Studies*, vol. 3, no. 2, 2011, pp. 1–28. doi: 10.5070/T832011622.

Lane, M. Travis. "At Home in Homelessness: The Poetry of Derek Walcott." *Dalhousie Review*, vol. 53, no. 2, 1973, pp. 325–38.

Latour, Bruno. *The Politics of Nature*. Harvard UP, 2004.

Lee, Maurice S. *Certain Chances: Science, Skepticism, and Belief in Nineteenth Century American Literature*. Oxford and New York: Oxford UP, 2012.

Lee, Wendy Lynne, and Laura M. Dow. "Queering Ecological Feminism: Erotophobia, Commodification, Art, and Lesbian Identity." *Ethics and the Environment*, vol. 6, no. 2, 2001, pp. 1–21.

Leithauser, Brad. "Ancestral Rhyme: *Omeros* by Derek Walcott." *The New Yorker*, 11 Feb., 1991, pp. 91–94.

Lewis, R. W. B. *The American Adam: Innocence, Tragedy and Tradition in the 19th Century*. U of Chicago P, 1955.

Leyda, Julia. *American Mobilities: Geographies of Class, Race, and Gender in US Culture*. transcript, 2016.

Liboiron, Max. *Pollution is Colonialism*. Duke UP, 2021.

Linford, D. Laurance. *Navajo Places: History, Legend, Landscape*. U of Utah P, 2000.

Liu, Ran. *Spatial Mobility of Migrant Workers in Beijing, China*. Springer, 2015. doi: 10.1007/978-3-319-14738-3.

Lowenthal, David. *George Perkins Marsh, Prophet of Conservation*. U of Washington P, 2009.

Luger, Moberly. "Toward a New Poetics of Witness: Juliana Spahr's *This Connection of Everyone with Lungs*." *Tulsa Studies in Women's Literature*, vol. 36, no. 1, 2017, pp. 175–200.

Magrane, Eric. "Mesquite." *The Sonoran Desert: A Literary Field Guide*, edited by Eric Magrane and Christopher Cokinos, U of Arizona P, 2016.

Magrane, Eric, et al. *Geopoetics in Practice*. Routledge, 2019. doi: 10.4324/9780429032202.

Majaj, Lisa Suhair, and Amal Amireh. "Preface: Situating Etel Adnan in a Literary Context." *Etel Adnan: Critical Essays on the Arab-American Writer and Artist*, edited by Lisa Suhair Majaj and Amal Amireh, McFarland, 2002, pp. 1–12.

Malpas, Jeff. *Heidegger's Topology: Being, Place, World*. MIT P, 2006. doi: 10.7551/mitpress/3467.001.0001.

Mares, Teresa M., and Devon G. Peña. "Environmental and Food Justice: Toward Local, Slow, and Deep Food Systems." *Cultivating Food Justice: Race, Class, and Sustainability*, edited by Alison Hope Alkon and Julian Agyeman, MIT P, 2011, pp. 197–219. doi: 10.7551/mitpress/8922.003.0014.

Martin, Wendy. "Emily Dickinson: The Poetics and Practice of Autonomy." *The Cambridge History of American Poetry*, edited by Alfred Bendixen and Stephen Burt, Cambridge UP, pp. 360–82. doi: 10.1017/CHO9780511762284.019.

Martinez, J. Michael. "Tidal Poetics: The Poetry of Craig Santos Perez." *American Poets in the 21st Century*, edited by Claudia Rankine and Michael Dowdy, Wesleyan UP, 2018, pp. 332–41.

Marzec, Robert P. *An Ecological and Postcolonial Study of Literature: From Daniel Defoe to Salman Rushdie*. Palgrave, 2007. doi: 10.1057/9780230604377.

Mason, David. "Derek Walcott: Poet of the New World." *The Literary Review*, vol. 29, no. 3, 1986, pp. 269–75.

Massey, Doreen. "A Global Sense of Place." *Marxism Today*, 1991, pp. 24–29.

—. For Space. Sage, 2012.

Mayar, Mahshid. *Citizens and Rulers of the World: The American Child and the Cartographic Pedagogies of Empire*. The U of North Carolina P, 2022.

McGrath, Campbell. *Road Atlas*. Ecco-HarperCollins, 1999.

McGurl, Mark. "'Neither Indeed Could I Forebear Smiling at My Self': A Reply to Wai Chee Dimock." *Critical Inquiry*, vol. 39, no. 3, 2013, pp. 632–38. doi: 10.1086/6700 49.

McKibben, Bill. *The End of Nature*. Random House, 1989.

Mejcher-Atassi, Sonja. *Reading Across Modern Arabic Literature and Art*. Reichert Verlag, 2012. doi: 10.29091/9783752000986.

Melas, Natalie. "Forgettable Vacations and Metaphors in Ruins: Walcott's *Omeros*." *Callaloo*, vol. 28, no. 1, 2005, pp. 147–68. doi: 10.1353/cal.2005.0028.

Mercer, Edward J. *Nature Mysticism*. George Allen and Company, 1913.

Merchant, Carolyn. *The Death of Nature: Women, Ecology, and the Scientific Revolution*. Harper & Row, 1980.

Merleau-Ponty, Maurice. *Le Visible et L'Invisible*. Editions Gallimard, 1964.

Merrill, Christopher. "'A Route of Evanescence': Agha Shahid Ali in America." *Mad Heart Be Brave: Essays on the Poetry of Agha Shahid Ali*, edited by Kazim Ali, U of Michigan P, 2017, pp. 88–98.

Metres, Philip. "From Reznikoff to the Public Enemy: The Poet as Journalist, Historian, Agitator." 5 Nov. 2007. <www.poetryfoundation.org/articles/68969/from-reznikoff-to-public-enemy>. Accessed 4 Apr. 2017.

—. "Remaking/Unmaking: Abu Ghraib and Poetry." *Comparative Racialization*, special topic of *PMLA*, vol. 123, no. 5, 2008, pp. 1596–610.

Metres, Philip, and Mark Nowak. "Poetry as Social Practice in the First Person Plural: A Dialogue on Documentary Poetics." *Iowa Journal of Cultural Studies*, vol. 12, no. 1, 2010, pp. 9–22. doi: 10.17077/2168-569X.1088.

Mill, John Stuart. "What is Poetry?" [1833]. *The Broadview Anthology of Victorian Poetry and Poetic Theory*, edited by Thomas J. Collins and Vivienne J. Rundle, Broadview Press, 1999, pp. 1212–27.

Miller, Perry. *Nature's Nation*. Harvard UP, 1967.

—. "The Romantic Dilemma in American Nationalism and the Concept of Nature." *Nature's Nation*. Harvard UP, 1967. Rpt. from Harvard Theological Review, vol. 48, no. 4, 1955, pp. 239–53.

Milne, Heather. "Dearly Beloveds: The Politics of Intimacy in Juliana Spahr's *This Connection of Everyone with Lungs*." *Mosaic: A Journal for the Interdisciplinary Study of Literature*, vol. 47, no. 2, 2014, pp. 203–18. doi: 10.1353/mos.2014.0019.

—. *Poetry Matters: Neoliberalism, Affect, and the Posthuman in Twenty-First-Century North American Feminist Poetics*. U of Iowa P, 2018. doi: 10.2307/j.ctvvnf7k.

Milton, John. *Lycidas: The Tradition and the Poem*. [1638]. U of Missouri P, 1983.

Moore, Marianne. "Poetry." *The Complete Poems of Marianne Moore*, The Viking Press, 1980, pp. 266–67.

Mootry, Maria K. "Three Caribbean Poets: Sea Imagery as an Index to Their African Consciousness." *Pan-Africanist*, vol. 1, no. 2, 1971, pp. 22–27.

Morton, Timothy. "The Dark Ecology of Elegy." *The Oxford Handbook of the Elegy*, edited by Karen Weisman, Oxford UP, 2010, pp. 251–71. doi: 10.1093/oxfordhb/9780199 228133.013.0015.

—. *The Ecological Thought*. Harvard UP, 2012.

—. *Ecology Without Nature: Rethinking Environmental Aesthetics*. Harvard UP, 2007.

Müller, Timo. "Transnationalism in Contemporary Black Poetry: Derek Walcott, Rita Dove, and the Sonnet Form." *Transnational American Studies*, edited by Udo Hebel, Winter Verlag, 2012, pp. 249–68.

Mullen, Harryette. *Urban Tumbleweed*. Graywolf Press, 2013.

Muñoz, José E. *Cruising Utopia: The Then and There of Queer Futurity*. New York UP, 2009.

Murray, Robin L., and Joseph K. Heumann. "Al Gore's *An Inconvenient Truth* and its Skeptics: A Case of Environmental Nostalgia." *Jump Cut: A Review of Contemporary Media*, vol. 49, 2007, n. pag.

Murray, Robin L., and Joseph K. Heumann. *Ecology and Popular Film: Cinema on the Edge*. State U of New York P, 2009.

Nabhan, Gary P. *The Desert Smells Like Rain: A Naturalist in O'odham Country*. U of Arizona P, 1982.

Needham, Lawrence. "'The Sorrows of a Broken Time': Agha Shahid Ali and the Poetry of Loss and Recovery." *Reworlding: The Literature of the Indian Diaspora*, edited by Emmanuel S. Nelson, Greenwood, 1992, pp. 63–76.

Newman, Amy. "'Separation's Geography': Agha Shahid Ali's Scholarship of Evanescence." *Hollins Critic*, vol. 43, no. 2, 2006, pp. 1–14.

Nixon, Rob. *London Calling: V. S. Naipaul, Postcolonial Mandarin*. Oxford UP, 1992.

—. *Slow Violence and the Environmentalism of the Poor*. Harvard UP, 2011.

Nolan, Sara. *Unnatural Ecopoetics: Unlikely Spaces in Contemporary Poetry*. U of Nevada P, 2017.

Nora, Pierre. "Between Memory and History: Les Lieux de Mémoire." Translated by Marc Roudebush, *Representation*, vol. 26, 1989, pp. 7–24. doi: 10.2307/2928520.

Nye, Naomi Shihab. *Fuel*. Boa Editions, 1998.

—. *Red Suitcase: Poems*. Boa Editions, 1994.

—. *Transfer*. Boa Editions, 2011.

—. *Yellow Glove*. Breitenbush Books, 1986.

O'Keeffe, Georgia. *From the Faraway, Nearby*. 1937, Oil on canvas, Metropolitan Museum of Art, New York.

O'Keeffe, Georgia, and Alfred Stieglitz. *My Faraway One: Selected Letters of Georgia O'Keeffe and Alfred Stieglitz*, edited by Sarah Greenough, Yale UP, 2011.

Olson, Charles. "The Kingfishers." *The Ecopoetry Anthology*, edited by Ann Fisher-Wirth and Laura-Gray Street, Trinity UP, 2013, 91–97.

—. *The Maximus Poems*. [1960, 1968, 1975], edited by George F. Butterick, U of California P, 1983.

Oppermann, Serpil. "From Ecological Postmodernism to Material Ecocriticism: Creative Materiality and Narrative Agency." *Material Ecocriticism*, edited by Serenella Ioviono and Serpil Oppermann, Indiana UP, 2014, pp. 21–36.

Orfalea, Gregory and Šarīf al-Mūsā. "Introduction." [1988]. *Grape Leaves: A Century of Arab American Poetry*, edited by Gregory Orfalea and Šarīf al-Mūsā, Interlink, 2000. xi-xxix.

Osorio, Jamaica Heolimeleikalani. *Remembering Our Intimacies: Mo'olelo, Aloha 'Āina, and Ea*. U of Minnesota P, 2021.

Osorio, Jonathan ay Kamakawiwo'ole. *Dismembering Lāhui: A History of the Hawaiian Nation to 1887*. U of Hawai'i Press, 2002.

Ostriker, Alicia. "Beyond Confession: The Poetics of Postmodern Witness." *The American Poetry Review*, vol. 30, no. 2, 2001, pp. 35–39.

Osundare, Niyi. *City Without People: The Katrina Poems*. Black Widow Press, 2011.

Patea, Viorica. "The Myth of the American Adam: A Reassessment." *Critical Essays on the Myth of the American Adam*, edited by Viorica Patea and María Eugenia Díaz, Editiones Universidad de Salamanca, 2001, pp. 15–43.

Paul, Heike. *Mapping Migration: Women's Writing and the American Immigrant Experience from the 1950s to the 1990s*. Winter Verlag, 1999.

—. *The Myths That Made America: An Introduction to American Studies*. transcript, 2014.

Paul, Heike, Alexandra Ganser and Katharina Gerund, editors. *Pirates, Drifters, Fugitives: Figures of Mobility in the US and Beyond*. Winter Verlag, 2012.

Payne, Elizabeth E. "Critters at Risk: Endangered Species and Habitats of Appalachia." *The Appalachian Voice*. 14 June 2016. <www.appvoices.org/2016/06/14/critters-at-risk/>. Accessed 18 March 2018. (link no longer functional)

Pease, Donald. "From Virgin Land to Ground Zero: Interrogating the Mythological Foundations of the Master Fiction of the Homeland Security State." *A Companion* to *American Literature and Culture*, edited by Paul Lauter, Blackwell-Wiley, 2010, pp. 637–54. doi: 10.1002/9781444320626.

Perez, Craig Santos. *from unincorporated territory [åmot]*. Omnidawn, 2023.

—. *from unincorporated territory [guma']*. Omnidawn, 2014.

—. *from unincorporated territory [hacha]*. Tinfish Press, 2008.

—. *from unincorporated territory [lukao]*. Omnidawn, 2017.

—. *from unincorporated territory [saina]*. Omnidawn, 2010.

—. *Habitat Threshold*. Omnidawn, 2020.

—. *Navigating CHamoru Poetry: Indigeneity, Aesthetics, and Decolonization*. U of Arizona P, 2021.

—. "The Page Transformed: A Conversation with Craig Santos Perez." *Lantern Review Blog: Asian American Poetry Unbound*. 12 Mar. 2010. <www.lanternreview.com/bl og/2010/03/12/the-page-transformed-a-conversation-with-craig-santos-perez />. Accessed 14 Oct. 2016.

—. "Praise Song for Oceania." *The Missing Slate*, October 1, 2017. <http://themissings late.com/2017/10/01/praise-song-oceania/>. Accessed 2 October 2017.

Pfefferle, W. T. *Poets on Place: Interviews and Tales from the Road*. Utah State UP, 2005.

Pollack, Eileen. *Woman Walking Ahead: In Search of Catherine Weldon and Sitting Bull*. U of New Mexico UP, 2002.

Protevi, John. *Political Affect: Connecting the Social and the Somatic*. U of Minnesota P, 2009.

Quint, David. *Epic and Empire: Politics and Generic Form from Virgil to Milton*. Princeton UP, 1993.

Ramazani, Jahan. *The Hybrid Muse: Postcolonial Poetry in English*. U of Chicago P, 2001.

—. "Poetry and Tourism in a Global Age." *New Literary History*, vol. 46, 2015, pp. 459–83.

—. *Poetry in a Global Age*. U of Chicago P, 2020.

—. *A Transnational Poetics*. U of Chicago P, 2009.

Ramchand, Kenneth. "Parades, Parades: Modern West Indian Poetry." *The Sewanee Review*, vol. 87, no. 1, 1979, pp. 96–118.

Rauscher, Judith. "From Planar Perspectives to a Planetary Poetics: Aeromobility, Technology and the Environmental Imaginary in Contemporary American Poetry." *A World on the Move*, special issue of *American Studies*, vol. 61, no. 4, 2016, pp. 445–67.

—. "'She Moves Through Deep Corridors': Mobility and Settler Colonialism in Sharon Doubiago's Proletarian Eco-Epic Hard Country." *Ecozon@*, vol. 11, no. 1, 2020, pp. 115–33. doi: 10.37536/ECOZONA.2020.11.1.3297.

—. "Toward an Environmental Imagination of Displacement in Contemporary Transnational American Poetry." *Geocriticism and Ecocriticism*, edited by Robert T. Tally, Jr. and Christine M. Battista, Palgrave Macmillan, 2016, pp. 189–206. doi: 10.1057/9781137542625_11 .

Ray, Sarah Jaquette. *The Ecological Other: Environmental Exclusion in American Culture.* U of Arizona P, 2013.

Reed, Brian M. *Nobody's Business: Twenty-First Century Avant-Garde Poetics.* Cornell UP, 2013.

Retallack, Joan. "What is Experimental Poetry & Why Do We Need It?" *Jacket2,* vol. 32, 2007. <jacketmagazine.com/32/p-retallack.shtml>. Accessed 28 Aug. 2017.

Retallack, Joan, and Juliana Spahr. "Introduction: Why Teach Contemporary Poetries?" *Poetry and Pedagogy: The Challenge of the Contemporary,* edited by Joan Retallack and Juliana Spahr, Palgrave Macmillan, 2006, pp. 1–12. doi: 10.1007/978-1-1 37-11449-5_1 .

Rigby, Kate. *Reclaiming Romanticism: Toward an Ecopoetics of Decolonization.* Bloomsbury, 2020.

Rinkevich, Baruch. "Rebuilding Coral Reefs: Does Active Reef Restoration Lead to Sustainable Reefs?" *Current Opinion in Environmental Sustainability,* vol. 7, 2014, pp. 28–36. doi.org/10.1016/j.cosust.2013.11.018.

Ritivoi, Andreea Deciu. *Yesterday's Self: Nostalgia and the Construction of Personal Identity.* Rowman & Littlefield Publishers, 2002.

Roberson, Ed. *City Eclogue.* Atelos, 2006.

—. *To See the Earth Before the End of the World.* Wesleyan UP, 2010.

Robins, Kevin. "Encountering Globalization." *The Global Transformations Reader: An Introduction to the Globalization Debate,* edited by David Held and Anthony McGrew, 2nd edition, Polity Press, 2003.

Rogers, Robert F. *Destiny's Landfall: A History of Guam.* Revised edition, U of Hawai'i P, 2011.

Ronda, Margaret. *Remainders: American Poetry at Nature's End.* Stanford UP, 2018.

Rukeyser, Muriel. *The Book of the Dead.* 1938. West Virginia UP, 2017.

Sanders, Scott. "Southwestern Gothic: Alienation, Integration, and Rebirth in the Works of Richard Shelton, Rudolfo Anaya, and Leslie Silko." *Weber Studies: An Interdisciplinary Humanities Journal,* vol. 4, no. 2, 1987, pp. 36–53. Reproduced online by *Weber Journal.* n. pag.

Sandilands, Catriona. "Desiring Nature, Queering Ethics: Adventures in Erotogenic Environments." *Environmental Ethics,* vol. 23, no. 2, 2001, pp. 169–88. doi: 10.5840/enviroethics200123226.

—. "Queer Life? Ecocriticism After the Fire." *The Oxford Handbook of Ecocriticism,* edited by Greg Garrard, Oxford UP, 2014, pp. 305–19. doi: 10.1093/oxfordhb/97 80199742929.013.015.

—. "Whose There Is There There? Queer Directions and Ecocritical Orientations." *Ecozon@* vol. 1, no. 1, 2010, pp. 63–69. doi: 10.37536/ECOZONA.2010.1.1.321.

Schlote, Christiane. "Generic Activism: Ahdaf Soueif's and Etel Adnan's Art of Creative Non-Fiction." *Experiences of Freedom in Postcolonial Literatures and Cultures,* edited by Annalisa Oboe and Shaul Bassi, Routledge, 2011, pp. 283–95.

Schlund-Vials, Cathy J. "'Finding' Guam: Distant Epistemologies and Cartographic Pedagogies." *Asian American Literature: Discourses and Pedagogies*, vol. 5, 2014, pp. 45–60.

Sennett, Richard. *Flesh and Stone: The Body and the City in Western Civilization*. W. W. Norton, 1994.

Seymour, Nicole. *Strange Natures: Futurity, Empathy, and the Queer Ecological Imagination*. U of Illinois P, 2013.

Seymour-Jorn, Caroline. "*The Arab Apocalypse* as a Critique of Colonialism and Imperialism." *Etel Adnan: Critical Essays on the Arab-American Writer and Artist*, edited by Lisa Suhair Majaj and Amal Amireh, McFarland, 2002, pp. 37–49.

Shankar, Lavina D. and Rajini Srikanth. "South Asian American Literature: 'Off the Turnpike' of Asian America." *Postcolonial Theory and the United States: Race, Ethnicity, and Literature*, edited by Amritjit Singh and Peter Schmidt, UP of Mississippi, 2000, pp. 370–87.

Sheller, Mimi, and John Urry. "The New Mobilities Paradigm." *Mobilities and Materialities*, special issue of *Environment and Planning*, edited by Mimi Sheller and John Urry, vol. 38, 2006, pp. 207–26. doi: 10.1068/a37268.

Sheridan, Thomas E. *Landscapes of Fraud: Mission Tumacácori, the Baca Float, and the Betrayal of the O'odham*. U of Arizona P, 2007.

Shoaib, Mahwash. "Surpassing Borders and 'Folded Maps': Etel Adnan's Location in *There*." *Studies in the Humanities*, vol. 30, no.1/2, 2003, pp. 21–28.

Simpson, Megan. *Poetic Epistemologies: Gender and Knowing in Women's Language-Oriented Writing*. State U of New York P, 2000.

Skinner, Jonathan. "Ecopoetics." *American Literature in Transition, 2000–2010*, edited by Rachel Greenwald Smith, Cambridge UP, 2017, pp. 322–42. doi: 10.1017/97813 16569290.022.

—. "Editor's Statement." *ecopoetics*, no. 1, 2001. pp. 5–8. <ecopoetics.files.wordpress.com/2008/06/eco1.pdf>. Accessed 8 June 2019.

—. "Somatics: Finding Ecopoetics on the Disability Trail." *Jacket2*, 24 Oct. 2011. <jacket2.org/commentary/somatics>. Accessed 28 Aug. 2017.

Slotkin, Richard. *Regeneration through Violence: The Mythology of the American Frontier, 1600–1860*. Wesleyan UP, 1973.

Slovic, Scott. "The Third Wave of Ecocriticism: North American Reflections on the Current Phase of the Discipline." *Ecozon@*, vol. 1, no. 1, 2010, pp. 4–10. doi: 10.37536/ECOZONA.2010.1.1.312.

Smith, Henry Nash. *Virgin Land: The American West as Symbol and Myth*. Harvard UP, 1950.

—. "Symbol and Idea in Virgin Land." *Ideology and Classic American Literature*, edited by Sacvan Bercovitch and Myra Jehlen. Cambridge UP, 1986. pp. 21–35.

Snediker, Michael. *Queer Optimism: Lyric Personhood and Other Felicitous Persuasions*. U of Minnesota P, 2009.

Snyder, Gary. *No Nature: New and Selected Poems*. Pantheon, 1992.

Sofaer, Anna, Volker Zinser and Rolf M. Sinclair. "A Unique Solar Marking Construct." *Science*, vol. 206, no. 4416, 1979, pp. 283–91.

Somerville, Siobhan B. "Queer." *Keywords for American Cultural Studies*, edited by Bruce Burgett and Glen Hendler, New York UP, 2007. pp. 187–91.

Soper, Kate. "Passing Glories and Romantic Retrievals: Avant-garde Nostalgia and Hedonist Renewal." *Ecocritical Theory: New European Approaches*, edited by Axel Goodbody and Kate Rigby, U of Virginia P, 2011. pp. 17–29.

—. *What is Nature? Culture, Politics and the Non-Human*. Blackwell, 2009.

Spahr, Juliana. *Everybody's Autonomy Connective Reading and Collective Identity*. U of Alabama P, 2001.

—. *Fuck You—Aloha—I Love You*. Wesleyan UP, 2001.

—. "Multilingualism in Contemporary American Poetry." *The Cambridge History of American Poetry*, edited by Alfred Bendixen and Stephen Burt, Cambridge UP, 2014. pp. 1123–43. doi: 10.1017/CHO9780511762284.054.

—. *Nuclear. Buffalo: Leave Books: 1991*. Republished via the out of print archive of Duration P. <www.durationpress.com/archives/index.html>. Accessed 04 Mar. 2016.

—. "Resignifying Autobiography: Lyn Hejinian's My Life." *Write Now: American Literature in the 1980s and 1990s*, edited by Sharon O'Brien, special issue of *American Literature*, vol. 68, no. 1, 1996, pp. 139–59. doi: 10.2307/2927544.

—. *Response*. N. p.: Sun & Moon Books, 1996. Re-published via the out of print archive of Duration P. <www.durationpress.com/archives/index.html>. Accessed 04 Mar. 2016.

—. *That Winter the Wolf Came*. Commune Editions, 2015.

—. *This Connection of Everyone with Lungs: Poems*. U of California P, 2005.

—. *The Transformation*. Atelos, 2007.

—. *Well Then There Now*. A Black Sparrow Book, 2011.

Spahr, Juliana, and David Buuck. *Army of Lovers*. City Lights, 2013.

Spencer, Eleanor. "'I hear America singing, the varied carols I hear': Introduction." *American Poetry since 1945*, edited by Eleanor Spencer, Bloomsbury, 2017, pp. 1–22. New Casebooks.

Stein, Gertrude. "Composition as Explanation." *A Stein Reader*, edited with an introduction by Ulla E. Dydo, Northwestern UP, 1993, pp. 493–503.

Steinbeck, John. *Of Mice and Men*. 1937. Penguin, 1993.

—. *Travels with Charley: In Search of America*. Viking Press, 1962.

Steingraber, Sandra. *Having Faith: An Ecologist's Journey to Motherhood*. Berkeley Trade, 2001.

Stuart, David E. *Anasazi America: Seventeen Centuries on the Road from Center Place*. U of Mexico P, 2000.

Suhr-Sytsma, Nathan. *Poetry Print and the Making of Postcolonial Literature*. Cambridge UP, 2017. doi: 10.1017/9781316711422.

Suleiman, Yasir. "On Arab American Literature." *Holy Land Studies: A Multidisciplinary Journal*, vol. 6, no. 2, 2007, pp. 212–14. doi: 10.3366/hls.2007.6.2.209.

Sullivan, Heather I. "The Ecology of Colors: Goethe's Materialist Optics and Ecological Posthumanism." *Material Ecocriticism*, edited by Serenella Iovino and Serpil Oppermann. Indiana UP, 2014. pp. 80–94.

Suzuki, Erin. *Ocean Passages: Navigating Pacific Islander and Asian American Literature*. Temple UP, 2021.

Swensen, Cole. *Noise That Stays Noise: Essays*. U of Michigan P, 2011. doi: 10.3998/mpub.1903627.

Tageldin, Shaden M. "Reversing the Sentence of Impossible Nostalgia: The Poetics of Postcolonial Migration in Sakinna Boukhedenna and Agha Shahid Ali." *Comparative Literature Studies*, vol. 40, no. 2, 2003, pp. 232–64. doi: 10.1353/cls.2003.0019.

Tagnani, David. "New Materialism, Ecomysticism, and the Resolution of Paradox in Edward Abbey." *Western American Literature*, vol. 50, no. 4, 2016, pp. 317–46. doi: 10.1353/wal.2016.0001.

Tatum, Stephen. "Postfrontier Horizons." *MFS Modern Fiction Studies*, vol. 50, n. 2, 2004, pp. 460–68. doi: 10.1353/mfs.2004.0049.

Teaiwa, Teresia. "Reading Paul Gaugin's *Noa Noa* with Epeli Hauʻofa's *Kisses in the Nederends*: Militourism, Feminism, and the 'Polynesian' Body." *Inside Out: Literature, Cultural Politics, and Identity in the New Pacific*, edited by Vilsoni Hereniko and Rob Wilson, Rowman & Littlefield, 1999. 249–63.

Thoreau, Henry David. *Walden: Or, Life in the Woods: Bold-faced Ideas for Living a Truly Transcendent Life*. [1854]. Ed. Laura Ross. New York: Sterling Publishing, 2009.

Thornber, Karen Laura. *Ecoambiguity: Environmental Crises and East Asian Literatures*. U of Michigan P, 2012.

Thurlow, Crispin, and Adam Jaworski. "Tourism Discourse: Languages and Banal Globalization." *Applied Linguistics Review*, vol. 2, 2011, pp. 285–312. doi: 10.3998/mpub.3867115.

Tölölyan, Khachig. "The American Model of Diasporic Discourse." *Diasporas and Ethnic Migrants: Germany, Israel and Post-Soviet Successor States in Comparative Perspective*, edited by Rainer Miinz and Rainer Obliger, Frank Cass, 2003, pp. 56–73.

Tomlinson, John. *Globalization and Culture*. Polity P, 1999.

Torres, Robert Tenorio. "Pre-contact Marianas Folklore, Legends, and Literature: A Critical Commentary." *Micronesian Journal of the Humanities and Social Sciences*, vol. 2, no. 1/2, 2003, pp. 3–15.

Trask, Haunani-Kay. *From a Native Daughter: Colonialism and Sovereignty in Hawaiʻi*. Revised Edition, U of Hawaiʻi P, 1999.

Trigg, Dylan. *The Memory of Place: A Phenomenology of the Uncanny*. Ohio UP, 2012.

Tuan, Yi-Fu. *Space and Place: The Perspective of Experience*. U of Minnesota P, 1977.

—. "Language and the Making of Place." *Annals of the Association of American Geographers*, vol. 81, no. 4, 1991, pp. 684–96. doi:10.1111/j.1467-8306.1991.tb01715.x.

Untalan, Fay F. "Chamorro Migration to the US." *Guampedia*. Guampedia. <www.g uampedia.com/chamorro-migration-to-the-u-s/>. Accessed 8 Mar. 2018.

Urry, John. *The Tourist Gaze: Leisure and Travel in Contemporary Societies*. Sage, 1990.

Vanderborg, Susan. *Paratextual Communities: American Avant-Garde Poetry since 1950*. Southern Illinois UP, 2001.

Vasseleu, Cathryn. *Textures of Light: Vision and Touch in Irigaray, Levinas and Merleau-Ponty*. Routledge, 1998. doi:10.4324/9780203047705.

Verghese, Abraham. "Foreword." *Contours of the Heart: South Asians Map North America*. Asian American Writers' Workshop, 1996, pp. xiii-xv.

Vestal, Stanley. *New Sources of Indian History, 1850–1891*. U of Oklahoma P, 1934.

Villa-Ignacio, Teresa. "Apocalypse and Poethical Daring in Etel Adnan's *There: In the Light and the Darkness of the Self and of the Other*." *Contemporary Literature*, vol. 55, no. 2, 2014, pp. 304–35. doi:10.1353/cli.2014.0013.

Vizenor, Gerald. "Aesthetics of Survivance." *Survivance: Narratives of Native Presence*, edited by Gerald Vizenor, U of Nebraska P, 2008, pp. 1–24.

Walcott, Derek. "The Antilles: Fragments of Epic Memory." *What the Twilight Says: Essays*. Farrar, Straus, and Giroux, 1998, pp. 65–85.

—. *The Arkansas Testament*. Faber & Faber, 1987.

—. *The Bounty*. Farrar, Straus, and Giroux, 1997.

—. *The Fortunate Traveller*. Farrar, Straus, and Giroux, 1981.

—. *Midsummer*. Farrar, Straus, and Giroux, 1984.

—. "The Muse of History." *What the Twilight Says: Essays*. Farrar, Strauss, and Giroux, 1998, pp. 36–64.

—. *Omeros*. Farrar, Straus, and Giroux, 1990.

—. *Tiepolo's Hound*. Farrar, Straus, and Giroux, 2000.

Weigle, Marta and Peter White. *The Lore of New Mexico*. U of New Mexico P, 1988.

Whitman, Walt. *Poetry and Prose*, edited by Justin Kaplan, Library of America, 1996.

Willis, Lloyd. *Environmental Evasion: The Literary, Critical, and Cultural Politics of "Nature's Nation."* State U of New York P, 2011.

Wilson, Rob. *Reimagining the American Pacific: From South Pacific to Bamboo Ridge and Beyond*. Duke UP, 2000.

Woodland, Malcom. "Memory's Homeland: Agha Shahid Ali and the Hybrid Ghazal." *English Studies in Canada*, vol. 31, no. 2/3, 2005, pp. 249–72. doi:10.1353/esc.2007 .0036.

Young, Julian. *Heidegger's Philosophy of Art*. Cambridge UP, 2000.

Zelinsky, Wilbur. *Not Yet a Placeless Land: Tracking an Evolving American Geography*. U of Massachusetts P, 2011.

Literaturwissenschaft

Julika Griem
Szenen des Lesens
Schauplätze einer gesellschaftlichen Selbstverständigung

2021, 128 S., Klappbroschur
15,00 € (DE), 978-3-8376-5879-8
E-Book:
PDF: 12,99 € (DE), ISBN 978-3-8394-5879-2

Klaus Benesch
Mythos Lesen
Buchkultur und Geisteswissenschaften
im Informationszeitalter

2021, 96 S., Klappbroschur
15,00 € (DE), 978-3-8376-5655-8
E-Book:
PDF: 12,99 € (DE), ISBN 978-3-8394-5655-2

Werner Sollors
Schrift in bildender Kunst
Von ägyptischen Schreibern zu lesenden Madonnen

2020, 150 S., kart.,
14 Farbabbildungen, 5 SW-Abbildungen
16,50 € (DE), 978-3-8376-5298-7
E-Book:
PDF: 14,99 € (DE), ISBN 978-3-8394-5298-1

**Leseproben, weitere Informationen und Bestellmöglichkeiten
finden Sie unter www.transcript-verlag.de**

Literaturwissenschaft

Elias Kreuzmair, Magdalena Pflock, Eckhard Schumacher (Hg.)
Feeds, Tweets & Timelines –
Schreibweisen der Gegenwart
in Sozialen Medien

September 2022, 264 S., kart.,
27 SW-Abbildungen, 13 Farbabbildungen
39,00 € (DE), 978-3-8376-6385-3
E-Book: kostenlos erhältlich als Open-Access-Publikation
PDF: ISBN 978-3-8394-6385-7

Renate Lachmann
Rhetorik und Wissenspoetik
Studien zu Texten von Athanasius Kircher
bis Miljenko Jergovic

Februar 2022, 478 S., kart.,
36 SW-Abbildungen, 5 Farbabbildungen
45,00 € (DE), 978-3-8376-6118-7
E-Book:
PDF: 44,99 € (DE), ISBN 978-3-8394-6118-1

Wilhelm Amann, Till Dembeck, Dieter Heimböckel, Georg Mein,
Gesine Lenore Schiewer, Heinz Sieburg (Hg.)
Zeitschrift für interkulturelle Germanistik
13. Jahrgang, 2022, Heft 1

August 2022, 192 S., kart., 1 Farbabbildung
12,80 € (DE), 978-3-8376-5900-9
E-Book: kostenlos erhältlich als Open-Access-Publikation
PDF: ISBN 978-3-8394-5900-3

Leseproben, weitere Informationen und Bestellmöglichkeiten
finden Sie unter www.transcript-verlag.de

GPSR Authorized Representative: Easy Access System Europe, Mustamäe tee
50, 10621 Tallinn, Estonia, gpsr.requests@easproject.com

www.ingramcontent.com/pod-product-compliance
Lightning Source LLC
Chambersburg PA
CBHW061606120626
46550CB00004B/1631